GENDER, RACE, AN
NATIONAL EDUCATION
ASSOCIATION

MW00790827

ROUTLEDGEFALMER
STUDIES IN THE HISTORY OF EDUCATION
FORMERLY GARLAND STUDIES IN HIGHER EDUCATION
VOLUME 10

Gender, Race, and the National Education Association
Professionalism and Its Limitations

Wayne J. Urban
Georgia State University

RoutledgeFalmer
New York & London
2000

Published in 2000 by
RoutledgeFalmer
29 West 35th Street
New York, NY 10001

RoutledgeFalmer is an imprint of the Taylor & Francis Group.

Copyright © 2000 by Wayne J. Urban

All rights reserved. No part of this book may be reprinted or reproduced
or utilized in any form or by any electronic, mechanical, or other means,
now known or hereafter invented, including photocopying and recording,
or in any information storage or retrieval system, without permission in
writing from the publisher.

10 9 8 7 6 5 4 3 2 1

**Library of Congress Cataloging-in-Publication Data is available from the
Library of Congress.**

Printed on acid-free, 250-year-life paper.
Manufactured in the United States of America

For Judy,
Always

Contents

Preface

I have spent much of my academic career working on various aspects of the twentieth-century history of the National Education Association (NEA). My first full-time teaching job in higher education was at the University of South Florida beginning in 1968. Earlier in that year thousands of Florida teachers walked out of their classrooms under the leadership of the Florida Education Association, the Florida affiliate of the NEA. During my three years in Florida much of my time was spent documenting and interpreting the walkout and talking to individual teachers about their participation, or nonparticipation, in it.[1] My conclusion about that walkout was that the Florida teachers allowed their own ideology of having undertaken the walkout "for the sake of the [school] children" to backfire on them to the point that it was used by school administrators, business leaders, and politicians opposed to the teachers to defeat the teachers and their education association. My unstated, or understated, assumption was that a more straightforward and economically oriented statement of objectives on the part of the teachers would have left them much less vulnerable to the counterattack that was waged against them.

In 1971 I moved to Georgia State University in Atlanta. Shortly after coming to Atlanta, one of my students discovered the records of the Atlanta Public School Teachers Association (APSTA), a group that was affiliated at one time or another with both the American Federation of Teachers (AFT) and the NEA. My initial research on the early years of the APSTA eventually led me to further study that culminated in *Why Teachers Organized*, published in 1982.[2] In that work I argued that teachers organized in the early twentieth century primarily for economic reasons and also to defend a traditional occupational orientation through policies such as seniority. In making that argument, I adopted an institutional labor history perspective that emphasized material pursuit as the essence of occupational organization and downplayed other motives such as political or social reform or occupational improvement as instrumental in the process.

In discussing the two national teacher groups of that era, the NEA and the AFT, I argued that both tried to respond to budding, local teachers' organizational activity but that neither, for different reasons, was successful. The AFT, which was at least partially in tune with local teachers' attempts to organize, gained members in the late 1910s but lost those gains in the 1920s. The post–World War I antiunionism that also permeated the 1920s and a bitter internal dispute, regional and ideological, over who would lead the union combined to cripple the teachers' union. The NEA, in contrast, never supported teachers' attempts to organize themselves, if such organization meant any sort of autonomy from the supervision of teachers by school administrators. Since organization of teachers at the least implied a lack of complete identity between them and administrators, the NEA tried to subvert independent teacher organizations by reorganizing itself and acknowledging teacher interests but incorporating them within the NEA umbrella.

I refined but did not discard these arguments in a chapter in Donald Warren's edited American Educational Research Association (AERA) collection, *American Teachers,*[3] published in 1989. Therein, I extended my discussion of teacher organizations by embracing the larger concept of teacher activism and ranged both backward from the Progressive Era to the nineteenth century and forward through the rest of the twentieth century. Additionally, I made an initial attempt to incorporate women and minority teachers' concerns within my framework. My interpretation continued to stress material occupational goals, however, as the essential element of teacher activity and to privilege teachers' organizations as the most appropriate agency through which to study teachers' occupational consciousness.

In all of this early work I held to a perspective on the two main national teachers' organizations, the NEA and the AFT, derived from my doctoral study days at Ohio State University in the mid to late 1960s. In those years I was one of a number of doctoral students hired to teach undergraduates at Ohio State while we worked on our advanced degrees. We always had our offices together, in a relatively large collective space, or "bullpen," as it was often called, and we learned a good bit from one

another in frequent, often heated, discussions about educational controversies of the time. The relative attractiveness of the two major teacher
organizations of that day, however, was not one of the issues over which
controversy raged among us. We were all males, and several of us had
substantial teaching experience in the public schools as well as some experience and rather fixed views on teacher unions and nonunion, NEA-
affiliated teacher associations. For us the AFT, the group that was
affiliated with the larger labor movement, was clearly the preferred organization. Second and last on our preference list was the NEA, the then
consciously antiunion professional organization. One of my fellow students had a wonderful way of expressing our disdain for the NEA as a
meaningful representative of teachers' interests. He used to say that he
knew one way that the NEA provided a valuable service to him when he
was a teacher. The NEA produced so many publications (largely useless
for any meaningful occupational purpose) that he saved all of them and,
in the wintertime when the roads were icy, he tied the NEA works into
bundles and put them in his trunk, where they made wonderful ballast for
his car and allowed him better control on the winter roads.

The preference for the labor-oriented AFT over the consciously anti-
labor NEA and the sarcasm with which my friend and I and most if not
all of our colleagues treated the NEA were characteristic of most of those
who wrote historically about teacher organizations in that and in later
years. I would characterize our views as embodying a distinct class, race,
and gender lens, the first aspect held to consciously and the latter two
semi- or unconsciously. This lens, or perspective, ideologically privileged the AFT and discounted the NEA. It was this white, working-class,
male point of view that drove much of my early work on teacher organizations. It might well be characterized as a distinctly male activist, militant, possibly even a macho, perspective.

In the latter pages of the chapter in the Warren volume of 1989, however, I began to give evidence of some recognition that there were other
perspectives that might profitably animate the historical study of teachers and their organizations. In those pages I welcomed the historical
work of several women scholars on teachers. In particular I mentioned
the studies of Geraldine Clifford, Polly Welts Kaufman, and Nancy Hoffman that dealt with America's women teachers, mostly but not exclu-
sively in the nineteenth century.[4] Also helpful in sensitizing me to the
significance and the variety of ramifications of the topic of women teachers was Clifford's essay in the Warren volume, "Man, Woman, Teacher."[5]
Yet at that time I did not acknowledge that for Clifford and the other

women historians, women teachers were the larger universe to be studied, the universe within which women teachers' organizations could, and perhaps should, be understood.

Also in my essay in the Warren volume I called attention to some international studies on the topic of teachers, their organizations, and other aspects of their work lives that I thought worthy of the attention of American historians. I pointed specifically to the work of Martin Lawn and Jenny Ozga in England and of Andrew Spaull in Australia.[6] From Lawn and Ozga I learned that teachers' perception of their work and their work lives, including the understanding they had regarding the professionalization of their occupation, was as important as, or more important than, their tendency, or hesitancy, to form occupational organizations. From Spaull I learned that Australian teachers often, in the nineteenth century especially, organized themselves in a consciously professional antiunion association just as they often, in a later time period, organized themselves into a powerful trade union. The reality of the nonunion, professional association form of organization was brought even closer to home when I replaced Spaull as external examiner on Harry Smaller's dissertation at the Ontario Institute for Studies in Education. That dissertation dealt with the organization in the nineteenth century of a teachers' association in Ontario, an organization that functioned practically as an appendage of the regional school administrator and in no way resembled an independent trade union.[7]

In subsequent years I continued to pay close attention to the work of both American women educational historians and of educational historians, men and women, in Canada, England, and Australia who wrote about teachers and their organizations. In 1990 I tried to summarize a little more fully the contributions of American women historians and international scholars, and I identified their works as some of the most interesting and important "New Directions in the Historical Study of Teacher Unions."[8]

At about the same time—that is, in the late 1980s and early 1990s—I was involved in another project completely unrelated to the topic of teachers' organizations. The published outcome of that project was my biography of Horace Mann Bond,[9] which carried on to at least partial fruition the development of another specialty area in my scholarly work, southern educational history.[10] From my study of southern educational history I learned to appreciate perspectives other than those of the white, male working class and to be prepared, at least to some extent, to respect views that clashed with my own leftward political leanings. Southern conservative ideas were especially attractive to me when they offered a profound critique of the accomplishments of liberal reforms, including public education, in the South and elsewhere.

My Bond biography was particularly important for two additional reasons. First, it sensitized me to the value of biography—intensive study of one individual—as an important way of understanding some of the larger issues in American educational history. I even went beyond biography and experimented on one occasion with an autobiographical essay.[11] Still more important, my study of Bond forced me to grapple with the concerns of African Americans and African American teachers as they struggled with the discrimination, especially the educational discrimination, they endured in the twentieth century. Or, to put it another way, my Bond biography brought the topic of race to the center of my historical consciousness.

While nearing the end of the Bond project, I received a phone call from the director of the Research Division of the NEA, Ronald Henderson, asking me if I was interested in writing the history of the division. After some negotiation I agreed to write the history and spent much of the first few summers of the 1990s at the NEA and in the NEA Archives. By 1992 I had produced a manuscript to honor the fiftieth anniversary of the Research Division. In 1998, with some additions to the earlier manuscript, I published a seventy-fifth-anniversary history of the Research Division.[12] In doing research for that history, I became aware of the myriad ways in which the nonunion NEA, through its Research Division and through many other agencies, had tried to honor a commitment to women teachers in much of the twentieth century. I also became aware of how the NEA for many years toyed with but did not embrace a relationship to black teachers and their own association, the American Teachers Association (ATA). The ironic reversal of these commitments in the processes of unionization and desegregation of the NEA in the late 1960s and 1970s—that is, the strengthening of the recognition of black teachers and a corresponding diminution of the attention paid to women teachers—struck me as important. Thus, as I labored on the history of the Research Division, I also began doing the research for and conceptualizing the larger history of the NEA that is contained in these pages.

Two other elements of historiographical work in the last decade are relevant to the perspective with which I approached this history of the NEA. The first is what historian Sol Cohen refers to as the "linguistic turn," or what might also be called postmodernism in educational history.[13] What this development has done for me is to increase my sensitivity to the ways in which a historian's conscious acknowledgment of her or his perspective and of the issues attendant to that perspective can enrich historical work. This preface is an attempt to indicate rather fully my own perspective so that readers will not have to search for it within the pages of the text. While I cannot go so far as to embrace the radical epistemological relativism championed by many postmodernists and thereby abandon completely any notion of historical truth, I can admit that the truths discovered by any historian are pragmatic and tentative, having as much to do with the assumptions he or she makes about the work as they do with the evidence adduced in its support. Further, any historical work, including my own, is never the last word on any topic. The attention of another historian with different assumptions and, perhaps, new evidence or at least a new reading of old evidence all lead to a new and different interpretation of any historical topic.

Finally, the recent work of several young women historians has played an important part in my understanding of the NEA. They have provided substantive insights that I have used to interpret my own research. Jackie Blount has shown that women were far more represented in the ranks of school administrators, particularly from the beginning of the twentieth century until 1950, than they were in the second half of the century. She thereby complicates, though she does not contradict, the identification of male gender with school administrators and female gender with teachers. Blount's work also suggests an explanation for why women teachers in the first half of the century were not as reflexively opposed to school administrators as were the men teachers who dominated the AFT, from the time of its inception.[14] Christine Ogren has studied normal schools, pointing out that these institutions, where many of the nation's teachers were trained, exhibited substantially more signs of gender equality than colleges and universities, even those that were coeducational.[15] She thereby complicates the category of male educational administrator, pointing to ways in which turn-of-the-century male normal school administrators did not take the same completely authoritarian point of view toward women teachers that the mostly male, big city superintendents did. And Kate Rousmaniere has looked at women teachers in the elementary schools of New York City, showing how they used clublike organizations, some of which were affiliated with the NEA, as an alternative to a teachers' union, which they found inimical to their interests. She shows that these organizations were part of a larger struggle by women teachers to carve a space for themselves and their work within the enormity that was the city school system and the dominance of that system by the superintendent.[16]

All of these works, by virtue of the particular topics they study and by overt discussion of gender issues, show that women teachers had, particularly in the first half of the twentieth century, substantial reasons to respond positively to the "professional," antiunion image promulgated by the NEA. These works, along with the various other works mentioned above, have all led me consciously to change the lens through which I view teachers and their organizations. In doing so, I am responding to the challenge posed by Joan Burstyn more than a decade ago.[17] I have changed from a mostly unconscious, white, working-class, male perspective to one that consciously seeks to understand the attractiveness of an avowedly professional, often overtly antiunion NEA agenda to women and women teachers, and the relationship of the association and its agenda to blacks and black teachers. To adopt such a stance in analyzing the NEA and other teacher organizations is to fly in the face of most of the work that has been done on these groups.

The major extant historical study of the NEA is unsatisfactory for a number of reasons. In addition to its ignorance of women teachers and black teachers as NEA actors, Edgar Wesley's centennial history, published in 1957, is marred by an uncritical description and an unabashed celebration of the organization.[18] Ever since Wesley, most histories of the NEA have attempted to correct his interpretation by stressing the top-down character of the organization, highlighting the weakness of its commitment to the cause of teachers and comparing it, usually unfavorably, to the unionized AFT.

Two more recent histories of teacher organizing by individuals who were directly involved in the process, one by an AFT officer and another by an NEA official, also echo the characterization of an NEA unresponsive to teachers until the 1960s. From that decade on, both histories show how the association was forced to remake itself and respond to teachers' concerns by the challenge of collective bargaining, as pursued successfully by the AFT in New York City and other large industrial centers.[19] All of these works, however, were written by men and, seemingly, for the men who led various teacher associations and teacher unions.

The most recent and comprehensive look at the NEA is not by a man but by Marjorie Murphy, a historian from Swarthmore College. She sees the NEA, however, within the context of its rivalry with the AFT for the allegiance of American teachers. Murphy, with a background in labor history, depicts the NEA as a formidable foe of the teachers' union but also as an organization hopelessly dominated by school administrators through the 1960s and, thus, largely unresponsive to the needs and concerns of teachers.[20] Although she is a woman and sensitive to women's issues and concerns as they played themselves out in the two national teacher organizations, Murphy is primarily a class-conscious labor historian who sees the fundamental problems in education as class oriented and dependent on class, or cross-class, organizing and political activism that links teachers with the parents of their students. For Murphy the early activism of women teachers, particularly as it intersected positively with lay and parent groups, is the most satisfying version of teachers' associational activity that has ever been practiced.

My work differs from Murphy's in several ways. First, I carry the story up to the end of the twentieth century, twenty years after she ends her account. Next, I reverse her relative emphasis between the two groups by concentrating on the NEA, its professional agenda from 1917 until the 1960s, and its subsequent embrace of unionism. The AFT is present in my account but takes a secondary position in my analysis. It comes to the fore when the NEA was forced to confront it as a formidable foe for the allegiance of teachers, first in the immediate post–World War I years and again in the 1960s. Finally, I give more credence than Murphy to the effectiveness of teachers' and administrators' attempts within the NEA to carve a meaningful "professional" occupational existence, attempts that were undertaken in conscious antipathy to the teachers' union and often without cooperation with lay and parent groups. None of these differences should obscure the point that I learned much from Murphy's work. I acknowledged her accomplishment in a review of her book several years ago, and close readers of the text and notes of this book will see the many particular places where I build on, or differ from, her analysis.[21]

My perspective on the NEA, then, stresses three themes—professionalism, race, and gender—all of which are contained in the title of this book. I will try here to give readers a brief, preliminary look at each theme and how it functions in my analysis.

First I want to discuss the theme of professionalism or professionalization. These are terms that can be defined with long lists of characteristics that often seem arid. Rather than do that, I would simply offer the following preliminary sketch of what professionalism meant for the NEA from 1917 until around 1970. In those years the first thing that professionalism meant was that the association was not unionized. Professionalism was an ideological term that the NEA used to distinguish itself from the unionized AFT. But professionalism also had more substantive meanings for the NEA, two of which were notions of improving occupational standards and serving school children and, thereby, the larger society. When the NEA itself unionized in the 1970s, it put its professional agenda on a back burner, only to attempt to resurrect it, within its union framework, in the 1990s. I will say more about this recent attempt at professionalization in the final chapter of the book and in the epilogue.

Additionally, this book is about how the themes of race and gender intersected with the professionalism that was first advocated, then downgraded, and finally reembraced by the NEA. In terms of race, the NEA basically ignored African American teachers, while occasionally paying them some lip service, until the 1960s. Then, embroiled in an internal dispute with its militant members over the issue of unionization, the association also undertook the task of desegregating itself, both nationally and in its many segregated state and local affiliates. That desegregation, though an often painful process, proved relatively successful, especially when compared with developments in the AFT in subsequent years. Yet the desegregation was also peripheral to the unionization of the association, which facilitated the process of racial amelioration. Furthermore, desegregation was an issue that was peripheral to the issue of responsiveness to women teachers, which preceded racial consciousness in the NEA, and to the subsequent attempts to rediscover a professional agenda for the association.

As suggested earlier, gender presents a reversal of the situation that occurred in the relationship between the NEA and race. For the period before unionization I argue that the NEA in its own way paid substantial attention to the women teachers whose membership it needed to build itself into a formidable organization. This attention was never complete and principled—that is, it never developed to the point that women teachers were understood to have an existence in schools or in the NEA that was independent of their usually male administrative superiors. Yet the NEA was responsive enough to women teachers to use their membership to build itself into the dominant occupational organization for teachers. When the militancy of the 1960s, largely the product of male high school teachers, eventually transformed the NEA into a teachers' union that competed with the AFT in the early 1970s, the attention the association paid to women teachers seemed to diminish drastically. This diminution took place alongside of, though not necessarily in relation to, the increased recognition of African American teachers that characterized the association in the same years.

Professionalism, race, and gender, then, constitute the major themes of this history of the NEA. Each ebbs and flows in significance at different times in the twentieth century, and I try to explain the factors behind the ebbing and flowing. In the epilogue I attempt to summarize the larger meaning of each for the past, present, and future of the NEA.

Having stated the many and complex factors that influenced my perspective on the NEA in this volume and indicated at least briefly the major themes of that analysis, what remains is simply to acknowledge the many individuals to whom I owe a special debt for help in completing this work.

I begin these acknowledgments by thanking, once again, the authors mentioned and/or cited in the preceding pages of this preface. I know that I have profited from their work, and I hope that they find that I have used it faithfully and productively. Additionally, I want to thank Edward Beauchamp, Geraldine Clifford, and Kate Rousmaniere, each of whom read the entire manuscript (Rousmaniere twice) and offered suggestions, corrections, and, just as important, encouragement to a colleague who needed it. Another reader of the entire manuscript, Czeslaw Majorek of the Cracow (Poland) Pedagogical University, provided me, along with his helpful reactions and suggestions, with a semester of congenial colleagueship and support that carried the manuscript almost to the stage of completion. And I want to thank my colleague at Georgia State University, Susan Talburt, for reading and commenting on parts of the manuscript just before I sent it to the publishers.

Ronald Henderson, director of the Research Division of the NEA, gave me the opportunity to work in the NEA Archives, a remarkably rich collection for my project as well as for numerous other projects related to almost any aspect of American educational history. Donald Walker, retired archivist of the NEA, introduced me to the wealth of material contained in those archives and pointed me to many parts of it that were necessary to the successful completion of this work.

I want to acknowledge also the work of Meredith Lester, senior secretary in the Department of Educational Policy Studies at Georgia State University. She has been enormously helpful to me on this and other manuscripts that I have completed in the past several years. Ms. Lester has done notable editorial and computer work that has made my labor on this manuscript an easier and often happier task.

Finally, this manuscript is dedicated to my wife, Judy Urban, who has experienced countless hours of eyes glazed over across the dinner table after a day at the word processor or in the library. Being a registered nurse with a substantial occupational consciousness, she has been supportive of my attempts to understand the process of how the NEA has interacted, or not interacted, with women teachers. Her patience is boundless, and her support is far beyond what I deserve. We have endured together for more than thirty years and, I trust, we will have many more years together.

NOTES

[1]See Wayne J. Urban, "Power and Ideology in a Teacher Walkout: Florida, 1968," *Journal of Collective Negotiations in the Public Sector* 3 (Spring 1974): 133–46.

[2]Wayne J. Urban, *Why Teachers Organized* (Detroit: Wayne State University Press, 1982). Also see Urban, "Organized Teachers and Educational Reform in the Progressive Era, 1890–1920," *History of Education Quarterly* 16 (Spring 1976): 35–52.

[3]Wayne J. Urban, "Teacher Activism," in Donald R. Warren, ed., *American Teachers: Histories of a Profession at Work* (New York: Macmillan, 1989): 190–209.

[4]Geraldine Joncich Clifford, "Home and School in Nineteenth Century America: Some Personal History Reports from the United States," *History of Education Quarterly* 18 (Spring 1978): 3–34; Polly Welts Kaufman, *Women Teachers on the Frontier* (Hartford, CT: Yale University Press, 1984); and Nancy Hoffman, ed., *Women's True Profession* (Old Westbury, NY: Feminist Press, 1981).

[5]Geraldine J. Clifford, "Man, Woman, Teacher: Gender, Family, and Career in American Educational History," in Warren, ed., *American Teachers*, 293–343.

[6]Martin Lawn, ed., *The Politics of Teacher Unionism: International Perspectives* (Dover, NH: Croom Helm, 1985); J. T. Ozga and M. A. Lawn, *Teachers, Professionalism and Class* (London: Falmer Press, 1981); Andrew Spaull, ed., *Teacher Unionism in the 1980s: Four Perspectives* (Hawthorn, Victoria, Australia: Australian Council for Educational Research, 1986); and Spaull, ed., *Australian Teachers: From Colonial Schoolmasters to Militant Professionals* (Melbourne: AE Press, 1986).

[7]Harry Smaller, "Teachers' Protective Associations, Professionalization and the 'State' in Nineteenth Century Ontario" (Ph.D. diss., University of Toronto, 1988).

[8]Wayne J. Urban, "New Directions in the Historical Study of Teacher Unions," *Historical Studies in Education* 2 (Spring 1990): 1–15. This article was

originally a vice presidential address given to Division F of the American Educational Research Association in 1989.

[9]Wayne J. Urban, *Black Scholar: Horace Mann Bond, 1904–1972* (Athens: University of Georgia Press, 1992).

[10]Wayne J. Urban, "History of Education: A Southern Exposure," *History of Education Quarterly* 21 (Summer 1981): 131–45.

[11]Wayne J. Urban, "Wayne's World: Growing Up in Cleveland, Ohio, 1942–1963," *Educational Studies* 26 (Winter 1995): 301–20.

[12]Wayne J. Urban, *More Than the Facts: The Research Division of the National Education Association, 1922–1997* (Lanham, MD: University Press of America, 1998).

[13]Sol Cohen, *Challenging Orthodoxies: Toward a New Cultural History of Education* (New York: Peter Lang, 1999). I also learned much about the linguistic turn and the value of perspectivalism from correspondence with Richard Angelo of the University of Kentucky.

[14]Jackie M. Blount, *Destined to Rule the Schools: Women and the Superintendency, 1873–1995* (Albany: State University of New York Press, 1998).

[15]Christine A. Ogren, "Where Coeds Were *Co*educated: Normal Schools in Wisconsin, 1870–1920," *History of Education Quarterly* 35 (Spring 1995): 1–26.

[16]Kate Rousmaniere, *City Teachers: Teaching and School Reform in Historical Perspective* (New York: Teachers College Press, 1997). Rousmaniere acknowledges the significance for her work of the oral history interviews of women teachers from the depression era in Hamilton, Ohio, conducted by her Miami University colleague Richard A. Quantz. See Quantz, "The Complex Vision of Female Teachers and the Failure of Unionization in the 1930s," *History of Education Quarterly* 25 (Winter 1985): 439–58.

[17]Joan N. Burstyn, "History As Image: Changing the Lens," *History of Education Quarterly* 27 (Summer 1987): 167–80.

[18]Edgar B. Wesley, *NEA: The First Hundred Years* (New York: Harper, 1957).

[19]David Selden, *The Teacher Rebellion* (Washington, DC: Howard University Press, 1985), and Allan West, *The National Education Association: The Power Base for Education* (New York: Free Press, 1980).

[20]Marjorie Murphy, *Blackboard Unions: The AFT and the NEA, 1900–1980* (Ithaca, NY: Cornell University Press, 1990).

[21]Wayne J. Urban, review of Murphy, *Blackboard Unions,* in *Educational Studies* 23 (Summer 1992): 221–26.

GENDER, RACE, AND THE NATIONAL EDUCATION ASSOCIATION

CHAPTER 1

Professionalism in Process
The Reform of the National Education Association, 1917–30

The National Education Association (NEA) was founded in 1857. In its first half century of existence its main purpose was to serve as a platform for the explication of ideas and ideals by the nation's leading educators. Included within this group were local, state, and national school officials (both educators and laypeople), educational journalists, college and university leaders, and high-status educators who usually served as university or secondary school teachers or as schoolmasters who supervised the work of teachers serving under their leadership. Membership in all of these groups was overwhelmingly male. Women teachers and other women were allowed to be present at NEA conventions but were forbidden to speak at them or to otherwise participate actively until the twentieth century.[1] In contrast, addressing some of the problems that plagued women teachers was a task that occupied much of the time and attention of the NEA in the twentieth century, though, as we will see, it did not occur in any regular, consistent, or principled manner. Nevertheless, it is a major thesis of this and the rest of the chapters of this book that, in a very real sense, the NEA, from its reorganization in the second decade of the twentieth century until the early 1970s, was to some extent responsive to the desires for recognition and for occupational improvement of the women teachers who composed the bulk of its membership. Further, for much, if not most, of this period, I would argue that the NEA proved more responsive to women teachers than did its rival, the American Federation of Teachers (AFT).

Near the turn of the twentieth century, classroom teachers, particularly women teachers in the primary classrooms of the newly or soon-to-be graded elementary schools, chafed under a set of working conditions that neither rewarded them financially nor recognized their value as educators. Under the direction of charismatic leaders such as Margaret Haley of Chicago, women teachers organized themselves into local groups such as her Chicago Teachers Federation. This group and other local teacher associations gradually became active and influential at NEA conventions to the extent that they became a force to be reckoned with by the association and its male leadership.[2] Increasingly, this leadership either consisted of, or needed to be accountable to, school superintendents, who were in the process of professionalizing a position, through graduate education and other formal qualifications for office, that had been more of a "calling" than a hierarchical, executive position.[3]

In this chapter I explain why and how the NEA responded to the occupational turmoil that characterized the lives of both teachers and superintendents and remade itself in the post–World War I years. The association transformed itself into a formidable organization of educators, consciously advertising itself as a professional association in a campaign designed to appeal to both occupational subgroups, teachers and administrators. The NEA's use of terms like *educator* and *professional* and the tendency to substitute them for the terms *teacher* and *principal* or *superintendent* allowed the association to mute rhetorically and symbolically the differences between the teachers and their organizational superiors that often surfaced in local school controversies. On the other hand, the NEA-sponsored notion of a single educational profession weakened somewhat the obvious patriarchy prevalent in an association that for a half century had not allowed women a voice, let alone a vote, in its affairs. In spite of this rhetorical invocation of one profession designed to appeal to women teachers, the educational professionalism advocated by the new NEA did not envision for them any organizational or occupational autonomy. In place of autonomy, women teachers were granted specific recognition of both their status and their occupational interests in the reorganized NEA, as long as this recognition was not allowed to proceed to the point that it provided any effective challenge to the power of school superintendents in the local schools or to them and the other educational administrators who controlled the new association. Thus, the NEA's new existence as an association of "professional" educators was built not only on a repudiation of the worst patriarchal excesses of the organization's past but also on both a clear understanding and affirmation of the existing hierarchy and patriarchy within the "profession" and a profound antipathy to any serious attacks on that patriarchal hierarchy from women teachers.

PROFESSIONALISM FORESHADOWED

In 1913 Henry Suzallo, a professor of philosophy of education at Teachers College, Columbia University, delivered a paper entitled "The Reorganization of the Teaching Profession" at the annual meeting of the NEA. There was some irony in Suzallo's choice of audience for his remarks; the body that heard his speech, the National Council of Education, was a small, exclusive subgroup of the NEA made up of the most notable educational leaders chosen from both schools and colleges. In his paper Suzallo advocated creation of a new national association of educators, a reformed NEA, that would have little need for small, select groups such as the National Council. The core orientation of the association envisioned by Suzallo was the encompassing task of service to the schools, to the teachers who worked in them, and to the children who attended them.[4]

Using language and voicing concerns borrowed from progressive political reformers, Suzallo claimed that the American educational enterprise was suffering from an acute crisis. He noted that an "educational machine"[5] had grown up in many American cities and that the public schools in those cities were plagued by enormous enrollment increases to which they had mounted little, if any, effective response. The educational machine in those cities was characterized by a stultifyingly prescriptive course of study and a regimen of prescribed teaching methods that was imposed on students and teachers by superintendents who believed that they needed complete control over what took place during every minute in every classroom. Thus, Suzallo characterized classrooms as places for a "monotonous drill and grind" that robbed both teachers and students of their individuality and creativity.[6] Teachers in schools were reduced to the level of closely supervised factory workers at exactly the time when substantial improvement of teaching practice was needed so that they could deal individually with the problems raised by their increasing number of charges. In addition to the challenge to teachers presented by the mushrooming numbers of students, Suzallo claimed that many of the parents of these students had never been to school and that some of the parents had not grown up in the United States but in foreign countries with habits and values different from those of

Americans who had been in the nation for several generations. All of these circumstances provided a severe test of teachers' abilities to succeed in their classrooms at the same time that superintendents were pushing for a uniformity that discouraged innovations that might respond to the new circumstances.

Suzallo argued that one way in which teachers had coped with their difficult work situation was by ignoring it and by emphasizing the economic return for their work. They had adopted this strategy, at least partially, because of the decline in the noneconomic rewards that had come with the mechanization of their teaching. They formed local associations in a number of cities that pursued pensions, tenure, and pay increases and implicitly abandoned the task of ameliorating their increasingly routinized working conditions. Suzallo advocated replacing these associations with a new kind of teachers' organization, one that would not neglect economic and material issues but would accompany their pursuit with activities geared to the more socially and ethically important matters of improving teaching and learning conditions in the schools. These concerns were the hallmarks of "professional" conduct, and they needed to be attended to if teachers were to take their proper place among the ranks of established professionals.

One of Suzallo's listeners was George R. Crissman, the principal of the Warrensburg Normal School in Missouri. This and other public normal schools in Missouri and other states educated women for the graded elementary schools. Crissman was quite sympathetic to the proposals of Suzallo, a Teachers College, Columbia University, professor whose institution was engaged in the training of school administrators and high school teachers. In a prepared response Crissman outlined three types of educational organizations and the abilities and inabilities of each to respond to the educational challenges identified by Suzallo. The first type of organization devoted itself completely to answering questions of educational policy and practice. The second concentrated on economic betterment, and the third adopted both of these emphases. The existing NEA, since its founding in 1857, had represented the first of these types of organization. The local teachers' federations in Chicago, New York, and other large cities represented the second type of organization. The third and preferred type of organization was at best in a formative stage in the activities of a few emerging state educational associations such as those in Ohio and California. For Crissman and for Suzallo, combining the two concerns—interests in educational questions and in occupational improvement—was the only way to "render to the [teaching] profession the kind of service needed."[7]

Better teacher education, both in subject matter and in pedagogy, was another aspect of a fully professional agenda for teacher educators like Suzallo who worked preparing high school teachers in universities and those like Crissman who worked preparing elementary teachers in normal schools. And better preparation of school administrators, another task of university education faculties, went hand in hand with improved teacher training. In fact, for Suzallo it was the insufficient preparation of school superintendents that had led to much of the deadening of teaching that was characteristic in many schools. The schools would improve substantially only if both groups, teachers and administrators, understood and responded to the need for occupational expertise and for a cooperative spirit and meaningful social service orientation within which that expertise would be practiced. The necessary occupational expertise was being nurtured in the emerging educator preparation programs of both normal schools and universities. Both of these institutions were moving toward an orientation that sought to induct their students into the type of educational practice necessary in truly "reformed" public schools. That orientation, however, needed to be reinforced in truly reformed professional organizations devoted to analyzing the problems and issues of educational service for the nation, as well as to the economic betterment of school people.

By linking the normal schools and the universities, giving each an important role in building a reformed educational profession, Suzallo was strategically acknowledging things as they were in the educational world outside of the public schools. The two institutions were in the process of solidifying their distinct roles in teacher training, and the enlightened leaders of both sets of institutions sought cooperation rather than competition in those efforts. There was more than enough work for both sets of institutions to engage in cooperatively, and the agreement at the NEA between Suzallo, from a university-affiliated institution, and Crissman, from a state normal school, testified to that spirit of mutuality.

Yoking the professionalization process with its emphasis on education and social service to the necessary pursuit of the economic improvement of teachers was a carefully crafted strategic move by Suzallo. He did this with full recognition of both emphases but without allowing the economic to supersede the professional, as he thought was the case in large city teacher associations, or without allowing the other emphasis to dominate, as was the case in the existing NEA.

Suzallo's advocacy of a multitiered structure for his teachers' association was another carefully designed aspect of his proposal. He proposed a rather complicated organizational hierarchy with local associations at the base, state associations in the middle, and the national organization at the top. The existing local associations for Suzallo, relatively few but growing in numbers, as already noted, operated mainly in the large cities. They were either teachers' federations that were often characterized by a narrow economic vision or associations of like-minded teachers formed into quasi social clubs with at best a vague occupational purpose.[8] Suzallo described the existing state associations as formally unrelated to the local associations, as well as to the national association. He added that there was no effective "method of cooperation among the state associations." And both the state associations and the existing NEA, in his view, had a "merely occasional purpose." The groups met but once a year and mainly existed to hear addresses.[9]

For Suzallo, the outcome of the existing organizational arrangement was that none of these associations exercised any real influence over educational affairs. Educational accomplishment still rested ultimately in the hands of various lay bodies, local and state school boards dominated by "the influence of partisan and personal politics." Suzallo complained that the "teacher or superintendent who stands against these influences encounters a pernicious hostility. Without the backing of an organized profession for his professional ideals of public service he is . . . likely to lose his position."[10]

Suzallo thus astutely blended the interests of teachers and superintendents by referring to the political dominance over both by lay bodies. Yet, this blending was threatened by divisions between the two sets of educators. Although, in the final analysis, the power of the organized profession Suzallo advocated depended on the large number of teachers who would enroll in newly invigorated associations, it had to exhibit more than the "merely coercive" orientation that characterized many local associations of teachers as they then existed. Suzallo believed that an "ethical cooperation which the true professional practice of education requires" needed to be added to the platforms of the proposed new associations. This cooperation was threatened by politically powerful lay bodies but its successful achievement was also threatened by the orientation of many school superintendents. Not all superintendents were the opponents of improved teachers' associations but some clearly were inimical to those associations—those who ruled tyrannically, ignored teachers' individuality, and justified their own arbitrariness with invocations that the schools were "for children, not the teachers." Suzallo's criticisms of these superintendents clearly implied that many of the chief executives of school systems needed to change their attitudes and actions toward teachers to ensure the success of new associations that encompassed all educational professionals.[11]

The attention Suzallo wanted his new association to pay to local educational affairs also threatened school superintendents who sought complete control over their school systems. He advocated increased emphasis on local organizations, issues, and concerns in place of the existing orientation of NEA-sponsored educational associations toward state and national meetings and discussions. For Suzallo, the new local associations should be organized by city, town, county, or some other geographical basis, and they needed to be kept small enough to ensure adequate discussion of problems. Whatever their locus, they were to be organized democratically, "from the bottom to the top rather than vice versa." Suzallo was clearly telling superintendents here that their teachers needed some degree of occupational autonomy in order to participate significantly and successfully in building a new educational profession.[12]

Turning to the state-level associations, Suzallo wanted those units to be composed of representatives from the local associations and to be governed carefully by a "representative council." This stipulation seemed geared to ensure that the state group clearly represented its local associations and their members rather than dictate to them or go its own way. Yet for Suzallo the state association was also to be more than an extension of its locals. It needed a permanent executive officer, a magazine with a paid editor, and an employment bureau for teachers if it was to facilitate the building of a true educational profession. Suzallo further believed that the new national association was similarly to be both representative of its constituent elements, the state and local associations, and able to deal with its own set of issues. He wanted each state to have the same number of representatives to the national educational body that it had in its congressional delegation and the representatives to be chosen by election from the state associations. The national meeting agenda was to consist of issues common to the states as well as all other educational matters that had important national scope. Suzallo felt that the national group also needed to maintain a central office with a paid secretary who, with participation by an elected executive committee, would administer its affairs.[13]

THE CHALLENGE OF TEACHER UNIONISM

Suzallo's proposal was laced with invocations of the word *professional* and the concept of professionalism as the fundamental building block of the new teachers' associations. This concept was broad and vague enough to animate the reform of the NEA that would be carried out several years after Suzallo had laid his plans. The ambiguities within the NEA's invocation of professionalism allowed the association to evade a number of conflicts that, if addressed directly, might have resulted in a stillbirth rather than a rebirth of the organization. The major conflict obscured by the concept of professionalism, as already suggested, was that which existed between teachers and school administrators. While much of the early history of the reformed NEA subdued that conflict, there was at the least a latent tension between these two groups that often came to the surface.

The prospect of open conflict between the two groups was raised in 1916, one year before the reorganization of the NEA executive office, when the AFT was created. Four local teachers' federations agreed to form the national teachers' union, which quickly affiliated with the American Federation of Labor (AFL), the national labor organization that represented primarily craftsmen and other skilled workers. Three of the four founding locals in the AFT were from the city of Chicago— Margaret Haley's overwhelmingly female federation of teachers from the elementary grades and two high school teachers' federations, one male and the other female. The final initial AFT affiliate was the teachers' federation from the city of Gary, Indiana, located quite near Chicago.[14]

The teachers' union reduced any overt expression of militancy or autonomy for its teacher members early on by adopting a cooperative stance toward the other major actors in school affairs and promising to participate with them in the improvement of American education. The NEA, not yet reorganized according to Suzallo's desires, noticed this apparently benign development of the teachers' union and did not perceive it as a threat. In fact, some early AFT meetings took place at NEA conventions.

The AFT increased its visibility nationally after the affiliation of a large local organization from New York City, a group dominated by men high school teachers though open to others. The New Yorkers brought with them their journal, *The American Teacher,* which quickly became the official organ of the national teachers' union. The early AFT program, though nonconfrontational, had stressed issues such as salaries, pensions, and tenure. The New Yorkers added to this emphasis a dimension of social reform, a flirtation with socialism, and some of the rough-and-tumble tactics that characterized New York political life. The dimension of social reform, socialism, and the activism were less prevalent in the other AFT locals and almost completely absent in the NEA.[15]

The early AFT quickly became embroiled in an internal dispute between the economically oriented midwesterners and the reform-oriented and politically conscious New Yorkers.[16] This conflict, along with the AFT's acknowledged official relationship with the AFL, caused the teachers' union substantial difficulties in recruiting large numbers of members, particularly women teachers, in many parts of the nation, especially in areas outside of the large industrial cities. Competition between the AFT and the NEA for members characterized the relations between the two groups for most of the rest of the twentieth century. It did not start, however, until the NEA undertook, one year after the founding of the AFT, an organizational reform that followed to a great extent the plans and provisions advocated by Henry Suzallo.

Normal Schools, Wartime Conditions, and NEA Reforms

The reform of the NEA would have been much more difficult to launch if the intervention of the United States in World War I had not occurred in 1917, three years after the war had begun in Europe. In the year or so before American entry into the conflict, the nation began to consider and discuss the ramifications of the prospective national involvement. Ironically, in educational circles it was this discussion that provided the impetus to change both the structure and the purpose of the NEA.

The change began in 1917, when a group dominated by normal school administrators began to implement a plan that resembled in large part the suggestions of Henry Suzallo. The NEA reformers, however, chose to begin at the top in their reorganization rather than follow Suzallo's admonition to start from the bottom. Given their status as the administrators of teacher training schools, the reformers saw little that was problematic in their strategy. An initiative starting from the bottom up required involvement begun by teachers such as that which had led to the formation of the AFT one year earlier. The normal school administrators, however, were not as overtly dominant in their relations with teachers as were the school superintendents, whose support they needed to facilitate the reform of the NEA. Rather than organizational superiors of teachers and supervisors of their work, the normal school executives were teacher educators who had an orientation geared as much to facilitation as to domination. Further, the normal school, in addition to its teacher training function, itself served a democratic purpose as a kind of "people's college," an institution characterized by relatively easy access to education for ordinary citizens who had been prevented for a variety of reasons from seeking a university education. And finally, there is increasing evidence that the early normal schools, despite their patriarchal authority featuring largely male administrations and faculty, were places where women students and staff carved spaces for statement and enactment of their own priorities.[17] Tensions between the normal schoolmen and school superintendents will be considered later in this chapter. For now the specific plans of the former group for the NEA's reformation are the topic of concern.

One crucial step in the NEA reorganization was to hire a full-time executive for the association to replace the part-time secretary who had previously served as facilitator of the organization's activities. Additionally, moving the NEA headquarters permanently to Washington, D.C., away from the institution and town where the previous, part-time secretary had held his full-time position, was in order. The new full-time secretary was a midwesterner, J. W. Crabtree. Born in Ohio, he had moved to Nebraska at an early age, attended a normal school in that state, and then served there as a teacher, school principal, and eventually state superintendent of education. He next became a state high school inspector, while serving on the faculty of the University of Nebraska. Ultimately, he rose to the presidency of the state normal school at Peru, Nebraska, where he himself had trained for teaching. After an eventful tenure in Peru, Crabtree moved to the presidency of a noted normal school in River Falls, Wisconsin. It was from that institution that he resigned and moved to Washington to head the reorganization of the NEA in 1917.[18]

Crabtree's roots in the normal school gave him some affinity for the women teachers who were trained in those institutions and who staffed the nation's graded elementary schools. Near the end of his almost two decades of service as the NEA's top officer, the official journal of the association described him as "a great commoner" who had always had a deep love and clear understanding of the interests of teachers. It added that he had long been concerned with improving teachers' salaries, an emphasis that he stressed was crucial to the building of the NEA.[19]

It was the entry of the United States into World War I in 1917 that gave Crabtree and his allies an opportunity to publicize widely their "newly reorganized" association and to use it to speak to teachers' salary grievances and other working conditions. In 1918 Crabtree and his allies chose to establish the Commission on the Emergency in Education and to use it to publicize the association and its work. The NEA cooperated in establishing the commission with its Department of Superintendence, a subgroup of the association that enrolled the most powerful school executives and that was equal if not superior in power and influence to the association. The major stated mission of the commission was to link the schools effectively to the war effort. Just as important for the growth of the new association, the commission also quickly linked the cause of teacher improvement to the wartime crisis conditions.[20]

The war had aggravated the already deteriorating working conditions of teachers in schools. Salaries had been and continued to be a problem. The supply of qualified teachers was threatened as more and more men left for war service and women left teaching for better-paying positions outside of the schools. The result was that increasing numbers of less prepared individuals were being thrown into the nation's classrooms. The negative outcome of this crisis was apparent, according to the NEA commission, in the large number of draftees who could not read or write.

One NEA response to these problems was to reignite a movement it had pursued, intermittently, since its founding in 1857. That movement was a campaign for increased federal involvement in education, most importantly federal financial support for schools and teachers' salaries. Institutionally, the NEA also fought for an increase in the status of the federal educational agency, then a bureau within the Department of the Interior, to that of a full cabinet-level agency with its own secretary. The push for salary improvement for teachers gave the NEA and its Commission on the National Emergency increased visibility among the nation's teachers, who were the victims of the ills that it publicized. Cabinet status for education was pursued to enhance the status of all who worked in the educational enterprise, whether teacher, administrator, or other official, and to bring them closer to the earnestly desired "professionalism."

While the armistice of 1918 ended wartime conditions shortly after the creation of the Commission, neither the economic problems of teachers nor the NEA's invoking of them as a spur for its own organizational agenda disappeared. The Commission on the Emergency in Education continued its work for another two years. Though it disbanded in 1920, its pursuit of federal aid for teachers and schools and a federal department of education was continued with the establishment of a new

Legislative Commission of the NEA. More will be said about the Legislative Commission later in this chapter, when the activities of some of the NEA's new central office staff are described. For now, it is sufficient to conclude that Crabtree and the rest of the new NEA leadership had managed to use the war crisis to publicize their commitment to financial and professional improvement for teachers and schools among both teachers and the larger public. The establishment of the Legislative Commission permanently institutionalized those efforts. In addition to that institutionalization, a structural reform of the NEA was accomplished that helped Crabtree in his larger renovation of the association.

A REMODELED STRUCTURE AND A MAJOR FAULT LINE

A few years before J. W. Crabtree assumed the first permanent secretaryship of the NEA, a movement had begun to streamline the organizational apparatus through which the association conducted its business. This alteration to a large extent fulfilled several of the recommendations of Henry Suzallo. As he had noted in 1913, the NEA's national meeting was largely an assembly whose major purpose was to listen to papers read by educational leaders. Little real "business" was conducted at the annual meeting, other than these presentations of papers and the reading of occasional committee reports. Any official action of the convention, such as the election of a president or the passage of committee-initiated resolutions, was taken by all the members of the NEA who were in attendance at that particular meeting. Of course, many of those who attended the NEA meetings did not do so to vote on resolutions or to otherwise conduct business. This was especially true of the usually large number of teachers who attended the meetings, particularly the teachers from whatever city in which the convention was held who often joined the association by paying yearly dues when they came to the meeting and then let their memberships go unrenewed. Their major purpose in attending was to establish or to confirm their own importance as teachers to this group of educational leaders or to absorb the atmosphere of an elaborate ritual that at least rhetorically confirmed the significance of the American educational enterprise in which they were enrolled.

Responding to the plea of Suzallo and others who sought a more efficient educational association that would address itself seriously to the educational problems and issues of its day, the NEA structural reformers developed a plan to revamp the form and the function of the national meeting. According to this plan, official convention delegates would be chosen to attend the national meeting as representatives of the various state educational associations. The delegates' duty would be to weigh seriously the issues presented in official business sessions of the convention and to cast their votes on the issues using their best judgment of the merits of the various proposals. In addition, the board of directors of the NEA, its executive body, was to be made up of representatives elected by the state education associations. Finally, under reorganization, the actual business sessions of the national convention would become longer and much more important than they heretofore had been. While Suzallo's proposal was for a national convention made up only of business sessions, the NEA reorganizers settled for an upgraded set of business sessions to be held in addition to the usual paper readings and committee reports. In fact, it was through a committee appointed under the prereform NEA, called the Committee on Reorganization, that the proposal was officially presented to change the national meeting. This committee was appointed in 1915 and was headed by William Owen, a normal school educator from Chicago, Illinois, and an ally of Crabtree.[21]

Ironically, it was teachers, the group that Suzallo saw as the core of the revamped educational professionalism that would be embodied in the new NEA, who balked at reorganization. Teachers had begun to attend the NEA in numbers and to raise their concerns at least a decade earlier. In 1905 an appointed Committee on Teachers Salaries reported to the NEA convention and called for improvement in teacher salaries nationwide. Since there was little way for the NEA to act officially on the proposal, and perhaps because of the diffidence of the many males who made up the NEA's leadership cadre, little was done, and another almost identical resolution was passed in 1912.

In that same year a subunit of the NEA, the Department of Classroom Teachers, was established in response to a strong push for representation from women teachers, most of whom were working in the primary grades. The new department was consciously geared toward the interests and desires of women teachers in the graded elementary schools. The 1910 election of Ella Flagg Young, superintendent of the Chicago, Illinois, schools, as the first woman president of the NEA was another sign of the emergence of women teachers as a force to be reckoned with in the NEA. In 1912, along with the salary resolution and implementation of the classroom teachers' department, passage of a resolution endorsing women's suffrage was still another indication of the increased recognition of women teachers. And in 1915, the same year that the Committee on Reorganization first made its proposal for change, an informal but effective policy was initiated in the NEA of choosing only presidential nominees who were women in every other year, thereby guaranteeing the presence of a woman in the top elected position in the association for half of the time. All in all, then, women teachers had made some headway in gaining recognition for their priorities in the as yet unreformed NEA. Increasingly in the first two decades of the twentieth century, they had made the national meetings a place where they voiced many of their occupational concerns.

In fact, it was in large part to protect their recently won gains within the NEA that the women teachers objected to reorganization. While the reorganization committee argued that the changes were necessary to improve the functioning of the NEA as a vehicle for the new educational profession, teachers feared that the change to a representative governance structure would diminish their voice and influence. Under the existing practices, which are well described as embodying a "town meeting" format, all NEA members who attended the meeting had a vote in any election or on any committee report or other business item. Under the reorganization proposal, the number of voting members—that is, the elected delegates from the state associations—would be drastically reduced, and nonvoting attendees at the meeting would have little ability to influence the business of the association.

As long as the NEA meetings were held in cities where there was a strong local teachers' association, which could turn out a number of teachers to vote on business, the proposal for reorganization was unlikely to pass. This was the case in 1918 and 1919 as teachers in the cities of Pittsburgh and Milwaukee, respectively, attended the meeting and defeated the reorganization. In 1920, however, the NEA leadership, including Secretary Crabtree, arranged for the annual meeting to be held in Salt Lake City, Utah, a city that did not have a strong local teachers' association. In addition, the political climate of Utah, a conservative state dominated by the avowedly patriarchal Mormon Church, made the possibility of a controversy over the issue of protecting the prerogatives of women teachers even more unlikely. The outcome of the Salt Lake City meeting, unsurprisingly and despite the opposition of a few non-Utah teachers' activists such as Margaret Haley of Chicago, was the approval of the Committee on Reorganization's proposal for structural reform. From 1920 on, the official business at NEA conventions was conducted only by vote of the official delegates chosen in the various state education associations.[22]

Despite the objections of Haley and other activist women, the Committee on Reorganization argued that relying on state education associations for delegates to conduct the official business of the NEA brought the NEA closer to more teachers. Yet the reorganization did little effectively to realize Suzallo's objective of building the professionalized NEA from the bottom up—that is, from a base of active affiliated local associations. While reorganization provided for affiliation on the part of local associations that could send delegates to the newly established business body, the Representative Assembly, it did not require that this be done. Rather, delegates had to come from state associations, which were under no requirement to work with local associations in choosing representatives.[23]

While the advocates of reorganization had outmaneuvered teacher opponents and passed their proposal for structural alteration, Crabtree and other NEA leaders knew that in a very real sense success for the new professional association depended on teacher membership. Building that membership base was made even more difficult during and after reorganization by the success of the AFT in increasing its number of local teachers' unions in the immediate postwar years. Thus, with reorganization the NEA moved vigorously to recruit teachers using a variety of strategies. One of these that was implemented in the early 1920s was to court Haley and other women leaders of local associations by emphasizing the Department of Classroom Teachers as the venue where the interests of grade teachers would be served. Another was to encourage superintendents to cajole, persuade, require, or otherwise convince their teachers to join the new "professional" organization. The response was overwhelmingly positive, judging by NEA membership statistics for the 1920s. Membership in the NEA grew from 8,466 in 1917, the year Crabtree became secretary and moved the headquarters to Washington, D.C., to 205,678 in 1929 and to more than 220,000 in 1931.[24] Though this figure was but half of what Suzallo had set as his goal for membership in 1913, it was a substantial accomplishment that provided considerable new dues income for the association to use to fund new programs and other initiatives.

Crabtree's accomplishment in building the NEA as a professional association with a large number of teacher members was remarkable. Yet within it was contained one substantial fault line that at least potentially threatened the success of the operation. Specifically, the potential problem was that although the bulk of membership came, had to come, from classroom teachers, the reins of power in the organization were clearly and firmly controlled by one or another group of school administrators.

School superintendents were firmly in command of most local school systems and also dominated the state education associations, which chose the delegates to the NEA Representative Assembly.

Crabtree and his normal school allies in the NEA, as already suggested, did not have precisely the same interests and orientations that the super-intendents had, but neither group advocated an independent-minded, teacher-led association. Crabtree sought to balance or at least to be somewhat responsive to the interests of both teachers and superinten-dents. Yet any and all of Crabtree's actions that spoke to teachers had to be undertaken with the concerns of the superintendents and their institu-tionalized voice within the NEA, the Department of Superintendence, clearly in mind. That department was by far the most powerful subunit of the NEA, both before and after reorganization. It met independently from the parent association, in a different place and at a different time of year, and it was open only to superintendents and those others invited by superintendents to participate. Crabtree could ill afford to lose the sup-port of this powerful group or to otherwise alienate the individuals who were its members. This almost came to pass in 1920, in the midst of the NEA's reorganization. At that time, the Department of Superintendence considered seceding from the NEA, with some of its members arguing that Crabtree and other leaders catered cravenly and unnecessarily to teachers.[25] Such conduct encouraged teachers to believe that they might have an autonomous existence in the schools, one not mediated through their superiors, as well as autonomy in the association. Needless to say, the chief executives of local school systems, with few exceptions, saw little merit in this type of autonomy.

The organizational embodiment of such wrongheaded autonomy was seen by many superintendents to be in the teacher unionism that had flourished with the establishment and early growth of the AFT, beginning in 1916. During World War I the federal government was intent on pur-suit of the war effort and consciously compromised with big business and craft unions on permissive labor policies that ensured that the pro-duction of war materials was not compromised in any way by work stop-pages. The result was a brief honeymoon period for unions and an increase in union membership, including teacher union membership. An-other spur to increased teacher unionism was the war and postwar infla-tion, which intensified teachers' long-held salary grievances.

A counteroffensive against organized labor quickly gained momen-tum in postwar America, however. Both the government and the citi-zenry, formerly intent on punishing anything German during the war, looked askance after the armistice at the emerging Soviet Union and its communist ideology as the new source of the subversion of American values. Strikes in several sectors, including a notable and notorious strike by Boston policemen in 1919, further inflamed the situation.[26] When a rash of bombings of unknown origins was publicized, one of which damaged the home of Attorney General A. Mitchell Palmer, he responded by leading a series of raids against suspected subversives across the nation. These and other various "red scares," at least one of which occurred in the New York City schools and in turn sparked a vigorous AFT defense of teachers attacked as subversives, brought trade unionism quickly into disrepute with the larger populace. Corporate and industrial leaders, along with the government, all of whom had cooperated with unions during the war, now reversed their position and fought organized labor with astonishing vigor. The development of various welfare capitalist plans to "take care" of workers, including company unions and other employee associations organized by ownership and management themselves, stopped the growth of independent unionism.

The NEA capitalized on this turn of events by sponsoring and publicizing the teacher representation, or teachers' council, movement as an alternative to teachers' unions. Councils, bodies of teachers chosen to provide advice to principals and the school superintendent of local systems, were advocated by numerous speakers at NEA meetings and within committees of the association throughout the 1920s. While the councils did not represent any movement toward autonomy for teachers, they often did speak to teachers' desire for some recognition as "professionals" whose opinion on educational problems and issues was worthy of being heard and heeded. It is impossible to the see councils as bottom-up vehicles for the building of a broad professional consciousness, as Henry Suzallo advocated. A better description of what the councils really signified was that they represented, at best, the desire of some administrators to attend responsively to their teachers' concerns and, at worst, the company-unionlike vehicle that educational leaders used to head off any genuine, independent teacher voice in school affairs.

Within the AFT and its local affiliates, where a more autonomous teacher voice might have arisen, internal disputes between leaders from different parts of the country with different approaches to teacher unionism combined with the growing antiunion political climate to close off that possibility. In turn, this combination of factors prevented the AFT from emerging as a serious threat to the NEA for the affiliation of most teachers. AFT membership declined severely through the 1920s, causing the union leaders to fear for the very life of their organization.[27]

The NEA's challenge in this period was to institutionalize nationally what had been accomplished in many local systems through the teachers' council movement. The NEA sought to harness the teachers and their interests firmly to its own structure and agenda and to use teacher dues to fuel association growth. To accomplish these purposes, teachers had to be provided with enough recognition and rewards from the national organization to maintain their interest and support. All of this had to be accomplished by J. W. Crabtree and the other NEA leaders without alienating the members of the Department of Superintendence, who were on the alert for any dilution of their authority, either in their own systems or in larger state or national arenas.

As already noted, Crabtree had to head off a secession movement from the NEA by the Department of Superintendence, and he carefully guarded his flanks from further attacks by superintendents or school principals at the same time that he encouraged masses of teacher members. Conflict between teachers and school administrators was a constant possibility to be warded off in whatever ways deemed necessary by Crabtree and his allies. He undertook a number of initiatives to build the NEA in the 1920s without provoking this conflict. For example, the creation of the Department of Elementary Education of the NEA in the 1920s gave elementary teachers another arena in which to express their concerns, along with the Department of Classroom Teachers, without threatening the already existing Department of Elementary Principals. This last group continued to cater to the organizational leaders of the graded elementary schools.

It was not just teachers who threatened the interests of school superintendents within the NEA. In 1922 the NEA abolished the Department of School Patrons, one place for lay influence in association affairs. In 1924, in response to pressure from the Department of Superintendence, the NEA Representative Assembly voted to abolish the Department of School Administration, the subgroup that had been created before reorganization to recognize the interests of school board members. The official reason given for this action was the overlap of interests between the Department of Superintendence and the Department of School Administration. It seems, however, that the move was related more to the desires of superintendents not to have their interests compromised by laypeople, even those elected to govern public schools, than to any genuine concern for overlap.[28] Superintendents had benefited from a variety of campaigns within their own districts to control lay board interference with school managers' prerogatives. Reforms such as the elimination of numerous neighborhood-based boards with substantial numbers of members and their replacement by one central board of education with few members were undertaken, particularly in large urban districts. These changes were advocated on the grounds of educational efficiency, an objective that also reinforced the substantial thrust for more power for the superintendent.[29]

Thus, the structural reform of the NEA—begun in 1915, achieved in 1920, and consolidated throughout the rest of that decade by Secretary Crabtree—did not succeed in finally reconciling completely the interests of teachers and administrators or of administrators and elected school lay officials. The reformed NEA did, however, manage to keep its teacher members happy—without alienating the superintendents. Crabtree undertook other improvements of the NEA operations, including the expansion of the association's central office, while never losing sight of the difficulties that might emerge within the association between its two major classes of members, teachers on the one hand and superintendents and their growing array of administrative underlings on the other.

THE EXPANSION OF THE NEA CENTRAL OFFICE

Additions to the staff and the responsibilities of the NEA's Washington office during the 1920s enhanced J. W. Crabtree's ability to court both school superintendents and the nation's classroom teachers as constituencies for the association and its programs. One innovation was his establishment of a new journal for the association in 1920 to call attention to the changes then taking place and their value for enhancing the educational profession. The *Journal of the National Education Association* replaced a newsletter-like publication of the association. The *Journal* was edited by Joy Elmer Morgan, a Nebraskan who had studied with Crabtree when the latter was president of the Peru Normal School in that state. Morgan had experience as a teacher, administrator, and school librarian, as well as experience as a newspaper reporter. This breadth of background helped him to make the new journal vital and responsive to all of the various interests represented within the new educational profession.

Like most NEA staff, Morgan had responsibilities in addition to editing the journal. In the area of membership he routinely navigated the fault line between superintendents and teachers with great success, encouraging the former to influence the latter to join the association without appearing heavy-handed. In an oral history interview made some years after his retirement from the NEA, he discussed how as the staff member whose major function was membership, he would visit a state, identify the best local superintendents, make appointments with them, compliment them on their outstanding leadership, and encourage them to induce their teachers to join the association.[30]

Morgan also had major responsibility for an alliance that the NEA forged with a noneducator conservative political group, an arrangement that managed to guard the association's right political flank.[31] Beginning in 1921, the NEA embarked on a relationship with the American Legion, a powerful voice for both American veterans and the superpatriotism that they often supported. Major outcomes of this alliance were legion speakers at NEA meetings, a series of patriotic booklets for use in schools, and annual cosponsorship of American Education Week by the two groups. This last activity, in which the legion pledged to support and publicize the work of the public schools nationally, gave the NEA and American public education an annual dose of support from a group that otherwise might have contributed criticism. The NEA's cooperation with this conservative group at least partially insulated the association from the charges of socialism or communism that the legion used to berate the AFT in the 1920s.

Growth in numbers is the most obvious way that Crabtree built the NEA central office staff. Starting with himself and only a few clerical assistants in 1917, by 1922 the headquarters staff had expanded to fifty people organized into five divisions. When Crabtree retired in the early 1930s, the number of staff had risen to 140 and the number of divisions to nine.[32] In addition to numbers, another way to look at NEA staff growth, at how it contributed to the pursuit of the association's professional agenda and how the association appealed both to teachers and superintendents, is to profile the career of the association's most visible woman staff member.

Charl O. Williams and the Legislative Services Division

Charl O. Williams began a notable career as an NEA staff member in 1922 that would last for more than a quarter of a century. Her experience in schools and in the NEA itself before taking a staff position made her an ideal candidate to pursue the reformed NEA agenda of a powerful presence in Washington, D.C., and the building of an organization that spoke to both teachers and school administrators without alienating either group. Before coming to the NEA, Williams had earned a reputation as an effective rural educator in the state of Tennessee. She started her work as a rural school teacher; she soon became a high school teacher and then a high school principal. Eventually, she became superintendent

of the Shelby County schools, the largely rural school district that encompassed the areas surrounding the city of Memphis, Tennessee. In addition to her school leadership, Williams also was active in women's
political work in the Volunteer State. She was a notable leader in the crusade to get the Tennessee legislature to ratify the nineteenth (women's
suffrage) amendment to the constitution.[33] Williams served eight years
as a county school superintendent, and in the last of those eight years she
was also elected as the president of the NEA.[34]

After completing her presidential year, Williams was chosen as one
of two field secretaries on the NEA headquarters staff, making her the
highest ranking woman staff member of the association. She would re-
tain that position and ranking for the better part of the next three decades,
retiring from the NEA late in 1949. This discussion of Williams's career
in the NEA will deal with her work as president and then as a staff member, placing it in light of the larger development of the association in the
period from the end of World War I to the early 1930s. It will highlight
both Williams's symbolic and real significance as a woman leader of the
association, as well as her accomplishments on behalf of women teachers. Further, it will show that her political ties to both school superintendents and Washington's political interest groups made both groups
confident that teacher advocacy in the NEA did not threaten their own
welfare.

Williams ascended to the NEA presidency in 1921, an important
time in its history. Her election occurred at the first convention in which
the association was governed by the Representative Assembly. Williams's
year as president, encompassing the period from mid-1921 to mid-1922,
furthered Crabtree's major objective of effective organizational development. Her picture was featured in the middle of an article outlining a new
NEA arrangement by which teachers would join and pay dues to their
local and state associations, as well as to the national association. This
plan enabled the creation of "a complete and effective organization of the
teaching profession, and the closest co-operation between local, State,
and National organizations." After declaring the success of the new form
of governance in making the NEA "the instrument of the teachers of the
nation," the article concluded with an announcement by President
Williams of a prize for the state that enrolled the largest number of members in the forthcoming year.[35]

Williams herself issued her own call to service to "educators of all
classes and ranks" in an article in the NEA's new journal. In this call,
which was placed within a larger article on better salaries for better

teachers, Williams indicated several challenges facing the NEA: enormous improvement in elementary education, particularly in rural areas, the universalization of secondary education "for every boy and girl," and appropriate growth in higher education to meet the challenge of providing leadership in a democracy. She concluded that professional unity of all teachers within the NEA was required to meet these and other challenges.[36]

Before becoming president of the NEA, Williams had served as chair of the association's Committee on Tenure. In an article published during her presidential year highlighting the work of the committee, Williams presented the NEA's argument for increased tenure protection for teachers. She invoked principles of both civil service employment and professional stability as the grounding for that protection. She identified tenure as the foundation of professionalism in teachers; it served their salary stability and facilitated their occupational improvement. In all of these particulars, Williams linked the interests of teachers directly to the program of the NEA, concluding with a plea to support the efforts of NEA affiliates in every state to achieve tenure legislation.[37]

In several addresses to the NEA convention that culminated her presidential year, Williams sounded themes that reinforced the association's relationship with the teacher. Her presidential address, titled "The Democratic Awakening and Professional Organization," touted the Representative Assembly form of governance and the other organizational changes pioneered by Secretary Crabtree as the impetus for the increase in the number of NEA members from fifty thousand to one hundred thousand in the past year. She spoke approvingly of the work being done by the NEA headquarters staff, the body that she shortly would join. Moving to larger themes, she tied the professional improvement of the nation's teaching force to the task of democratic awakening throughout American society. After brief mention of the special problems of rural schools, she concluded with an invocation of public education as a vehicle for national greatness. "We are here to dedicate ourselves anew to . . . further improvement . . . to the end that education of the people, by the people, and for the people shall make good the glorious promise of democracy."[38]

In another speech to the NEA convention at the end of her presidential year, Williams sounded themes that reassured the women teachers who had joined the NEA that their investment in the association was well spent. After noting that the "classroom teacher is the very heart of the public-school system of America," she spent considerable time on the improvements that were necessary in teachers' salaries in order that the heart of the system be maintained in a healthy state. She then acknowledged the importance of pension legislation, minimum salary provisions, and a single salary scale to the educational improvement of the nation. The single salary scale was particularly important to women teachers, since it offered "the same salary to all men and women of equal training and equally successful experience, regardless of the grade or department in which the work is done." Here Williams was espousing a crusade that built on the earlier equal pay movements women teachers had waged in many of the nation's cities. While these crusades resulted in women teachers who did the same work as men receiving equal pay, the single salary schedule moved the women's equity movement one step further: women elementary teachers who had the same training and years of experience as men high school teachers were to be paid the same salaries. This equity reform would not be realized fully until the time of Williams's retirement from the NEA at mid-century. She made support of the single salary scale a constant theme of her work for the association.[39]

In two other speeches to the NEA convention in 1922, Williams decried the low average salary of the American teacher of $700 per year, bemoaned the fact that many teachers received even less than this paltry sum, and outlined the provisions of a model teacher tenure law for the forty-one of the forty-eight states that did not have such legislation.[40] Williams almost always combined her program for improved teacher welfare with a call for increased professional training, establishment of codes of ethics or other devices to insure professional practice, and larger enrollment of teachers in local, state, and national educational associations. Like Crabtree and other NEA power brokers, she realized that the success of the NEA rested on its ability to attract teacher members through appeals to both their material and professional interests. Also like her colleagues in the NEA leadership, she never couched her ideas about improving teacher welfare or building an educational profession in ways that pitted teachers' interests against those of school superintendents or other administrators.

After Williams's presidency of the NEA ended at the mid-summer 1922 convention, she returned to the superintendency of the Shelby County school system but only for a brief period. By November of that year, she was chosen to be a member of the NEA's permanent staff at its Washington headquarters. Williams's first official title was that of field secretary. She was one of two individuals named to that position, replacing the first-ever field secretary, who had served in the position since

being appointed by Crabtree several years earlier. The two new field secretaries divided their labor: Williams was assigned to publicize and develop the NEA program with lay audiences; her counterpart was to work
within the constituency of educational professionals.[41] Within two years
Williams's co–field secretary resigned from the association and was not
replaced. Williams was then the association's top field-worker, assigned
both lay and professional responsibilities. She retained this position and
was the NEA's most visible female presence for the next quarter century.

Though Williams had a wide-ranging assignment, particularly after
she became the association's only field secretary and head of the newly
established Legislative Services Division, the bulk of the work that she
did for the NEA in her first decade on its staff was as the major lobbyist
and publicist for its campaign to establish a federal department of education. Within the NEA's larger crusade to become the leading professional
organization in the nation, the campaign for a federal department had
an important role. A United States Department of Education would increase the visibility of the nation's educational effort, which was obscured by the place of the federal Bureau of Education within the
Department of the Interior. More prominence and significance for education in Washington would, in turn, bring more respect for the NEA from
the nation's political leaders. And this, in turn, would enable the NEA to
pursue its program of professional and occupational improvement more
effectively. Williams had been involved in the NEA's effort to establish a
federal department of education during her presidential year. As the
elected leader of the association, hers was the first signature on "A Petition for a Department of Education" that was also signed by the leaders
of thirteen other national organizations. Prominent among these organizations were six women's groups (several of which Williams either had
served or would serve as an officer), the American Federation of Labor,
the American Council on Education, and national groups in the library
and music fields.[42]

Williams worked assiduously on behalf of the federal department
for her first ten years at the NEA. A recent study of federal involvement
in education in the 1920s highlighted the way that the NEA combined
the occupational agenda of better teacher salaries with the pursuit of professionalism, two consistent themes of Williams in her work. Also, the
tactic of directly lobbying Congress and the president, pioneered under
the Commission on the Emergency in Education but expanded in a
greatly sophisticated fashion by Williams, was identified as a prototype
of the "new lobbying" that came to characterize national politics in the

early twentieth century. This new lobbying was "institutionalized, public, and conducted by voluntary associations," in contrast to the activities of earlier decades, which had been informal and secretive and carried out by those who represented individual corporations.[43]

An important part of Williams's participation in lobbying for federal involvement in education was her charge to maintain friendly and productive relations with allied groups, particularly club women and organized labor. She also developed close alliances with a number of politicians who favored the NEA cause. In analyzing the sources of her own commitment to the NEA program, the parallel between her earlier work for women's suffrage in the state of Tennessee and the NEA's political campaign deserves special notice. Williams herself remarked to the 1927 NEA convention, in the context of a report on her efforts for the federal department, that "What we really need is some of the old spirit of the suffrage campaign." She added that many of the women at the NEA convention were familiar with that earlier struggle and that the decades-long campaign for suffrage that eventually bore fruit was a perfect model for the NEA's effort for a federal department of education, which was now entering its second decade.[44]

As part of her work with women's organizations, Williams held office in a number of those groups, including the National Federation of Women's Clubs and the National Congress of Parents and Teachers (NCPT). She served as a vice president of the parent-teacher group and as director of its Department of Education. In that capacity she wrote several articles in the NCPT magazine, *Child Welfare,* that supported the establishment of a federal department of education as a major step in accomplishing the improvement of education desired by the organization. She performed similarly in her role as an officer in the National Federation of Women's Clubs, serving as spokesperson for the cause of the federal department within the organization and as a writer of articles advocating the cause and other aspects of the NEA program in its publications.[45]

Williams's interactions with the AFL also deserve comment. Her longtime cooperation with that group harnessed the national labor federation to the NEA's campaign for the federal department at the same time that it helped maintain a wedge between the AFL and its own constituent body representing teachers, the AFT. Support from Williams and the NEA for a child labor constitutional amendment that was a cornerstone of the AFL's program, as well as Williams's successful interactions with AFL leaders at a personal level, cemented the alliance between the professional educators and the group of craft union leaders of the AFL. Marjorie Murphy has commented on Williams's effectiveness in hampering the AFT. Further, she contrasted Williams's "free rein" within the NEA to pursue affiliation with other women's groups and to appeal directly to women teachers with the plight of women activists in the AFT, who had to contend with the male dominance of their own organization as well as with the conservatism of the larger AFL toward women's rights and other social and political reforms.[46]

Murphy also highlighted Williams's effective cooperation with Republican women, a critical alliance in the 1920s when three different Republicans held the presidency. Some of these women believed that Williams herself might become the first secretary of the new department of education when it was established. In addition to women Republicans, Williams interacted on behalf of the federal education department with several other more conservative groups that might have been expected to oppose it. Williams's reports and correspondence for this period reveal political alliances in support of the federal department with a group of southern governors, the Women's Christian Temperance Union, the Daughters of the American Revolution, the Scottish Rite Masonic Order, and several different national Protestant religious groups. Many Protestant denominations were conspicuous in support of the federal department, while Catholics were prominent opponents of the legislation.[47] Catholic fears of the federal department were linked to their campaign support for and their fear of government control of their own private schools.

Williams led the formation of a substantial lobby for the federal department of education that acted throughout the 1920s into the early 1930s. Although the effort to establish the federal department was unsuccessful, Williams's political accomplishment in forming and maintaining the political coalitions that supported it was unprecedented in educational circles. The Williams-NEA type of political lobbying nationally can be contrasted with the local orientation and political pressure tactics of local teachers' associations some decades earlier. For example, Margaret Haley and her Chicago Teachers Federation were more than willing to confront the economically and politically powerful who sought and won favorable tax treatment that hampered severely the funding of public schools. Williams and the NEA, in contrast, were unwilling to wage public conflict with political enemies, preferring to seek alliances by which the enemies would be overcome. Also, Haley and other early teacher leaders cultivated ties to local parent groups, seeking to work with them in the interests of community involvement, which the teacher leaders did not fear. Again in contrast, Williams and the NEA sought national alliances with club women and other socially prestigious groups who were interested in the larger picture of reform and improvement and who were unimpressed, if not downright fearful, over the prospect of community control of local schools.[48]

Charl O. Williams was clearly the kind of staff member needed to win friends for the NEA in Washington political circles, from the teachers interested in proper conduct on behalf of their interests and the larger cause of education, and from school superintendents who recognized that she was one of them before coming to work for the NEA and was unlikely to take action that was inimical to their interests. Her visibility as the highest ranking woman staff member at the NEA reinforced the professional image of the association, its reputation for service to women teachers, its abilities to interact effectively in the developing political environment of Washington, D.C., and its increasing number of occupational associations. In short, Williams was competent and confident in her role in the NEA and proud to be the visible leader of the women on the NEA staff.

Of course, Charl Williams was not the only woman on the NEA staff, and the Legislative Services Division was not the only, or even the most important, part of the central office. The body that became the most important and reputable part of the NEA central office was the Research Division.

THE NEA RESEARCH DIVISION AND ITS AUDIENCES

The first official mention of a research body as part of the NEA central office occurred at the national convention in 1921. At that meeting two proposals surfaced regarding the research enterprise. One came from the Commission on the Coordination of Research, headed by the noted superintendent of the Denver, Colorado, public schools, Jesse Newlon. For Newlon and his commission, research was a function that would primarily aid school superintendents who needed solid justification for ongoing and increased school expenditures in the stringent financial conditions that characterized the post–World War I era. Superintendents required proposals and policies "based on facts" rather than on sentiment or simple assertions.[49]

A second proposal from the Committee on Sources of Revenue repeated the focus of the first proposal but broadened the audience for the proposed research operation beyond superintendents to include state and local education associations. This committee asked that the association "establish a bureau of economics" to be headed by a "scientifically trained student of economics and statistics." The bureau, in conformity with the purpose of the recent organizational alteration of the NEA, was to provide "service to the affiliated state and local associations with respect to school revenues and finances."[50]

The two calls were heeded almost immediately and the Research Department of the NEA was founded on March 1, 1922. In discussing its activities, suggestions were made for the department to be a "clearing house," to contain a "reference library of information" gathered from city and state reports, and to gather information and formulate statements on current and future educational problems. In fact, the Research Department did establish a library and did serve as a coordinating body that planned, conducted, and disseminated studies to state and local associations. It met still another important association objective when it was asked to supplement and support the activities of the federal educational agency. One of the proposing bodies wanted the new department to be organized so that its activities could be "turned over to the Research Department of the National Department of Education when it is eventually organized."[51]

While the creation of the Research Division was largely the work of J. W. Crabtree, specific decisions regarding its configuration, staff, and program were within the purview of John K. Norton, its first director. Norton came to the NEA from the position of director of the Bureau of Research and Extension at the San Jose State Teachers College, which had formerly been titled a state normal school. Son of a school principal, Norton had served as a teacher and principal in Oakland, California, as well as a director of research in that city's school system. His teaching and normal school background echoed the orientation of Crabtree and his organizational allies, and Norton's many years of experience in California made him attractive since that state and its teacher associations were regarded as a model of professional activity that the national association should encourage in other states. Norton had degrees in education from the University of California at Berkeley and from Stanford University, studying at the latter institution with the noted educational administrator Ellwood P. Cubberley. Norton's training and experience in a school system research bureau and his other wide-ranging experiences in education made him a popular choice with school superintendents, directors of research bureaus in city school systems, and officers and staff of state education associations for the position of director of the Research Division.[52]

In his report on his first four months in office at the 1922 NEA convention, Norton highlighted his efforts in the area of school finance as well as his activities with state and local associations—the priorities of the commission and the committee that had proposed the new division. In a nod to teacher interests in the association, he added that he had worked with the Committee on Salaries, Tenure, and Pensions.[53] Thus Norton managed to highlight activities that pleased every interest and interest group important to building the new NEA. His political acumen proved as good a qualification for his position and for helping build the NEA as were his experiences in research and other educational activities.

The title of the Research Division's first publication, which came in 1922, was "Facts on the Cost of Public Education and What They Mean." In twin prefaces to the report, Norton and Crabtree restated priorities that clearly emphasized the major goals of the reorganized NEA. Crabtree noted that the Research Division would gather and publish information, a function that was not then being performed by the federal government's Bureau of Education. He called this situation "neglect of education on the part of the Government" and said that it had provoked the NEA to establish its own agency and, in a sense, do the government's work. Norton's preface emphasized the coordinating role of the new department. Data for the first report had been gathered from cooperative school administrators as well as from within the Bureau of Education, in response to a request from the NEA's teacher-oriented salary committee. He added that the Research Division's success depended ultimately on the numerous school systems of the nation and urged them to forward results of their own investigations for compilation and distribution to others.[54]

Norton moved quickly to build his new division by enhancing his budget and increasing the number of professional and clerical staff. While the budget for the Research Division was $18,000 for its first year of existence, it had increased to $48,000 five years later.[55] The Research Division's growth was greater than that of any other division in the NEA headquarters operation, a testimony to the high status that it assumed from the earliest days of its development and that it maintained and enhanced throughout the 1920s. Much of the Research Division's importance depended on its ability to relate to two major constituencies—teachers and superintendents.

The Research Division and the Classroom Teacher

A major constituency that the Research Division needed to cultivate was composed of classroom teachers. From the beginning, salaries and other issues of material interest to teachers constituted a focus of the work. For example, of the five issues of the *Research Bulletin* published in the first year of the work of the division, each devoted to a single topic, three dealt with tenure laws for teachers, salary schedules, and retirement systems, respectively. These topics reappeared regularly in issues of the *Research Bulletin* published in the rest of the 1920s. In a forward to a May 1927 issue of the *Bulletin* devoted to teacher salaries, Secretary Crabtree noted that as one of its two most important objectives, the NEA "has sought to secure social and economic recognition for teaching comparable to that of other professions requiring equivalent training, character, and responsibility." In a bow to the NEA's professional posture of cooperation with all interested parties, he added that the information presented would be of use to "superintendents, committees of citizens, and teacher organizations." He concluded, however, with a return to a focus on teachers, indicating that the intended result was "better salaries for teachers."[56]

This issue of the *Bulletin,* like most issues, devoted a substantial number of its pages to the presentation of tables and charts; almost as many pages contained these graphic representations as were devoted to text. The objective of the presentation of the graphic information was clear: it was intended to provide ammunition for the crusade to raise teachers' salaries. For example, readers of one chart in the *Bulletin* saw that the average teacher salary of $1,275 was roughly two-thirds of the $1,908 salary of high-grade clerical workers, just above the $1,200 salary of ordinary clerical workers and slightly below the $1,309 paid annually to manufacturing workers. More dramatically, readers learned that the average teacher's salary was more than $700 below the average for all employed persons ($2,010) and about half of the $2,500 earned yearly by trade union members. In case readers might not draw the proper conclusion from the charts and graphs, the text drew it for them: "Teachers' salaries are completely outclassed by the returns for other forms of professional service . . . and are lower than the wages received in many occupations calling for little training and the performance of service of no greater significance to the general welfare."[57]

The combination of frequent invocations of teaching as a profession worthy of substantial remuneration with the presentation of actual salary data was a characteristic of all publications of the Research Division devoted to the topic. In fact, from the beginning, the Research Division produced a new study of teachers' salaries every two years, a project designed to keep the NEA and its activities clearly in the forefront of the minds of teachers, who knew they were worthy of occupational improvement and who believed that the publication of the information was mainly what was necessary to arouse a lethargic public to act on their behalf. Publications on tenure and retirement featured the same combination of data and text and the same rationale that characterized the salary works.

Teacher benefits were also the focus of the publicizing of the efforts of the Research Division in the pages of the *NEA Journal.* For example, in early 1928, John K. Norton began a series of articles on teachers' salaries that used data from a previous year's issue of the *Research Bulletin* as well as other sources. Norton introduced the series in the first article by noting that each was "based on authentic data in the files of the Research Division to which school systems throughout the country turn constantly for the latest information on every type of salary question." In a 1922 contribution to the *Journal,* Norton had compared static teacher salaries to a rising cost of living and noted that "there is no reason why teachers' salaries should not keep pace with the cost of living in so far as the country's income represents its ability to pay." And in 1925 an article in the *Journal* based on an issue of the *Bulletin* published one month earlier contained numerous pages of charts on teachers' salaries as well as those of other school employees. A discussion after several pages of charts reached the following conclusion: "Salaries must be raised to the amount that will not only attract the best of the Nation's youth to the teaching profession, but also give adequate tangible tribute for service rendered." Thus, in articles geared to teachers that featured allusions guaranteed to appeal to both their pocketbooks and their sense of themselves as professional social servants, the statistical data contained in the *Bulletins* was distilled and presented with the proper conclusion explicitly drawn in the *Journal.*[58]

The Research Division and School Administrators

One should not conclude from the above discussion that the work of the Research Division was geared solely, or even mainly, to teachers' interests. In fact, if there was one major audience to which the division marketed its wares, it comprised school superintendents and other school administrators. The data gathered on teachers' salaries came from reports generated by school systems and were in turn useful to superintendents as ammunition to obtain funding increases for their systems. Further, many discussions of salaries published by the Research Division dealt with administrators' salaries as well as with those of their employees. And the occasional noneconomically oriented publications of the division were almost always of more direct interest to those who managed the schools than to those who taught in them. Issues of the *Research Bulletin* devoted to the curriculum dealt with the makeup of the "course of study" in the schools rather than with innovations in particular subjects in classrooms, a clear sign that administrators were the target audience.[59] Other issues devoted to topics such as record keeping and state education laws also were clearly geared for school leaders. On the rare occasion when instructional reform became a focus of the Research Division, the emphasis was on the administrator, not the teacher. In the one (and only) issue of the *Research Bulletin* devoted to progressive education in the 1920s, the orientation to school administration was well illustrated in the title: "The Principal and Progressive Movements in Education."[60]

There is more direct evidence than scanning titles and content of publications that the Research Division had school superintendents and other administrators as its major client group. In the same year that the Research Division was established, and shortly after the Department of Superintendence decided to remain with the NEA and not become an independent organization, the secretary of the department became a full-time employee of the association. The new secretary of the Department of Superintendence moved into the NEA's new headquarters building and joined the Research Division and its director as the inhabitants of one floor in that building. Almost immediately the two groups cooperated in establishing the Educational Research Service (ERS), an agency that served as a subscription service for school superintendents. The mandate of the ERS was to respond to requests for data from school superintendents about any aspect of the conduct of school business. In response to the large demand from the school executives for information, the ERS quickly increased its staff. The secretary of the Department of Superintendence reported to that body that the ERS, a joint venture of the department and the Research Division, provided "studies prepared by cities, universities, and other agencies not available for general distribution" as well as "detailed salary distributions" prepared regularly by the Research Division. The two bodies, the Research Division and the Department of Superintendence, worked so closely with each other that they shared staff. One employee of the ERS reported that early on she worked for both agencies without any thought that they were separated in their responsibilities or in the NEA.[61]

Clipping and summarizing articles on education in newspapers and magazines was another service provided by the Research Division staff to all but that was utilized much more frequently by superintendents than by any other group. Twice in 1927 the clippings were combined and published as circulars of the ERS. Thus, in a sense, one is hard-pressed to distinguish between the employees or the products of the Research Division and the Department of Superintendence. The comfortable personal relations between Secretary Shankland of the Department of Superintendence and Director Norton of the Research Division, as well as between both of them and Secretary Crabtree of the NEA, further reflected symbiosis. The primary affiliation of all of these men with the field of school administration reinforced the affinity between the Research Division, all NEA operations, and school superintendents.[62]

The questions that the subscribers asked of the ERS provide still another indication of the similarity, if not the identity, between the Department of Superintendence and the Research Division. School salaries and costs were two of the most frequent issues on which subscribers sought information from the ERS, whose publications included a clear majority of items that paralleled the concerns of the Research Division's publications. Examples of ERS publications illustrating this overlap included "Financial Statistics of Cities and Schools" in 1926 and "Salaries of Teachers and Principals" in 1928–29.[63]

A final indicator of sympathetic relations between the Research Division and the Department of Superintendence was provided when John K. Norton left the NEA in 1930. Initially, he took a leave of absence from the association to serve in a temporary position on the faculty of Teachers College, Columbia University, in the field of school administration. A year later he officially resigned to accept a permanent position at Teachers College. Resignation, however, did not prevent Norton from being active in the NEA. He continued to participate in the affairs of the association and of the Department of Superintendence for many more years.

In 1932, the same year of his resignation from the Research Division, Norton commented on recent NEA accomplishments. He began with praise for Secretary Crabtree and proceeded to identify the progress made in each of the headquarters' divisions under the chief executive officer. In considering his own Research Division, Norton declared that it had "made the association the principal source of information on teachers' salaries and renders direct service annually to hundreds of communities each year in the field." He attributed the teachers' salary gains that had taken place in the 1920s to the work of the Research Division. He went on to note that the Research Division's studies "in the fields of school finance and educational administration are everywhere accepted as authoritative and have exercised important influence in promoting educational advance." Moving from the accomplishments in educational administration of the Research Division, he next noted the comparative work the division had done with the Department of Superintendence. He then recounted how the cooperation between the Research Division and the department had helped move relations between the NEA and school superintendents from a posture of conflict to one of amity. The Research Division, in 1930, was as much a branch of the Department of Superintendence as it was a component of the NEA.[64]

Clearly, the closeness of the Research Division with the Department of Superintendence reflected the fact that superintendents had an interest in teachers' salaries related to that of classroom teachers. Raising their teachers' salaries was a way for superintendents to affirm their own worth, at the same time that it benefited their employees. On the other hand, knowledge of comparative salary data could also help a superintendent respond to salary initiatives from teachers that were "out of line" compared with what was paid in other systems. The ERS and the Research Division made it their business to provide superintendents with ammunition that they needed to succeed in salary discussions with teachers or with school boards. The national improvement in teachers' salaries in the 1920s, when compared with the preceding or following decades, was an obvious sign of the success of the NEA salary efforts.[65]

Yet all of this evidence of affinity and amity, of cooperation and cordiality, between the Department of Superintendence and the Research Division should not be taken as a sign that the association was one happy family. Members of that family could and did endure strained relations with one another.

PROFESSION OR "PROFESSIONS"

As shown in this chapter, the major objective of the reorganized and professionalized NEA of James W. Crabtree and his staff was service to teachers and to school administrators. Meeting the needs of these two audiences guaranteed that the NEA would grow in numbers and in influence, as it did in the 1920s. Embedded within this attention to teachers and administrators were at least two possible cracks in the wall of affiliation: one between men and women teachers and the other between teachers and administrators.

In the 1920s, as in its earlier history, the NEA recognized neither fault line. Occasionally, however, the reality of disputes within the teaching force or between teachers and administrators came close to being recognized in NEA publications. For example, the September 1926 issue of the *Research Bulletin,* devoted to the topic of teacher personnel policies, contained a section on men and women teachers' salaries that exposed the disparities between the two groups. Comment on the figures was sparse and dispassionate but the clear direction of the act of reporting the figures in these categories was toward alleviating the differential. Two years later another NEA publication, this one devoted to the topic of married women teachers, detailed salary figures that clearly showed that women earned substantially less than men. While no comment in the article specifically addressed the issue of salary discrimination, again the very data clearly made the point for readers.[66] And Charl Williams's advocacy of the single salary scale, discussed earlier, was also a prominent theme in many NEA forums and publications. Thus the NEA in the 1920s went on record, subtly but clearly enough, as enrolled in the campaign of women teachers who were seeking salary equity.

In the next two decades, as will be shown in subsequent chapters, the NEA emerged more actively on the side of salary equity for women and for an end to discrimination against women teachers. The means for this advocacy would continue to be mainly the publication of salary and other data on employment and working conditions. For women such as Charl Williams, the data were the basis for pointed, though not overly shrill, statements in support of the cause. The reaction of men teachers to this advocacy was largely missing from the NEA's presentations and discussions on the topic. Men were clearly in the minority in the teaching force, and this fact, plus the attractiveness of equity in salaries for an occupation that claimed professional status based on the selfless provision of a service, helped mute any male advocacy of salary superiority that might have occurred.

In contrast, in the area of salary differences and power relations between teachers and administrators, the NEA was absolutely silent, avoiding any suggestion of conflict throughout the 1920s. The existing hierarchical relations between the two groups were clearly and fully acknowledged, and the NEA never gave any evidence of an interest in challenging the authority of school superintendents and other administrators

over their teachers. The admonition of Henry Suzallo to build the profession from the bottom up was ignored, though most of the rest of
Suzallo's suggestions were honored. The NEA's constructed ideology of
"professional service" never contemplated a profession that was divided
hierarchically into groups that might at times have divergent interests.

This situation was understood clearly and perhaps even viscerally
by J. W. Crabtree and the others who rebuilt the NEA. Men like Crabtree,
John Norton, and Sherwood Shankland dealt easily with one another and
blended their concerns into a single effort that joined the interests of
teachers to those of administrators. The occasional woman in the NEA
hierarchy, typified by Charl Williams, was carefully chosen for her own
ideology that, while it might call for salary equity for women teachers,
would not challenge the power of administrators. And yet, all of this
should not be taken to imply only manipulation of the teachers in the
NEA. Cooperation between teachers and administrators was institutionalized in the association and advocated in its constituent organizations
and in school systems. Judging by the NEA's increasing membership
numbers, women were persuaded that cooperation was the proper stance
to take. While the impetus on behalf of cooperation was real and consistent, it was not always necessarily successful. Some administrators, particularly within the Department of Superintendence, could and did
question the NEA's advocacy of a cooperative stance between teachers
and administrators as a dilution of their power and prerogatives, while
some teacher advocates went beyond advocating cooperation to choosing confrontation in pursuit of their objectives.

Yet these voices of dissent over the NEA perspective were muffled
successfully in the 1920s. In that decade, as already noted, the association managed to recruit substantial numbers of new teachers and to keep
the Department of Superintendence securely within its embrace. One can
infer from this result that most women teachers were unaware of, or ignored, the cracks in the foundation of the professional solidarity that was
advocated by the NEA. Of course, pressure on teachers by administrators
to join the NEA was a very real phenomenon in the 1920s that served to
patch or perhaps hide the cracks then and in later decades. Nevertheless,
women teachers were satisfied enough with the NEA and its polite and
professional pursuit of their welfare to pay both formal allegiance and
membership dues to the association to a substantial degree.

The success of the cooperative stance between administrators and
teachers was crucial to the NEA in subsequent decades. And symbiotic
relations between constituent bodies such as the Research Division and

the Department of Superintendence supported that cooperative impulse. Yet both these sets of relationships underwent stresses and strains as the NEA and the nation endured the economic depression of the 1930s.

NOTES

[1]On the early NEA, see Edgar Wesley, *NEA: The First Hundred Years* (New York: Harper, 1957), and Paul Mattingly, *The Classless Profession: American Schoolmen of the Nineteenth Century* (New York: New York University Press, 1975).

[2]Wayne J. Urban, *Why Teachers Organized* (Detroit: Wayne State University Press, 1982), ch. 5. Kate Rousmaniere is at work on a biography of Margaret Haley that promises to shed new light on her and her leadership of women teachers.

[3]The standard sources on the school superintendency are Raymond E. Callahan, *Education and the Cult of Efficiency* (Chicago: University of Chicago Press, 1962), and David Tyack and Elisabeth Hansot, *Managers of Virtue: Public School Leadership in America: 1820–1980* (New York: Basic Books, 1982).

[4]Henry Suzallo, "Topic: The Reorganization of the Teaching Profession," *Journal of the Addresses and Proceedings of the National Education Association* 51 (1913): 362–79 (hereafter cited as *NEA Proceedings*).

[5]The antipathy of political progressives for local political machines, often controlled by immigrants or those who used the allegiance of immigrants to foster a system seen by progressives as plagued by graft and corruption, was well known. For a classic scholarly study of turn-of-the-century politics that emphasizes this antipathy, see Richard Hofstadter, *The Age of Reform: From Bryan to FDR* (New York: Knopf, 1955).

[6]*NEA Proceedings* 51 (1913): 363, 366.

[7]Ibid., 376–77.

[8]On material interests as dominant in local associations in Atlanta, Chicago, and New York, see Urban, *Why Teachers Organized,* chs. 2, 3, and 4. Kate Rousmaniere has shown that the quasi social club type of organization in New York City in the 1920s served more than social purposes. See her *City Teachers: Teaching and School Reform in Historical Perspective* (New York: Teachers College Press, 1996).

[9]Suzallo, "Reorganization of the Teaching Profession," 370–71.

[10]Ibid.

[11]Ibid., 372–73.

[12]Ibid., 373. Suzallo's advocacy of small local associations may well have been a criticism of the large city teacher groups such as Margaret Haley's Chicago Teachers Federation, which was agitating politically at the local and state level for occupational improvement and nationally within the NEA for recognition of women teachers.

[13]Suzallo, "Reorganization of the Teaching Profession," 373.

[14]William Edward Eaton, *The American Federation of Teachers, 1916–1961: A History of the Movement* (Carbondale, IL: Southern Illinois University Press, 1975).

[15]On the early AFT, see Urban, *Why Teachers Organized,* ch. 6; Eaton, *The American Federation of Teachers;* and Marjorie Murphy, *Blackboard Unions: The AFT and the NEA, 1900–1980* (Ithaca, NY: Cornell University Press, 1990).

[16]Haley's more militant Chicago Teachers Federation was forced to abandon its union affiliation after losing a bitter fight with the board of education over that issue.

[17]On the early normal schools, particularly in the Midwest, see Juergen Herbst, *And Sadly Teach: Teacher Professionalization and American Culture* (Madison: University of Wisconsin Press, 1989). On women and their creation of space in these institutions, see Christine Ogren, "Where Coeds Were Coeducated: Normal Schools in Wisconsin, 1870–1920," *History of Education Quarterly* 35 (Spring 1995): 1–26.

[18]For additional description of the change in the NEA, see Urban, *Why Teachers Organized,* ch. 5. On Crabtree and his career, see James W. Crabtree, *What Counted Most* (Lincoln, NE: University, 1935).

[19]"The Service of J. W. Crabtree," *Journal of the National Education Association* 24 (January 1935): 1–4 (hereafter cited as *NEA Journal*); and the obituary "James W. Crabtree," *NEA Journal* 34 (October 1945): 130.

[20]On the genesis and life of the commission, see Wesley, *NEA,* 246–48, 300–302.

[21]On the reorganization, see Urban, *Why Teachers Organized,* ch. 5, and Wesley, *NEA,* 328–32.

[22]On the issues and outcome of the Salt Lake City meeting, see Frederick S. Buchanan, "Unpacking of the N. E. A.: The Role of Utah's Teachers at the 1920 Convention," *Utah Historical Quarterly* 41 (1973): 150–61.

[23]As we will see in later chapters, particularly in Chapters 3 and 4, local associations became a priority for the NEA in subsequent decades.

[24]Wesley, *NEA,* 397. The 1931 figure was a high-water mark that would not be equaled again until 1944 because of the negative impact of the depression economy and World War II labor markets on membership.

[25]On the possible secession of the Department of Superintendence, see John K. Norton, "A Survey of the National Education Association," *School and Society* 36 (July 16, 1932): 75.

[26]Francis Russell, *A City in Terror: The Boston Police Strike* (New York: Viking Press, 1975).

[27]Urban, *Why Teachers Organized,* ch. 6.

[28]*NEA Proceedings* 62 (1924): 96, 739.

[29]For a specific account of the centralization of school boards in large cities, see David Tyack, *The One Best System* (Cambridge, MA: Harvard University Press, 1974).

[30]Interview with Joy Elmer Morgan (August 17, 1976), NEA Archives, box 3117.

[31]Ibid.

[32]Wesley, *NEA,* 376–77; "The Service of J. W. Crabtree."

[33]*NEA Journal* 2 (November 1922): 371. As a county superintendent, Williams held the one level of school leadership that was relatively frequently occupied by a woman in the early twentieth century. For an account of the number of women in this "intermediate" superintendency in this period and their subsequent decline in numbers holding that position later in the twentieth century, and the reasons for both the rise and fall, see Jackie M. Blount, *Destined to Rule the Schools: Women and the Superintendency* (Albany: State University of New York Press, 1998).

[34]Material related to Williams's career is found in several boxes in the NEA Archives, reached through the association's headquarters in Washington, D.C. Biographical details are in an undated (1949?) special issue of the *NEA Journal,* in box 462 of the NEA papers.

[35]"Effective Professional Organization," *NEA Journal* 10 (September 1921): 119–20.

[36]Charl O. Williams, "The Call to Service," *NEA Journal* 10 (October 1921): 135.

[37]Williams, "Tenure—An Important Problem," *NEA Journal* 10 (November 1921): 151–52.

[38]Williams, "The Democratic Awakening and Professional Organization," *NEA Proceedings* 60 (1922): 208–10.

[39]Williams, "Actual Results of the Year," *NEA Proceedings* 60 (1922): 482–84.

[40]Williams, "The Hope and the Result of American Education," *NEA Proceedings* 60 (1922): 378–81, and "The Improvement of the Teaching Profession through Tenure Legislation," ibid., 685–88.

[41]See insert, with photographs and description of Williams and her counterpart, J. O. Engleman, in *NEA Journal* 11 (November 1922): 371.

[42]NEA press release (October 1921), including a copy of "A Petition for a Department of Education," addressed "To the President of the United States"; NEA Archives, box 323.

[43]Lynn Dumeil, "'The Insatiable Maw of Bureaucracy': Antistatism and Education Reform in the 1920s," *Journal of American History* 77 (September 1990): 499–524, especially 505 and 510.

[44]Charl O. Williams, "The Policy of the National Education Association Towards Federal Legislation," *NEA Proceedings* 65 (1927): 152–56; quotation, 156.

[45]For example, see Williams, "The Challenge," *Child Welfare* (July–August 1931): 662–63; "A Wise Economy in Education," ibid. (May 1932): 531–32; "Are You Posted on Committees? Department of Education," ibid. (October 1932): 88–89; and "A Message for American Education Week," *Independent Woman* 17 (November 1934): 338.

⁴⁶Murphy, *Blackboard Unions,* 115.

⁴⁷Box 594 of the NEA papers contains substantial correspondence to and from Williams in regard to the creation of a federal department. The signers of these letters constitute a veritable who's who of American educational leadership in this period. The contents of the letters give fascinating insight into the politics of a federal lobbying effort by Williams and the NEA. For a listing of the national organizations supporting a federal department, see Williams, "Report of Legislative Division, National Education Association," *NEA Proceedings* 64 (1926): 1139–40.

⁴⁸Murphy, *Blackboard Unions,* ch. 1.

⁴⁹*NEA Proceedings* 59 (1921): 170. For a more detailed look at the Research Division in this period, see Wayne J. Urban, *More Than the Facts: The Research Division of the National Education Association, 1922–1997* (Lanham, MD: University Press of America, 1998): ch. 1.

⁵⁰*NEA Proceedings,* 59 (1921): 138–39.

⁵¹Ibid. Shortly after its founding, the Research Department was changed to a research division within the NEA headquarters, to avoid confusion with most NEA departments, which were subunits of the larger organization such as the Department of Classroom Teachers or the Department of Elementary Principals.

⁵²*NEA Journal* 11 (April 1922): 134. Also see the clipping on Norton entitled "Like Mother, Like Son," NEA Archives, box 323.

⁵³*NEA Proceedings* 60 (1922): 146–49.

⁵⁴"Facts on the Cost of Public Education and What They Mean," *Bulletin One of the Research Division of the NEA* (June 1922): 2; hereafter cited as *NEA Research Bulletin.*

⁵⁵*NEA Proceedings* 60 (1922): 410; ibid. 65 (1927): 1181.

⁵⁶*List of NEA Research Bulletin Articles from June 1922 to May 1972* (n.d.), NEA Archives; and "The Scheduling of Teachers' Salaries," *NEA Research Bulletin* 5 (May 1927): 134.

⁵⁷*NEA Research Bulletin* 5 (May 1927): 157, 156.

⁵⁸John K. Norton, "Teachers' Salaries Before the War," *NEA Journal* 17 (January 1928): 27; Norton, "Have Teachers Salaries Been Increased?" *NEA Journal* 11 (April 1922): 172; ibid. (May 1922): 216; and ibid. 14 (April 1925): 131–32.

⁵⁹"Facts on the Public School Curriculum," *NEA Research Bulletin* 1 (November 1923); and "Keeping Pace with the Advancing Curriculum," *NEA Research Bulletin* 3 (September and November 1925).

⁶⁰Ibid. 7 (March 1929).

⁶¹Sherwood D. Shankland, "The Department of Superintendence—1891–1931," *American School Board Journal* 82 (March 1931): 61–121; Shankland, "The Department of Superintendence of the National Education Association, Report of the Executive Secretary," (April 13, 1927), NEA Archives, box 323; and Hazel Davis interview (June 17, 1988), NEA Archives, box 3117.

[62]Hazel Davis interview (June 17, 1988), and J. W. Crabtree, "The School Board Journal and the N.E.A.," *American School Board Journal* 82 (March 1931): 61. Crabtree published this article in the same issue of the school board magazine in which Shankland's article, noted previously, appeared.

[63]"Publications of the Educational Research Service" (May 18, 1988), NEA Archives.

[64]John K. Norton, "A Survey of the National Education Association," *School and Society* 36 (July 16, 1932): 75–76.

[65]Lois Scharf, *To Work and to Wed: Female Employment, Feminism, and the Great Depression* (Westport, CT: Greenwood Press, 1980), 67.

[66]"Practices Affecting Teacher Personnel," *Research Bulletin* 6 (September 1928), contained a titled section on "Salaries of Men and Women Teachers" and appendixes.

CHAPTER 2

Professionalism and Educational Equity
The National Education Association in the 1930s

In the 1930s the Great Depression was by far the most obvious and powerful influence on the NEA, the nation's schools, and the United States as a whole. NEA employees, like teachers in schools, suffered direct monetary losses because of the catastrophe. For a substantial period NEA staff members were paid only part of their salaries, the smallest portion in the period being one-half of the scheduled amount.[1] Yet, comparatively speaking, again like classroom teachers—at least like those who did not lose their jobs—NEA employees escaped the most devastating consequences of the depression. Salary cuts were endurable, particularly in the deflationary spiral of an economic depression. NEA staff members did not lose their jobs because of depression conditions.

A significant positive outcome of the depression for the NEA was the silencing of any possible division between teachers and administrators in the schools or within the association. Economic crisis put teachers and administrators squarely on the same side of the most important educational issue, the side of preserving funding for salaries and other educational expenses from the threats of business groups and taxpayer groups, both of which sought relief from any and all taxation. These groups sought to use the depression-era economic crisis as a wedge against current and future public spending in most, if not all, areas, particularly in the public schools, which constituted the single largest public expenditure in most locations. Protecting jobs, salaries, and school funding was a cause that teachers and administrators could and did embrace together, enthusiastically.

Perhaps an even more significant outcome of the depression for the NEA, however, was that it spurred a fiscal equity push at the local and state levels in America's schools. Adding to this equity thrust, equity-oriented concerns about the salary and employment conditions of black teachers, women teachers, and rural teachers came to the forefront of the NEA's consciousness in the latter half of the 1930s. The first of these groups, black teachers, received the least amount of attention from the NEA. The reasons for this neglect were several—mainly related to the segregation that existed in many state education associations, as it did in the nation's schools, particularly those in the South. Rural and women teachers received a more positive response from the NEA in their quest for equity. Women teachers, especially, saw in the 1930s an intensification of the single salary scale movement, begun in the previous decade, that eventually resulted in their enjoying a position of substantial salary equity.

Advocacy of the cause of women teachers in the NEA also kept Charl Williams in the limelight in NEA affairs and attracted attention to some other women staff members. Williams's efforts and those of another NEA woman staff member, Hazel Davis, are highlighted in this chapter. These two and other NEA women staff members endured a changing of the guard at the top of the NEA as J. W. Crabtree retired in 1935 and was replaced by Willard Givens. Givens was faced initially with a crisis sparked by discontent with the NEA program in the Department of Superintendence, much like what Crabtree had endured early in his tenure. Givens, however, also proved able to placate school administrators and prevent them from leaving the fold. The stance taken by Givens and his successor, William G. Carr, in relation to the place of women teachers in the program of the NEA constitutes another theme of this chapter. Carr came to the NEA as a relatively young man in 1929 and helped shape the NEA response to the depression. While Carr was closely associated with the equity thrust in school finance, neither he nor Givens seemed overly interested in women's issues. Both men, however, maintained association allegiance to teachers' economic betterment throughout the decade.

One might conclude that the 1930s was an equity decade or a women's decade in the NEA. Neither Givens nor Carr, however, as will be shown, wanted to embrace anything like the social and political radicalism that was plaguing the AFT in the depression decade. For a time, something like that radical impulse made its way into NEA circles. Both fiscal equity and the cause of the woman teacher could be construed as signs of political and social radicalism in the association. Neither Carr nor Givens was interested in any kind of radical reputation for the NEA, and they were careful to smother any hint of radicalism that might surface and deface its reputation as a careful, professional group. Yet, both fiscal equity and women teachers remained in the forefront of NEA concerns through much of the decade.

THE GREAT DEPRESSION

The stock market crash of October 1929 is said to have marked the beginning of the Great Depression. That particular event did not, however, have a measurable impact on the NEA or most of the nation's schools until a year or two later. In fact, in February 1930 the association acted as if the future were rosy, economically, for itself and for the public schools. The NEA embarked on construction of a new building on land that it had purchased in downtown Washington, borrowing the considerable sum of $325,000 to finance the project. Only two members of the board of directors voted against the new venture, and they apologized as they explained the reasons for their vote, lest they be interpreted as naysayers who feared the future.[2]

The first few years of economic downturn also had hardly any adverse effect on the NEA's pursuit of teachers' economic improvement. In 1930 the association expanded its appeal explicitly to include high school teachers along with elementary teachers as groups that needed upward salary adjustments. In a June article in the *NEA Journal* of that year, a high school teacher commented critically on every aspect of her working life, except the relation between it and the national economy. Titled "Teacher or Factory Hand?" the article enumerated several of the onerous working conditions that plagued this high school English teacher: five class periods a day, each with between thirty-five and forty-five students, were accompanied by study hall duty for an additional period, mandatory attendance at university courses to earn a salary increase, general faculty and English teacher meetings, grading and planning activities, extracurricular duties with the debating team, and extensive work-related reading. It all added up to overwork and underpay, at a time when (in perhaps a veiled reference to the emerging economic depression) the board of education was on the verge of adding a sixth period of teaching in the high schools. This teacher saw herself performing at the same pace as a worker in a bobbin factory. Of course, she noted that young people were not bobbins and that to treat them as such, which was the ultimate effect of her working conditions, was to shortchange them dearly.[3]

Not long after this article appeared, the depression economic downturn began to affect the NEA. In December 1930 NEA secretary J. W. Crabtree wrote to school superintendents and other interested educators alerting them to the recent creation of the NEA Commission on Unemployment. Chaired by Professor William C. Bagley of Teachers College, Columbia University, the group sought contributions from educators who had not lost their jobs to support teachers who had suffered such a loss because of a wide range of factors, including the economy. These teachers had been discharged because of cost-cutting measures in school systems, or because they were widows or had children or aged dependents, or were aged and infirm themselves and suffered job loss because of their disabilities, or were younger people who had completed teacher training but could find no job. Bagley's group tried to keep in touch with state associations and to circulate information about employment from one state to another. Educators who made salaries of more than $4,000 were encouraged to contribute slightly more than 0.5 percent of their salaries to locally based emergency funds for the unemployed. For those earning under the $4,000 threshold, the suggested contribution was a lesser percentage.[4] Response to the Bagley Commission's letter evidently was not overwhelming. It took a more overt crisis to provoke a more assertive reaction from the leadership of the association.

That reaction began two years later. In a circular published at the beginning of the 1932–33 school year, Secretary Crabtree outlined the particulars of a growing educational calamity with drastic occupational consequences for those who worked in schools. In many local school systems, depression-initiated cost-cutting measures threatened music, art, recreation, health programs, kindergartens, and vocational and home economics studies, as well as a shortening of the school year and/or an increase in teacher load. Appealing to the NEA's traditional link between economic welfare and status-conscious professionalism, Crabtree noted that teachers' salaries were being cut to levels comparable to those of unskilled workers. To compensate for these threats, Crabtree urged intensified NEA membership drives in every school system. He hoped that "every teacher can see this letter" and, in response, join the effort to "maintain efficient service and to prevent the loss of additional thousands."[5]

By early 1933 Crabtree was notifying school leaders that, nationally, upward of fifty thousand NEA members, close to one-fourth of the total association rolls, had lost their jobs. He added that NEA efforts to help ameliorate the situation were being hampered by the association's own troublesome financial situation. Staff had recently taken a 50 percent salary cut, and $75,000 of NEA funds were on deposit at a recently closed bank. In other words, Crabtree commented, "We are up against the same thing here at headquarters that teachers are up against over the nation. We are making the same sacrifices to keep the schools open that teachers are making." Seeking to recover dues money lost to teacher dismissals, the NEA secretary pleaded for an increase in recruitment activity as an antidote for financial ills.[6]

Crabtree's pleas for more members went largely unheeded, as had the appeals for help for teachers who had lost their jobs. Both the NEA and the nation's school systems managed, however, to escape the most devastating ravages of the depression. Teachers who were able to keep their jobs fared reasonably well economically because the reality of their salary cuts was often cushioned by the decrease in prices for goods and services that accompanied the economic downturn. NEA employees, similarly, avoided layoffs and instead took reduced salaries that still provided them with relatively good purchasing power. With respect to the long-term future of the association, however, there were issues related to the depression that would have more of an impact than the negative economic conditions.

FISCAL EQUITY AND NEW LEADERSHIP

The NEA tried to turn the negative economic consequences of the depression into a positive result for public education by embarking on a quest for a massive funding reform in the states. This school finance equity drive was spearheaded by John K. Norton with the help of William G. Carr, who had been hired by Norton in the Research Division in 1929. In January of that year, Carr came to the NEA as an assistant director in research. He spent the next four decades at the association, rising quickly to the top position in the Research Division and later to the top association staff position of executive secretary. Carr thus became a figure of substantial significance in NEA history.

Born in England, Carr had moved with his family to rural Canada at an early age and soon migrated again with his family, this time to Los Angeles, California. Here he attended and was graduated from the Manual Arts High School.[7] His higher education began at the southern branch of the University of California (now known as the University of

California at Los Angeles [UCLA]), where he first studied mining and engineering. He finished his undergraduate education at Stanford University, from which he eventually received bachelor's, master's, and doctoral degrees. The first two degrees were in the fields of English and education, and the final one was in education. After finishing his bachelor's degree, he taught for a year at a junior high school in Glendale, California, close to Los Angeles. On completion of his master's degree he served as a faculty member in the education department, again for one year, at a private college in Oregon.[8]

While at Stanford, Carr came under the tutelage of several noted faculty members. He coauthored, with John C. Almack, an article based on Carr's master's thesis, which dealt with the application of a mathematical method of calculating and graphing phenomena to the field of educational research. Carr completed his dissertation, a historical contribution, under Ellwood P. Cubberley, dean of the School of Education at Stanford. The topic was a biography of John Swett, noted nineteenth-century California school reformer. The dissertation was published in 1933. Carr also reported being greatly reinforced in his interest in international affairs by Stanford's president, David Starr Jordan, who arranged publication by the Stanford University Press of a book Carr had written earlier on international relations.[9]

While working on his doctorate, Carr took a part-time job as research director of the California Teachers Association. He reported that this experience, along with NEA research director Norton's reading his book on international education, resulted in his being offered a position with Norton at the NEA. Norton's ties to California, to Stanford, and to Cubberley undoubtedly worked in Carr's favor. In fact, as dean of the School of Education at Stanford and author of successful textbooks on educational administration and the history of education, Cubberley was clearly one of the undisputed leaders nationally in the professional educational world.[10]

Like all NEA employees, though assigned to duties in one unit, the Research Division in his case, Carr also devoted time to a variety of tasks as assigned by his superiors. Early on he worked with the Committee on Propaganda, which was conducting a study of the undue influence on the public schools by large business interests, a focus to which Carr returned in his fiscal equity work of the 1930s. Particularly threatening to public schools were electric companies, which feared that success in public education made very real the possibility of public ownership of their own enterprises.[11]

Carr's early assignments in the Research Division were in an area, school finance in the states, that had not received extensive attention previously. It was significant, however, especially given the statements regarding the importance of the states as a site for research work that were aired when the division was begun. Shortly after his arrival in 1929, Carr began work on a project, "Studies in State School Administration," that he would not finish until 1933. By November of that year, a total of twelve monographs on various aspects of the topic had been published, eleven of them completed between December 1929 and February 1932.[12]

The titles of several of these monographs reflected the NEA's ongoing commitment to teacher welfare as the spur behind its reform push. For example, Study 3, published in February 1930, was entitled "Group Insurance for Teachers," while Study 7, published in January 1931, was entitled "Flat-Rate and Percent-of-Salary Retirement Systems." Carr was careful to note, on occasion, the direct link between his various state studies and the interests of teachers. In a 1930 article in the *NEA Journal,* he reviewed the activities of state legislatures in the preceding year (most of which had taken place before the stock market crash), emphasizing the laws that had been passed that had led to improved teacher benefits. Retirement, tenure, and leaves of absence were among the specific topics discussed by Carr. He concluded the article with the prediction that, because of the enlightened leadership of state departments of education, along with reinforcement from "the cooperative activity of state and national education associations, . . . the years 1930 and 1931 are likely to inaugurate a new stage of progress in legislation affecting the welfare of the nation's million teachers."[13]

What was novel in Carr's work was certainly not the emphasis on teacher welfare, a staple of the NEA program since reorganization and the ascendancy of J. W. Crabtree. Rather, Carr's innovation was that he was applying analyses based on tested school finance principles and practices in arenas outside of the local school districts where they had been developed. Carr's work was concentrated on state houses, state legislatures, and state departments of education. In keeping with this focus, three of the state school administration monographs—the first, sixth, and tenth, respectively—were on "State School Legislation" in the years 1929, 1930, and 1931. Still another, published in March 1931, considered "Staffs and Salaries in State Departments of Education."[14] In these works Carr took the NEA beyond studies of local school costs, salaries, and funding, and beyond its advocacy of federal aid to education, both of which had begun in earnest in the 1920s. Now the NEA was involving itself at the state level, in the governmental arena that had heretofore escaped its attention and that held the only substantial promise of alleviating educational fiscal crises in the turbulent depression climate.

This emphasis on state school finance also reinforced Secretary Crabtree's long-stated objective, dating to 1917 when he took office, of strengthening the NEA through service to its state affiliates. Although he had succeeded in building NEA membership through the state associations, dealing with state school finance gave Crabtree a way to involve the national association directly in matters of concern to those affiliates, their leaders, and their members, thereby cementing the ties that had been built largely through personal relationships.

It was not that studies of the states had been neglected completely prior to William Carr's arrival at the NEA. The *Research Bulletin* for January 1929, the month in which Carr was first employed, was devoted to the topic of "Can the States Afford to Educate Their Children?" This publication continued a line of work that had developed two years earlier in the Research Division under John Norton. In that year two issues of the *Research Bulletin* considered "The Ability of the States to Support Education." In those issues Norton showed that the states varied substantially in their wealth and, consequently, in their ability to support public schools. These publications were, mainly, however, analyses of factors that accounted for the variance in levels of state support rather than attempts to identify and pursue a policy that would address the situation. The direction in which this line of inquiry seemed to lead, though not explicitly stated, fit nicely with a long-held NEA priority—federal involvement in state school finance for the purpose of redressing the grossest inequalities in the states' abilities to support public education.[15] Thus, an important focus of NEA activity spurred by the depression was the pursuit of equity in school funding through federal aid to poorer states that would allow them to approach parity with their wealthier counterparts.

William Carr's coming to the NEA clearly had something to do with his prior work in state school finance. Much of what he accomplished for the California Teachers Association had dealt with this field, and it clearly qualified him for the work he would do for the NEA.[16] Carr expanded on Norton's descriptive work in the state studies in at least one important way. He looked at various aspects of state legislation and administration, especially at different approaches to taxation, in terms of their relationship to school finance. Thus, rather than simply show that inequities existed within and among states, Carr investigated the possible impacts on school funding of various kinds of taxes in the several states—for example, individual and corporate income taxes. These types of taxation promised an improved and more equitable outcome, especially for poorer districts in states, than the existing and increasingly controversial local property tax.[17]

In these efforts the NEA was not abandoning the pursuit of equity through federal aid to local schools but supplementing it by putting the various state laws and policies under the same comparative microscope it had used to study local school systems. And as the depression deepened in the early 1930s, John Norton, William Carr, and the NEA discussed politically controversial topics such as recommending taxation changes in the states in the effort to ameliorate the increasingly critical fiscal situation of the public schools.

The investigations into state school finance culminated in 1934 with the establishment of the State Legislative Reference Service at NEA headquarters. The object of that service was to provide a "clearinghouse on state school legislation" and to make the legislation available to teachers, school administrators, and state legislators and executives who were interested in what states other than their own were doing to combat the depression.[18]

William Carr's early work for the NEA involved topics other than state school finance. Late in 1931 the Research Division published a report he wrote, *Childhood in the Depression,* another attempt to show that the NEA was capable of a creative response to the new situation. This report, by title and much of its content, broke new ground. It showed how the schools were facing increasing enrollment in areas such as vocational education because youngsters in the depression found it less and less likely to find work as an alternative to finishing their schooling. Similarly, an expansion of social services was desirable as schools, responding to the negative effects of the depression on families, attempted to compensate by developing a variety of new initiatives. In the conclusion of the report, however, Carr returned to two familiar themes for the NEA. One was the necessity to implement the school finance reform efforts that he was developing in his other work. The second was the need to stop the thoughtless cutting of teachers' salaries, a policy certain to decrease the effectiveness of schools in meeting the challenge of serving children. Thus did Carr, much like Crabtree, Norton, and other NEA leaders in the 1920s, unite the obviously "professional" goal of service to children and families in need with the long-sought priority of improving teachers' economic welfare.

Again reprising an earlier initiative, that of the 1917 Commission on the Emergency in Education caused by World War I, in 1933 the NEA and the Department of Superintendence appointed a Joint Commission on the Emergency in Education to investigate the conditions and consequences of the economic crisis on the schools. John Norton was appointed to head this commission, and William Carr was quickly chosen as its executive director. The policies that the joint commission advocated to meet the crises were obvious, at least for the NEA—federal aid to education and financial equity reform in state and local school support. One of the joint commission's major activities was the sponsorship of a large national conference on the financing of education in July and August 1933. Its output included reports on taxation that echoed points made by Carr in his series of reports on state school administration. Following Carr's earlier analysis and recommendations, the joint commission hoped to persuade states to place less reliance on the property tax and to embrace corporate and individual income taxes as solutions to state revenue crises and as a way to mitigate inequities between school districts.[19]

Like much else of what the NEA attempted, the joint commission proved more successful in maintaining the morale of school employees than in implementing federal aid or equity-oriented tax reform in the states. Unprodded by any concrete result of NEA efforts, the economy and the schools nevertheless seemed on the road out of the depression by 1935. The joint commission acknowledged this and prepared to disband itself. Before doing this, however, it recommended that a new NEA body be created, the Educational Policies Commission (EPC), that would prevent similar disaster from befalling the schools in the future.

Jointly sponsored by the NEA and the Department of Superintendence, the EPC proved to be a vehicle for what is now called long-term planning of the educational enterprise. Changing social needs were to be anticipated and their ramifications for schooling understood. The membership of the EPC read like the pages of a who's who in American education. Leading school administrators, university professors of education, and normal school teachers and administrators were represented in its ranks. William Carr was made the executive director of the body when it began its activities in January 1936.[20] For the next several years Carr's major assignment for the NEA was to be his leadership of the EPC. In the 1950s he became the executive secretary of the NEA, replacing Willard Givens, who had ascended to the position after J. W. Crabtree retired in 1935.

A New Leader with New and Old Priorities

Like William Carr and John Norton, Willard Givens came to the NEA from a background of school service in the state of California. He had a bachelor's degree from Indiana University and a master's degree and a theological diploma from Columbia University. He had taught at the army officers' training schools in California and Hawaii during World War I. After the war he stayed in Hawaii, serving as a high school principal, and then moved to Oakland, California, back to Hawaii, and then to San Diego. He assumed a series of increasingly important administrative positions. He rose eventually to become superintendent of schools in the territory of Hawaii and city school superintendent in Oakland.[21]

Generally speaking, Givens continued the policies of his predecessor, J. W. Crabtree. The fiscal equity thrust of the late 1920s and 1930s, as well as the pursuit of teacher welfare emphasized in the 1920s, were reinforced under Givens. Givens's personal views on these and other issues of interest to the future of the NEA were unclear when he arrived at headquarters, however.

Initially, Givens faced several political controversies, some of which had challenged his predecessor and some of which had not. Soon after becoming secretary, Givens faced one problem that Crabtree also encountered early in his NEA career, a movement for secession on the part of the Department of Superintendence. The exact reason for the rift this time, as in 1920, was not clearly revealed in extant sources. It seems, however, that administrative discontent was at least partially related to an increase in size and power in the Department of Superintendence—to the extent that the school superintendents thought that they might be able to "go it alone."[22] Like Crabtree, Givens proved equal to the task of keeping the superintendents in the fold, though, as we will see soon, it was not an easy task.

Developments around the issue of teachers' political activities constituted a relatively new problem that Givens had to face. In late 1934 and 1935 the NEA began to discuss whether teachers needed to move directly into politics in order to respond to budget cuts, salary reductions, and loss of jobs due to the depression. In 1934 the Department of Superintendence had made clear its belief that it was inappropriate for teachers to engage in, or otherwise endorse, the radicalism then sweeping the ranks of a few large city locals of the AFT and a scattered but prominent minority of university education professors, most coming from Teachers College. The school administrators thought that the radical teacher unionists and their professor allies were contemplating and sometimes advocating unhealthy changes in the American economy as well as in its schools. While the Teachers College radical George S. Counts could ask in 1932 *Dare the School Build a New Social Order?*[23] the superintendents made it clear that for them this was a wrongheaded, inflammatory, and totally inappropriate question.

Not all superintendents shared the view of their organization, however. In January 1935 Superintendent Samuel Burr of New Castle, Delaware, published an article in the *NEA Journal* entitled "The Teacher's Part in School Reform."[24] In it he acknowledged that some teachers were persuaded by the radical analysis of Counts and others that society was in drastic need of change. He also noted that many others, of course, were not so persuaded. What Burr wanted was for teachers, whatever their personal views, to address the current crisis in their classrooms by emphasizing the facts of the situation and using them to spark a discussion of the views of radicals and others. This was the appropriate educational strategy to use in relation to the social scene, and Burr believed that this approach, fact finding, was revolutionary in its own right. Heretofore, he argued, the public schools had been involved largely in indoctrination of students into a social and political status quo.

John Norton also addressed the role of the teachers-in-politics issue in another *NEA Journal* article. Norton saw teachers as a force to be reckoned with in politics but cautioned that their appropriate role was not as partisans of one political party or candidate. Rather, they should inform political candidates of all parties on issues of educational concern. Additionally, teachers should enthusiastically undertake their duties as citizens, informing the general public about educational needs. Norton praised the Connecticut teachers' association, which had managed to get an educational plank installed in the platform of both that state's political parties in a recent election campaign. He also favored the actions of a local teachers' association in Wisconsin that had "interrogated" all candidates on educational issues before an election and had then prepared a list of those candidates who were "preferred." Norton summarized his position as follows: "Teachers should—avoid indorsement [*sic*] of particular candidates and parties; inform and poll all candidates on crucial educational issues; [and] play a more dynamic role in the whole realm of public affairs." He concluded, "When they do these things vigorously and wisely, they get results."[25]

The views of Burr were anathema to most members of the Department of Superintendence, and even Norton's opinions seemed to allow teachers the possibility to deviate from whatever political position their superintendent endorsed. Most teacher views on the issue published by the NEA in this period were somewhere between those of Burr and Norton and far different from the official position of the Department of Superintendence.

One example of teacher radicalism was voiced by the president of the Pennsylvania State Education Association, who began an article in the *NEA Journal* by noting that the depression had threatened to crush the spirit of teachers. To combat this negative outcome, he advocated an "inspiriting [*sic*] of fight and stamina" into teachers. New spirit could come only with proper "leadership and organization" of the teaching force, accomplished through their local associations. In particular, the Pennsylvanian advocated vigorous opposition to antieducation groups such as the U.S. Chamber of Commerce and local and state taxpayer associations that espoused the chamber's single-minded cut-the-budget message. Other enemies of teachers included journalists and politicians who followed the probusiness, antitaxation line. Only an organization motivated by professional solidarity could ensure the protection of schools, teachers, and children.[26] Superintendents and other school administrators were noticeably absent as actors in this teacher leader's analysis.

The politically charged issue of academic freedom for teachers came to the fore at the 1935 NEA convention. Teacher delegates from New York, notably former AFT leader Abraham Lefkowitz of New York City, were vocal advocates of teachers' rights. Lefkowitz noted that vested interests were trying to prevent the teaching of the truth in public schools. He and his colleagues joined with a group of university professors, many from Teachers College, to gain the appointment of a committee on the issue of academic freedom. The committee's purview was to expose and combat legislation that sought to curb the freedom of teachers in their classrooms. In addition, the committee was charged to cooperate with other national organizations that were pledged to fight for teachers' academic freedom. According to one report, no doubt exaggerated to some extent, the outcome was that the association had been "turned into a militant organization to fight for academic freedom."[27]

The strong action in favor of teacher rights overcame the hesitancy of the Resolutions Committee of the NEA, controlled by the leadership, which had earlier refused to endorse cooperation between the NEA and other national groups on academic freedom or other issues. It had also ignored a request to allow resolutions on the topic to be proposed and acted on from the floor of the convention rather than to go through the committee process before reaching the floor.[28]

Some saw the 1935 convention action on academic freedom as a repudiation of the cautious leadership of J. W. Crabtree and his colleagues who had either ignored or downplayed earlier declarations on the topic. Willard Givens, just appointed as Crabtree's replacement, was able to turn the criticism to his own advantage by appearing to embrace it. Yet Givens also had to act in an environment that had many crosscurrents, as evidenced by another resolution passed by the convention. In response to the academic freedom dispute, a resolution was passed noting that the American form of government was "the best so far devised by the mind of man to govern a free people."[29]

Givens quickly emerged with his own version of increased political activity by the NEA when he publicly criticized the administration of President Franklin D. Roosevelt, a tactic that had never been adopted by his predecessor. In an article entitled "New Deal a Raw Deal for Public Schools," Givens criticized Roosevelt for failing to follow through on his promises to "make infinitely better the average education which the average child receives." Particularly troubling to Givens was Roosevelt's tendency to bypass the Bureau of Education and the nation's public schools and, instead, to create a variety of new educational programs administered by other federal agencies. The Civilian Conservation Corps (CCC) and the National Youth Administration (NYA) were two prominent examples. Givens added that most recently the administration had through the Social Security Act appropriated funds for the education of handicapped children that were to be administered through the Department of Labor. He questioned why all of these dollars for education were not going to the public schools, where the administrative costs would be substantially lower without any sacrifice of efficiency. In contrast to expensive new programs in noneducation-related agencies, the NEA stood for increased federal support of the public schools.[30]

Givens's criticism of the president by name represented his version of the new NEA political thrust. It was calculated, however, to win the allegiance of superintendents in the local schools, who would benefit much more directly from the NEA approach and who faced loss of students to Roosevelt's new programs. Thus, Givens used the increased politicization of educational issues simultaneously to distinguish himself from the cautiousness of his predecessor in the eyes of teachers and to criticize the federal government in the interests of school superintendents.

In the area of teacher welfare, Givens built on and invigorated the emphases of his predecessor. Givens undertook steps to strengthen both the Department of Classroom Teachers and local teachers' associations. He streamlined the operation at NEA headquarters to allow the staff member who served as director of the Division of Classroom Services to oversee the Department of Classroom Teachers, an obvious attempt to upgrade services to teachers. In turn, he made the Department of Classroom Teachers formally responsible for work with local education associations, designating it as the group that certified locals and specified their official representation at the annual meeting. The increase in significance of the local associations was reflected late in the decade when Givens changed the name of the Division of Classroom Services to the Division of Affiliated Associations.[31] This effort to expand and invigorate local associations through rearranging the national office was intensified with expanded services to locals early in the next decade.

RIVALRY WITH THE AFT

All of Givens's efforts at energizing the NEA's dealings with teachers can be seen in the context of the continuing rivalry with the AFT. Although the teachers' union had suffered a severe decline in membership in the 1920s, the depression presented the AFT with a new opportunity. It responded with a vigorous organizing campaign in several cities and renewed activism in those few large northeastern and midwestern cities where it had a relatively large membership. Union membership totals increased substantially during the depression, thus making the AFT a more viable alternative to the NEA.

In contrast to the AFT membership growth, the NEA suffered from a largely stagnant membership in the 1930s. In the first half of the decade, the period from 1931 to 1936, the NEA lost almost one-fourth of its members, going from a total of 220,000 to 165,000. Willard Givens was aware of this situation when he took office in the NEA in 1935, and clearly it claimed a great deal of his attention and effort. An upturn in NEA membership did take place in 1937, a few years after his arrival and implementation of a vigorous recruitment campaign. Slow increases in membership would continue from that year for the next several but not until 1944 would the NEA again reach its 1931 membership total.[32]

In 1937 NEA president Orville Pratt, speaking to the annual meeting, praised Givens's reorganization of the headquarters operation. Pratt noted that reorganization was undertaken to regain lost members, to attract new members, and to allow the association to become the authoritative voice in educational affairs at the national level. This last objective, for Pratt, would make the NEA (and obviously not the AFT) equivalent to the American Bar Association and the American Medical Association as the leading professional bodies in their respective fields. Pratt noted, however, that as long as the NEA represented only one-fifth of the nation's teachers, as it did in 1936, its influence was undermined. The major competitor for the allegiance of teachers was the AFT. Pratt commended the union for the value it placed on classroom teachers and the "aggressiveness" with which it advocated their cause. He also noted the renewed life added to the labor movement by the recent challenge to the American Federation of Labor (AFL) from the Congress of Industrial Organizations (CIO). Pratt concluded by warning his listeners that "the National Education Association is in danger of finding the fertile field of classroom teacher membership sown and reaped by another organization if it fails of aggressiveness in furthering teacher welfare."[33]

Later that year the *NEA Journal* featured an article that publicized the association's accomplishments in several areas related to teacher welfare. For example, substantial improvement in teachers' tenure rights had been accomplished through the efforts of the association's Committee on Tenure, which had conducted a dozen studies on tenure in the past two decades that had resulted in a fivefold increase in the number of states having tenure laws. Further, the Committee on Tenure had investigated several cases of unfair dismissal of teachers and, most recently, had been involved in a reinstatement of teachers dismissed in a Michigan district. The Committee on Tenure had also cooperated with the recently established Committee on Academic Freedom and teachers in the District of Columbia schools to repeal the notorious congressional "red rider" provision. Each month before they could receive their paychecks, teachers in Washington, D.C., were required to testify by signature that they did not advocate or teach communism. The result was a terrible decline in teacher morale as well as a tangible reduction in the amount of information taught in the schools about the Soviet Union. These problems were redressed completely with the repeal of the "red rider."[34]

A discussion of retirement in the article on association accomplishments mainly echoed the language of past discussions of the topic. It noted that whereas in 1917 only three states had retirement systems for teachers, by 1937 the number had increased to twenty-nine, with three states adding a system in the immediately preceding year. Notably absent from this discussion was any reference to the recently passed and Roosevelt-initiated Social Security Act. This likely reflected the strain that existed between the association and the administration. In discussing teachers' salaries, there was not much achievement to publicize. According to the article, current salaries were woefully low, and whatever progress was being made was due to the salary services of the NEA. The article reminded readers that since 1922 the NEA had published a biennial survey of teachers' salaries and that it also distributed salary tables to school systems in the spring, to be used in the preparation of budgets for the next school year.[35]

Given the stasis or decline in salaries during the depression, it was not a surprise that Willard Givens undertook to reinvigorate the NEA's traditional salary advocacy after he became secretary late in 1935. In 1936 two issues of the *Research Bulletin* discussed teachers' salary schedules. In the face of little prospect of salary increases because of the depression, discussing salary schedules allowed the association to keep the issue of salaries firmly in the foreground, to appeal to women teachers who sought pay equity with men within the schedules, and to show senior teachers that the existence of a schedule rewarded them for their years of service, all without encouraging unrealistic expectations.[36]

Givens's alterations in NEA recruitment efforts managed to contain a budding AFT membership drive in the 1930s and, more important, to set the stage for an NEA rebound in succeeding decades. While the number of AFT members increased from 7,000 in 1930 to 30,000 in 1940, the NEA managed to stop the attrition of the early 1930s and achieve its own increase from 172,000 in the middle of the decade to 203,000 by 1940. And in the next two decades, when neither group drastically altered its approach to recruitment, the NEA dwarfed the AFT with an increase to 454,000 in 1950 and 714,000 in 1960, compared with the union's numbers for those years of 41,000 and 59,000, respectively. Thus, Givens's reorganization of headquarters, his embrace of work with local associations, and his publicity of salary scales all proved, in the long run, moderately successful.[37]

The inability of the AFT to build on its early 1930s gains deserves some attention, particularly in terms of its failure to make headway with women who belonged to the NEA. An in-depth study of women teachers in a small Ohio city in the 1930s, the type of teacher and district that provided fertile ground for NEA recruitment, is instructive. Oral interviews with these women showed them to be of a middle-class background, which implied accepting authority in the workplace and rejecting any group that appealed to them to do otherwise. These women also tended to return to where they had lived as children to teach and were hired by administrators who favored safe and compliant employees. The orientation of teachers to their jobs was characterized in this study as "competent conformity." Furthering this conformity, and thereby frustrating unionism, were the actual conditions under which the women worked. The schools were hierarchical, managed by men, and characterized by classroom relations in which the teachers were dominant. Both these patterns of dominance replicated the patriarchal authority in the small-town families in which the teachers were raised, where mothers were responsible for children but fathers ruled the larger world within which child-rearing took place. Women in teaching thus reinforced women as mothers and the maternal virtues of propriety and docility. Marriage, in this milieu, meant retirement from the "public" familial sphere of the school and return to the authentically "private" realm of the prototypical family. Background and culture for these women teachers thus combined to frustrate dangerous actions such as union membership. On the other hand, joining a "professional" organization like the NEA was well within the confines of expected activity for these teachers.[38]

The NEA appeal to "professionalism" was clearly geared to women like those in the small Ohio town, who also existed in large numbers throughout much of the rest of the country. Only the relative anonymity of large, industrial cities provided shelter for women of non-middle-class backgrounds that countenanced occupational militancy or middle-class women who wished to transcend their traditions and culture and join the teachers' union. In the largest cities, however, the most fertile grounds for organizing union locals, the AFT was hampered by an ideological conflict over communism that spoke to few women teachers. Further, the conflict was waged, as was much union business, by a leadership that was largely male dominated within an organization that turned a relatively deaf ear to women teachers as women.[39]

EQUITY FOR WOMEN AND MINORITY TEACHERS

Given the relationship between the union and women teachers, it should not be surprising that even the NEA's relatively mild advocacy of equity looked good in comparison with what the AFT offered. Salary scales, for example, were justified by the NEA as the appropriately "professional" way to reward teachers for long service and as an antidote to the politicization that resulted when a board or superintendent could simply decide each year what each teacher was worth. A proper schedule meant success for a school system in securing, improving, and retaining good teachers. Again, in the words of the NEA publication on salary schedules from the mid-1930s, "From the strictly professional point of view these things are important because they help to maintain the morale of teachers and to improve generally the efficiency of our schools."[40] Thus, for the NEA, a salary scale was a necessary professional improvement for teaching and teachers and for children.

There was, however, a controversial issue lurking below the surface of the salary schedule question. NEA publications revealed that existing scales were of two types, either position or preparation. The former paid high school teachers more than elementary teachers and, in fewer cases, elementary teachers in the higher or grammar grades more than those in the primary grades. In contrast, preparation schedules paid teachers according to the amount of professional training they had received, regardless of the level in which they worked within the system. All teachers with a graduate degree were paid on the same scale, those with an undergraduate degree on a lesser scale, and those with no degree still less. The most significant issue being addressed in this discussion was "Sex As a Basis for Variations in Salary." The NEA lauded the trend away from paying men more than women, a direct outcome of position-based salaries, and reaffirmed its long-standing commitment to equal pay for women as institutionalized in the preparation scale. The preparation scale was a giant step toward the single salary scale advocated by the NEA since the early 1920s and an arrangement that brought women elementary teachers into a far more equitable relationship with high school (where most of the men were concentrated) teachers. The issues of sex equity and the thrust toward the single salary scale were subordinated to the terminology of position and preparation scales in the pages of the NEA publications of the mid-1930s. Yet these larger issues were clearly there for the women teachers who wanted to construe NEA policy as favorable to women's interests.[41] Such a construction was even more likely to be made near the end of the decade as the association began to be more explicit about sex-equity issues.

Increasing enthusiasm for equity for women teachers and others in the schools led to the creation of a Committee on Equal Opportunity in 1935, shortly after Willard Givens became secretary. The resolution creating the committee stated: "That a committee of men and women be appointed to make a thoro [*sic*] study of discrimination because of sex, race, color, belief, residence, or economic or marital status, with particular reference to the teaching profession." In spite of this specification of mixed membership by sex, the actual makeup of the committee was all female: three teachers (one at a university laboratory school), one college professor, and one junior high school principal. Slowly but surely, the committee investigated the issues surrounding the topic of equal opportunity. In 1936 it reported that equal opportunity was basically a "slogan," not near to being an accomplished fact.[42]

That assertion was supported with a lengthy report, published in 1939, that detailed evidence relating to the inequalities endured, especially by women teachers. The report began with a familiar issue: how low salaries in general harmed the entire teaching profession by constricting "professional growth" and lowering "the standing and effectiveness of teaching in general." Quickly, the report moved to three specific issues: salary differences between elementary and high school teachers, between men and women teachers, and between black and white teachers. This last topic received the least attention in the report, though the information was explicit. In states where segregation was the law, 70 percent was the highest fraction of white teachers' salaries earned by black teachers. At the other extreme was the state of Louisiana where blacks earned only 35 percent of what was paid to whites. Little else was said other than these statements of fact about the inequalities endured by black teachers. This caution was characteristic of all NEA efforts with black teachers. While the association had appointed a Committee on Relations with Black Teachers in 1926, it had been chaired ever since by a succession of southern whites who served their states as superintendents of black schools and who could not be expected to advocate, even if they harbored within themselves any real equity concern.[43]

The other sections of the report were similarly data based but much more adventuresome in that they drew conclusions from the information presented. For example, after documenting that elementary teachers had earned a median amount that was from 76 percent to 78 percent of high school teachers' median in 1924–25, and that the comparative figures for 1938–39 were between 78 and 83 percent, the report drew a few conclusions. Two changes were necessary to close the gap between elementary and high school teachers: the first was to adopt a preparation schedule and the second was to raise the level of training required for elementary teachers to the same required for high school teachers, thereby approaching a true single salary scale.[44]

The discussion in the report on sex differentials in salaries highlighted a slow closing of the gap between men and women at the high school level. Much progress had been made in the 1920s, but little improvement had taken place during the depression. Progress, where it occurred, was usually accomplished through a preparation or single salary scale and by curtailing the bonuses that still were often paid to men in addition to their scheduled salaries. While some argued that bonuses were necessary to lure men into the high schools where they were needed, particularly for disciplining boys, the committee reported that it had found no relationship between salary differentials and the ratio of men to women teachers. The relationship that explained the ratio of male to female salaries, if there was one, was likely to be the result of "a complex of social factors, typical of the locality or the region" in which teachers worked, rather than any salary provisions that privileged men over women. This time the committee went well beyond merely stating the facts, as it had done in the case of black teachers' claims. In this case interpretations were made that showed what the salary figures of men in relation to women meant in regard to the issue of women's equity.[45]

Equity for Married Women

The NEA's willingness to advocate for women teachers in the late 1930s was again illustrated by a 1938 report from the Committee on Equal Opportunity. Beginning with an invocation that linked professionalism and equity, the report argued for a merit system of remuneration so that teaching would be made a career service. What was meant by merit system became clear when the report noted that only by eliminating nonmerit criteria such as marital status could the proper professional goal of teaching as a career be reached. Most states, according to the report, had little if any legal protection for the married woman teacher. Tenure laws were seldom inclusive of married women, and extending that protection to married women often required litigation. Even this process was difficult, because a married woman who did not contest a dismissal when it happened forfeited her rights. The fundamental professional priorities for the NEA committee were merit and competence. Studies showed little difference in efficiency between married and single women teachers. In addition, employing married women would cut down on turnover in teaching, which clearly hampered efficiency.[46]

Economically, the committee met directly the arguments used to force married women to resign their positions. First, in countering the argument that married women should not teach because they did not need to—that is, because properly they were supported by their husbands—the NEA claimed that married women teachers contributed to the support of dependents as well as to their immediate families. In dealing with the argument that employing married women increased the unemployment of single men and women teachers, the response was that married women often employed others in domestic service in numbers that equaled if not surpassed the number of positions that would be created with their dismissal. Noting a trend against discriminating in employment of married women in public employment other than teaching, the committee attributed it to an increased antipathy to discriminatory policies as well as to an improving economy. To further the fight against discrimination, three recommendations were offered. First, carefully drawn tenure laws were necessary that ensured that efficiency was the sole criterion of employment and continuation. Next, supply and demand studies were necessary to adjust the numbers of teachers being trained to coincide with employment needs. Finally, public enlightenment was required to develop respect for the merit principle in employment and retention decisions. The report's last sentence reiterated the NEA's long-standing belief that the facts, particularly if in this case as interpreted properly by a professional organization, yielded the best results. "By frequent reiteration of the 'facts,' public opinion must be developed against any employment policy that cannot be defended as a means to better teaching service."[47]

Equity for Rural Teachers

A 1937 pamphlet of the NEA Committee on Tenure dealt with still another salary equity issue that became acutely visible in the depression decade, though it had long been a concern of the NEA—the plight of rural teachers. The pamphlet, like some other NEA equity efforts, began with an invocation of efficiency in education as the professional objective to be obtained through achieving equity. Particulars such as certification standards, tenure provisions, retirement planning, uniform contracts, and minimum salary laws all were seen as avenues to such efficiency in rural schools. In fact, it was inefficiency in those schools that had sparked the investigation and report, stated the committee, which argued that "Never again should teachers, particularly the less favored in rural areas, be subjected to reductions in salaries which have too frequently characterized recent years." Rather than call for a national uniform minimum salary such as the $100 monthly that the Department of Superintendence had recommended, the Committee on Tenure advocated as the solution for rural teachers' salaries minimum salary laws for each state that were flexible enough to accommodate the unique conditions in the various states. General principles that were needed to undergird all the laws included, most important, a statewide scope that protected all the rural teachers in the state. This would prevent rural areas from crying poverty when confronted with the legitimate claims of their teachers to the minimum salary. Similarly, the committee noted NEA state finance studies from earlier in the decade that provided alternative taxation such as state individual and/or corporate income taxes as a way to achieve equitable rural teacher salaries.[48]

One more issue confronted in the report was the argument that minimum salary laws exerted downward pressure on salaries, which forced them toward the minimum. Earlier NEA research was cited to show that salaries in rural one-teacher schools were higher in states with minimum salary laws than in adjoining states without them. Further, the median salary for all teachers and school administrators was significantly higher in minimum salary law states than in the others. And in a final declaration, the committee noted that minimum salary laws were particularly effective in raising the salaries of rural teachers and black teachers in the South.[49] This mention of black teachers is the only one that occurred in the NEA materials on women and rural teachers. It is the exception that proves the rule that black teachers were the least likely beneficiaries of NEA equity activity in the 1930s as well as in the next two decades.

Two years after the 1937 report, the NEA published another lengthy study on the rural teacher. This effort was based on the responses from rural teachers to an extensive survey of their working conditions. In addition to documenting the severe salary penalties endured by many rural teachers, the NEA dealt here with the entire complex of conditions they faced. Rural teachers had substantial family responsibilities, lacked sufficient resources to own a home, and suffered from a lack of facilities and opportunities for cultural or professional improvement.[50]

Again, as in most of its other equity efforts, the cautious NEA urged rural teachers to be "professional." This meant that they should familiarize themselves with the contents of the report and bring the report's findings to the attention of "influential individuals and organizations." If these groups could be aroused, then a positive response was assured. Unfortunately, in this case as in the case of black teachers and, somewhat less consistently, in the case of women teachers, the hope for attaining equity went largely unrealized.

WOMEN AND EQUITY ON THE NEA STAFF: CHARL WILLIAMS

As was the case when she was first employed by the NEA in the 1920s, Charl Williams was the NEA's most important woman staff member in the 1930s. Presently, the discussion will focus on the significance of Williams for teachers' involvement in the NEA program. Before that, however, a brief discussion of her political value to the NEA in the decade is in order.

Franklin Roosevelt's election to the presidency in 1932 meant a substantial decline in NEA influence in Washington for the next two decades. That decline and its circumstances have been effectively analyzed by David Tyack and other educational historians.[51] Unlike the male NEA leadership, most of which came from midwestern Protestant stock and was aligned with Republican interests, Charl Williams's southern roots linked her to the Democratic Party. In the 1930s and in the next decade, she was the major, if not the only, link between the NEA and the Democratic administrations. Her work at the NEA lasted through all four of Roosevelt's administrations and into that of his successor, Harry Truman. Vigorous lobbying for the federal department of education, however, was not the approach Williams and the NEA used in the 1930s. Roosevelt's antipathy to such an idea and his distaste for most of the NEA leadership tended to put the federal department on the back burner.

Given this political climate and the dire economic crisis of the depression, it should not be surprising that, like the rest of the NEA, Williams downplayed federal aid and a federal department of education. Already discussed in this chapter has been the NEA addressing the deepening financial crisis that was increasingly affecting American schools by sponsoring a number of studies in the area of taxation and using them as a forum to push for more equity in state school finance. One aspect of the traditional bias inherent in discussions of the topic of school finance, namely that it was the purview of males, ensured that the association bodies that considered it would be overwhelmingly male.

Charl Williams accepted this reality in her own work life and chose to stress her activities in women's groups and the parent-teacher congress rather than try to break into the closed male circle of NEA finance reformers.[52] As already noted, Williams had multiple affiliations and responsibilities outside of the NEA, all of which served to complement her professional NEA endeavors. Late in the decade, however, Williams hit on a new program that facilitated her return to the limelight within the NEA. It enabled her to remain prominent in the women teachers' movement within the NEA and to capitalize in her activities on the dominant NEA theme of "professionalism" and its positive image in the minds of many women teachers.

In the fall of 1938 Williams helped organize the first of a series of institutes on professional relations, this one at George Peabody Teachers College in Nashville, Tennessee, the capital of her home state. In an article describing the conference, Williams remarked that she enjoyed the chance to hear speakers from several established professions recount their own problems, which were remarkably similar to those faced by teachers and the NEA. The differences, however, were as important as the similarities. Teachers had a social heritage that, in Williams's words, "has ridden our shoulders like an incubus." Part of this was due to teachers' status as public employees, which meant that they depended more closely on public support than traditional professionals. A major goal of this and future institutes was to develop a public relations emphasis for teachers' associations that would communicate the importance and significance of their work to the community at large.[53]

Williams went on to note that the rapidly building body of pedagogical knowledge was a boon to the movement to professionalize teaching. Similarly, the development of codes of ethics for teachers was a positive sign. The cause of professionalization was put at risk, however, because, as Williams noted, "teaching is not considered a life career by thousands of men and women who enter its ranks." She went on to bemoan the high rate of annual turnover among teachers. She then noted that "teaching can never truly attain professional status until certain discriminations are removed. Prominent among these are the regulations in many places concerning the married woman teacher." Williams here referred to the customary practice in many school districts of removing a woman from the teaching force if and when she married. As already noted, the NEA late in the 1930s began to highlight the discrimination against married women in teaching in an effort both to eliminate the policy and to win substantial membership support from women teachers. Williams thus effectively harnessed her own emphasis on increasing professional development to the NEA's larger thrust to increase teacher membership.[54] She spent much of her last decade at the NEA developing, promoting, and attending NEA-sponsored institutes on professional relations. While they did not always consciously espouse the cause of women teachers, married or unmarried, Williams rarely passed up an opportunity to tie these institutes to those larger commitments.

The institutes on professional relations were almost always held in the summer, on college or university campuses. The clientele was the

teachers who were students in the summer schools at the various higher
education entities. The official goals, as stated by Williams herself, were
threefold:

> 1. Unify the profession thru [*sic*] the cooperation of various agen-
> cies, foremost among them the teacher education institution itself, the
> state education association, and the National Education Association,
> and thru [*sic*] the evolving of a yardstick to measure a profession.
> 2. Democratize the profession thru [*sic*] the principle of democratic
> teacher-participation put concretely to work.
> 3. Make the profession vocal on its problems by encouraging frank
> discussion of vital problems.[55]

During the years after the professional relations institute was first
developed, Williams was tireless in its advocacy. For example, at a national seminar on building strong education organizations, held at the
1940 NEA meeting, Williams reported on the three-day institute program. In addition to acquainting all those attending with the concept and
practice of the institute on professional relations, she stressed the emphasis on public relations that characterized many of the institute agendas.
She added, however, that "placing the emphasis . . . on public service
[in institutes and in the seminar] . . . did not suggest that loyal efforts
toward better salaries, tenure, retirement, and other teacher benefits be
diminished." Instead, she added, such efforts should be "increased, believing that a profession cannot be evolved in poverty, and that by giving
the teacher a more secure place in society public welfare is served."[56]
Williams then went on to describe a situation that hampered the NEA's
membership efforts, the weakness of the tie between the local, state, and
national associations. Although professional relations institutes did little
to directly address this relationship, they could at the least alert the teachers who attended them that the NEA was interested in better organizational development in all of its existing organizations.

Other Women on the NEA Staff

Although she was the most prominent woman on the NEA staff, Charl
Williams was certainly not the only female employee. The women on the
NEA staff in the first two-thirds of the twentieth century can be divided
into two groups. The first, represented by Williams and a few others, consisted of those who came to the NEA after a career in schools and, usually, work in local associations and election as an NEA officer. Another

such prominent woman on the NEA staff was Agnes Winn, appointed in 1922 to the position of assistant secretary of the association. Winn came to her position from a career in the Seattle, Washington, public schools. In Seattle Winn had been active in the local Grade Teachers' Club. She reported on that club's activities, its affiliation with the NEA, its membership in a City Federation of Women's Clubs, its cooperation with the local chamber of commerce in a school improvement effort, and its membership campaign, which yielded close to a 100 percent result. Winn's task on the NEA staff was to help organize local teacher groups like the one in Seattle throughout the country. She praised the NEA for its advocacy of a single salary scale as a major vehicle through which to attract women members and urged it to use its influence in placing in school management positions "men and women of broad, constructive leadership to whom any teacher can look for justice and inspiration." For Winn, the classroom teacher was the "true leader, the real guide" to be followed in the American educational enterprise. To reach this leader, the NEA had to place greater stress on classroom teachers and their work. The objective of that work for the grade teacher was that "greater recognition and compensation must follow."[57]

Winn was the NEA staff member who became liaison to the Department of Classroom Teachers, after it was raised in status in 1924. She worked in the area of classroom teachers until her retirement in the early 1940s, when she was replaced by another activist from a women teachers' association, Hilda Maehling, from the state of Indiana.[58]

Williams, Winn, and Maehling all came to the NEA from established careers in the public schools and, in the case of Winn and Maehling, in local associations affiliated with the NEA. They all were placed in visible positions to show the nation's women teachers that the NEA was a friend of the woman teacher. Advocacy of the single salary scale, starting in the 1920s and continuing until its eventual adoption nationwide in the 1950s, furthered the image of the NEA as a friend of women teachers. The strategy of appointing high-profile women helped build the NEA into a large-membership, professional association that competed effectively for the allegiance of women teachers with the AFT, from the 1920s to the 1960s. The employment and the responsibilities of Williams, Winn, and Maehling were intended to help the NEA court women teachers, whose allegiance was necessary to achieve its objective of mass teacher membership.

In addition to Williams, Winn, Maehling, and other high-profile women from the schools on the NEA staff, there was a second group.

These individuals came to the NEA not from the public schools. For some, the NEA was an early employer, and they stayed with the association and built a career there. Others came from elsewhere in the workforce and used the NEA as the place to bring to fruition what they had begun elsewhere. Most of these women, unlike Williams, Winn, and Maehling, began their service in the NEA in positions of lesser rank but rose in the staff hierarchy through a combination of educational improvement and excellent performance of their assigned responsibilities.

The Research Division was one place that hired numerous women employees. For example, Madeline Remmlein came to the Research Division as a research assistant, the level reserved for those employees who had a bachelor's degree, in 1936. She previously had worked for the Psychological Corporation and the Pennsylvania State Department of Education and had a doctorate from the Sorbonne in France. Her experience made her conversant with issues in psychology as well as in educational administration, a combination that made her also one of the more versatile members of the Research Division staff. She also had a clear specialty area, however, in the area of school law. Remmlein earned a law degree at George Washington University Law School while she worked at the Research Division.[59] After receiving her law degree, she was made an assistant director of the Research Division. Remmlein's specialty in law stood her, and the Research Division, in good stead for the rest of her career.

Like Remmlein, Mildred Sandison Fenner worked her way on the NEA staff to a position of leadership. Fenner started on the NEA staff in 1931 as a writer for the *NEA Journal.* She was author or senior author of a series of articles on women in education published in the *Journal* in the 1941 and 1942 volume year, which will be discussed in the next chapter. While on the *NEA Journal* staff, Fenner completed her master's (1938) and doctoral degrees (1942) in education at George Washington University. Her dissertation, a history of the NEA, was published in an abbreviated version by the association in 1945.[60] In 1949 she was appointed managing editor of the *Journal,* the second-ranking post on the staff. In 1954, when the longtime editor of the *NEA Journal* retired, Fenner was first appointed as acting editor and then, early in 1955, as editor of the association's flagship publication.[61]

Like Madeline Remmlein and Mildred Fenner, Hazel Davis built her career at the NEA. Unlike her two colleagues, Davis spent almost her entire work life there. She was employed by the NEA on September 15, 1926, after attending the Harrisonburg (Virginia) Normal School and

Strayer Business College in Washington, D.C. Her first assignment was to help Sherwood Shankland, secretary of the Department of Superintendence, establish the Educational Research Service (ERS). She spent her entire career in the NEA Research Division, which shared space and employees with the Department of Superintendence.[62]

Almost immediately after she started working at the NEA, Davis began to enroll in evening classes at Washington-area universities. After a few terms she started summer school at Columbia University and its Teachers College. For the rest of the 1920s and almost all of the 1930s, Davis attended summer sessions, mostly at Columbia and Teachers College but also for a few summers at the University of Chicago. She reported that she was able to attend summer school without a pay loss because of the interest and encouragement shown in her and her work by her superiors at the NEA, particularly by Dr. Shankland. She had no vacations during these years, using whatever vacation time she accumulated for summer school. As a result of these summer studies, Davis earned a bachelor's degree from Columbia University in the late 1920s, a master's degree in education from the University of Chicago in 1936, and, after more summer study and a one-year leave of absence for full-time study, a doctorate in education from Teachers College in the late 1930s. The subject of her master's thesis, state minimum salary laws, and the subject of her doctoral dissertation, teacher employment as a function of school personnel work, became the topic of NEA publications.[63]

Davis worked mainly for the ERS until she completed her doctoral studies. Among her duties at the ERS, in addition to providing information to subscriber superintendents, she was responsible for the compilation and reporting of teacher salaries. This subject was important to the NEA, for it helped to cultivate not only teacher members who valued the information as a means to enhancing their own remuneration but also school administrator members who valued the information to build their own reputations as enlightened employers.[64] While the Research Division had concentrated on providing salary information from its inception, Davis's work added a new wrinkle, the reporting of the actual salary schedules according to which teachers were paid. This work, which published minimums, maximums, and steps in between in various local school systems, was of direct benefit to women teachers who were intent on using the NEA information as a weapon in the campaign for a single salary schedule in their districts.[65]

Throughout the 1930s, while attending graduate school in the summers, Davis continued her work for the ERS and for the Research

Division on teacher salary schedules. On completion of her master's degree in 1936, she was promoted to the rank of research assistant in the Research Division. A few years later, after completion of her doctorate, she was made an assistant director of the Research Division, one of four people, all of whom held doctorates or advanced professional degrees, who served immediately under the director of the division.

Each of the four assistant directors carved their own niche within the division, taking responsibility for one or more of the areas of study undertaken by the division. Davis's responsibility in the 1930s was in teachers' "salaries as a phase of personnel administration." Her work became widely known to teachers through articles that she published summarizing the contents of NEA *Research Bulletins* that she had produced. Davis was the NEA staff member who was most likely to be called on to provide staff assistance to committees such as those that produced the reports on minimum salaries and other salary-related concerns. She also was involved in preparing the report (discussed earlier in this chapter) that advocated on behalf of married women teachers.[66]

While she was clearly and enthusiastically committed to the cause of women teachers, Davis never allowed those commitments to endanger herself or the NEA. She was committed to the careful professionalism that the NEA advocated as the basis for all its commitments, and she no doubt was indoctrinated in this professionalism in her graduate education at Teachers College and the University of Chicago. Davis's commitment to cooperative NEA professionalism was doubtlessly enhanced by her early work for the Department of Superintendence, through which she had developed an affinity for school executives that was much like what she felt for teachers. In fact, immediately before coming to the NEA, she had worked briefly as secretary to the superintendent of the Washington, D.C., public schools, who recommended her for employment at the association. Given her own lack of teaching experience in public schools, it should not be difficult to see why Davis could work for teachers in a spirit that seldom considered that their interests might conflict with those of school administrators. However, though it would be an exaggeration to say that Davis devoted herself to the cause of women teachers rather than to that of teachers in general, there is much in her work that shows that she was keenly conscious of the conditions of women teachers as women and as teachers.

For Davis and many others, then, the NEA provided an occupational mobility track that allowed them to develop as professional staff members of the avowedly professional NEA. That commitment to professionalism was also a hallmark of the careers of Charl Williams, Agnes Winn, and Hilda Maehling, who came to the NEA staff from positions in the schools. It should not be surprising, then, that this professionalism never embraced any militant activity on behalf of women's issues. It was enough, for Davis and the others, and for the NEA, to call attention to the issues and, perhaps, to suggest ways to ameliorate situation. The belief was that those in power in the educational world would do the right thing.

THE 1920s AND THE 1930s

The major difference between the NEA in the 1920s and the 1930s was that conflict between teachers and administrators was highly unlikely to erupt in the latter decade because both groups combined to respond to the challenge of economic depression. Teachers and administrators often found common cause as they together faced self-styled taxpayer organizations committed to reducing public expenditures. The existence of a common problem and a common enemy combined to reduce any tension between the two groups like that which had lain closer to the surface in school affairs in the 1920s. Certainly, the 1930s were in this sense an ideal decade for the NEA to advocate its own cooperative version of professionalism as the vehicle for teachers' occupational improvement.

Willard Givens's ascension as secretary of the NEA in the middle of the 1930s allowed a shift to occur in association activities and commitments. That shift involved paying much more attention to equity claims on the part of women and rural teachers and less attention to the claims of black teachers. It also enabled the NEA to reverse a dismal membership situation in the first half of the decade that showed it losing to the teachers' union, the AFT.

The push for recognition of the claims for equity of women, rural, and black teachers in the second half of the decade took place in a climate where resistance from school administrators was not prominent. One should not conclude from this lack of overt resistance, from the existence of the various equity-oriented movements, or from the successful response to teacher unionism that the NEA was becoming a militant or radical group that would fearlessly pursue the interests of all teachers. In conscious contrast to militant advocacy, almost every NEA statement on occupational issues was couched first in terms of benefiting children and the larger society through educational improvement. For example, the 1937 publication on minimum salary laws for teachers began with the following sentence: "The purpose of minimum-salary laws for teachers is to guarantee a minimum standard of effective teaching service for all children in the state."[67]

Also, the NEA's advocacy of teacher equity was often accompanied by acknowledgment of the relationship between good personnel policies and intelligent school administration. For example, consider the opening lines of the report on married women teachers: "In school administration, as in every phase of public administration, good service rests fundamentally and prominently upon *personnel.* Organization and management are important; adequate finance is important; public law and public relations are significant; but *personnel* is generally conceded to be the most vital issue of all."[68] Thus, fairness to married women as teachers was as much or more an aspect of good school administration as it was a response to an ongoing occupational crisis.

In 1939 Willard Givens made explicit in his remarks to the Department of Superintendence, now renamed the American Association of School Administrators, the fundamental orientation underlying the NEA's equity activities. Improvement, if it took place, would come from the top down. In his talk, titled "The Challenge of a United Profession," Givens argued that the superintendent was the one charged with making democracy work in his school system. Those school executives who failed to democratize relations with teachers were not getting all that they could out of the teachers for the children in the schools. He ended the talk by urging each superintendent in the audience to take a solemn vow to be sincerely democratic and participatory. Only then would education have a truly united profession.[69]

Thus, under Givens, NEA advocacy of the cause of teachers as well as of the equity interests of women, rural, and black teachers, never was couched in egalitarian or in power-sharing terms. Equity was desirable not primarily because it was just but because it improved educational efficiency. And democracy in schools was a process that depended on initiative from the top and that would fail miserably without such an initiative.

As the 1930s drew to a close, the depression and its negative consequences for public education had receded in importance. The prospect of World War II, however, brought a new crisis to the public schools, to teachers and administrators, and, thereby, to the NEA.

NOTES

[1]Hazel Davis interview (June 17, 1988), NEA Archives, box 3117.

[2]Minutes of the Board of Directors (February 26, 1930), NEA Archives, box 323.

[3]"Teacher or Factory Hand?" *NEA Journal* 19 (June 1930): 171–72. It is significant that the NEA used a woman teacher as the protagonist of this article, even though the number of men teachers in the high schools had been steadily increasing since the 1920s. The similarity between the work life of this English teacher and that of a male English teacher described in the late-twentieth-century minor educational classic by Theodore Sizer is remarkable; cf. Sizer, *Horace's Compromise: The Dilemma of the American High School* (Boston: Houghton Mifflin, 1984).

[4]J. W. Crabtree to Dear Friend (December 9, 1930), NEA Archives, box 323.

[5]J. W. Crabtree, "Here Is a Fundamental Point of View: Read Every Word" (n.d. [September? 1932]), NEA Archives, box 323.

[6]J. W. Crabtree to Dear Friend (April 21, 1933), NEA Archives, box 323.

[7]All biographical material, unless otherwise noted, is based on William G. Carr, *The Continuing Education of William Carr: An Autobiography* (Washington, DC: National Education Association, 1978).

[8]Carr's total full-time teaching experience of two years, one in a junior high and one in a college, testified to the fast track to administrative accomplishment on which he ran, along with many other ambitious young men of the period. It also suggests why he acquired a reputation later in his career as not in tune with the interests of classroom teachers.

[9]John C. Almack and William G. Carr, "The Principle of the Nomograph in Education," *Journal of Educational Research* 12 (December 1926): 340–55; Carr, *John Swett: An Educational Pioneer* (Santa Ana, CA: Fine Arts Press, 1933), as listed in "Chronology of William George Carr Prepared at the Request of Alice Morton" (January 1983), NEA Archives, box 3066; and Carr, *Education for World Citizenship* (Palo Alto, CA: Stanford University Press, 1928).

[10]Carr, *Autobiography,* 35.

[11]Ibid., 38–40.

[12]*Studies in State School Administration* [all twelve in] NEA Archives, box 808.

[13]Ibid., and William G. Carr, "The 1929 Legislatures and the Teacher," *NEA Journal* 19 (February 1930): 61.

[14]*Studies in State School Administration.*

[15]"List of NEA Research Bulletin Articles from June 1922 to May 1972," NEA Archives; and John K. Norton, "The Ability and the Effort of the States to Support Education," *Journal of Educational Research* 16 (September 1927): 88–97.

[16]As discussed in Chapter 1, professionalizers in the NEA had a view of the work of the California Teachers Association as exemplary of what they wanted done in their new association at the national level. Norton's and Carr's hiring followed this statement of priority.

[17]"The Personal Income Tax and School Support," Study no. 8 (February 1931), and "The Corporation Income Tax and Its Relation to School Revenue Systems," Study no. 11 (August 1932), NEA Archives, box 808.

[18]Mildred Sandison Fenner, *NEA History: The National Education Association: Its Development and Program* (Washington, DC: National Education Association, 1945), 81.

[19]*Joint Commission on the Emergency in Education Official Records, 1933–35,* Vol. 7, "National Conference on the Financing of Education" (July 31–August 11, 1933), NEA Archives, box 925. In addition, the joint commission published a volume, coauthored by Carr, on school taxation; see Harley R. Lutz and William G. Carr, *Essentials of Taxation* (February 1934), NEA Archives, box 461.

[20]"The Association Moves Forward," *NEA Journal* 24 (October 1935): 207.

[21]J[oy]. E[lmer]. M[organ]., "Secretary Willard E. Givens," *NEA Journal* 24 (January 1935): 5.

[22]See the discussion in Murphy, *Blackboard Unions,* 140.

[23](New York: John Day Company, 1932). For the superintendents' response, see Charles H. Judd, "Conclusions of the Cleveland Conference," *NEA Journal* 23 (April 1934): 104.

[24]*NEA Journal* 24 (January 1935): 27–28.

[25]John K. Norton, "When Teachers Enter Politics," *NEA Journal* 24 (February 1935): 55.

[26]"The Strength of a National Organization," *NEA Journal* 23 (November 1934): 210.

[27]"The Strength of a National Organization," *NEA Journal* 23 (November 1934): 210; L. A. Chapin, "Convention Stampeded by Liberals: Delegates Support American System of Government," newspaper clipping (1935), NEA Archives, box 323. Lefkowitz was a longtime leader of the New York local of the AFT. Along with his colleague Henry Linville, he lost control of the union to communists in the 1930s and established a new local in response; see Murphy, *Blackboard Unions,* 151–60.

[28]"Liberals Defeated on 3 Major Points in Hectic Sessions," undated clipping (1935?), NEA Archives, box 323.

[29]"The Strength of a National Organization," 210.

[30]Willard E. Givens, "New Deal a Raw Deal for Public Schools," *NEA Journal* 24 (September 1935): 195.

[31]*NEA Proceedings* 74 (1936): 917.

[32]Wesley, *NEA,* 397.

[33]Orville C. Pratt, "Then and Now in the National Education Association," *NEA Journal* 26 (September 1937): 165–68; quotations, 166, 167.

[34]"Achievements in Professional Advancement," *NEA Journal* 26 (November 1937): 250, and "The 'Red Rider' Repealed," *NEA Journal* 26 (September 1937): 193.

[35]"Achievements in Professional Advancement."

[36]"The Preparation of Teachers' Salary Schedules: 'Part I: Administrative and Fact-Finding Procedures,'" *NEA Research Bulletin* 14 (January 1936): 5, and "The Preparation of Teachers' Salary Schedules: 'Part II: Drafting the Schedule,'" *NEA Research Bulletin* 14 (March 1936): 57–59, 77.

[37]Murphy, *Blackboard Unions,* 277.

[38]Richard A. Quantz, "The Complex Vision of Female Teachers and the Failure of Unionization in the 1930s," *History of Education Quarterly* 25 (Winter 1985): 439–58.

[39]Murphy, *Blackboard Unions,* 150–74.

[40]"The Preparation of Teachers' Salary Schedules: 'Part I,'" 5.

[41]"The Preparation of Teachers' Salary Schedules: 'Part II.'"

[42]NEA Committee on Equal Opportunity, *Progress and Problems in Equal Pay for Equal Work* (Washington, DC: National Education Association, June 1939): 4; and *NEA Proceedings* 74 (1936): 859.

[43]Committee on Equal Opportunity, *Progress and Problems in Equal Pay,* 24–28. On black teachers and the NEA, see Michael John Schultz, *The NEA and the Black Teacher* (Coral Gables, FL: University of Miami Press, 1970).

[44]Committee on Equal Opportunity, *Progress and Problems in Equal Pay,* 13–23.

[45]Ibid., quotation, 21.

[46]Committee on Equal Opportunity, *Status of the Married Woman Teacher* (Washington, DC: National Education Association, [Junc] 1938). The NEA's advocacy of the cause of married women teachers in this publication was in marked contrast to its stance on the matter ten years earlier. In "Married Women Teachers," *NEA Journal* 17 (December 1928): 297–98, the association settled for a discussion of various points of view on employing and retaining married women teachers and the provision of some statistical data on the subject.

[47]Committee on Equal Opportunity, *Status of the Married Woman Teacher.* The NEA's commitment to professionalism and merit as total solutions for all the issues involved in the employment of married women stands in stark contrast to the situation in South Australia in a similar period, when a teachers' union fragmented into distinct bodies representing married women and single women, respectively. See Kay Whitehead, "The Women's Teachers' Guild, 1937–1942," in Adrian Vickery, *In the Interests of Education: A History of Education Unionism in South Australia* (St. Leonard's, New South Wales: Allen & Unwin, 1997): ch. 4. For extended discussion of the NEA's efforts on behalf of married women teachers, and the limitations of those efforts, see Scharf, *To Work and to Wed,* 70–71, 76–77, and 80–81.

[48]"Minimum Salaries for Teachers" (January 1937): 4–5, NEA Archives, box 764.

[49]Ibid.

[50]Committee on the Economic Status of the Rural Teacher, *Teachers in Rural Communities* (Washington, DC: The Association, 1939).

[51]See David Tyack, Robert Lowe, and Elisabeth Hansot, *Public Schools in Hard Times* (Cambridge: Harvard University Press, 1984), and Edward A. Krug, *The Shaping of the American High School, 1921–1940* (Madison: University of Wisconsin Press, 1972).

[52]Marjorie Murphy has noted the depression years as a time of particular difficulty for women teachers in both the NEA and the AFT. Her account of the NEA reads as if Williams had left the association and no comparable advocate remained. This was not true. Williams remained with the association, but her profile was reduced substantially. See Murphy, *Blackboard Unions,* 172.

[53]Charl Ormond Williams, "How Professional Are Teachers?" *Peabody Journal of Education* 16 (September 1938): 118.

[54]Ibid., 119.

[55]Charl Ormond Williams, "Field Service," *NEA Proceedings* 78 (1940): 921.

[56]Willie A. Lawton and Charl Ormond Williams, "National Seminar on Building Stronger Professional Organizations," *NEA Proceedings* 78 (1940): 104–5.

[57]Agnes S. Winn, "Education and the Classroom Teacher," *NEA Journal* 11 (April 1922): 137–39.

[58]On the Department of Classroom Teachers and its first two leaders, see "Spotlight on the Classroom Teacher: Draft of the 50-Year History of the NEA Department of Classroom Teachers," and T. M. Stinnett and Alice Cummings, "Sixty Years of Classroom Teacher Advocacy: An Historical Account," both in NEA Archives, box 1824.

[59]"Research Division's Silver Anniversary," *NEA Journal* 36 (April 1947): 288–89.

[60]Fenner, *NEA History.*

[61]"Meet the New Editor," *NEA Journal* 44 (April 1955): 193.

[62]Hazel Davis interview (June 17, 1988).

[63]National Education Association, Committee on Tenure, "Minimum Salary Laws for Teachers" (January 1937), NEA Archives, box 764, and "Teacher Personnel Procedures," *Research Bulletin* 20 (March and May 1942). In her interview Davis stated that both her thesis and dissertation were published in the *NEA Research Bulletin.* No article on state minimum salaries was in any issue of the *Research Bulletin* in the 1930s or early 1940s. See "List of NEA Research Bulletin Articles," NEA Archives. Since Davis received her master's degree in 1936, this would surely have been the period in which it would have been published. The foreword to the Committee on Tenure's 1937 report acknowledges the "Research Division of the National Education Association for this significant contribution to teacher welfare" (p. 5). Since individual members of the division were not acknowledged by name in its publications until the 1950s, my strong infer-

ence, though only an inference, is that this is the publication that contained the information from Davis's master's thesis.

[64]For a look at how the Research Division from its very inception reflected the NEA's twin commitments to teachers and administrators, as well as its commitment to administrators as the superiors of teachers, see Urban, *More Than the Facts.*

[65]Davis interview. While the *preparation schedule,* the term used by the NEA to distinguish it from the *position schedule,* helped minimize the difference in men's and women's salaries by paying according to preparation and not to position held, the high school men usually had more advanced preparation than the elementary women, thereby meaning that the single salary schedule did not end the differences in salaries completely.

[66]"Research Division's Silver Anniversary," 289; *Status of the Married Woman Teacher.*

[67]*Minimum Salary Laws for Teachers,* 6.

[68]*Status of the Married Woman Teacher,* 5.

[69]Willard E. Givens, "The Challenge of a United Profession," *NEA Journal* 28 (April 1939): 103–4.

CHAPTER 3

War and Professionalism
The National Education Association, 1940–49

The NEA's activities just before, during, and immediately after World War II were more similar than dissimilar to those of the preceding two decades. In many ways the NEA of 1950 bore close resemblance to what James W. Crabtree began to build in the 1920s and to what he and Willard Givens presided over in the 1930s. This is not to say that there were no significant initiatives undertaken during the war years and during the rest of the decade of the 1940s, however. Some of these initiatives looked very much like earlier NEA activities and at least a few extended those activities without breaking significantly from the NEA's commitment to professionalism in education. The most dramatic single activity of the NEA in the decade was the creation of a new commission to try and link the NEA and public education to the war effort, as had been done during World War I.

The creation of the commission and the addition of substantial new responsibilities for it and for other parts of the operations of the NEA's headquarters demanded expansion of the association budget to support these activities. This would be accomplished only through additional dues income, which, in turn, required intensification of the always-present membership and recruitment efforts. They expanded in two different ways. The pursuit of teacher welfare increased and, in direct relation to problems in the AFT that provided the NEA with an opportunity for recruiting new members, was sometimes accompanied by the most militant language ever used by the association, particularly by its staff. Along with this activity, a vigorous effort was made to develop local associations, again with an emphasis on staff support from the national office through fieldwork with the locals.

Larger dues income, however it was raised, could come from only one source: teachers. Building on efforts from the 1930s, the NEA engaged in a variety of attempts to reach teachers, especially the women teachers who still constituted the majority of the occupation.[1] These efforts were diverse and imaginative, though they never became intemperate or strongly feminist in an ideological sense. This chapter highlights a series of articles in the *NEA Journal* on famous women educators that illustrated the cautious commitment of the association to women teachers. Further light on the careful but conscious NEA brand of pragmatic, women-oriented professionalism and its distinct limits is shed through a look at women staff and their work in the association in the 1940s. Of special interest is the relationship between women staff and the male NEA leadership in this period. I will argue that the same ambiguities and ambivalences that plagued women teachers on the job were evident in the work lives of women at the NEA.

The result of all of this activity was that by the end of the 1940s the NEA had increased its membership substantially, though it fell far short of the membership goals it had projected. While the NEA was becoming more powerful, in the second half of the decade it largely ignored the postwar militancy of many classroom teachers who, beset by low salaries and increasing numbers of students, chose to strike in several of the nation's towns and cities. The NEA in the late 1940s, then, with a similar but somewhat invigorated professional agenda very much like it embraced in 1920, was an organization at least somewhat out of touch with many of the teachers whose allegiance it needed to fuel its efforts.

ANOTHER EMERGENCY, ANOTHER OPPORTUNITY, AND ANOTHER COMMISSION

By 1940 it was clear that the nation, its schools, and its teachers had survived the Great Depression. Ominous war clouds were gathering, however, and a new crisis for the teachers and the schools was on the horizon, a crisis that the NEA hoped to turn into a new version of an old crisis to which it had successfully responded. This new crisis provoked a flurry of activity as the NEA sought to develop a way to harness it and to assess its implications for education and for the association. After several initiatives were proposed, the one that was eventually implemented built consciously on the model of the NEA's responses to World War I and to the

Great Depression. During World War I, as discussed in Chapter 1, the NEA had created a Commission on the Emergency in Education to pursue its goal of organizational enhancement at the same time that it worked vocally on behalf of the war effort. Similarly, during the depression, as seen in Chapter 2, a Joint (with the Department of Superintendence) Commission on the Emergency in Education and, then, an Educational Policies Commission were created to address problems in educational finance and planning that had been exacerbated by the poor economy. In each of these cases, the creation of a committee or commission yielded substantial public relations benefits for the NEA in the larger society and among the teaching force.

The 1940–41 school year for the NEA was punctuated by several discussions of how to address the challenge of the coming wartime conditions in the schools. Consensus was quickly reached on developing a commission, as had been done in the past. One document circulated in the highest NEA circles contained four suggested names for the new commission, and the one to be chosen was a topic of considerable and sometimes acrimonious debate within the NEA staff. The four names suggested were: National Commission for the Defense of Education, National Commission to Safeguard Education, National Commission on Public Relations in Education, and National Commission on the Security of Education. Three of the four names used war-oriented metaphors that sought to turn the war crisis into an educational crisis. The one non-war-oriented title, the "public relations" commission, pointed to a major dimension that had characterized all of its predecessors, was a significant part of most NEA work, and would surely be important in this effort.

The nature of the war's impact on education, at least as seen by the NEA, was indicated in a discussion of the new commission within the association's Washington staff: "The vital long-time defense function of the American school system must be maintained even in times of unusual expenditures for the military defense of our country." The only way to finance the military expenditures in the war was through the raising of significant new tax revenue. This action would necessarily create a reaction in the form of a movement to reduce other taxes, particularly those in states and local communities that provided the bulk of support for the public schools. Wartime conditions also would likely result in "patriotic" movements to create distrust in the public schools generally, and teachers in particular, as insufficiently loyal to the national cause. There already were organizations in existence that were moving to implement the antitax, antischool, antiteacher agenda, and the new commission, whatever its name, needed to respond vigorously and successfully to these threats.[2]

The president of the NEA for 1940–41, Donald DuShane, made a case for the wartime importance of public education in a radio address given in conjunction with the NEA's annual public relations effort with the American Legion, American Education Week. In his address DuShane noted that the "present world crisis had made it imperative that in our country the schools shall rededicate themselves to effective citizenship training." For the NEA president, pursuit by teachers of effective citizenship education was hampered by their poor pay and by working conditions that threatened their job security. He added that already various "groups are unjustly criticizing and attacking teachers, school management, school expenditures, textbooks, and courses of study." DuShane here was adroitly linking the ideological threat to schools and teachers presented by right wing groups and the financial threat to public school health presented by organized business and other taxpayer interests to the traditional focus of teachers and the NEA on job protection through policies such as tenure.[3]

These links were made not only by the NEA's president but also by its staff. The NEA professional employees were asked to respond to a variety of plans to invigorate the association's efforts in teacher welfare activities. One response highlighted the weakness of the commitment of some of the NEA staff to any aspect of a teacher welfare agenda. The respondent noted that the teacher tenure work that had been pioneered by Donald DuShane and an NEA committee before he became president had been made more difficult by some NEA staff opposition to the cause. According to this response, existing staff tended to be "hidebound by traditions of a non-militant NEA" and "full of inhibitions that would interfere" with the effective pursuit of teacher welfare. For this member of the NEA staff, what was needed was new blood whose purpose was to animate "an assembly plant—a central agency familiar with all phases of educational and teacher welfare, able to produce and carry out a total program; empowered to call on any existing committee for needed parts; and expected to make the whole machine do a thorough and effective job of teacher protection." Those on the NEA staff who looked for an infusion of new blood and new ideas were provoked in part by the relative indifference of teachers to the NEA's traditional efforts in the teacher welfare arena. Activist-oriented NEA staff reasoned that the tepid "reaction of teachers to our present program of 'furnishing the ammunition' with which they must do the fighting is indicated in a membership plateau which may become permanent." These staffers believed that teachers were "not satisfied with aid short of war."[4]

Another staff member noted a further reason to invigorate teacher welfare activity: it could be a vehicle that presented "a timely opportunity to take advantage of A.F.T. troubles." This individual was referring to the pitched battle that was then taking place within the national teachers' union, and that had taken place earlier in some locals, over the issue of communism. The AFT was in the process of expelling communists from its membership rolls, and the battle over this issue was bitter and long lasting. If the NEA could make good on its commitment to the defense of education and the related commitment to the defense of teachers, it stood to gain significant allegiance from rank-and-file teachers who, otherwise, might have looked to the teachers' union to protect them.[5]

To summarize the situation, then, the proposed national commission, whatever its title, needed to carry forth a three-pronged effort: a public relations move to counteract the financial and ideological threat to public education and teachers from the right, a citizenship education effort that would successfully ally the teachers and the schools with the war effort, and a renewed and more powerful push for teacher welfare protections that would compete successfully with a weakened AFT. While these three prongs were not mutually exclusive, they could vie with one another for the lion's share of the new commission's resources just as easily as they could reinforce one another to gain the allegiance of teachers, parents, and the public for the NEA's program.

Primacy of the public relations aspect of the effort, as well as a presumably accompanying de-emphasis of teacher welfare, was the goal of one proposal for the commission's makeup. It sought a group of nine professional educators and eight prominent laypersons, chosen from the following categories: labor, business and industry, women's organizations, school boards, and parents' associations. This was not the proposal that was chosen for implementation, however.[6]

The plan that was eventually adopted was the work of a three-person committee comprising President DuShane, Secretary Willard Givens, and another high-ranking official. This group chose not to involve laypeople but, instead, to include a wide-ranging group of professional educators for the commission. The new body was to be composed of sixty educators, a ten-member executive committee to be appointed by the NEA Executive Committee, and the remaining members appointed by the state education associations. The goal was to build "a strong,

nationwide, unified public relations program for the defense of education." This and other commission business was to be initiated by the
commission secretary, who would be chosen by the ten-member executive committee.[7]

This proposal was circulated to a wide range of NEA officials at the
national and state levels for response. Despite some mild objections,
based on arguments that the existing NEA staff and committee apparatus
could handle the responsibilities of the new commission, the body was
officially created at the summer 1941 NEA annual meeting. One month
before the convention, voting delegates were apprised of their status as
"Soldiers of Civilization." This titled editorial in the NEA's magazine
stressed that, as soldiers in their own right, teachers had to wage the war
effort by uniting behind it in their actions with students and parents and
by looking ahead to the peace and the reordering of the world that would
come with that peace. Most important, teachers needed to be ready to approve the NEA plan for a commission that was being perfected "to defend America by safeguarding the schools."[8]

In his presidential address at the 1941 NEA convention in July, Donald DuShane outlined the larger social justification for the commission
as well as some items on its educational agenda. He began by mentioning
a large adult literacy problem in the nation as well as a large number of
school children who were not enrolled in school. Both of these situations
threatened a manpower loss that could hamper the war effort. DuShane
went on to detail the salary and working conditions that prevented teachers from effectively addressing these problems. For example, while
tenure laws existed in several states, there were still "over 500,000
American teachers" who had no civil service or tenure protection and,
thus, faced discharge "without reason, justice, or recourse." Given this
situation, DuShane concluded that it was "as important to support and
improve our schools as it is to support and develop our army and navy."
Such support was needed, he added, to respond to movements already
afoot in state chambers of commerce and various taxpayers' associations
to drastically reduce school taxes. DuShane noted that attacks "upon the
loyalty and patriotism of the teaching profession" made by long-standing
enemies of public education were even more destructive. He went on to
describe the NEA as composed of a group "that was more devoted to
American freedom and democracy" than any other profession, a group
that would make "every effort to use the schools fully for the defense and
improvement of American democracy." To protect themselves and the
schools, DuShane concluded, teachers must "win from the public a new

and more understanding loyalty to education," must protect themselves "from fear and intimidation and unjust discharge," and must see that the schools function so that "the youth of today may be prepared to live effectively in a changed but democratic world of tomorrow."[9]

Not surprisingly, given the high rhetoric he invoked and his long service to the NEA in a variety of elected and appointed positions, Donald DuShane was chosen as the secretary of the Commission on the Defense of Democracy in Education. In order to take the new position on the NEA staff, DuShane resigned as the school superintendent of a medium-sized district in Indiana. From that time on, his work and that of the defense commission went forward in earnest.[10] A close look now at the commission as it developed its actions shows that, like many other activities in the NEA, it was more oriented to issues of improper political influence in the educational arena and protection of administrators from that undue influence than it was to the defense of teachers' academic freedom or other interests.

Less than a year after the commission's creation, Secretary DuShane reported to NEA members on a teacher-oriented matter that had attracted the attention of his commission. Amendments to the Hatch Act (the federal law preventing political activity by government employees), designed to free teachers from unwarranted restrictions on their political activities, had passed Congress. NEA staff and officers testified to Congress on behalf of these desirable changes. Yet this brief homage to teachers was dwarfed by the commission's attention to issues of improper political influence in school policy and its defense of school administrators from that influence.[11]

To facilitate investigations by the commission, the NEA Executive Committee adopted a set of procedures in September 1942 to be used by all NEA commissions and committees. The procedures to a large extent were modeled on the rules of the American Association of University Professors (AAUP). The educators sought the same image of nonpartisanship and fairness that was enjoyed by the professors' group.[12]

Less than a year later the commission embarked on a high-profile investigation of charges that New York City Mayor Fiorello LaGuardia had inappropriately involved himself in the running of the city's schools. That investigation was conducted according to the recently developed procedures and resulted in a finding that the mayor had, indeed, intruded into school affairs. According to the commission, LaGuardia had interfered in the school board's expenditure of educational funds and had sought to gain financial control over school affairs through sponsorship of measures to that end in the state legislature. While the Defense Commission, like the AAUP, had no formal means other than publication by which to enforce remedies for its findings, the result of this investigation was positive. After the commission conducted its examination into New York City, the mayor retreated in his efforts to manage school finances, and a bill was introduced in the state legislature to give the New York City schools financial independence from the mayor.[13]

In 1944 the commission successfully defended a New Mexico rural school supervisor who had been dismissed for refusing to contribute a portion of his salary to the local political machine. Cooperating with the educator's attorney and the state education association, the Defense Commission authorized an attorney from the NEA staff to prepare a "friend of the court" brief, which was presented to the New Mexico Supreme Court as it considered the case. The eventual reinstatement of the rural supervisor with back pay constituted a significant victory for that administrator as an individual, for the Defense Commission, and for the NEA in its efforts to thwart unwarranted political interference in professional educational affairs.[14]

In 1945 the Defense Commission successfully participated in expelling the superintendent of schools in Chicago from his membership in the NEA because of "flagrant" political favoritism in teacher appointments and numerous other violations of professional personnel policies. In the immediate postwar years the commission also continued its involvement in unfair dismissal cases in Chandler, Arizona, in Grand Prairie, Texas, and in Sebring, Florida. Although not always successful in reversing politically induced dismissals, the Defense Commission succeeded in keeping the issue of unfair dismissals prominent in the consciousness of NEA members and in continuing to make the matter a significant part of the organizational agenda of the association.[15] If its success was achieved more often in defending administrators than teachers, the NEA could accept this situation given that it always had stressed the identity between the interests of the two groups.

THE CONTINUING PURSUIT OF TEACHER WELFARE

In addition to its investigations of political interference in school affairs and personnel decisions, the Defense Commission also became involved in the pursuit of the NEA's long-standing objective of higher salaries for teachers. Shortly after its formation, the commission, in cooperation with the Research Division, conducted a survey of teacher supply and

demand. The results indicated an acute teacher shortage in rural schools
and in some high school subjects, as well as a drop in enrollment in the
nation's teachers' colleges.[16] The commission linked the shortages of
teachers and teacher candidates to the increased cost of living that teachers were enduring in wartime and the lack of a corresponding salary increase. It noted that when the NEA published the survey results, several
salary campaigns began in state and local affiliates that bore fruit. Progress, however, was sporadic, and the increases granted often did not
match the rise in living costs that teachers experienced. The commission
concluded that additional increases were a necessity to truly offset the
inflated cost of living for teachers.[17]

In 1943, one year after the supply and demand survey, the NEA published a *Research Bulletin* that dug more deeply into the salary question
and tried to relate it to the public good. In this pamphlet the NEA presented in full the argument that it had hinted at a year earlier. The later
publication opened with the following question: "Why do teachers in
general and in the National Education Association in particular keep advocating higher salaries for teachers, even in time of war?" Thirty pages
of tables and text proceeded to answer the question. Several arguments
were made: that teacher pay was too low to maintain life at a professional
standard, that the real but modest monetary gains teachers had made in
the 1920s and 1930s had been quickly eroded by wartime inflation, that
teachers' salaries could be raised substantially without running afoul of
recently enacted federal wage ceilings, that because of the situation thousands of teachers had left the schools for better-paying positions, that because of the same circumstances the number of teachers being trained in
teachers' colleges was down substantially, that this lack of trained teachers directly threatened the national welfare (using the argument that it
was the uneducated who did not qualify for the draft), that increased taxation was not an obstacle to better salaries since state and local tax revenues had risen significantly because of the war, that the amount of
federal money necessary to aid teachers' salaries was small compared
with the amount spent on the war itself, and that local action by teachers
was needed to gain the needed salary increases.[18] Many, if not all, of
these arguments had been made in the past quarter century by the NEA,
some in the World War I era, and their restatement here in the midst of
the presentation of new data on salaries belied the novelty of that data.

These same points were reiterated in various NEA publications as
the association tried to combat the worsening economic conditions of
teachers. At times, partial success was the result of the campaign, but on

the whole, schools and teachers suffered under wartime conditions. In April 1942, for example, the NEA reported that only 640 replies from a survey of more than 2,100 city and county school systems reported provision for any salary increases in the 1942–43 school year. While the 640 positive replies gave reason for hope, the larger number of negative replies, or nonreplies, to the salary question indicated that things were not improving in most localities.[19]

Advocating state minimum salary laws was another way that the NEA borrowed from its earlier campaigns, this time from the 1930s, to wage the battle for teacher improvement during the war. Again, as in the earlier decade, this type of law was especially important for the rural areas where teachers often encountered either a lack of any funds available for decent salaries or an unwillingness to commit funds to that purpose. To counter this situation, the NEA argued that minimum salaries should be set on a statewide basis, should be enforced legally, and should be achieved when necessary with supplementary support from the state to districts that were unable to pay the minimum with local funds.[20]

There were some specific additions to the NEA's wish list in the World War II era that enabled it to put a few new arrows in its teacher welfare bow. For example, the association closely monitored threatened changes in various titles of the Social Security Act to make sure that they did not result in a decline in state or locally supported teacher retirement benefits. Also, periodic reports indicated how various provisions of the income tax code for a particular year affected teachers. In conjunction with this last topic, teachers were reminded that NEA dues, travel to NEA conventions and other meetings, and other professional expenses were fully deductible.[21] The serving of the association's well-being in this latter appeal is evident, though it also seems fair to say that service of individual teachers was an objective. And it also is clear that the NEA made great efforts to link the welfare of teachers to its own activities, as it had in all of the years after its remodeling in 1917.

The NEA managed to use its wartime campaign for improvements in teachers' salaries and other aspects of their welfare to keep itself prominent in the eyes of its members, who were concerned with their working conditions. Yet the funds were in short supply for the NEA to support its long-standing activities such as salary campaigns and research and publications, new initiatives such as the Defense Commission, and the fixed costs of staff salaries as well as the challenge of their improvement. As a nonprofit entity and as an employer, the NEA was buffeted by the same wartime financial conditions that threatened the public schools. Inflation made NEA salaries worth less to employees, and they, in turn, were subject to offers of better salaries in the for-profit, corporate sectors of the economy. The situation grew more acute for the NEA as the war dragged on through the first half of the decade.

ASSOCIATION FINANCE IN A TIME OF CRISIS

The activities of new groups such as the Defense Commission increased the pressure on NEA finances, particularly when the group contained a new, highly compensated staff member like commission chair Donald DuShane. The issue of how to finance the commission, its staff, and its work had been widely discussed when the idea was initially proposed. One suggestion had been to obtain a grant from a philanthropic foundation for start-up expenses. Another was to support those activities with a loan. Neither of these suggestions was followed since the final proposal, rather than call for any new resources, chose another method of support. "The Executive Secretary of the National Education Association will endeavor to reassign personnel at the headquarters building in order to form a staff for the National Commission without materially increasing the personnel budget of the Association other than the added cost of the Secretary of the Commission." This attempt to launch the commission without addressing its revenue needs quickly proved an inadequate response to the problem. Commission Secretary DuShane, in an early report on the group's activities, noted that the "commission has been prevented by a lack of funds and inadequate facilities from instituting a number of activities called for by the emergency." He requested additional funds to assist in opposing taxpayer groups, in winning the cooperation of right-minded lay groups, in maintaining an investigative apparatus to look into political intrusion in school affairs, and in creating state-level defense commissions.[22]

In 1942, in an attempt to raise new revenue, the NEA proposed that its several affiliated "departments" force all of their members to pay dues to the parent association. Some departments, like the Department of Superintendence (renamed the American Association of School Administrators in the 1930s), traced their origins to the pre–World War I era before the reorganization led by J. W. Crabtree. These departments could thus invoke their own lengthy history, along with a variety of other arguments, in opposition to the NEA dues enforcement initiative. The stated reason of many departments for refusing mandated NEA dues was that they had been given prior commitments that their members would not have to join the NEA. Whatever the reasons for opposition within the departments, they proved successful as the departmental leaders coalesced into a strong block within the NEA that refused to implement compulsory dues for department members. Departmental leaders voiced support for voluntary rather than compulsory relations between their members and the NEA, a position that meant no change in the status quo and, therefore, no improvement in the association's budgetary situation.[23] What was evident in this situation was that there were many cracks in the foundation of the "professional" association Crabtree had built.

By the spring of 1943, the NEA financial situation was precarious enough that two additional initiatives were launched to find new sources of revenue. First, a "War and Peace Fund" was established to which teachers were invited to contribute to help the NEA in its war effort. Invoking the Defense Commission by name, the NEA appeal sought to raise $400,000 in new money from existing members to help bear the financial burden that had arisen because of the national emergency.[24] The tepid response to this appeal was unsurprising.

More important, in the same year the NEA moved to address its financial condition more permanently by increasing membership dues. The proposal was to raise annual dues from two dollars to three dollars per member. The NEA's magazine editorialized on behalf of the dues increase, noting that dues had been two dollars since 1875, and that wartime inflation had reduced substantially what that two dollars yielded in results for the association. The editorial added that a membership increase was just as important as a dues increase for the long-term welfare of the association. It pointed out that the current NEA membership of 220,000 was less than one-fourth of the nation's teaching force of more than one million members. The combination of a dues increase and a membership increase, according to the editorial, meant that the association would be able to wage successfully its multifaceted effort on behalf of teachers and public schools.[25]

One more aspect of the NEA's effort at financial improvement deserves attention here. As a corollary of the War and Peace Fund and a way to reap maximum benefit from a dues increase, the NEA engaged in a drive to unify membership so that a teacher who joined a local or state education association also joined the NEA. This campaign exposed a major organizational weakness in the NEA. Teachers could and often did pay dues to their local or state association without contributing to the national association. Local and state associations were chartered as groups by the NEA with nominal attention paid to the number of members in the group. Thus, once chartered, the number of members in a local or state association paying national dues had little impact on the body's standing in or relationship with the NEA. In a way it was a situation analogous to what the NEA faced with its departments, though at least the national association could argue that, unlike in many departments, there was little deviation in purpose between the national program and the interests of the members of its local and state affiliates. However, the NEA had to move carefully in this campaign, since formal action by the local and state education associations was required for unification to occur. In November 1943 a proposal was made that seven states adopt unification per year for the next seven years, thereby guaranteeing complete unification of all states by 1950.[26] Unification did not proceed on this schedule, though a number of states did unify during the 1940s. It would take two more decades, however, before the association was fully unified.

Opposition to the proposed dues increase to three dollars was substantial enough that the NEA delayed consideration of its implementation for one year from the 1943 to the 1944 national meeting. In that year the NEA magazine published a series of articles telling teachers what publications, programs, and other services they received for their NEA dues and which states had been successful in increasing their number of NEA members.[27]

Shortly before the 1944 meeting, the NEA announced a formal plan that combined its various membership initiatives into a "Five Year Program" for organizational improvement. The essentials of the plan were the dues increase, unification by one-fifth of the states for each of the next five years, and a specific membership goal for each state for the next five years. The rocky road for approval of the plan, as for any initiative in the unification or dues arena, was indicated in its provision that after adoption by the national convention, it would have to be approved by each state at its convention before it could be implemented in the particular state. The NEA prodded the states to approve the five-year plan through the publication of articles in the national journal by state officials pointing out what the NEA had accomplished for their state and what it could do for all the states if it obtained increased resources. Published articles also called to the attention of NEA members actions taken in states to comply with provisions of the five-year plan.[28]

As the war drew to a close, the NEA was obviously experiencing some success in its financial campaigns. Expanded services for the 1945–46 school year were announced in the association's magazine. The nature of the expansion, however, indicated that the NEA's emphasis on teacher welfare would be competing with some new emphases. International activity was one such new initiative in NEA efforts, as well as the activities sponsored by three new divisions of NEA headquarters: adult education, audio-visual education, and a travel service. While the last of these spoke to NEA members in terms of their individual interests and personal desires, it did not speak to their occupational interests as teachers. All of these additions enlarged the association's professional agenda while they simultaneously threatened any coordinated effort in teacher welfare by calling attention to nonwelfare issues and concerns.[29]

The expansion of its headquarters' activities did not mean that NEA was abandoning salaries or other teacher benefits as a concern, however. In fact, one month after the expanded services were announced, readers of the NEA magazine were treated to an editorial demand for increased teachers' salaries along with a reprint of an article from *Reader's Digest* that pronounced the level of teacher remuneration disgraceful throughout the nation.[30] Yet it is also the case that the more the NEA diversified its services, the harder it was for it to maintain a coherent organizational commitment to teachers and their welfare. Of course, much of this entire study of the NEA has shown the forces and the factors that relativized, though they did not completely neutralize, that commitment.

In the middle of 1946 the NEA announced that it had expanded again, this time in the field of rural education, with an increased budget and staff earmarked for the Division of Rural Services. This emphasis had already born some fruit with the establishment of a White House Conference on Rural Education in 1944 as well as several regional conferences on the topic. What the expanded rural division promised now was more publications, field service to state teachers' associations and to state officials in rural states, more conferences on rural life, and organization of rural teachers into local and state professional educational associations.[31] Given the NEA campaign for equity in rural teachers' salaries in the 1930s, those teachers may well have had reason to expect a positive outcome from this effort.

Later in 1946 the NEA moved to address an imminent postwar teacher shortage when it convened a national "emergency" conference on the topic. That conference in turn resulted in the creation of the Commission on Professional Standards for Teacher-Preparing Institutions, which would be prominent in NEA affairs for the next two decades. The successful outcome of World War II also enabled the NEA to repackage its various membership initiatives into a "Victory Program," thereby taking advantage of an opportunity to state its accomplishments and restate its objectives for the coming five years. All in all, then, the various measures designed to raise NEA revenues and the national visibility of the association as the group that addressed the problems of teachers and schools were yielding some results.[32]

Yet none of this should be taken as an indication of complete, or even substantial, membership recruitment and fund-raising success. The five-year plan adopted in 1944 set large membership increases for the next five years as a goal, culminating in a membership of 800,000 by the end of the 1940s. The first year of the plan saw an increase in membership from 271,000 to 330,000, well below the goal set for that year of 400,000 members. In the rest of the decade the actual totals would fall even further below the projections. Instead of the desired membership of 800,000 in 1950, the NEA reported 454,000 members for that year.[33] The partial success in membership, along with a severe postwar inflation, meant that early in 1948 the NEA had to mount a campaign for another dues increase, this time from three dollars to five dollars per year. Although the association had not increased its dues in the sixty years before 1940, twice in the 1940s it was forced to increase dues to keep itself in business. After the second increase the annual dues of five dollars amounted to a 150 percent increase over the two dollars that teachers had paid in 1940.[34]

In addition to the NEA membership campaigns and the catchy slogans of a War and Peace Fund and a Victory Program to help support its programs, the association engaged in one relatively constant and mundane but organizationally critical activity throughout the 1940s in order to maintain and increase its teacher membership. That activity—field services to state and local associations and publicity for these field services—was crucial to the NEA membership effort. The halting, intermittent, and ultimately indifferent record of accomplishment in this effort provides the fundamental explanation of why the NEA did not achieve the major membership increases it set as its goal. A close and critical look at the relations between national, state, and local associations and how they were affected by field services provides a revealing analysis of the factors underlying the unsatisfactory membership outcome.

BUILDING LOCAL ASSOCIATIONS

Following up on some of its initiatives toward local associations in the late 1930s, in 1941 the NEA acted as if its future rested to a significant extent with the state and local education associations. In that year the association publicized the unification that had recently taken place in the territory of Hawaii as the wave of the future. After unification, no teacher in the territory could join a local association without joining the territorial association and the NEA. Further, the NEA was pleased that Hawaii had also adopted a salary deduction plan for collecting the unified dues of all three levels of organizational affiliation. This was greatly preferred to existing cumbersome plans whereby local officers were forced to collect dues for all associations individually from members. Also receiving favorable publicity was a "contract" plan of dues collection where a local superintendent made it part of a teacher's contract that the unified dues for all associations be deducted from the teacher's salary. Although for the NEA this plan was as effective as payroll deduction, it also betrayed the NEA's willing dependence on school administrators to secure dues payments from teachers. In turn, this dependence made the development of any teacher welfare program independent from administrative influence much more difficult.[35]

In 1942 the NEA addressed specifically the problems that local associations talked about as impediments to getting and maintaining members. Here again, a top-down plan akin to superintendents' enforcing membership and collective dues, this time from the state of Georgia, was given favorable notice. In the Georgia plan state association officials joined with local school administrators to boost membership. Also garnering positive comment were an all-inclusive membership card used in one region of the state of Illinois and payroll deduction of dues. A revealing conclusion of this presentation noted that most existing plans were antiquated, relying on separate recruitment and dues collection by local, state, and national associations and resulting in "much lost motion and wasted effort" as well as irritated teachers having to respond to three different pleas for money.[36]

Lost motion and wasted effort were two of the problems that the NEA tried to address through its many unification initiatives later in the 1940s. Slowly but surely, the association was coming to realize that the local associations were the places it needed to go to build a strong teaching profession. A series of articles in the NEA magazine alternately suggested, cajoled, and exhorted local associations to engage in recruitment and chapter development. The range of suggested activities was dizzying, from salary campaigns to teas for retired teachers to public forums on educational issues. The general purposes to be achieved, whatever the activity chosen, were threefold: professional improvement, teacher and pupil welfare, and community service.[37]

In 1943 Willard Givens, now somewhat pretentiously called the NEA executive secretary rather than secretary, addressed the annual convention on the topic of the future of the teaching profession. In his address Givens remarked that the association's chief weaknesses were in the area of teacher welfare and in ensuring legislative action on behalf of that welfare. The way to remedy the weaknesses, said Givens, was to organize effectively like labor unions and business associations such as chambers of commerce had done. He added that most professional workers were plagued by organizations that did not know how to pursue their welfare, but that teachers had in their hands the ability to make their associations into powerful groups that acted effectively on behalf of their members. To accomplish this, Givens advocated that local associations be permitted to negotiate with boards of education over working conditions. Lest he be seen as favoring an autonomous approach to negotiations such as the collective bargaining engaged in by trade unions, Givens emphasized that the negotiations could be "informal." If local associations had this base of informal negotiations from which to build, then they could serve as the foundation for an invigorated state and national association.[38]

The role of the state associations, according to Givens, was to provide integration and coordination activities for the locals and to develop a form of "federation in cooperation with the NEA." The national, in turn, had an obligation to be "an effective instrument in helping the state and local organization to deal with employment problems." This meant that national field-workers were required in order to help improve employment conditions in the states and local schools. In one sense Givens was restating priorities that had been advanced ever since the NEA remodeling of the early 1920s. His concluding statements were rather distinct echoes of the past. He called one more time for federal aid to education and made it clear that the invigorated teacher association he was advocating would not be a labor union. Instead, its orientation was to cooperate "with all friendly groups" but affiliate with none. And his final peroration made clear that the NEA's commitment to teacher welfare was undertaken for a larger purpose than teacher benefits: "If we *do our full part now* intelligently and courageously, we shall make a lasting contribution to our fellow teachers, to youth, to public education, and to our country."[39]

The combination of occasional almost-tough talk with reassuring allusions to cooperation and to the general welfare characterized the NEA's approach to local associations in the 1940s. Many reports written by local leaders from rural states emphasized cooperation as the solution to their organizational problems. For example, in an article on "Democracy within the Local Education Association," two officials from teacher associations in Manhattan, Kansas, advocated teacher-administrator cooperation as preferable to either separate organizations for teachers and administrators or a top-down, administrator-dominated association. Separate organizations, for these Kansans, meant a tendency toward a pressure-group environment with the groups vying for supremacy, a setting that "was a breeding ground for disunity and distrust." Domination by administrators meant a "social club"–like atmosphere pervading teacher involvement, a situation in which "dissent is seldom evident, but professional alertness is usually at a low ebb." Teacher cooperation with administrators in the local association, the most viable alternative, prevented teachers from becoming like American workers who did not know what to do with their powers when they were obtained through unionization. Intelligent cooperation meant a steady gain in power and skill for all members of the local association as well as the development of a leadership that was geared to address and to solve problems rather than to apportion power on some predetermined basis. The unity that came from a properly democratic and cooperative local association would also be reflected in the workings of the group with the state and national associations. The closest that this discussion of cooperation and democracy came to talking about teacher welfare was a muted reference near the end of the article to the objectives to be gained through collective action. "The local association should not, of course, limit its program to philosophy and policy formation. It should promote those things from which the membership . . . can benefit to a greater extent by group rather than individual action."[40]

For two years in the mid-1940s the NEA magazine ran a series of articles titled "Building Strong Local Associations." The first issue in the series contained three separate contributions. The lead article reiterated the NEA's position that the local association was the mainstay for a three-level "professional citizenship": local, state, and national. The second article described the range of activities available to the local associations for their program planning: civic projects, legislation, organizational problems, public relations, teacher welfare, and good fellowship projects. The third article described the services that the NEA had available for local associations: research, publications, and public relations. It also mentioned the reports of the numerous NEA committees and commissions that were available to locals, including the output of the Educational Policies Commission, the Defense of Democracy Commission, and the Legislative Commission. The last article concluded with a plea for unity of local, state, and national associations, noting that "They must advance together if the best interests of the schools are to be served."[41]

If there was one pervasive theme running through the two-year series of articles on local associations, it was cooperation. Even when the articles addressed topics oriented to teacher welfare such as salaries and used the language of organization to consider the topic, they made sure to stress cooperation with school administration as an integral part of the organizational effort. For example, in a late 1943 contribution to the series, a compilation of four reports from several local associations titled "They Work on Salaries," two mentioned how local associations made progress on salaries through cooperation with the school superintendent, one spoke of cooperation with a salary "expert" appointed by the local school board, and the final one discussed cooperation between the local classroom teachers' association and other groups such as two elementary principals' clubs. Discussion of other reports in this compilation emphasized diverse ways of obtaining cooperation: "community goodwill is the key" said one; another noted that the local association was "asking" for consideration rather than demanding it, and still another spoke of the effectiveness of "personal conferences with each member of the board." In summing up the secrets of success of the several reports, the article, after advocating getting teachers together as the first secret, followed with advice to work "with the school administration, not against it" and to make sure to use "good public relations" in pursuit of the goal. All of this testified to the NEA's acceptance of the existing hierarchical school structure. As the NEA pursued the potentially controversial goal of salary increases, and advocated a bottom-up strategy of building local associations as the vehicle to engage in that pursuit, it also reinforced a long-held priority of non-confrontation with existing authorities as essential to the success of these efforts.[42] The contradictions within this structure and program were many, even if they were not evident to the NEA leaders who proposed it or the state and local leaders who tried to enact it.

In an article that dealt with taxation and school finance as local association problems, subjects that might well involve a group in controversial activities, the author, a high-ranking NEA staff member and former school administrator, advocated setting up a special committee of the

local association that was to be guided by the knowledge that "time and
time again a local education association had improved school conditions
by carrying the problem to the people of the community." Here again the
manner in which the problem was to be addressed by the local association was in no way to include any challenge to community authority in
school affairs. Professional unity that included cooperation with the
board of education and the superintendent was also recommended as a
productive strategy. In the interests of these various cooperative initiatives, the author assured the local association that strategic information
in support of its effort for financial improvement was available from the
state association, and relevant statistical data were easily obtained from
the national association. The article said nothing about times when cooperation proved unproductive or when missing information was not the
problem in achieving a solution to a difficulty.[43]

In the one article that reported actual field assistance to a local association from the NEA central office, the nature of that assistance and
the purpose that it served were clearly in keeping with the cooperative,
nonconfrontational approach emphasized in the articles. In Mobile,
Alabama, a series of salary cuts during the 1930s had been followed in
the early 1940s by a deluge of new students that seemed to preclude any
success in reversing the salary decline. The result was a salary crisis that
deeply disturbed the city's teachers. One group responded by forming a
union and issuing a series of "demands" to the board of education. The
Mobile Education Association (MEA), in contrast, formed a committee
that, with the superintendent, sought a meeting with the board to discuss
the situation. Responding positively to this "professional initiative," the
board resolved to develop a salary schedule in cooperation with the MEA.
Further, the board approved a working agreement between the MEA and
the superintendent that would ensure that the "point of view, wishes, and
considered opinion of the Mobile public-school teachers on matters of
concern to them may be revealed to the board for proper consideration."
Pursuant to this agreement, the MEA appointed a contract committee,
which included both teachers and school principals, to work with the superintendent on a new salary schedule. This committee was assisted by a
member of the NEA staff in drafting a new salary schedule for consideration by the superintendent and the board. The proposed schedule recognized that teachers' salaries should not be increased at a level any greater
than the increases in other legitimate financial claims on a school budget
such as books, buildings, and nonteaching school employees. The article
concluded that the teachers and school authorities in Mobile "have laid

the foundation for a constructive approach to the problems of educational adjustment that will face Mobile" in the future. The article clearly endorsed the MEA approach and just as clearly criticized the unprofessional confrontationalism of the unionized teachers. It ended by noting that "Success in this cooperative venture by a board of education and a professional association may inspire other communities to similar endeavors."[44]

While the article reported a successful outcome, it did not detail the particulars of the successful settlement. Additionally, it did not consider that one reason for whatever success the NEA had might have been the existence of the teachers' union. A board of education faced with demands from an independent union of teachers had substantial incentive to deal with an avowedly cooperative group of teachers and administrators. And finally, the article illustrated just what the NEA meant by fieldwork. Rather than organizing or strategic or tactical advising of local associations, for the NEA fieldwork meant the provision of expert advice on the makeup of salary scales. It is difficult to see this activity in Mobile as exemplary of a consistent, effective, building-from-the-bottom approach to teacher association development.

Two other articles in the series on building strong local associations touted the products of the NEA Research Division as valuable information. One article described a recently released pamphlet based on a substantial Research Division study of teacher leaves of absence. It argued that such leaves were a cornerstone of a professional advancement program, a valuable tool for a local association. The other dealt with the topic of credit unions, again detailing the contents of a recently published pamphlet based in turn on data generated by the Research Division. Credit unions were touted as a practical, everyday service that could be provided by the local association to help build professional welfare among its members.[45] While leaves of absence and credit unions no doubt have their place in any full occupational agenda, it is difficult to see them as a building block of an organizational effort designed to ameliorate the conditions of an occupation in considerable financial crisis. Rather, they represented the kinds of benefits that might come to a mature occupational organization that had already solved its members' basic needs. This hardly characterized the situation of teachers, at least as presented in the many NEA publications that stressed their salary problems in this decade.

The two pamphlets just discussed were the result of joint sponsorship between the Research Division and the Department of Classroom

Teachers (DCT) of the NEA. The DCT had been established in 1912 to recognize directly the interests of grade teachers. After the association reorganized at the end of World War I, the DCT became the sole body that regularly dealt with initiatives from teachers. In the late 1930s the DCT became associated with the NEA effort to build local associations. For most of the period since its founding, the DCT itself, however, had addressed pedagogical topics and other issues unrelated to teacher welfare. The crisis of the early 1940s and the NEA's effort to build local associations energized the DCT and moved it more in the direction of teacher welfare. The DCT was assigned a full-time staff member by the NEA in the early 1940s. This move was expected to result in increased membership for the NEA. As part of its new orientation, the DCT held a series of regional conferences to establish or invigorate classroom teachers' departments in state and local associations.[46]

The newly appointed executive secretary of the DCT issued a "Call to Action" in December 1944 that firmly put this group in line with the full NEA membership agenda of the period. Addressed to local associations, the call sought to involve classroom teachers in the NEA's five-year program of unification of national, state, and local associations. According to the DCT executive, local associations had been ineffective because many of them "existed on *paper* only" and met for meals or for tea or to hear speakers. This emphasis on social activity, while laudable in one sense, prevented teachers from considering the many unresolved problems facing them and from constructing action programs to address those problems. In many respects, teachers were their own worst enemy: "Teachers pay so little attention to the only organizations that *can* and *will* remedy these situations. When will classroom teachers learn how to use the instruments at hand and work together to improve their status." For the DCT leader, the instruments at hand were the NEA and its five-year membership program. She charged the local associations with the task of "collecting dues for the local, state, and national organizations." After mentioning that many teachers objected to superintendents who imposed association dues on teachers as a condition of employment, she went on to answer the objection. As she saw the situation, the fault lay with the teachers, not the superintendent: "Pity the superintendent who has teachers on his staff who have to be told and reminded over and over concerning their debts to the profession."[47]

This article makes clear that in the particular sector of the NEA assigned major responsibility for the classroom teacher membership effort, as well as in the local association initiative, activities or ideas that could

in any way be construed as questioning the existing hierarchy of authority in the schools or the NEA were not entertained. While local and classroom teacher groups existed to respond to teacher concerns, they
responded only insofar as those concerns dovetailed with and supported
the plans and policies of teachers' organizational superiors.

This commitment to the existing school administrative hierarchy,
through "cooperative" campaigns to build strong local associations, was
consistently reinforced. In the opening year of the local association campaign, an article on "Democratic Participation in Local Administration"
noted that the first threat to democratic participation came from school
teachers themselves, those who refused to cooperate in the administration of democratically developed school policies. This threat was often
evidenced in unjust and unjustified complaints from teachers about
salaries or a course of study that had been adopted democratically,
through procedures that utilized teacher participation without ceding
control to them. The article recommended that teachers use a "soft" approach, not confrontation, in initiating teacher participation. A year later
the NEA's top-down approach to building local associations was again
epitomized in an article that profiled five local associations that were
functioning successfully as much or more because of the cooperation of
the superintendent than of the enthusiasm of the teachers.[48]

The formal series of articles on building strong local associations
halted at the end of the 1945–46 school year, though the topic would continue to be addressed. Subsequent articles on local associations repeated
the same cooperative theme that had characterized the series. For the rest
of the 1940s, the articles on local associations decreased in numbers,
were shorter, and were mainly devoted to anecdotal reports from various
communities. A typical report came from the city of Zanesville, Ohio,
and told of the local association's success. The components of that success included establishing a mental hygiene institute, sending five of
its members to a state association–sponsored leadership conference,
publishing a mimeographed association bulletin, and forming a salary
committee that sought "to encourage professional growth."[49]

The few thematic articles in the new "Our Affiliated Local Association" series that succeeded the "Building Strong Local Associations" series addressed efforts to strengthen the NEA or to improve the image of
local teachers. Typical of the latter emphasis was an article in late 1947
that argued that teacher and student welfare were inextricably linked and
that, therefore, the prime path to be taken to reach the goal of teacher
welfare was over a "bridge of understanding" that needed to be built

between the local association and parent and community groups. Another version of the theme of primacy of cooperation was found in a January 1948 article. In it, an editor of an Arkansas newspaper told how his preconceived view of the local classroom teachers' association was corrected by the president of the association. The editor learned from speaking to the local teacher and from literature that she handed to him that members of the local association were first and foremost concerned with each pupil individually, with the effectiveness of their own teaching efforts, and with the improvement of those efforts. The editor concluded that the local classroom teachers' association was "not a teachers union," that the "salaries, tenure, and retirement plans come far down the line" in its priorities, and that its task was "to serve all humanity and to advance the general welfare."[50] Thus, the NEA in this and other late 1940s articles seemed to retreat somewhat from its rather mild pursuit of teacher welfare earlier in the decade and in previous decades.

Additionally, the emphasis in the discussion of local associations in the second half of the decade was even more devoted to cooperation between teachers and administrators than it had been earlier in the decade—and, as we have seen, it was prominent in that earlier work. Themes of cooperation, hierarchy, unity, public relations, and community conciliation also permeated the series of articles that the NEA magazine began on the topic of state education associations in the mid-1940s. Again, the major stated priorities were the successful implementation of the NEA's membership program and support for dues increases. The major strategic and tactical advice given in the series was for teachers to cooperate and conciliate in their relations with school administrators, with state school officials, and with governors and state legislators.[51]

The intensification of the NEA's commitment to cooperation with school administrators, at times in a context of discussing teacher welfare, was not in any sense problematic for the association's leadership or for its staff. What was problematic, or at least should have been problematic, was that this NEA commitment flourished in the post–World War II era when teachers in several places were using the strike and the threat of a strike to gain salary increases and improved working conditions. The NEA officially had a no-strike policy, as did the AFT, but both organizations were lagging behind the teachers who shocked the American educational power structure in 1946, 1947, and 1948. One could conclude that the NEA never countenanced the strike and, thus, turned a deaf ear to striking teachers. What characterized the strikes, though, was the desperation of the teachers who engaged in them. NEA's choice to ignore the situation was understandable from a public relations perspective, but what was less understandable was the association's offering teachers a policy that bore so little relevance to what they were experiencing in their schools. The NEA offered an ideal world of educational cooperation in the midst of a period far from ideal for the nation's teachers. Further doubt on the wisdom of the NEA's position arises when one considers that one of the most notable teacher strikes of the postwar period was waged by the NEA's local association affiliate in the town of Norwalk, Connecticut.[52]

The NEA publications of this era and the extant documents of the association are all but silent on the strikes, even the one in Norwalk. No article ever appeared on the topic of teacher strikes in the *NEA Journal* in 1946, 1947, and 1948 when the strikes were taking place. On one occasion, however, the situation in Norwalk was discussed in the magazine. It was in a one-column, unsigned treatise buried in the back pages of the November 1946 issue. It informed the readers that since teachers in Norwalk had refused to sign contracts that abrogated a pay increase that the board of education had agreed to in February 1946, their refusal to come to work when school began in the fall of 1946 could not be considered a "strike." The report went on to detail how the final settlement of the dispute gave teachers $65,000 of the $90,000 that they had been promised by the board. Further, the report noted that the board had also agreed to recognize the Norwalk Teachers Association, the local NEA affiliated association, as the "bargaining agent for the teachers."[53]

In this case the NEA had an opportunity to publicize a remarkable victory for teacher militancy undertaken by one of its own local associations. And there was still a series on local associations being published in the *NEA Journal.* Teachers might have wanted to know more about what it was that provoked the members of the Norwalk Education Association to leave their jobs, what the tactics were behind the scenes during the strike, and what the positive outcome portended for their own work lives. Instead of providing this understanding, instead of trumpeting the teacher victory to the high heavens as evidence of the NEA's commitment to teachers, the association chose to discuss the situation by quibbling about whether it was a strike and, thereby, essentially ignoring the one significant victory that one of its local associations earned. All this occurred in an era when the NEA was committed to publicizing the work of its local associations. Of course, the reasons behind this neglect should be clear to the readers of these pages. In late 1946 a case had surfaced that illustrated the positive consequences of an approach distinctly different from the NEA's conciliationist stance to teacher welfare, to local associations, and to teachers in general. As long as the association had to serve both teachers and school superintendents, and as long as administrators had the ear of the NEA hierarchy, independent teacher initiatives, no matter how successful, were ignored.[54] Just as problematic as the NEA's commitment to teachers and to local teachers' associations in the 1940s was its commitment to the equity concerns of women and minority teachers.

WOMEN TEACHERS AND BLACK TEACHERS

As outlined in the last chapter, the NEA moved to make salary equity for women teachers a prominent part of its agenda in the second half of the 1930s and, at roughly the same time, made more hesitant attempts to recognize the salary and other inequities facing black teachers. In the 1940s the emphasis on salary equity for women continued, though in a distinctly muted manner. The most likely explanation for the diminution in emphasis was that wartime conditions had depleted the number of men teachers in the schools and also reduced to near nil the number of men intent on entering teaching. These realities meant a diminished visibility for the salary differentials that still existed between men and women. During the 1940s, and in particular during the war years, the NEA continued to mention its support of a single salary scale and the direct benefit this scale meant to women elementary teachers, but this emphasis had to take a place behind the association's support of the war effort as well as its efforts to increase both membership and dues.

None of the membership or dues activities spoke directly to women teachers as women. This did not mean, however, that the NEA forgot completely about women as women. For much of the war period, the NEA publicized the historical contributions of pioneer women educators, perhaps as a way to inspire women to increased organizational consciousness in years when equal pay initiatives were clearly on the back burner. The historical discussions of women educators were, like NEA discussions of all issues, suffused with appeals to traditional values and orientations that mollified any concerns that the NEA male hierarchy, including male school superintendents, might have about the association taking radical positions on women's issues. Similarly, the conservatism of many women teachers themselves on gender issues was reinforced by the traditionalism exhibited in the articles. And by the very act of having such articles at all in NEA publications, even those that took a cautious approach to the topic, the association spoke to the more forward-looking among the ranks of women teachers.

The first mention of a woman educator by the NEA in the 1940s occurred in a February 1941 article on Alice Freeman Palmer. Leading off with a reminder that February was the month in which noted national leaders such as George Washington and Abraham Lincoln received their due, readers were reminded that "February has illustrious daughters as well as sons. It is fitting, therefore, that . . . tribute be paid to a great woman educator whose birth month was February." Next came a description of the career of Palmer, who lived in a time, from 1855 to 1902, when women progressed from a condition of substantial educational deprivations such as not being allowed membership in the NEA to an era when the association eulogized Palmer after her death "as the ideal of the educated woman."[55]

The article stressed the zeal for education that burned in the young Alice Freeman and caused her to convince her reluctant parents that she should have a college education, also sending a clear message from the NEA to women of the 1940s that college and teaching were appropriate destinations. Next came a description of Freeman's graduation from the University of Michigan and three years of high school teaching that presaged her becoming the chair of the history department at the new women's college in Wellesley, Massachusetts. Readers then learned that by the unusually early age of twenty-six, Freeman became president of Wellesley College and led the college to a position of national prestige and a firm financial foundation, all without alienating the male educational establishment in Massachusetts. According to the article, Wellesley pioneered in women's higher education while simultaneously developing a "homey" spirit that reassured parents uneasy about sending their daughters to college. Palmer reinforced Wellesley's image as a guardian of the virtue of young women when she married a Harvard University professor. Though she soon gave up the presidency, she remained on Wellesley's board of trustees. She went on to become president of the forerunner of the American Association of University Women and to serve as dean of women at the University of Chicago. She accepted that position, the article demurely noted, only when she was assured that she would need to be resident in Chicago (and thus away from her husband in Cambridge) no more than three months a year.[56]

Palmer was described as the motivating spirit in the "personal and professional growth" of hundreds of women. Thousands more, though not touched directly, had benefited from her legacy. And surely, women teachers reading the article were to see themselves as among the long-term beneficiaries of Palmer's work. As if to reinforce this and to build up Palmer's somewhat distant relationship to the NEA, the article quoted at length the NEA memorial to Palmer by a male association leader. This memorial simultaneously paid tribute to her accomplishments and upheld her traditional womanliness: "She has left us the ideal of the educated woman: scholarship without a particle of pedantry; optimism with no blinking of unpleasant facts; efficiency unsevered from winsomeness; power unspoiled by pride; all rooted, as women's best influence must ever be, in the affections of a loving heart, and radiating from its center in a happy home."[57]

This combination of honoring women educational pioneers while simultaneously assuring readers that they were in no way threatening to traditional womanly and familial values and virtues characterized all in a series of seven articles in the NEA magazine devoted to "Great Women Educators." The series began six months after the publication of the Freeman article. Proceeding with one article published in every successive month, the series profiled Emma Willard, Mary Lyon, Dorothea Dix, Elizabeth Peabody, Frances Willard, Susan B. Anthony, and Clara Barton. The articles had a reassuringly formulaic quality about them: they were each two pages long; wherever possible they associated their subjects with school teaching experience—even when, as with Palmer, it had been a minor factor in the woman's biography; and, most important, they simultaneously pointed to the unprecedented nature of the women's educational or other accomplishments while downplaying any cultural, social, or political disruption that might have also resulted.[58]

In the case most problematic for this traditionalist theme, Susan B. Anthony and her campaigns for women's political and educational equality, the article harnessed Anthony's political feminism to the NEA's pursuit of equal pay for women teachers, thus inoculating her for readers from any image of political radicalism. Anthony was described as someone to whom "all the people of this nation, especially the men and *women* teachers, owe a debt of gratitude." The reason for the debt was that "Susan B. Anthony exemplifies our profession at its best. Today the platform of the National Education Association provides that teachers of equivalent training and experience should receive equal pay, *regardless of sex* or grade taught; and that they should not be discriminated against because of race, color, . . . or economic or *marital* status."[59]

A related article, though not identified as one of the series, was published in May 1942, two months after the last article in the series. This article brought the series of portraits of famous women educators more directly into contact with the history of the NEA. Its subject was Ella Flagg Young who, in 1909, rose to the superintendency of the Chicago, Illinois, schools and who, one year later, became the first woman president of the NEA. The article repeatedly referred to Young as Mrs. Young, thereby reinforcing her married status while ignoring the early death of her husband and the gender bias and political corruption she confronted in much of her school career as well as within the NEA.[60] Young was depicted not as a politically astute leader but as a "selfless" giver of herself to teachers and children as she took on increasingly responsible administrative tasks in Chicago. Her devotion to teachers and their welfare was also highlighted, as well as her social invitations to teachers to come to her home for tea and discussions of educational issues. While her one-year presidency of the Illinois State Teachers Association was mentioned, her relationship with Margaret Haley and Catherine Goggin, who formed the militant Chicago Teachers Federation and eventually affiliated it with the NEA, was ignored. Her relationship with John Dewey during and after her tenure on the education faculty at the University of Chicago was highlighted, but the politics surrounding her dismissal from the Chicago schools before her tenure at the university, as well as the politics involved in her dismissal and reappointment to the Chicago superintendency, also went unmentioned. Thus the Ella Flagg Young that the NEA readership, male and female, encountered was a depoliticized school administrator, robbed of the gendered political dimension that was intimately related to her success in the schools and the association.[61]

With the publication of the article on Young, the treatment of women in the NEA magazine ceased for a four-year period. Early in 1946, however, readers again received a profile of a prominent woman educator. This time the subject was Catharine Beecher, and this time the subject's accomplishment as a developer of a novel, yet traditional, approach to women's education was juxtaposed to her political activism on behalf of women in a way that saw little contradiction in the commitments. Beecher's founding of the American Woman's Education Association in 1852 was counterposed, with no acknowledgment of any problematic aspect to any of the work, to her development of domestic science and household arts courses in schools and colleges as well as to her writing of "several cookbooks and texts on household hints." And six months after the Beecher article, readers of the NEA magazine learned about an Alabama woman educator, Julia Tutwiler, who, in the late nineteenth century, pioneered the establishment of a woman's female academy in that state that eventually became a state normal school. The career of this women educator also had an NEA culmination, in her selection as president of the Department of Elementary Education in the late 1890s. The gap in accomplishment between Tutwiler and the other women profiled in the series was large. Perhaps she was included to reassure southern women that they, too, could be represented in the NEA pantheon of women's achievement.[62]

The frequent historical articles on women educators ended with the publication of the Tutwiler article near the end of World War II. A few years before the end of the war, however, the long-standing but temporarily on the back burner focus on salary equity, as institutionalized in the single salary scale, resurfaced as a center of NEA concern. Two 1944 articles reported on school districts, both in southwestern Ohio, where the single salary scale was adopted. The absence of a focus on gender in the articles was significant, yet it was not difficult to read between the lines and see the significance of gender. The articles clearly showed that elementary teachers gained equity with high school teachers through the single salary scale, thereby indicating to anyone familiar with the gender makeup of the two groups that women were gaining equity with men. The NEA's choice not to discuss the gender issue openly in these two accounts continued its long-standing preference for the implicit over the explicit, for the pragmatic over the ideological, in its advocacy of equity for women teachers.[63]

Later in the decade the association trumpeted substantial progress in its cautious pursuit of equity in teacher pay. In a summary article on city teachers' salaries for the 1948–49 school year, the director of the NEA Research Division pointed to a substantial rise in median salaries during the decade and also noted a significant increase in the number of systems using a single salary scale. He showed that in a ten-year span the percentage of cities reporting a single salary pay scale had risen from 30.6 to 94.8. Care was taken in the article to credit these increases to "the participation of school employees in local and state salary committees" who operated using "NEA salary information." As in almost all cases, gender as a significant concern in the equal pay movement was ignored.[64]

Contemporary women as politically active, and women teachers' political concerns, did occasionally appear in NEA publications in this period; however, the focus was usually on making a direct link between the activity and the welfare or reputation of the NEA, rather than on stressing other aspects of the issues. For example, a 1944 article on the involvement of women in planning for postwar peace highlighted the presence of women NEA members at a conference on the topic. To make sure that readers were not put off by an image of women meddling in policy areas for which they had no background, the article explained: "All that concerns the home and the child is woman's special domain. Some of the most vital postwar problems deal with just these matters— homes to be rebuilt, children to be clothed and fed. To omit women from leadership in these phases would be uneconomical and impractical." And in its conclusion the article urged women teachers to act as the NEA members involved in the peace planning had acted, reassuring the teachers of the probity of those actions. "To the development of an enlightened public opinion in their own communities, teachers can make substantial contributions and can lead in a mobilization of women to their obligations as citizens with a stake in the future."[65] Thus the NEA's advocacy of the educational and occupational interests of women teachers remained in the 1940s, as it was in the 1930s, an intermittent, subdued, usually implicit but often featured theme.

The interests of black schools and teachers received substantially less attention than did those of women in these years, as in previous years. When issues germane to this racial minority were discussed, they received an even more cautious treatment than that given to women's issues. There was one relatively pointed description of black educational conditions in an NEA forum in the 1940s, when Mordecai Johnson, president of Howard University, spoke to the 1941 NEA convention. Johnson decried the caste quality that pervaded the economic, educational, social, and political condition of African Americans. Specifically, he identified the gross inequities between teachers' salaries for blacks and whites in the South, though he did not stress the NEA's tepid efforts on behalf of the redress of this inequity. He pointed out how these inequities could be used by Hitler and other wartime enemies to embarrass the United States in Central and South American nations with sizable black and Indian populations. Turning to domestic concerns, he praised the recent efforts in Missouri and Oklahoma to spend more money on black education in an effort to overcome the legacy of previous neglect.[66] The major reason that the NEA chose to listen to the relatively frank talk from this black educator became apparent in the latter part of his speech when he advocated a tried-and-true NEA remedy of federal aid to education as the vehicle to get more educational funding to the southern states where blacks were still concentrated.[67]

During the rest of the 1940s, the NEA never again allowed a black educator to remind its members of the educational harm being inflicted on African Americans. Instead, a number of articles appeared in the NEA magazine that highlighted not the issue of educational inequality but the contributions of individual black educators. In a sense mimicking the treatment of women educators discussed earlier, readers were regaled with the contributions of Booker T. Washington, George Washington Carver, and the founder of a black college in Louisiana, all of whom advocated the conservative strategy of racially separate, practical education for blacks. The articles did not note that this approach guaranteed superiority in educational achievement to the whites who would receive the academic training that these "practical studies" assiduously avoided. Of course, the Washington approach was the one that was officially sanctioned in the southern states, where the NEA had substantial numbers of members, and implemented by the white educators who were appointed in those states as supervisors of "Negro" education. One of these supervisors wrote an article for the NEA in which he lauded the virtues of this pragmatic, practical approach to the education of black citizens for whom he was responsible.[68]

The NEA's treatment of minorities in the 1940s, then, like that of women in this decade and of women and minorities in previous decades, couched issues in terms of professional problems to be solved rather than as instances of social or political conflict. Further insight into this treatment and its ramifications is gained by considering how the NEA treated its own women staff members in this decade.

WOMEN ON THE NEA STAFF: MOBILITY AND ITS LIMITS

The courting of women teachers by the NEA has been a prominent theme throughout this book. Yet I have also stressed the limits of that courting, as institutionalized in the patriarchy of the men who led the NEA and the other men who superintended the nation's schools. The NEA as an employer of women, as discussed initially in the last chapter, had to be sensitive both to the desires of women employees for improvement and to the concerns of high-ranking men that the improvement not develop to the point that anything approaching genuine equality between the sexes be institutionalized in education or in the association. Such an equality, in addition to threatening the hegemony of the male NEA officials, also would have threatened the patriarchy institutionalized in the nation's school systems. The NEA engaged in a high-wire balancing act as it promoted the achievement of women teachers and its women staff members and simultaneously made sure that the promotion was accomplished within a context that maintained a clear set of limits to that achievement.

As had been the case since the 1920s, Charl Williams continued to be the NEA's highest ranking staff member until her retirement late in the 1940s. Her activities in this decade mainly continued in directions she had established in earlier decades. For example, her work in the first half of the decade was largely in developing professional relations institutes, begun late in the 1930s. She continued to combine in this work the public relations approach to the advocacy of the "professionalism" so important to the NEA with occasional invocations of teacher welfare or women's issues. In the early 1940s Williams was tireless in her advocacy of professional relations institutes. For example, at a national seminar on building strong education organizations, held at the 1940 NEA meeting, Williams reported on a three-day program for professional relations institutes. In addition to acquainting all attending with the concepts and practices of the institute on professional relations, she stressed the emphasis on public relations that characterized many of the institute agendas. She added, however, that "placing the emphasis . . . on public service [in institutes and in the seminar] . . . did not suggest that loyal efforts toward better salaries, tenure, retirement, and other teacher benefits be diminished." Instead, she added, such efforts should be "increased, believing that a profession cannot be evolved in poverty, and that by giving the teacher a more secure place in society public welfare is served."[69] Williams then went on to describe a situation that hampered the NEA's membership efforts, the weakness of the tie between the local, state, and national association. Though professional relations institutes did little to directly address this relationship, they could at least alert the teachers who attended the institutes that the NEA was interested in better organizational development in all of its existing organizations.

Two years later another national seminar was held that was specifically devoted to building stronger local and state associations. As we have seen, this concern received major emphasis in NEA activities in the 1940s. In reporting on that seminar, Williams noted the twofold purpose of local associations as "the promotion and advancement of education and the promotion and advancement of teacher welfare." The work of the local associations was so important that the 1942 seminar resolved to concentrate on that topic alone in the seminar session at the next year's meeting. In her local association work as well as in her professional institute work, Williams was effectively linking a variety of professional policies and commitments to the material interests of teachers.[70] Probably because of her popularity with women teachers, Williams was the NEA staff member assigned to work with all of these seminars, and her commitment to the strengthening of NEA local associations, linked with all of her work on behalf of women teachers, remained prominent throughout the rest of her years at the NEA.

Throughout the war years Williams continued to work on behalf of professional relations institutes and local associations. In conjunction with the former, she wrote an article on teacher ethics for the Illinois NEA affiliate. In the article she summarized the NEA's work on a code of ethics, dating to the 1920s, and concluded with an endorsement of professional relations institutes as the proper arena in which to address ethics and other professional problems.[71] She gave a feminist twist to the institutes, one that came close to seeing women teachers and male administrators as having divergent interests, in an article published in the NEA's magazine in 1943. In that article, titled "Yes Mr. Rawlings," Williams began with the male administrator's admonition to Miss Giles, an elementary teacher, that her first and most important task was "to do the best possible job in her classroom." While Miss Giles agreed with her superior, she also understood that there were other priorities for teachers besides effective student contact. Williams then spoke of the professional relations institutes as the appropriate vehicle through which teachers could address their out-of-class concerns. The theme of conflict between woman teacher and male administrator was at best implicit in the article. No NEA publication would have dared to describe direct antagonism between teachers and administrators, men and women. Nevertheless, the choice of Mr. Rawlings as the administrator in the article and Miss Giles as the teacher, as well as the endorsement of Miss Giles's belief that out-of-class concerns were a proper focus for her own energies, indicated that Williams was pushing the NEA to recognize that the occupational subordination of the woman teacher was a problem to be acknowledged in educational work and an issue to be addressed in the development of the NEA program.[72]

One year later Williams highlighted the theme of teachers' legitimate concern with out-of-class issues in an article published in the magazine of the NEA's Department of Elementary Principals. Here the focus was on "Miss Bonny," whom legend said spent so much time on the nuts and bolts of her work of washing pots that she ignored the uses to which the clean pots were to be put. She scrubbed the pots so diligently and so repetitively that she even ignored her "Prince Charming" when he came to "cure her from her work." The result of this misplaced single-mindedness was that "her own fair face came to look—horror of horrors—like one of her pans." Williams went on to note the resemblance between Miss Bonny and those teachers who prepared their students diligently for the inspection of the supervisor or principal, the official who "beams on the automatons lined up for his scrutiny and devoutly hopes that Teacher will continue the good work, [thereby] keeping herself well within the bounds of the schoolroom, where she belongs." Williams countered this scenario with the admonition that the teacher had "duties and obligations beyond the walls of the schoolroom" and that the "wise principal will know this situation" and take steps to facilitate appropriate teacher activity directed to those ends. Williams concluded that institutes on professional relations were a most effective vehicle for teachers to develop their external relations. She added that the Department of Elementary Principals had made a great contribution in its support of the movement for such institutes.[73]

In this article, written for the women elementary principals, Williams used feminine imagery that was more traditional than she had used in the article in the NEA's magazine, perhaps because she was addressing an audience of older women who had served long enough to gain a principalship. Whether using more or less traditional language, Williams was consciously speaking to women in the educational profession and alerting them to the gains that women teachers could make through participation in larger educational affairs.

Williams made her boldest statement on the potential of the professional relations institutes as a vehicle for realizing the occupational goals of women teachers in a 1946 article in the NEA magazine. Perhaps here reflecting the militance that would soon cause teachers to strike in several of the nation's cities, Williams began the article with the description of a teaching force with an 80 percent women majority. The morale of those women, according to Williams, determined "in great measure the success of efforts to make teaching truly a profession." She went on to enumerate the obstacles to high morale for women teachers. First, the marriage bar meant that, unless it were altered as the NEA desired, "marriage will automatically end the career" of those who married. Women teachers, according to Williams, "should be able to lead normal women's lives and still continue their career—indeed they should be encouraged to marry and have children and yet continue teaching." Additionally, women "should have a chance to take administrative positions in school systems and in their professional organizations which they largely support." These problems, and others, were, for Williams, peculiar to women teachers who were unable to "speak their minds freely without fear of reprisal." All of these matters were "appropriate to the alive Institute on Professional and Public Relations. . . , the place that any teacher could sit down on an equal basis with the administrator, the supervisor, . . . or the college president, to discuss problems in professional and public relations common to all members of the profession." Williams then described the progress that had been achieved in many states in establishing professional relations institutes and other innovations such as professional relations workshops and leadership schools. In these schools, as in the other NEA-sponsored forums, "she noted that each worker 'counted one' regardless of sex or teaching position." She commended the professional relations institutes "to every teacher who believes in such general welfare objectives as equality of opportunity in education, cooperation, and organization as a means for curing existing ills" and concluded that institutes were for "all who believe in these goals, or even have thoughts on them."[74]

Williams's increased boldness in raising women's issues in an NEA forum was characteristic of her activism on several women's issues in the last years of her service at the association. Williams was instrumental in the establishment of two White House conferences, one discussed earlier in this chapter on the topic of peace and a second, also mentioned earlier, on a topic that was of long-standing personal concern to her as well as to the NEA: rural education. In the publication arising from that conference, Williams wrote an introductory essay that profiled the history of earlier White House conferences and detailed the steps taken to prepare for the current one. Williams paid homage to President Franklin D. Roosevelt for his support of the conference. She spent more space, however, in acknowledging the effort of Mrs. Roosevelt, who had responded immediately when asked for support. Williams recounted that the idea for the conference was hatched as she sat in "the mezzanine section of the Republican National Convention" earlier in that year. Positive response to the idea from both Republican and Democratic politicians emboldened her to proceed with the planning and to vet her plans to Mrs. Roosevelt "during an overnight visit to Hyde Park." Eleanor Roosevelt's positive response meant that the conference became a reality, fueled by the participation of NEA leaders at the national and state levels. The conference and its ten study groups produced reports that would receive nationwide distribution. While she demurred from predicting what the resulting recommendations would be, Williams ended her essay with a final homage to the president and his wife: "I cannot close my remarks without expressing my deep and abiding appreciation to Eleanor Roosevelt, without whose cooperation and vision this Conference could not have been held, and to our great President—my friend of long standing—Franklin Roosevelt, whose talk to us this afternoon will give significance to the cause to which this group of men and women have devoted their lives."[75]

Williams's political connections with the Rooscvelts clearly had been instrumental in establishing this conference and her high-profile role in the earlier conference on women and world peace. Her interactions with women's clubs and with the parent-teacher group, as well as her work as an advocate of the NEA's various federal involvement schemes, culminated in her personal triumph in the two White House conferences. Her longtime activism in the Democratic Party, as well as Roosevelt's affinity for the South and southern Democratic votes, probably also contributed to her political influence. As discussed in the previous chapter, the male, midwestern and western NEA male leadership's affinity for the Republican Party and for conservative causes such as Prohibition, and its enmity for Franklin Roosevelt, all made Williams the association's most effective communicator with the White House during Roosevelt's terms in office. Her personal relationship with Eleanor Roosevelt, forged to a great extent through Williams's work with the various women's clubs, reinforced her image as a formidable political leader of the NEA.

The memorial article published by the NEA at the time of Williams's retirement in 1949 highlighted the Roosevelt connection, pointing out the two White House conferences discussed above as well as Williams's personal presentation in 1947 to Eleanor Roosevelt of several mementos of their interactions. Additionally, the article noted Williams's friendship with the former secretary of state and Mrs. Cordell Hull, with Republican president Calvin Coolidge in the 1920s, and with numerous other Washington luminaries.[76] It also contained a commendation of Williams's work by Executive Secretary Willard Givens. On the surface, all appeared amicable between the male executive and his highest ranking woman staffer, as indicated in Givens's tribute:

> You have given the best years of your life to a great cause—that of helping to improve and strengthen our system of free, public, tax-supported schools. . . .
>
> The officers and members of the Association are deeply indebted to you for the fine, constructive work which you have done. The members of the headquarters staff value your friendship.

> You leave the active service of this Association with our best
> wishes for health, happiness, and a deep sense of satisfaction which
> comes from knowledge of important work well done.[77]

Below the surface of these sentiments, however, lay some unresolved
difficulties. They will be discussed in detail shortly, after the accomplishments of another notable NEA woman staffer are discussed.

In the last chapter I described Hazel Davis's coming to the NEA
staff in the 1920s and her working her way up in the Research Division
during the 1930s as she earned an undergraduate degree and two graduate degrees. Davis's studies of salaries and other aspects of teacher
personnel work became widely known to teachers through articles in
the *NEA Journal* in the 1940s that summarized her larger studies. For example, in an article entitled "The Teacher As an Employee," she summarized the two issues of the 1942 *Research Bulletin* on teacher personnel
that were based on her dissertation.[78] In the article Davis discussed various aspects of teachers' working conditions, using the format of a quasi
advice column to beginning and experienced teachers. The reference in
the article was to a teacher named "Mary Brown" and, throughout the article, the teacher was referred to as "she." Much of the article was devoted to handicaps faced by married women teachers. For example, in 87
percent of the districts studied by Davis, married women could either not
be employed at all or could be employed only in special circumstances.
Similarly, in a discussion of tenure protection, she noted that untenured
women in two-thirds of the districts lost their positions if they married.
She then commented on the fact that also in two-thirds of the districts,
high school teachers made more money than elementary teachers, regardless of their training. Even when women taught in high school, they
faced salary penalties compared with men. While gender discrimination
was not the direct focus of the article, Davis made it clear that women
teachers, and especially married women teachers, were second-class citizens when compared with men in salaries and working conditions.

Davis never went overboard in her advocacy of salary equity for
women teachers, however. In fact, she often underplayed the gender
angle in her research and writing. Even in these cases, however, it was
never far from the surface of her work. For example, in 1947 she produced an issue of the NEA *Research Bulletin* devoted to single salary
scales and published an article based on the research in the *NEA Journal*.[79] Each publication began with an acknowledgment of the NEA's
decades-long advocacy of the single salary scale. Both also noted that as

of the late 1940s, there was finally a majority of school systems reporting adoption of the single scale. The explicit gender consequences of this were noted later in the report with the conclusion that "Salary differentials on the basis of sex alone appear to be on the decline. Ten percent of the 452 schedules analyzed reported some provision for higher salaries to men teachers as compared to about 25 percent in the 1943–45 study."[80] This notion of progress was tempered elsewhere in the report, however, where it highlighted the casual nature of some of the documents that contained the schedules and added that many school systems reported having schedules but did not forward them to the NEA for analysis.

Davis's article addressed an issue that was unmentioned in the research report: the reasons for having a single salary scale. Here, however, in conformity with the NEA's careful approach to the topic, she did not stress the gender issue but rather preferred an indirect approach. She argued that single salary schedules put into action the "long supported theory that elementary education plays a fundamental part in the development of an individual."[81] There is little doubt, however, that Davis and her readers knew that the major outcome of a single salary schedule was a more equitable salary for women elementary teachers in relation to men high school teachers. In fact, by the late 1940s advocacy may no longer have been necessary. The report and the bulk of the article on it were devoted to more technical issues, such as how experience was to be recognized in the schedule, where teachers transferring from other districts might be placed, where teachers who had no degrees but substantial experience were placed, and the size of the differential for each step on the schedule. Clearly, Davis was a master of the salary situation experienced by women elementary teachers in the public schools.

In a long interview about her career, in which the interviewer acknowledged Davis's contributions to women teachers, Davis was asked at several points about discrimination against women in their employment at NEA. At each time the issue was raised directly, she stated that women were not second-class citizens in the NEA, that she herself was not discriminated against, and that she never felt personally demeaned because she was a woman. Yet at other times in the interview, Davis reported on events and circumstances that might well lead to a different conclusion.

For example, in discussing her relationship with Frank Hubbard, a man who came to work in the Research Division in the same year that she did, and with whom she worked side by side for almost thirty years, she recounted a somewhat different story. In the 1940s, when Hubbard became director of the Research Division, Davis reported that she encountered some difficulties with her new superior. At one point in her interview, Davis described her relationship with Hubbard as "embattled," and later she remarked that he considered her "too aggressive" in the conduct of her duties. She pointed to one specific characteristic of Hubbard's: his irritation when women teacher leaders from local or state associations would jump the chain of command in the Research Division and approach her directly for information on topics such as teachers' salaries, rather than begin their inquiries by going through the director. Davis concluded that Hubbard was overly concerned with his authority, that he made too much of minor occurrences such as the women seeking information directly from her. She also added that he was jealous that her salary program of research was proceeding so smoothly. Although she concluded that her relationship with this director was manageable, "reasonably polite," and one that did not get in the way of either one of them performing their duties effectively, she also spoke sufficiently of the tensions between her and her director that one wonders whether things were as manageable as she claimed. This conclusion is reinforced by Davis's response to a question asked near the end of her interview: Did she have any regrets about her career? She remarked that she "might have stood up more to Hubbard than I did."[82]

Davis reported another at least subtly gender-related difficulty she encountered in her dealings with Executive Secretary Willard Givens. She clashed with Givens over the issue of a credit union for NEA employees. One of Davis's responsibilities in the Research Division was to be the staff liaison to the NEA Committee on Credit Unions. One of the tasks of this committee was to promote credit unions in local teachers' associations as a means both of membership enhancement and service to teachers. Obviously impressed with what credit unions accomplished for teachers, Davis took a leading role in the drive to establish a credit union for NEA employees in the 1940s. Davis reported that Givens was opposed to the idea, though employees managed to establish it despite his objections. From that point on, she remarked, Givens always regarded her with a certain amount of suspicion.

In discussing her difficulties with Givens, Davis described another relationship of Givens's that strengthens the conclusion that the issues involved were gender-related. Givens, according to Davis, had an uneasy relationship with Charl Williams. The point of contention Davis mentioned in explaining the problem was the issue of the importance of local teachers' associations. Davis remarked that Williams saw the local association as the foundation stone, the building block in constructing and maintaining the NEA. Davis herself was in agreement with Williams on this issue. In contrast, Givens was less enthusiastic about supporting local associations, preferring to stress the top level of the NEA rather than build from the bottom. Davis never mentioned gender in the discussion of Williams, Givens, and local associations, but it seems more than plausible to conclude that gender was operative in this dispute, with Williams seeing the local association as a prime setting for women to earn their spurs as teacher leaders and Givens declining to stress the significance of an arena where the women were reasonably active.

In completing the discussion of the Williams-Givens relationship, Davis pointed to other tensions, remarking that Williams always took herself seriously, demanding the best in personal accommodations while traveling and holding herself to the highest standards in personal appearance. Givens's reluctance to grant Williams what she considered her due was, to Davis, an inexcusable slight.

What is to be made of Davis's protestations of satisfaction that she was not discriminated against in the NEA when compared with her accounts of her relationship with Frank Hubbard and her relationship (and Williams's) with Willard Givens? It is not that Davis directly contradicted herself. Logically, one can reconcile the absence of discrimination as policy and one's personal belief that she did not suffer it with the reality of personal tensions between male and female coworkers as pertaining to two distinct realms of experience. Yet, the intensity of feeling in Davis's discussion of relations with Hubbard and Givens requires more than a logical parsing to do it justice.

One possibility is to note that Davis's favorable account of her interactions with male superiors spoke specifically to individuals involved in the early phases of her career, and her unfavorable experiences with Hubbard and Givens occurred in midcareer. Early in her NEA years, Davis was a low-ranking employee whose aspirations for advancement were sponsored by male superiors such as John Norton and Sherwood Shankland, who, in no sense, saw her as a rival. In the 1940s, however, as Davis was making her reputation in the Research Division, her accomplishments could and did threaten people like Frank Hubbard, who conceivably saw in her a challenge to his own ascendancy to the directorship of the Research Division. Similarly, Davis's clash with Givens over the credit union at the NEA came at a time when she was extremely active as an employee, was greatly respected by the other employees, and stood as a potential and, in this case, a real and successful opponent of the designs of the NEA's top officer.

There is little doubt that the NEA was a patriarchal organization during Davis's tenure. The top manager of the association, as well as Davis's own administrative superior, was always a man. The negative consequences of that patriarchy for her, at least as she saw them, were experienced infrequently and at a personal level with men who were overly concerned with their authority. In these infrequent cases, Davis did not see the situation as casting a shadow over her accomplishments. Her relations with all other male administrators at the NEA, like her relations with the school superintendents with whom she worked directly early in her career, were positive. Thus, the two occasions of bad relations, in her mind, could be seen as exceptions to the rule of pleasant and productive interactions with superiors.

Whatever the ultimate explanation of her relationships, it seems that Davis was extremely generous in her evaluations of gender relations at NEA. One can speculate that interviews with some of Davis's women coworkers might have yielded conclusions about gender relations that would be in tension with or in contradiction to Davis's conclusions. In any event, the particulars of gender relations between NEA executives and women staff members indicate that conflict, though subdued, was clearly present. This occurred at the same time that the association increased the visibility of its women staff members in order to enhance its appeal to women teachers.

NOTES

[1]Feminization of teaching had peaked in intensity in the first two decades of the twentieth century. As salaries improved in the 1920s, and as a teaching job looked desirable compared with other positions in the 1930s, the proportion of men in the ranks increased, though slowly. Women in teaching declined from more than 80 percent of the occupation in the 1920s to about 75 percent in 1940. See Lois Scharf, *To Work and to Wed,* 66–67, 84–85.

[2]"Proposed National Commission for the Defense of Education" (n.d.), NEA Archives, box 1012.

[3]Donald DuShane, "The Task of Education in Our Democracy," *NEA Journal* 30 (January 1941): 28.

[4]"Memo to Dr. Givens" (January 17, 1941), NEA Archives, box 1012.

[5]"Memorandum to Dr. Givens" (February 17, 1941), NEA Archives, box 1012. I have discussed the problems in the AFT and their negative impact on

rank-and-file teachers in an article coauthored with Joseph W. Newman, "Communists in the American Federation of Teachers: A Too Often Told Story," *History of Education Review* 14 (1985): 15–24. Also see Murphy, *Blackboard Unions,* ch. 8.

[6]"Proposal for the Consideration of the Executive Committee of the National Education Association at Its Atlantic City Meeting on Friday, February 21, 1941," NEA Archives, box 1012.

[7]"Proposed National Commission for the Defense of Education" (March 29, 1941), NEA Archives, box 1012.

[8]Joy Elmer Morgan, "Soldiers of Civilization," *NEA Journal* 30 (May 1941): 129.

[9]Donald DuShane, "A Challenge to the Teaching Profession," *NEA Journal* 30 (September 1941): 163.

[10]Joy Elmer Morgan, "Our New Commission at Work," *NEA Journal* 30 (October 1941): 193.

[11]"NEA at Work on the Legislative Front," *NEA Journal* 31 (September 1943): 166.

[12]"The NEA Assumes a New and Important Responsibility," *School and Society* (August 4, 1943): 99.

[13]Donald DuShane, "Defense Commission's New York City Investigation," *NEA Journal* 33 (April 1944): 85.

[14]Donald DuShane and Frank W. Hubbard, "Victory for Teacher Freedom in New Mexico," *NEA Journal* 34 (March 1945): 61.

[15]"Ethics Committee Expels Chicago Superintendent from NEA Membership," *NEA Journal* 35 (March 1946): 161; "Dismissal Procedures: Fair or Fearful?" ibid. 37 (December 1948): 577; "Are Teachers Citizens?" ibid. 38 (December 1949): 622; and "A Dismissal in Sebring, Florida," ibid. 39 (February 1950): 110.

[16]By this period many American normal schools had changed their names to teachers' colleges, an indication that they were now granting bachelor's degrees—in education and, in some cases, in other subjects.

[17]Donald DuShane, "The NEA Salary Campaign," *NEA Journal* 31 (May 1942): 137.

[18]"Teachers, Salaries, and the Public Welfare," NEA *Research Bulletin* 21 (December 1943): 93.

[19]Research Division, "The Current School Salary Situation," *NEA Journal* 31 (April 1942): 110.

[20]"State Laws on Teacher Salaries," *NEA Journal* 32 (February 1943): 51.

[21]"Teachers and the Social Security Act," *NEA Journal* 30 (September 1941): A120, A122; "Federal Social Security Legislation," ibid. 30 (December 1941): 268; "The Teacher's Income Tax," ibid. 31 (January 1942): 10; and "Income Tax on 1942 Income," ibid. 32 (January 1943): 6.

[22]"Proposed National Commission for the Defense of Education" (n.d.); "Proposal for the Consideration of the Executive Committee of the National

Education Association" (n.d.); and "Commission for the Defense of Democracy in Education" [prepared by Donald DuShane] (n.d.); all in NEA Archives, box 1012.

[23]M. S. Robertson [president of the Department of Adult Education] et al. [presidents of six other NEA departments] to Mrs. Myrtle Hooper Dahl, President, Mr. Willard E. Givens, Executive Secretary, and Other Officers, National Education Association (July 29, 1941), NEA Archives, box 323. The relatively autonomous existence of the departments was an issue that Crabtree had left unresolved in his reorganization of the association. This situation was now presenting financial problems that, in a sense, masked the larger problem of any overarching sense of purpose being imposed over the multitude of activities carried out under the banner of the NEA and its many allied organizations. This problematic situation would not be resolved until the 1960s and early 1970s.

[24]"The War and Peace Fund Marches On," *NEA Journal* 32 (September 1943): 155.

[25]Joy Elmer Morgan, "Our Association at the Crossroads," *NEA Journal* 32 (May 1943): 119.

[26]Joy Elmer Morgan, "Planning for Unified Professional Membership," *NEA Journal* 32 (November 1943): 213.

[27]"What Do I Get for My NEA Dues?" *NEA Journal* 33 (January 1944): 11; and "Three Cheers for West Virginia," ibid.: 25.

[28]"A Five-Year Program for Professional Organization," *NEA Journal* 33 (April 1944): 83; "One Profession Now," ibid. (December 1944): 205; and "Oregon—The *First* for United Education Associations," ibid. 34 (March 1945): 57.

[29]Willard E. Givens, "Expanded NEA Services for 1945–46," *NEA Journal* 34 (October 1945): 127.

[30]Joy Elmer Morgan, "Teachers' Salaries Must Be Increased," *NEA Journal* 34 (November 1945): 145; and Robert Littell, "Teachers' Pay: A National Disgrace," ibid.: 157–58.

[31]"NEA Enlarges Its Rural Service," *NEA Journal* 35 (April 1946): 193.

[32]"NEA Acts to Meet Teaching Crisis," *NEA Journal* 35 (September 1946): 291; and "Victory Program Goals," ibid.: 304.

[33]Membership figures in Wesley, *NEA,* 397.

[34]"The NEA Faces Increase in Membership Dues: The Executive Committee Presents the Problem," *NEA Journal* 37 (January 1948): 15.

[35]T. D. Martin, "A Vital Project for Local Associations," *NEA Journal* 30 (May 1941): 148.

[36]T. D. Martin, "How Shall We Enroll Our Members?" *NEA Journal* 31 (October 1942): 189.

[37]Agnes Winn, "Foundation Stones of the Profession," *NEA Journal* 31 (November 1942): 222.

[38]Willard E. Givens, "Our Profession Faces the Future," *NEA Journal* 32 (September 1943): 157–58.

[39]Ibid.: 158.

[40]"Democracy within the Local Association," *NEA Journal* 32 (April 1943): 107–8.

[41]"Threefold Professional Citizenship," "Activities of Local Associations," and "Some Services of the NEA," all in *NEA Journal* 32 (October 1943): 193–97; quotation, 197.

[42]"Building Strong Local Associations: They Work on Salaries," *NEA Journal* 32 (November 1943): 227.

[43]Frank W. Hubbard, "What the Local Association Can Do—Programs of Taxation and Finance," *NEA Journal* 34 (March 1945): 67–68.

[44]Hazel Davis, "Mobile Makes Educational History," *NEA Journal* 33 (September 1944): 141–42.

[45]Clayton D. Hutchins, "Teacher Leaves of Absence," *NEA Journal* 35 (February 1946): 85–86; and Frank W. Hubbard, "Credit Where Credit Is Due," ibid. (March 1946): 132–33.

[46]"Building Strong Local Associations: The Southeastern Regional Conference," *NEA Journal* 33 (March 1944): 73–74; and "State Departments of Classroom Teachers," ibid. (April 1944): 99–100. On the DCT, see "Spotlight on the Classroom Teacher: Draft of the 50-Year History of the NEA Department of Classroom Teachers," and T. M. Stinnett and Alice Cummings, "Sixty Years of Classroom Teacher Advocacy: An Historical Account," both in NEA Archives, box 1824.

[47]Hilda Maehling, "A Call to Action," *NEA Journal* 33 (December 1944): 206.

[48]"Democratic Participation in Local Administration," *NEA Journal* 33 (November 1944): 193–94; and "School Administrators Advocate Strong Local Associations," ibid. 34 (April 1945): 89–90.

[49]*NEA Journal* 36 (October 1947): 519.

[50]Frank Potter, "Do You Want to Make History?" *NEA Journal* 36 (November 1947): 583; and "Layman Appraises Locals," ibid. 37 (January 1948): 40.

[51]In 1948 the Research Division published a substantial report on the activities of state education associations. It included a thirty-page summary of state activities and 150 pages of reports from individual states. See *State Education Associations: Their Organization, Programs, and Staffs in 1947–48,* Microfiche Document no. 430, S48.1, NEA Archives.

[52]On the strikes, see Wayne J. Urban and Jennings L. Wagoner, Jr., *American Education: A History* (New York: McGraw-Hill, 1996), ch. 10.

[53]"The Facts about Norwalk—," *NEA Journal* 35 (November 1946): 533. My conclusion that this was the only NEA mention of post–World War II teachers' strikes is based on a reasonably diligent search in the various NEA publications of the late 1940s, of the association *Proceedings* of the annual meetings for those years, and of the documentary record left by the association for the period.

[54]It should be noted, as mentioned briefly above, that the AFT did not handle this situation in a substantively different manner. While AFT affiliates in Minneapolis and St. Paul, Minnesota, and in East Detroit, Michigan, undertook

strikes that achieved at least partial victories like the one in Norwalk, the AFT refused to alter its own official "no-strike policy" and thereby refused to bring the union along to the point that it agreed with what its own affiliates were doing. See Murphy, *Blackboard Unions,* 182–84.

[55]Mildred Sandison Fenner, "Alice Freeman Palmer, February 21, 1855–December 6, 1902—An Appreciation," *NEA Journal* 30 (February 1941): 35–36, quotation, 35.

[56]Ibid.

[57]Ibid.: 36.

[58]The articles, all written by Mildred Fenner and Eleanor Fishburn of the staff of the *NEA Journal,* were as follows: "Emma Willard and Her Plan for Improving Female Education," *NEA Journal* 30 (September 1941):177–78; "Mary Lyon and Mount Holyoke College," ibid. (October 1941): 205–6; "Unto the Least: Dorothea Dix, Crusader," ibid. (November 1941): 241–42; "Elizabeth Peabody and the Kindergarten," ibid. (December 1941): 275–76; "Frances E. Willard, Educator," ibid. 31 (January 1942): 13–14; "Susan B. Anthony, Apostle of Freedom," ibid. (February 1942): 49–50; and "Angel of the Battlefield: Clara Barton, Teacher and Philanthropist," ibid. (March 1942): 85–86.

[59]Quotes from article on Anthony in *NEA Journal* 31 (February 1942): 50.

[60]For this aspect of Young's career, see Blount, *Destined to Rule the Schools,* 77.

[61]Mildred Fenner and Eleanor Fishburn, "Ella Flagg Young: School Administrator," *NEA Journal* 31 (May 1942): 147–48. On Haley, Young, and the Chicago Teachers Federation, see Urban, *Why Teachers Organized,* ch. 3.

[62]Jean Conder Soule, "Catharine Esther Beecher: Pioneer in the Education of American Women," *NEA Journal* 35 (February 1946): 104–5; and Mildred Fenner and Jean Conder Soule, "Julia Tutwiler—Southern Pioneer," ibid. (November 1946): 499–500.

[63]Claude V. Courier, "Consider the Single Salary Scale," *NEA Journal* 33 (April 1944): 93; and Courier, "Hamilton, Ohio Adopts a Single Salary Scale," ibid. 34 (January 1945): 18.

[64]Frank W. Hubbard, "Salaries in 1948–49," *NEA Journal* 38 (May 1949): 352–53. Also left unmentioned in this article was any opposition to single salary scales on the part of high school teachers, particularly the men. The next chapter shows that such opposition in New York City sparked the formation of militant teacher unions in that city in the late 1950s.

[65]"If the Women of America . . . ," *NEA Journal* 33 (September 1944): 149.

[66]These states acted after the 1939 *Gaines v. Canada* [Missouri] Supreme Court decision that required that a good-faith effort be made to legitimate the "separate but equal" doctrine of the 1896 *Plessy v. Ferguson* decision. While the southern states had accepted the principle enunciated in *Plessy,* they had systematically ignored its implementation as they awarded school funds and teachers' salaries to whites in amounts far exceeding those given to blacks. *Gaines* was the forerunner of a number of equalization suits won by blacks in various southern states in the 1940s.

[67]Mordecai W. Johnson, "Negro Opportunity and National Morale," *NEA Journal* 30 (September 1941): 167–68. The budget demands of the war effort made federal aid to education less plausible and the NEA, correspondingly, de-emphasized its advocacy during the war, without abandoning it completely.

[68]"Booker T. Washington," *NEA Journal* 33 (April 1944): 95–96; "George Washington Carver—The Wizard of Tuskegee," ibid. 35 (December 1946): 580–81; "[Grambling] College Close to the People," ibid.: 576–79; and Roscoe H. White, "A Southern Program of Negro Education," ibid. 30 (April 1941): 111–12.

[69]Willie A. Lawton and Charl Ormond Williams, "National Seminar on Building Stronger Professional Organizations," *NEA Proceedings* 78 (1940): 104–5.

[70]Joe A. Chandler and Charl Ormond Williams, "National Seminar on Making the Teaching Profession More Effective Thru [*sic*] Local, State, and National Associations," *NEA Proceedings* 80 (1942): 70.

[71]Charl Ormond Williams, "Teacher Ethics and Professionalization," *Illinois Education* (March 1942): 198–99.

[72]Charl Ormond Williams, "Yes, Mr. Rawlings," *NEA Journal* 32 (March 1943): 82.

[73]Charl Ormond Williams, "The Legend of Miss Bonny," *The National Elementary Principal* 23 (June 1944): 41–42.

[74]Charl Ormond Williams, "Professional Institutes," *NEA Journal* 35 (January 1946): 29.

[75]Charl Ormond Williams, "Background of the Conference," *Proceedings of the White House Conference on Rural Education* (Washington, DC: National Education Association of the United States of America, October 3, 4, and 5, 1944): 27, 28.

[76]Special Number, *NEA Journal* (n.d., 1949).

[77]Ibid.

[78]Hazel Davis, "The Teacher as an Employee," *NEA Journal* 31 (May 1942): 138.

[79]"Analysis of Single Salary Schedules," *NEA Research Bulletin* 25 (October 1947): 74–111; and Hazel Davis, "Single Salary Schedules Today," *NEA Journal* 36 (December 1947): 638–39.

[80]Hazel Davis, "Single Salary Schedules Today," *NEA Journal* 36 (December 1947): 639.

[81]Ibid.: 638.

[82]Hazel Davis interview (June 17, 1988), NEA Archives, box 3117. This interview was undertaken by a consultant hired to conduct a number of interviews with former NEA staff members. It consists of three tapes that have not been transcribed. For more information on Davis, see my unpublished paper "A Woman Educator in the Twentieth Century: Hazel Davis and the National Education Association, 1926–1966."

CHAPTER 4

An Exaggerated Sense of Accomplishment
The National Education Association in the 1950s

Because the Korean War had an economic impact on the nation's teachers, it also affected the NEA. The fact that the war remained undeclared officially, however, made it much less significant as a publicity vehicle for association purposes and programs than either of its two twentieth-century predecessors. In terms of other federal relations, the NEA's increasing international role, sparked by its participation in post–World War II planning for peace activities, drew it close to a national administration enmeshed in a cold war with communism. And ironically, the implementation of federal aid to education legislation late in the 1950s took place in a way that found the NEA, a longtime advocate of the objective, hardly happy with the results.

In terms of most other aspects of its activities in the 1950s, the association continued and expanded on emphases pioneered in earlier decades. The pursuit of teacher welfare and the enhancement of state and local associations were both long-standing commitments that were renewed, though in somewhat subdued fashion, in the 1950s. The key event for the leadership in this decade had little to do with either of these commitments; rather, NEA officials spent prodigious amounts of time and money planning and executing the association's one hundredth anniversary celebration in 1957.

Change at the top of the NEA occurred when Executive Secretary Willard Givens retired in the early 1950s. While there were some significant differences in the backgrounds and priorities of Givens and his successor, William G. Carr, there was also substantial continuity in their approach to the association and their desire to have a proper recognition of the centennial. Both of these men, the rest of the headquarters staff, and the NEA elected officers did everything they could in the early and middle years of the decade to enlist NEA members, the majority of whom were still women teachers, to participate in the centennial celebration. Addressing members in the same ways that they had in earlier decades, NEA leaders alternately urged, cajoled, and pleaded with teachers to recognize the significance of and to help celebrate the centennial. The anniversary also provided an occasion for the NEA to announce a new organizational initiative, catchily named like its predecessors, to increase membership and to invigorate the association. The Centennial Action Program of the 1950s, like the membership initiative of the 1940s, also involved a substantial increase in dues.

In the midst of the NEA centennial celebration, however, critics of the association, some friendly and some not, weighed in with searching assessments of what had been accomplished. One of the main points made by the critics was the failure of the NEA to acknowledge and respond to a newly emerging group of activist, largely male, teachers. The gender of these activists and the gendered nature of their rhetoric challenged the NEA's devotion to professionalism and its commitment, if only an indirect one, to the concerns of women teachers. Some teacher discontent with the NEA had surfaced earlier in the decade. It was muffled, however, by a hesitant, ultimately tepid, but still somewhat effective association response. For a time the discontent was successfully buried under the avalanche of publicity for the centennial celebration and the constant beating of the drums for the NEA's service to the teaching profession and to public education. Near the end of the decade, however, new drums were beating among America's teaching force, and they were not in tune with the tempo of the NEA.

THE NEA AND THE FEDERAL GOVERNMENT

As discussed in Chapter 1, a major purpose of the NEA's remodeling in the post–World War I era was to get the federal government to recognize its responsibilities to public education, especially in the area of financial support. The attainment of this goal proved elusive, however. In spite of this difficulty, by 1950 the NEA, largely through the efforts of Charl Williams, had managed to establish itself on the Washington scene as a formidable, if not always effective, lobby. Like many interest groups, it proved more capable of blocking legislation it opposed than of implementing measures it supported, like its long-held dream of federal aid to public schools.

In wartime the NEA had always done its best to support the national effort at the same time that it sought to turn that effort toward association purposes. The Korean War was unlike the previous two wars of the twentieth century, however. Korea was an undeclared war, a "conflict" in a far-off land that was unfamiliar to most Americans. Because of these circumstances, the NEA's traditional strategy of officially endorsing the war and using the wartime climate to build the association could not be employed, since the nation never declared itself at war. The association thus this time was unable to reap the organizational benefit from wartime conditions that it had managed to realize twice before.

One concrete indication of the indifferent success of any Korean War–related NEA enterprises was manifested in the activities of the group established by the association at the onset of World War II, the Commission on the Defense of Democracy in Education. In the 1950s, in spite of the Korean conflict, the group became popularly known simply as the "defense commission." The connotation of defense that was featured prominently in the NEA publicity of the commission was the defense not of the national interest but of educators who were unjustly dismissed from their positions or who were otherwise under ideological attack. Unlike in the two prior wars, the link between the defense of educators and the ongoing defense of the nation was missing in NEA publicity regarding the work of the defense commission.

One internal development related to the defense of teachers was the establishment of the DuShane Memorial Defense Fund to provide financial support to educators who were in dire economic conditions. An example of the circumstances under which defense fund money was granted occurred in the case of a midwestern married couple, both of whom were teachers. The wife had been shot in a schoolyard incident in 1951 and had not received proper compensation for her injuries from her local school system or from the state. Her husband was unfairly dismissed from his position in the following year. Both were pursuing suits to redress their situation, with financial help from the "defense fund."[1]

Despite its failure to capitalize on the Korean War, the NEA was able to publicize its own pursuit of teacher salary enhancement when salaries were threatened by wartime price controls. From the beginning of the controls early in 1951 until they were withdrawn in February 1953, the NEA published eight "Wage Stabilization Memos" that were sent to state education association secretaries. These officials were advised to provide the "memos" to state and local school officials, as well as to local associations.

The theme of the memos was that federal wage controls did not apply to public school teachers. This point was made in the first memo and subsequently endorsed by the head of the federal "Wage Stabilization Board." The NEA position was that in an arrangement of joint governmental responsibility like the American "federal" constitutional system, public school teachers who were employed under contracts granted by state and local governments were exempt from wage controls imposed by the national government, primarily on private employers. The NEA also argued that teachers could receive salary increases granted under new state or local contracts, that local boards of education could grant new contracts with upward adjustments to existing salary scales, and that boards of education could create new salary scales in cases where none existed.[2] One thing that the memos ignored was that it was precisely the argument made here by the NEA, the constitutionally based primacy of local and state government in educational affairs, that was used by opponents of its campaign for federal aid to education throughout the twentieth century. The opponents argued that the federal government had no right to involve itself in educational finance or other educational concerns, which were properly under the purview of the states and local school districts.

The NEA was able to ingratiate itself in the eyes of the federal government in the 1950s through an involvement in peace activities begun after World War II. Specifically, the association had participated enthusiastically in planning for the United Nations and took steps to ensure that the United Nations would involve itself in educational improvement activities. It had also offered assistance to the reconstruction efforts, particularly their educational components, in Germany and Japan. Educational planning was integral to this reconstruction process, and the NEA achieved a highly visible role in that planning process. In still another venture, in 1946 the NEA had facilitated the revival of an international organization of teachers' associations that it had been involved with since the 1920s. Dormant during World War II, the World Federation of Education Associations (WFEA) was succeeded in 1946 by the World Organization of the Teaching Profession (WOTP), which, in turn, gave way to the World Confederation of Organizations of the Teaching Profession (WCOPT) in 1952.[3]

The WOTP and the WCOPT allowed the NEA to proffer its "professional" approach to teachers' associational activity to the world, in the context of an international political struggle by the U.S. government against the communist menace. The NEA's peaceful, cooperative approach to teacher organizing could be counted on by the federal government to combat militant, more ideological teacher groups that subscribed to international trade unionism and/or to communism. While this waging of a cold war in teachers' international organizing activity might have caused some difficulty for an NEA pledged to defend domestic teachers or administrators who were being tarred with a communist label, the NEA leadership ignored any inconsistency and followed diligently its anticommunist course internationally. This practice allowed association leaders to gain favorable attention from the foreign policy leadership in the national administration, particularly after the election of the Republican, Dwight Eisenhower, as president in 1952.

Domestically, one development in the late 1950s should have given the NEA substantial reason for celebration. In 1958 Congress passed and the president signed the National Defense Education Act (NDEA). The law resulted from a public outcry about poor national educational achievement, especially in the sciences. The public reaction was sparked by the successful launching of the *Sputnik* satellite by the Soviet Union in 1957. While this might have signaled a successful end to the NEA's long quest for federal aid to education, it was not seen as such by the association. Rather, the NEA initially and persistently opposed the NDEA because the association's historic advocacy had been for general federal aid to education—funds for public schools that were unrestricted as to their purpose and that could be used by state and local education agencies in the ways that they desired. The NDEA, in contrast, provided aid for specific subjects—the sciences, mathematics, and foreign languages—as well as for specific services such as school guidance programs. Also, the NDEA provided substantial support for colleges and universities, thereby diminishing the amounts going to school systems.

As it became clearer and clearer that the NDEA would pass, in spite of the NEA's objections, the association officially embraced the legislation. It could never bring itself to support this federal aid measure enthusiastically, however. And though the NEA before the NDEA had consciously downplayed its commitment to unrestricted federal aid in order to embrace modest, new, targeted federal aid policies such as the Eisenhower administration's support of school building construction, the

1958 law went even further in this unacceptable direction of using federal dollars for restricted purposes and rankled the NEA leadership.
Thus, at a time when it might have trumpeted a victory after over three
decades of unsuccessful effort to achieve federal aid to education, the
NEA chose instead to officially approve but not to embrace enthusiastically the NDEA.[4]

TEACHER WELFARE: OLD AND
(A FEW) NEW APPROACHES

Throughout the 1950s the NEA approached teacher welfare in ways fundamentally consistent with what it had been doing in the three previous
decades. Even older goals such as teacher retirement, which traced its
roots to the time before the NEA post–World War I reorganization, retained their prominence. Similarly, the association continued its biannual
surveys of teachers' salaries, which had begun in the 1920s, and its publicity of the results of the surveys in the NEA magazine.[5]

Early in the 1950s, however, at least one new wrinkle began to appear in the association's approach to teacher welfare. A spate of articles
devoted to the problem of large class size peppered the NEA's publications in this period. Undoubtedly related to the mushrooming school en-
rollments caused by the post–World War II "baby boom," the articles
sometimes alluded to the negative impact of large classes on children's
school achievement, while at other times they simply counted the increasing student numbers that were threatening to inundate the schools.
Occasionally, teacher reactions to the pedagogical problems caused by
the large classes were also featured. The one angle of the situation that
never surfaced in NEA accounts was that larger classes were an intensification of teachers' work without a corresponding increase in remuneration. Emphasizing this aspect of the situation would have been a
violation of the NEA's "professional" approach to teacher organization
and an approval of a less than professional trade unionism; thus, the entire line of argument about improving teachers' working conditions was
assiduously avoided in discussions of class size.[6]

In the area of salary schedules, the NEA's efforts in the 1950s were
continuous with those of earlier decades but were characterized by an increasingly specific indication of desired salary numbers and an increasing tendency to be prescriptive. In terms of salaries, for example, the
1953 NEA convention resolved that any salary scale provide for a minimum of at least $3,600 per year and a maximum of at least $8,200. The

NEA magazine's report on this resolution emphasized that it was a continuation of an approach begun in 1946 but now buttressed by a substantially enhanced minimum and maximum that were geared to the fiscal realities of the 1950s.[7]

One year later, a mass-mailed newsletter, intended to reach a larger audience than the readership of the *NEA Journal,* summarized the NEA's efforts to attain "professional salaries" for American teachers. Starting off with the good news that many small systems had improved salaries and that some state legislatures had also moved in an appropriate direction, the newsletter then gave what it called "The Other Side of the Story." From this point of view, salaries were piteously low in many places, and advances of as much as 50 percent were needed to address these situations. Further, salaries even in the higher-paying city systems were far short of the minimum and maximum that had been recommended in the previous year. Eight specific principles on which the scheduling of appropriate, professional salaries should be based ended the newsletter. These eight were a condensation of several emphases that had been stressed by the association for many years. They included appropriate minimums and maximums, equity for elementary and secondary teachers, annual increments, incentives for advanced study, periodic upward adjustments in the entire scale, administrative increases in line with those granted to teachers, and "participation by classroom teachers in the development and administration of salary policies." Despite the increase in the mention of specific policies in this and other accounts of salary issues in the 1950s, the NEA never assumed a strident tone that might have compromised its commitment to nonconfrontational "professionalism."[8]

When other new publications in the area of teacher welfare were inaugurated by the NEA in this period, they more often reinforced the traditional approach to the topic than they broke new ground. For example, the Research Division in the 1950s began a series of "Special Memos" on various topics—a new publication project. The subjects of these memos, however, were hardly new for the NEA. For September 1952 the topic of the "Special Memo" was "State Minimum Salary Laws," for August 1953, "Class Size in Elementary Schools," and for May 1954, "Salary Schedule Policies" affecting principals and other school administrators.[9]

The topic of the July 1956 Special Memo was merit rating and merit pay for teachers, a relatively new issue to which the NEA Representative Assembly had declared its opposition in 1955. Needless to say, the special memo on the topic had little of a positive nature to say about merit pay. The fundamental objections of the NEA were twofold. First, given the existing low level of salary support for all teachers, provisions to pay some more than others out of the existing paltry allotment were unwarranted and impractical. Second, teachers were suspicious of rating systems that were much more likely to be indications of which teachers were the favorites of school administrators than they were to be sound judgments of teaching quality.[10] What the NEA did not notice, or at least did not publicize, was that in this case their argument was based as much on trade union principles of self-protection as it was on a notion of a non-combative professionalism. This is not to say that trade unionism as a principle of occupational organization was wrong for teachers, but rather that it was occasionally embraced by an NEA that assiduously opposed it as a principle inimical to its own obsessively careful approach to organization.

Other topics that were traditional for the NEA but that related indirectly to teachers' salaries continued to be highlighted in the 1950s, as they had been in previous decades. School finance, which had been an association theme since the 1920s, and the policies of state equalization aid for school districts and equalization in local property assessments, both of which had come to the fore during the depression, were given renewed attention in the 1950s. And when the NEA needed an outside expert in the midcentury decade to weigh in on the side of its teacher salary agenda, it turned to John Norton, a prominent professor of educational administration. Readers of the earlier chapters of this volume will remember that Norton had worked at the NEA as director of the Research Division in the 1920s and had kept in constant contact with the association, participated in its committee work, and supported its agenda ever since. This reliance on old voices recycling old ideas testified to a distinct sense of fatigue in the NEA's efforts at teacher welfare that increasingly characterized them as the 1950s wore on.[11]

This stale quality permeated the series of articles devoted to various aspects of NEA advocacy of teacher welfare in the 1955–56 school year. The topics of each article were quite familiar to readers: salaries, tenure, defense of teachers, economic status, teacher load, sick leave, credit unions, and ethics. Similarly, the contents of each article were a rehash of ideas and positions that had been advocated for years by the NEA. For new readers of the NEA magazine, the articles might well have contained novel ideas. But for longtime members of the association facing what they considered to be deteriorating working conditions and looking for new ideas or issues to guide a response, they must have seemed utterly dull and repetitive. The chronic nature of the conditions highlighted in the articles, as well as the relative lack of improvement despite the NEA's efforts, could hardly have constituted heartening news.[12]

PROBLEMS WITH LOCAL AND STATE ASSOCIATIONS

As discussed in the last chapter, the NEA spent much of the 1940s trying to build up its local associations and to involve them in national affairs and concerns. From the NEA point of view, the major motive for this drive was the need for dues revenue from classroom teachers. That continued to be a need that drove the NEA to try to energize its local associations in the 1950s, with results that are best described as mixed. The focus for this latter effort, given the absence of an officially declared war as a peg on which to hang it, was the NEA centennial, which was to be celebrated in 1957. The specific membership goal established for the centennial year was one million, certainly a formidable number given that the association was only halfway there in the early 1950s.[13]

The Centennial Action Program was the vehicle that the NEA developed to meet its membership target. This program formally recognized the association's dependence on its state and local affiliates by designating the first of its twenty-five specific goals as "an active, democratic local in every community" and the second as "a stronger and more effective state education association in every state." This indication of the NEA's reliance on local and state associations did not translate into effective action, however. The 1956 membership of less than seven hundred thousand was far short of the goal of one million. That shortfall, combined with the inflation of the 1950s, led to the consideration and passage of still another dues increase, this time a doubling from five dollars to ten dollars per year. After the increase was passed at the centennial convention in 1957, membership declined for the following year. Thus, in the last two years of the decade, the association struggled to restore its membership to the 1956 level, which was well short of the number of members it had projected.[14]

The ways in which the NEA publicized the work of its local associations in the 1950s paralleled, to a large extent, earlier approaches. Favorable reports on the accomplishments of various locals were a mainstay in NEA publications, as they had been previously, particularly in the 1940s. In the 1950s the reports were often thematically organized—for example, showing how several locals dealt with issues such as legislative advocacy, salary problems, or agenda planning for a meeting. Similarly, an article on small, county associations in rural states showed how several had organized to overcome their size problems.[15]

Another thematic similarity in many local association accounts of the 1950s reached back to all of the predecessor decades since the NEA had reorganized after World War I. The invocation of cooperation with school administrators, with school boards, and with influential lay groups was frequently reiterated as a priority as it had been in the past. And, also as before, teachers again were enlightened about the virtues of cooperation through articles by a school board member and a superintendent advocating NEA membership. The image of one, big, happy family of all those interested in children's and teachers' welfare was prominent in NEA publications. In support of that image, particularly as it pertained to superintendents and local teachers' associations, the 1956 convention of the American Association of School Administrators (formerly the Department of Superintendence) featured a symposium on teacher-administrator relations. The symposium included comments on various instances of successful cooperation as well as analyses of instances of failure to achieve that cooperation. The latter examples constitute some of the few occasions on which the NEA acknowledged that all might not be well between teachers and administrators. Teachers' associations, as well as superintendents, were advised to relax and trust one another as the basic stance from which to base positive and productive contacts.[16]

The NEA's failure in the 1950s to understand how its own internal procedures hampered its membership efforts with local associations also repeated earlier actions. In an article titled "On the Question of Affiliating," local associations learned that all it took to join the NEA was to fill out a registration form and to make a five dollar dues payment. While for a local to have a voting representative at the NEA meeting required at least fifty dues-paying members, any number of members less than fifty brought all other privileges of association membership to a local. The incentive for a local to enroll all its members in the NEA—suspension of the yearly local dues of five dollars—hardly served to encourage all-out effort in support of the objective. Thus, the ease with which local associations affiliated without the payment of national dues by all of their members continued to hamstring the NEA drive for membership and funds.[17]

Occasionally in the 1950s, the association resorted to showy devices such as scorecards or score sheets to encourage members to rate their local associations. The text appended to these graphics, however, indicated that the NEA had not moved beyond its earlier, ineffective approaches to local organizational development. For example, in 1955, following a two-page, forty-two item rating sheet to "Size Up Your Local Association," the reader learned little about the specific items. Rather, he or she was told that the local association works for the profession and then given a long list of examples including "recruiting, morale-building, improving instruction, . . . raising economic and professional status," developing "community understanding," and cooperating "in educational and civic growth." The contrast between the specificity of the rating items and the generality of the examples was stark.[18]

The fundamental problem was that the NEA was prescribing local association activities and orientations from its national office, rather than trying to analyze exactly what situations and problems the locals were facing in their school districts and communities. For example, an editorial in the NEA magazine in 1952 suggested that improvement in local associations was the result of such activities as urging local leaders to attend the NEA and state association conferences and workshops, issuing a local directory according to a format in an NEA leaflet, formally affiliating the local with the state and national association, and adopting the Centennial Action Program as the model for a local's own action program. Similarly, another article discussed a recent book on group process as a source of ideas for invigorating local associations. What all of this advice had in common was utter inattention to the circumstances that existed in the local associations and their communities.[19]

Perhaps a high point in fatuousness in treating the issues of local associations was reached in a 1957 article on East St. Louis, Illinois. This account described how a local association in that city had been enlivened through a "Mexican carnival motif" that included entertainment by a teacher dressed as "Pedro the Pedagog." According to the article, this innovation resulted in a positive judgment of the meeting by 198 of the 200 participants who completed an evaluation form. Not as outlandish but similarly unhelpful was a 1956 article on dues and budgets by an officer of the Department of Classroom Teachers. She apprised her readers of the results of a survey of local associations but provided little or no analysis. For example, in discussing the finding that almost all locals relied on dues income, she concluded that "few locals engage in money-raising activities" rather than discuss what such activities might mean in terms of programs. She ended her contribution with the following statement of the obvious: "Evidence shows that a well planned budget adopted at the beginning of the fiscal year and put into operation promptly lays the foundation for a worthwhile program."[20]

The NEA's approach to state educational associations, an area marked for significant enhancement in the 1950s, also suffered from deficiencies like those that plagued the local association effort. Fundamentally, the NEA served as a cheerleader for the state associations at the same time that it tried, albeit rather aimlessly, to direct their efforts. Through much of the decade, national publicity of state association activities was confined to brief reports from several states with little thematic unity. For example, a 1951 published survey of state association activities reported on thirty-two states that were involved in school finance, school construction programs, equalization efforts, increased limits on bonding authority, retirement, pensions, tenure, salary scheduling, improvement of teacher education, public relations, teacher supply and recruitment, local association work, and other miscellaneous activities. The lack of seriousness in the enterprise was indicated in the published account of the survey in the NEA magazine. In the three-page article, all that could possibly be done was to list the activities rather than provide any analysis of the efforts.[21]

A little more than a year later, the NEA Research Division profiled the activities of the state education associations in various aspects of teacher welfare. Again, the various activities were presented in rapid-fire, short paragraphs organized under topics such as placement, salaries, defense, retirement, insurance, recreation, publicity, fact gathering, fieldwork, and legislative work. This article, again a two-page effort, simply recited the facts about what was happening in various state associations without undertaking any evaluation or otherwise serious analysis. One wonders what the teacher readers of the article were supposed to conclude from the presentation.[22]

By the middle of the 1950s, the focus of discussions of state associations seemed to shift from multistate surveys to single-state accounts. Here again, however, neither the intent nor the impact of the efforts was clear. A report from New Jersey by that state association's president, for example, recounted how research, fieldwork, and public relations had resulted in achieving passage of successful salary legislation in the state legislature. In Montana the state association executive secretary described a successful effort to enroll members in local, state, and national associations. In New Mexico the Committee on Insurance and Investment of the state association had been successful in teacher welfare by publishing three articles for members: one on insurance, one on investments, and one on savings. In Louisiana, the state association cooperated with the state superintendent and the state school boards' association to form the United School Committee, which considered proposals for legislation prior to their going before the legislature. And in Hawaii the state association had supported successful legislation to allow teachers to engage in state political activity. None of these presentations considered the relationship between its activity and any possible alternative that might have been employed. What was characteristic of every contribution, however, was the celebration of the activities, the naming of the various officials involved, and the indirect commendation of the entire state association membership through the praise given. Any serious effort to gain knowledge from the activities described that might have been useful in another setting was totally absent in all of the articles.[23]

All of these accounts ignored the reality that the states were at best participating fitfully and ineffectively in the NEA effort to begin or to enhance local associations as the fundamental building block in the association. As state associations developed their own membership rolls, staff, and budgets, they tended to elaborate themselves organizationally according to the NEA model. State associations hired field-workers whose roles overlapped with NEA field-workers, and state associations developed journals and research operations that seemed able to do little but duplicate the NEA's efforts. The problems were that the overlap was so severe and that analyses of the situation and identification of the ways that it could be turned to the benefit of teachers in the local associations were almost totally absent.

Occasionally, a glimmer of insight into the problems of duplication and the ineffectiveness of service to members came to the surface. For example, in 1953 the NEA Research Division issued a report on the problems of fieldwork and field-workers in state associations. The topic was of considerable interest to state organizations and their leaders, many of whom were cooperating financially with the national association to fund field-workers. The report cataloged the activities of the field-workers as well as the dissatisfaction of many executive secretaries of state associations with the limited provision from the national association for such work. The negative consequences of the lack of a formula through which NEA assistance to the states was allotted were clear in this report. The document also noted that "A significant number of executive secretaries are not satisfied with the NEA's present policy with regard to financial arrangements with state associations for joint field work. Over one-third of those reporting would like to see aid extended to all states on a uniform policy basis." In contrast, national field services or national assistance to state field services was provided on an ad hoc basis, often as the result of contracts signed several years in the past for purposes that had since been forgotten.[24]

Similarly, there was an unplanned, unsystematic, and largely ineffective quality in the field service being offered by the state associations, with or without NEA assistance. For example, in the section of the report devoted to the goals of fieldwork in the states, the item most often mentioned was "interpreting the state association program." Other goals receiving attention were "[h]elping strengthen programs of local associations" and "securing membership in the NEA." The three least frequently mentioned goals included securing "membership in local associations," "providing welfare services to individual teachers," and "providing welfare services to local associations." What seems clear is that if the local associations really were the foundation for the state and national groups, then the goals for membership and teacher welfare would have been just as prominent as, or more prominent than, interpretation of the state program. Still another problem evident in field services was indicated by the listing of "making speeches to local associations" as the most frequently used method of carrying out fieldwork juxtaposed to the later evaluation of speech-making as the least effective procedure that field-workers used.[25]

When the Research Division surveyed state associations again, three years later, on the personnel practices they used in employing professional and nonprofessional staff, the variety of relationships reported between executive directors of state associations and their elected boards of governors indicated the structural problem that hampered any effort to harness the states to a local recruiting movement. Also, the diversity in responses to issues such as recruitment, employment procedures, contracts, benefits, reorganizations, and use of staff personnel committees testified again to the lack of uniformity within the state associations and the weakness of the NEA as a dispenser of information or any type of guidance about desirable policies and procedures for its state affiliates.[26]

All of this information testifies to the fact that the NEA was spending a considerable amount of its dues money in the state associations without getting anything substantial in return in terms of membership development in the local associations. The publicity given to NEA efforts toward state associations was surely a way that the NEA could show its affiliates that they were important, but any additional outcome was not really planned for and, if achieved, came about serendipitously.

TROUBLE AT THE TOP

Willard Givens retired as NEA executive secretary early in 1952. He had served in the position for more than seventeen years and could point to a number of accomplishments as having taken place in that period. Among those mentioned in an editorial in the NEA magazine announcing Givens's retirement were a tripling of NEA membership to half a million; a fivefold expansion of the budget from less than $500,000 to more than $2.5 million; increases in the number of NEA headquarters divisions from eight to fourteen, in affiliated departments from twenty-four to thirty-one, and in headquarters-staffed NEA commissions from one to five; and the establishment of the War and Peace Fund (1944–46), the Victory Action Program (1946–51), and the Centennial Action Program (1951). Additionally, Givens had increased the budget of the *NEA Journal* from $75,000 to $430,000, the Research Division from $62,000 to $150,000, and the Department of Classroom Teachers from $10,000 to $95,000.[27]

Embedded in this number-laden litany of accomplishments were some signs of the organizational problems that Givens had failed to solve. For example, the increase in affiliated local teachers' associations from 620 to 4,010 looks less significant when compared with the tripling of the total membership. This indicates that the size of the average local association was little greater in the 1950s than it had been in the 1930s and may well have been smaller. Additionally, the size of the Representative Assembly, the official body that conducted the business at the NEA annual meeting, was 3,315, meaning that the meeting bore more resemblance to a political convention than it did to an efficient organizational apparatus.[28] The plethora of divisions, departments, commissions, committees, and so on, when added to the overlap between national and state associations, meant that the NEA's organizational structure was exceptionally complicated, beset by overlapping jurisdictions, and largely incapable of undertaking any mass activity that would earn the allegiance of a majority of its members. In a sense, Givens had abetted the creation of a monster or at the least an elephant that was incapable because of its size (as well as its internal diversity) of nimbly responding to events.

Not surprisingly, this negative aspect of Givens's organization building was ignored by the school administrators, college administrators, and officials from the NEA and state education associations who praised him highly for his accomplishments. Givens's work had largely been a continuation or extension of what had been begun by J. W. Crabtree. The

NEA of 1952, though much larger than it had been in the post–World War I era when Crabtree remodeled it, fulfilled most of the wishes and reinforced the fundamental orientations of its creator.[29]

The one genuinely novel dimension that was identified in the official NEA presentation of Givens's career, his international focus in the post–World War II reconstruction of the defeated nations of Germany and Japan, was unrelated to teachers and their welfare. International relations was also a commanding interest of Givens's successor, William G. Carr. Another similarity between Givens and Carr was their service in California and in that state's education association before coming to the NEA. By 1952 Carr had been in the position of associate executive secretary of the NEA since 1940, making him in every sense the "heir apparent" to Givens. Unlike Givens, Carr held an earned doctoral degree that, when combined with his experience in the Research Division and the Educational Policies Commission, led him to project a consciously professorial aura. The editorial announcing his appointment to succeed Givens stressed Carr's academic credentials and his international experiences with UNESCO immediately after World War II as his major qualifications for association leadership.[30]

Carr's early actions as NEA executive secretary followed up on Givens's programs and commitments. Carr embraced the Centennial Action Program as the core of the NEA's organizational development effort as the centennial year of 1957 drew near, and he continued to advocate the professionalism so cherished by both Givens and J. W. Crabtree as the raison d'être of the NEA. Carr also moved to do something about the NEA's cumbersome internal structure by reorganizing the headquarters staff and operations in 1955. He appointed five assistant executive secretaries, each of whom was responsible for one or more of the several divisions in the headquarters. These five, along with the business manager and the secretaries of the Educational Policies Commission and the Legislative Commission, formed the executive secretary's "cabinet." This pattern, modeled on the presidential administration in the federal government, testified as much to Carr's own status consciousness and aspirations as it did to any genuine reform instincts. Though the reorganization was touted as a "simplification" of the NEA structure, the creation of a new bureaucratic layer between the executive secretary and those employed in the NEA's various divisions was more a complication than a simplification of the situation. When Carr later established and staffed several regional NEA offices as a way to enhance cooperation with state and local associations, he provided another organizational elaboration that was promulgated as a move toward enhanced effectiveness.[31]

Carr gave further insight into his own vision for the NEA in one of what became his regular monthly contributions to the NEA magazine. In discussing the association's "unique character," he pictured the NEA through the use of three adjectives: as an "inclusive" organization, one that enrolled elementary and secondary teachers together with school administrators; as an "independent" organization, one that had no official relationships to government or to any organized economic, political, or social group; and as a "voluntary" organization, one whose members came together to pursue their objectives without any coercion. The three characteristics made the NEA unique in the world of educational organizations and also made it a model for teachers' associations in other countries to emulate. While Carr did not mention teachers' unions in this article, its content suggests that he was distinguishing his association from unions here, as much as he was serving any other purpose.[32]

In a later discussion of "What Is a Member" in the *NEA Journal,* Carr expanded on his own sense of the NEA. Rather than couch the association's achievements in terms of its services to individual members, he remarked that the NEA's achievements were "the profession's achievements." Consciously expanding on the idea of inclusiveness that he proffered in the earlier article, he stressed not only teacher-administrator affinity and cooperation but the identity between the teacher and the NEA staff member as well. All "are working at different parts of the same job," he remarked, and therefore the issue of what the NEA does for a teacher was better put as "What do the members of my profession do for each other?" and "What do I as an NEA member do for the profession?" Carr here was submerging any trade unionlike idea of an independent teacher consciousness within the NEA image of an overarching educational profession intent on bettering itself without any notice of occupational segmentation.[33]

Carr's vision of an educational profession and association encompassing all involved in educational work characterized the NEA as it approached and celebrated its centennial year in 1957. In the midst of the centennial celebration, he described the variety of ways that the diverse and inclusive NEA was involved in internal policy making: through the Representative Assembly, the board of directors, the headquarters staff, the Executive Committee, and the Educational Policies Commission. What he did not discuss was the opportunity this plethora of policy-making bodies provided for conflict in policy positions among themselves and the lack of obvious means available to resolve that conflict. Also, he revealingly de-emphasized the state and local associations, invoking them only in his final paragraph. And there he noted that each NEA member was a policy maker "either by means of *suggestions* to his state and local associations or by actions of his representatives at the national meeting." Carr's final comment that "NEA policies are what the members say they should be" stands as a gross oversimplification of a highly complex, clumsy, and often contentious process, the outcome of which represented countless steps and bodies intruding themselves between members and results.[34]

In William Carr's world of the inclusive, independent, voluntary educational profession and association, the place of teacher welfare was less prominent than it had been for his predecessors. One indication of this change came one month after his discussion of NEA members as policy makers, in an article by the executive secretary of the California Teachers' Association. A longtime associate of Carr's on the Educational Policies Commission, the Californian addressed himself specifically to teachers and posited the fundamental goal of associational activity as the assurance for teaching of its "rightful place among the professions." This meant that individual teachers must embrace the cooperative effort to raise standards in their profession. These higher standards were to be achieved through a fivefold program of enhancement in personnel relations, teacher education, educational service, community relations, and, last, professional and economic security. The relative place of occupational security, last in order and in significance compared with the other objectives, was made clear in the penultimate paragraph. Here teachers were instructed as follows: "Economic security is a symptom of professional maturity but is not necessarily the cause of its attainment. The immediate doubling of teachers' salaries would not of itself guarantee professional status for teachers . . . higher salaries alone will not be enough."[35] Thus were teachers' salary grievances and claims relativized within the NEA program of professional associational activity to a place near the bottom of the priority list.

William Carr's approach to the NEA and its activities, then, can be characterized as one of organizational elaboration and programmatic multiplication. Its intended effect on teachers, if any, seemed to be to reduce their commitments to themselves as teachers. Unfortunately for the NEA, this shift in orientation from the more conscious "teacher" emphasis of Crabtree and, to a lesser extent, Givens, occurred at about the same time that teacher consciousness, at least among an increasing segment of the teaching force, was headed in a substantially different direction. Before exploring that difference, which was largely the result of an activism arising among men teachers, however, a look at how the NEA related explicitly to women teachers is in order.

THE NEA AND THE WOMAN TEACHER IN THE 1950s

The approach that the NEA took toward the woman teacher in the 1950s was much like what it had followed in the preceding decade, though a diminution in the public attention given to women and the significance of the women's cause and their concerns for the NEA leadership also occurred. The essentials of the earlier effort, as described in the preceding chapter, were to publicize the careers of notable women, to honor some of the women who were high-ranking members of the NEA staff, and to diligently seek the implementation of the single salary scale. Each of these thrusts was repeated in the 1950s, though often less vigorously and enthusiastically than in the preceding decade. For instance, by the 1950s the single salary scale had been largely institutionalized in the nation's larger school districts and was on the way to being adopted in the other districts. Thus, the NEA's muffling of its public drumbeat for salary equity for women was at least partially related to the success of the effort, though one wonders why the association did not pay much more attention to celebrating the victory than it did.

In terms of the mention of women in NEA publications and other activities, there also was a distinct diminution in the 1950s. No series of articles on the accomplishments of women reformers and educators appeared in the NEA magazine in this decade to rival the effort of the 1940s. The number of mentions of women teachers seemed to be less frequent in NEA publications, and when mentioned, the gender of the teachers or their position on controversial issues such as salary equity was less prominently in focus. Also, when women teachers were discussed, their allegiance to traditional values and accepted feminine traits received attention, rather than any questions or quarrels they might have with those traditions.

For example, a 1950 article in the NEA magazine by the famous New York financier Bernard Baruch was titled "A Real Teacher" and subtitled as a tribute "to a great teacher from a great man." Only by reading the text of the article did the reader learn that the great teacher in question was Katherine Deveraux Blake, an activist for equal pay for women who also ran, unsuccessfully, for the NEA presidency in the 1910s. The substance of Baruch's tribute reinforced Blake's traditional feminine qualities rather than her activism. He described his teacher using words such as *beloved* and possessing a *beautiful character.* Intended as an inspirational piece to raise teacher morale, this article blithely ignored the political dispute or gender angle to that dispute that operated in the New York City schools and in the NEA during Blake's career.[36]

One year later NEA members were treated to an article called "I Like Teaching" in which the woman writer praised many of the aspects of the occupation that others, particularly men teachers and administrators, were wont to criticize. The article began with a statement of pride in being a teacher and went on to praise the salaries that teachers received as well as the prospects of regular salary increases and other benefits. Though the financial remuneration did not mean "affluence," it did provide financial "security" for teachers. Also receiving favorable comment were the weekends off that teachers enjoyed, summer vacations, and the breaks of a week or longer that occurred frequently during the school year. Addressing directly the matter of being a woman teacher, the author gloried in the status that the teaching profession brought to its woman practitioners. Maternity leaves, where "allowed," were another benefit provided for women, as was the coincidence between a woman teacher's working hours and the school day of her children. Friendliness and a cooperative spirit rounded out the positive aspects of teaching for and by women.[37]

Several points can be made about this article. First, the author's reveling in traditional women's roles and orientations seemed obviously intended to reassure the traditional women who composed the majority of the teaching force and NEA members. Second, the approval of the salaries was an endorsement of the NEA's salary work over the past several decades as well as a rebuke to those in the NEA and elsewhere who were complaining about low salaries. What was not said but clearly implied in the article was that the equality of women's salaries with those of men was in some sense a substitute for higher salaries—a point of special significance for those women who were earning a second income in their families. And finally, the identification of the author as a professor at the University of Southern California called the entire essay into question. While readers were assured that the author had "taught at every level," their degree of skepticism about how much of this woman's satisfaction was related to her salary and status as a college professor is impossible to estimate.[38] Clearly, the article was intended to serve as an endorsement of the traditional NEA agenda: salaries for teachers, an acceptance of traditional authority in schools and the larger society, and a refusal to see classroom teachers as a group with interests in any sense separate from those of other professional educators.

The NEA took conscious steps in the 1950s to link teaching with reassuring, traditional images of women, a strategy that was less in evidence in earlier decades. In the same issue of the NEA magazine that contained the article discussed above, readers were also introduced, through photographs, to two teachers who were contestants in the Miss America beauty pageant. The brief article accompanying the photos, entitled "Pedagogic Pulchritude," began with the note that "Not all teachers, of course, win beauty contests. But some do!" It went on to argue that apprising the public of the beauty of some women teachers was an antidote to cartoonists who drew physically unfavorable caricatures of teachers. The text and photos did not even occupy a full page in the magazine; thus, one should not make too much of its publication. The title, the photos, and the cheerleader-like text led toward the conclusion, however, that the NEA was as interested (or more interested) in praising the physical attributes of women and in clearly invoking passive, traditional imagery as it was in emphasizing women's contemporary challenges or accomplishments.[39] The contrast between this article and the 1940s accounts of the accomplishments of Susan B. Anthony, Mary Lyon, and other famous women suggests a difference in the prevailing social orientation toward women's issues in the two decades, as well as the NEA's willingness to play up that difference in an effort to reach what it considered a major portion of its audience.

Other aspects of the NEA's relationship to women teachers in the 1950s reflected little or no reduction in commitments made in earlier decades. For instance, if pictures were worth a large number of words, then the publication by the NEA in 1951 of the pictures of elected state association leaders, of state association executive secretaries, and of chief state school officers gave some encouragement to ambitious women in education. Of the first group, state association leaders, eleven of the fifty-three individuals pictured were women. Although the presence of only four women state school officers and two state executive secretaries was less encouraging, the very presence of any women in these two groups gave some reinforcement to women interested in occupational advancement.[40]

The topic of women in school administration received special attention in two articles by Kathryn Steinmetz, who was a district superintendent in the Chicago schools and who also was president of the NEA's

National Council of Administrative Women in Education. The data in her article on women administrators in K–12 schooling were, however, anything but reassuring. Steinmetz pointed out that the number of women administrators in a variety of positions had diminished substantially since the 1920s. While in the earlier decade, eight state departments of education had been headed by women, the number was four in 1951. More significant, the number of women who were city superintendents had plummeted from forty-six in 1939 to eight in 1951. Analysis of other statistical information revealed that small cities were a more fertile field for women administrators than large ones, though no explanation for the phenomenon was advanced. In measured tones, Steinmetz told her readers that "most school executives think the distribution of administrative positions between men and women about right," again without following up the statement with any analysis or explanation. She offered three suggestions for further exploration of the issue: studying the personal qualities of administrators and comparing them with personal profiles of men and women, looking at promotion policies to determine if the "apparent" discrimination against women was intentional or if the situation had come about by chance, and increasing efforts to encourage women to obtain the education that qualified them for administrative posts. Steinmetz concluded that formal research was needed to determine if causes other than real prejudice contributed to the situation, the extent to which marriage was implicated as a factor, the nature and impact of public attitudes toward women school administrators, and the comparative ratio of women school administrators to women in other occupations.[41]

Less than a year later, Steinmetz published a second article on women administrators in higher education. Here the relatively large proportion of women administrators of 27.6 percent was mitigated by the number who were in traditional female positions such as dean of women. The percentage of women in the highest administrative positions, as well as on governing boards, was substantially lower. Steinmetz ended the article with a plea for further research and a somewhat rhetorical question: "Are women who are adequately prepared for administrative positions fairly considered when college administrative posts are being filled?"[42]

Steinmetz was timid in the face of her own statistics, which clearly indicated that discrimination operated in both sectors that she studied. One reason for her timidity may have been that the NEA was a timid organization, more interested in describing problems than in solving them, particularly if the solution pitted one of its constituent groups against another. Steinmetz did indicate that the National Council of Administrative

Women in Education, as a department of the NEA, was "interested in this problem but had sponsored no feminist movements." Rather, with the NEA, the women administrators' group had sought to "get the facts for consideration by the profession." What the profession was to do with the facts was not a stated concern of Steinmetz or of NEA articles on the issue. Description was enough for the NEA and was all that it would allow. And for many, if not most, women in education, description of difficulties seemed a sort of, if not a real, solution to problems.[43]

The image of the NEA as an impartial arbiter rather than an advocate in controversies surrounding women's roles in education held, even in cases where publication of the facts was not the sole purpose of an article. For example, a discussion of the proper curriculum for women in college featured a polite debate between academic administrators from two women's colleges. One argued for curriculum change geared toward the practical needs of women in mid-century society—courses such as consumer economics, child development, religion and values, and the arts—all reflecting women's dominance in traditional internal family life. The other defended the established liberal arts curriculum as desirable for women, calling the development of different courses for women a step backward toward the idea of a limited feminine sphere. The polite tone of both articles was characteristic of the NEA in the 1950s, as well as in earlier decades. The refusal to weigh in with an evaluation of the points of view was also characteristic, though it must be said that the NEA in earlier years was more open to a wider variety of opinion on women's issues than it proved to be in the 1950s.[44] Still, the publication of articles such as those discussed herein was an acknowledgment of the wide women's readership of NEA publications and the best response to that readership that the NEA of the 1950s was capable of offering. Evidently, the readership was reasonably satisfied with the notice that women received, even if that notice was only a notice.

The visible character of women on the NEA staff was a feature of the 1950s that replicated the situation in previous decades. The accession of Mildred Sandison Fenner to the editorship of the *NEA Journal* in 1955, succeeding the retiring Joy Elmer Morgan, meant that for the first time in its history a woman supervised the association's flagship publication.[45] Despite the appointment, a diminution in the attention given to women's education and other women's issues occurred in the rest of the decade. This may have meant that Fenner was less free to explore women's roles and concerns as an editor than she had been as a writer for the magazine, and/or that a male editor had more freedom to explore

issues related to the role of women in education than did a female. The
most obvious explanation for this situation, however, is that the centennial celebration and its aftermath so consumed the attention of William
Carr and the rest of the NEA staff that other concerns were simply put on
the back burner.

One aspect of women in the teaching profession did become clear to
the NEA in the 1950s. The married women who were becoming more
prominent in the teaching ranks claimed an increased share of NEA attention. Of course, this in a real sense was a vindication of earlier NEA
efforts, however gentle, on behalf of married women teachers. That was
the theme played out in the opening sentences of Hazel Davis's brief account in the NEA magazine of her larger study of the status of the American public school teacher, published in April of the NEA's centennial
year, 1957: "What happened to those funny old rules against employing
married women as teachers? Today more than half of women teachers
are married. In fact, four out of 10 of *all* the teachers are married
women." After this pointed introduction, however, the phenomenon of
the married woman teacher was quickly lost as the discussion moved on
to other topics.[46]

A more problematic account of married women in teaching was
published by the NEA less than a year after Davis's report. The author of
this article, Isobel Brown, was pseudonymous, identified as representing
the ideas of "several teachers who wanted one person to put their
thoughts into a single article." The general theme of the article was that
the unprofessional attitude of many teachers was hampering occupational development. Teachers' complaints about extra classroom duties,
summer school, and salaries constituted prime examples of this anti-
professionalism. Women teachers came in for special condemnation. A
young woman teacher who bragged about not being recognized physically as a teacher—that is, about being better looking than the average
teacher—was depicted as guilty of betraying her profession. The article
also criticized those young married women who taught for only a few
years in order to put a husband through school as a drag on salaries,
along with married teacher couples who took two substandard salaries as
a substitute for one genuinely professional reward. The inclusion of married women as special targets for opprobrium in this article testified to
the existence of some less than sanguine interpretations of the place of
married women teachers within the large, complex NEA, which had
spent much of the past twenty years acting on their behalf.[47] While the
NEA never went on record as agreeing formally with the ideas of Isobel

Brown, it is hard not to conclude that publication of this article meant, at the very least, that some powerful people within the association were uncomfortable with its own victories on behalf of women teachers, especially married women teachers.

William Carr never publicly revealed his own attitudes and commitments toward women teachers. His personal penchant for internationalism at the expense of domestic concerns such as teacher welfare, however, combined with his rather pretentious organizational alterations of the NEA staff, lead toward a conclusion that he was not an enthusiastic supporter of underdogs like women in teaching. His testimony to Hilda Maehling, longtime secretary of the Department of Classroom Teachers, at the time of her retirement also lends support for this conclusion. Carr's account of Maehling's career was a recitation of offices she held in state and national associations, the formal accomplishments of the Department of Classroom Teachers under her leadership such as conferences at the NEA convention and on college campuses, and the strong coordination she brought to teacher welfare activities after her appointment as assistant executive secretary for professional development. Carr's one mention of any gender-related aspect to Maehling's career subordinated it to his own priority of international affairs. He noted that Maehling had "represented American teachers at the UNESCO Conference on Educational Opportunity for Women" in 1949.[48] While all of this is indirect evidence, at best, it points toward the conclusion that Carr was further removed from the causes of women teachers than was J. W. Crabtree and as far removed from them, if not more so, than was Willard Givens.

If in the 1950s Carr and the NEA retreated to some extent from earlier commitments to women teachers, the record in terms of black teachers was even bleaker. Most notable here was the NEA's failure to acknowledge the significance of the *Brown v. Board of Education* Supreme Court decision of 1954 that proscribed legal segregation in schools. The association simply printed the decision in the *NEA Journal* without any comment whatsoever.[49] Since the NEA had several dual affiliates—that is, separate organizations for black and white teachers in the segregated southern states—as well as numerous white southern members who were unlikely to stray from their regional political leaders' vehemently stated opposition to the *Brown* decision, its diffidence is explainable, if not defensible. The notable lack of attention given to black teachers and the educational welfare of the nation's black communities in the 1950s, however, indicates that more than strategic concerns were involved in the organization's actions.

Thus, the 1950s can be seen as a time of retreat on a number of fronts by the NEA from its earlier commitments: to teacher welfare, to women teachers, and to minority teachers and students. Generally speaking, the NEA of the late 1950s was a more politically and occupationally conservative organization than it had been in the earlier decades of the twentieth century. This conservatism and its consequences were commented on by several students of the association during the decade and particularly at the time of its centennial. The nature of those comments, as well as the issues they brought to the surface and the NEA's response, are topics of concern in the final two sections of this chapter.

THE SPECTER OF UNIONIZATION

As discussed in the previous chapter, the immediate post–World War II period saw an increase in the incidence of teachers' strikes and in the publicity given to those strikes nationally, as well as a failure to respond meaningfully to this phenomenon on the part of both the NEA and the AFT. Despite the seeming paralysis of the two organizations and the decline in the number of strikes in the 1950s, in some sense the cat had been let out of the bag and would not be put back in. While the number of strikes diminished significantly after the postwar outbreak, discussion of the issues raised both by the 1940s strikes and the existence of teachers unions in the United States as well as elsewhere in the world began to make its way into educational discourse. Unfortunately, the discussion and the issues it considered did not make their way into the forefront of the consciousness of the NEA.

A 1951 issue of the *Phi Delta Kappan,* journal of an all-male honorary fraternity in the field of education, carried several discussions of issues surrounding the "closed shop," or compulsory membership, in teachers' unions. One article in this issue might have assuaged the fears of NEA members about teachers' unions. In it the leader of the National Union of Teachers of England and Wales (NUT) described how his union had beaten back an attempt by a local educational authority in an industrial city, one obviously controlled by the trade union–dominated Labour Party, to make teachers enroll in their union before getting a teaching position. The NUT leader characterized his organization as committed to the freedom of teachers to join associations and against coerced membership. He saw the closed shop as a despotic device and argued that compulsory membership deprived teachers of their freedom to act and hampered a teachers' union by loosening the tie between members, leaders, and polity.[50]

In a symposium in the same issue in which the English union leader wrote, several American authors discussed the issue of compulsory membership in teachers' associations. The contribution to the symposium by the former membership director of the NEA revealed an irony in the association's position on the issue. After paying much obeisance to the principle of voluntarism, the NEA official argued for compulsory membership on the grounds that it effectively built a unified profession. Another contributor put his finger on the reason why the NEA favored compulsion, the same strategy that was embodied in the trade union advocacy of the closed shop. He noted that the NEA was an organization of both administrators and teachers and that compulsory membership in this kind of organizational context harnessed teachers firmly to the agenda and designs of school administrators. Since teachers and administrators had distinctly different employment circumstances as well as distinctly different responsibilities and problems, compulsory membership hampered development of teachers' interests by subordinating them to those of administrators. Only in an organization that had separate mediums for discussion and deliberation for its different classes of members, argued this contributor to the symposium, did compulsory membership offer a chance at service to all of its members. He concluded that the NEA, with its emphasis on unity, was far from this type of "sectored" institution. Thus, for him, compulsory membership in the NEA and its subsidiary organizations was not advisable for teachers interested in their own welfare.[51]

In another contribution to this symposium, the author largely ignored the theme of compulsory membership but sounded a discordant note about the NEA, raising an issue that caused it significant difficulty in dealing with a rising teacher militancy in the late 1950s and the succeeding decade. First of all, he noted that teachers were moving "towards collective bargaining." Given this movement, and taking pointed aim at the NEA without mentioning it by name, he argued that "we cannot afford to be represented by an organization controlled by spinsters." He went on to testify to his love for women like his wife and daughters at the same time that he decried the economic gains that women teachers had made at the expense of men teachers through devices such as the single salary scale. Now that women had salary equality, he concluded, "the public thinks of teacher's salaries in terms of the needs of a spinster." The problem with this conclusion was that "the same point on . . . [a] monetary scale means prestige to a spinster and stigma to a familied man!" To "solve" the problem, he suggested two equally sarcastic possibilities: that all teachers be women without dependents or that men teachers remain unmarried. If neither of these situations prevailed, he argued, then the reasonable solution to the problem was to "Let men organize separately, and insist on dependency allowances, like the army." Within organizations like the NEA, with their numerical dominance by women teachers, he opined that this type of representation was impossible since the female majority could hardly be expected to vote for it. "Women just don't see that it's a problem."[52]

These last two contributors to the symposium identified two aspects of the NEA that would hamper it severely in its attempts to respond to the tide of militant, masculinist unionism that developed later in the 1950s and 1960s. First, the NEA was dominated by administrators, and its own organizational program and priorities reflected that dominance and looked askance at any independent teacher initiatives. Second, the NEA responded more positively to the interests of women teachers who composed the majority of its members than it did to the demands of men teachers for preferential salary treatment. All of this was less clear in 1951 when this symposium was published than it would become at the end of the decade and throughout the following decade.

As the 1950s evolved, the NEA began to identify some of its major membership problems as coming from the nation's largest cities, an insight that also pointed to its future difficulties. For example, in an early 1953 discussion of the local NEA affiliate in Cleveland, Ohio, the president of the organization noted that membership had plummeted from a high of nearly 90 percent of those eligible in the 1930s to its early 1950s level of less than 25 percent. While the local officer offered little analysis of the reasons for the decline, several months later, an editorial in the NEA magazine concluded that the problems of Cleveland were not limited to that city. Rather, the NEA's membership efforts were the least successful in the most populous cities and states. For example, 250,000 teachers eligible for membership but not enrolled in the association— a number almost large enough to close the gap between the NEA's projected and actual membership numbers—came from eight large-population states. Within those and other states large cities accounted for the overwhelming majority of missing members. While the contours of the problem were clearly identified in the editorial, it offered no analysis, strategy, or remedy to rectify the situation.[53]

Subsequent efforts at building support for the NEA in large cities continued previous association orientations and followed earlier initiatives that had never worked. For example, in a 1956 discussion at a Department of Classroom Teachers conference on the problems of large city locals, the following were suggested as productive responses: determining the "ideal length" of the term for officers, seeking release time for association officers, and seeking public recognition of building representatives. The rest of the article featured ways to improve communications between teachers and local association officers, an unwitting adumbration of a 1960s movie satirizing the unequal relations between a guard and a prisoner whom he had just beaten, concluding that "what we have here is a failure to communicate."[54]

Earlier in the same year, a local in another Ohio industrial city reported that it overcame traditional difficulties in recruiting building representatives by holding a full-day conference for these officials on the first Saturday of each school year. The description of that conference revealed, however, a devotion to the trite and polite rather than to the problems of teachers. In that conference one morning session had been given over to briefings from state and national officials while another was made up of smaller "buzz groups" that dealt with whatever questions were raised. A "purely social luncheon" followed, which, in turn, was succeeded by the afternoon session, the first regular meeting of the building reps, at which "the keynote of the year's cooperative endeavor is sounded and the practical mechanics of operation are covered." Other suggestions for help included a "calendar of coming events" and a "kit containing information about how to collect and record local, state, and national dues." While the president of the local association stated that she was "convinced that this kickoff meeting is important to the making of a good year," it is hard to take that sentiment as a plausible substitute for a meaningful response to the special problems of overcrowding, poverty, and race relations beginning to face teachers in this and most other large industrial cities.[55]

There was a similar, ethereal quality to the NEA's announcement in November 1958 that it was creating a new editorial information center in New York City at a time when the city's male teachers were organizing militant union locals in the junior and senior high schools. This NEA action testified clearly to the distance between the association and the occupational movements then stirring among the nation's big city teachers.[56]

As the NEA celebrated its centennial year in 1957, at least some of the external reflection on the past, present, and future of the association pointed to its problems. Internally, the NEA celebrated its centennial with no recognition of any difficulties in the present or on the horizon. A committee had been planning the series of centennial events for several years. Part of the celebration was the publication of a centennial history of the NEA that looked at the association, in retrospect and in prospect, through a set of rose-colored glasses.[57] In addition, the NEA was also about to complete a remodeling of its headquarters building.

Not all analysts were enamored of the NEA and its programs, however. Around the time of the centennial celebration, Myron Lieberman, a scholar of teachers' associations and teacher professionalism, turned a critical eye on the association in several publications. Author of a notable book written in 1956, *Education As a Profession,* as well as an article in that same year on the topic of teachers' strikes, Lieberman also wrote an article critical of the NEA's diffidence on civil rights in 1957, the year of the NEA centennial. Finally, in that same year, he edited a series of articles in an issue of the journal *Progressive Education* devoted to analyzing the association.[58]

Lieberman's critical position on the NEA was clearly articulated in his 1956 article on teachers' strikes. First of all, he made clear that teachers could strike without compromising their professionalism; in fact, it was the case that a strike could be undertaken in pursuit of professional goals. This was a direct challenge to those in the NEA and elsewhere in the educational world who declared any strike an unprofessional act. Lieberman also pointed out that the NEA had no official, on-the-record policy on strikes, though its officers had spoken and acted many times as if the association did have a policy against them. And finally, he added that the NEA had lent some support to the actions of its local association in Norwalk, Connecticut, in 1946 when it encouraged teachers who had not yet signed a contract not to report for work. Although the NEA itself did not call this action a strike, preferring to label it a decision not to work without a contract, Lieberman argued that for all practical purposes this was a distinction without a difference.[59]

In his book Lieberman developed many of the arguments he made in his article. In particular, he made several points about the NEA, in addition to his discussion of its position on teachers' strikes. In the area of collective bargaining, a process often linked in the popular mind, and by many in the NEA, to strikes, he noted that the NEA Executive Committee had in 1947 issued a statement endorsing the principle of collective action by teachers on behalf of improving their salaries. He quoted this statement at length:

> Group action is essential today. The former practice where teachers
> bargained individually with the superintendent of schools or the board
> of education for their salaries is largely past. For years, there has been a
> steady movement in the direction of salary schedules applying to all
> teachers.
>
>   In the present crisis it is especially important that there be profes-
> sional group action on salary proposals. A salary committee composed
> of capable and trusted members of the group is necessary. This com-
> mittee should be chosen by the entire teaching group and should have
> the authority to represent and act for the local education associa-
> tion. . . . It is essential that the teaching group give this committee full
> authority to act and then stand back of it.

Lieberman pointed out that in spite of this endorsement, many if not
most in the NEA, including its elected and staff leaders, were opposed to
collective bargaining because they saw it as an unprofessional act.[60]

Lieberman was an evenhanded analyst of teacher organizations. He
also criticized the AFT. He noted that the teachers' union had an official
no-strike policy, which it had to ignore in the several cases when its locals went on strike. For Lieberman, however, the fundamental difference
between the NEA and the AFT was that whereas the association enrolled
all educators, the union proscribed superintendents from membership
and confined the ranks of its locals to only classroom teachers. Administrators other than the superintendent—that is, principals and assistant
principals—could join the AFT only by forming their own local organizations apart from the teachers' local. What the AFT policies recognized
and what the NEA policies ignored, argued Lieberman, was the fundamental reality that the occupational interests of teachers were not the
same as those of school administrators.[61] Because of this, legitimate
steps to improve the teaching profession might well be opposed by
school administrators. As long as the NEA embraced teachers and administrators as members of the same association, it ignored this fundamental reality.

Lieberman ended his book by predicting that the process of collective bargaining would become more common in the nation, especially in
the larger cities. In terms of teachers' choice of the NEA or the AFT to
represent them in collective bargaining, he concluded that unless the association did something about the issue of administrator membership, it
was the clear second choice for teachers.[62]

In a May 1957 issue of *School and Society,* a leading educational periodical, Lieberman took his criticism of the NEA in another direction.

Ostensibly considering only the issue of the NEA's record in protecting the civil rights of teachers, Lieberman skillfully linked that concern
to the matter of racial minority rights. He did this by noting that at the
time, the "most critical threat to the civil rights of teachers grows out of
the resistance to racial integration in the public schools." Racially discriminatory employment and dismissal policies, taken in reaction to the
integration or possible integration of public schools, constituted his
major case in point. While the NEA's official policies bespoke a firm resolve to protect teachers' rights, its practical actions in the area of race
and teaching were equivocal at best. For example, he noted that the NEA
Committee on Professional Ethics had refused to issue a statement on
the propriety of appointing or dismissing teachers on racial grounds.
Similarly, the NEA Committees on Tenure and Academic Freedom had
demurred from judging the actions of two southern states that had elimi-
nated teacher tenure policies in an effort to intimidate black teachers
who might be inclined to push for racial equity in the schools. Generally,
for Lieberman, the NEA had "avoided any head-on collision with any of
the strongly entrenched segregationist forces in and out of education
which are leading the assault on the civil and professional rights" of
teachers.[63]

Lieberman also noted that the NEA's timid commitment to minority
teachers' civil rights was long-standing. Despite the fact that it had a
thirty-year relationship with the segregated national organization of
black teachers, the American Teachers Association (ATA), the NEA had
seldom if ever acted vigorously to support positive and constructive relations between black and white teachers. As a recent example, Lieberman
characterized the 1957–58 project of the NEA's joint committee with the
black teachers' group as "the promotion of a project designed to aid publishers to improve materials on . . . minority groups . . . in encyclope-
dias." He concluded that this "picayune enterprise makes it easy to
understand why the prosegregationist elements in the N. E. A. show little
concern over the N. E. A.'s verbal affirmations for freedom and equality
of educational opportunity."[64]

Lieberman was not the only scholar who was critical of the NEA as
it celebrated its centennial year. George Male, a professor of education
from the state of Michigan, compared the NEA unfavorably with the
NUT. He noted that while both groups embraced the dual objectives of
social service and professional enhancement of teacher welfare, the
NUT was much more straightforward in its pursuit of teacher welfare
than the NEA. Male also pointed out that although the NEA, since 1920,

had been more aware of teacher welfare and, since the 1930s, had taken a more positive stance in search of it, the association was still hesitant to act decisively and aggressively in favor of teacher welfare, particularly when compared with the NUT as well as with the NEA's domestic organizational rival, the AFT.[65]

In the same month in which the NEA officially celebrated its centennial, July 1957, *Progressive Education* published an issue in which several of the articles critically analyzed the NEA. The editor of the six articles, Myron Lieberman, introduced the collection by noting that the NEA seemed singularly incapable of self-criticism. In spite of the torrent of published materials that it turned out, for Lieberman there was a "surprising absence of evaluative materials relating to the Association." The NEA centennial, which the association was using solely as an occasion to celebrate, should, according to Lieberman, therefore "be an occasion for genuine evaluation of the Association." The six articles he edited set out to achieve just that purpose.[66]

The lead article in the series, written by Lloyd Jorgensen, an educational historian from the University of Missouri, noted that the NEA had taken a conservative position on most political issues in its history. Jorgensen discussed four main issues that had occupied the national stage in the last half century—agrarianism, industrialization and labor unrest, child labor legislation, and racial integration—noting that in every case the NEA stood as a flat-footed opponent of politicians and legislation that sought to redress the grievances of oppressed groups. The NEA's reluctance to move positively to meet any of these problems did not bode well for its future prospects, according to Jorgensen.[67]

Another article, written by Maurice Hunt, a noted social studies educator, decried the NEA's failure to act as a critical analyst of the nation's schools. The association exhibited a reflexive defensiveness about public schooling, according to Hunt, that meant that the schools were left helpless in the face of external critics who had little regard for the complexities and significance of the educational enterprise. The context for Hunt's analysis was the unremitting criticism of progressive schooling by academics and others who claimed that progressive pedagogy was anti-intellectual. By refusing to admit room for any criticism, argued Hunt, the NEA abetted the negative and largely unfair image of schools and teachers that was offered by these ignorant critics.[68]

In the context of a discussion of teacher welfare, George Male's article analyzed the rivalry between the NEA and the AFT. Although the NEA had begun its interest in teacher welfare early in the twentieth century (with, as shown in Chapter 1, the arrival of J. W. Crabtree and his remodeling of the association), its constant rivalry with the AFT since that time had caused the association to mitigate its own commitment while charging that the teachers' union was overly concerned with teacher welfare to the neglect of other relevant issues. Now, according to Male, as the nation's teachers were becoming increasingly concerned with their own welfare, the NEA was in a poor position to consider the development of strategies and tactics that it had denounced for a number of years. Male described the NEA's own commitment to teacher welfare as real but lukewarm, needing to be intensified in order to keep pace with the AFT. Male believed that the NEA seemed unwilling to make such a move, however.[69]

In an article on the publications of the NEA, William Brickman showed that the prodigious number and diversity of NEA publications—yearbooks, reports, pamphlets, leaflets, and several journals—militated against any attempt to communicate effectively a single message to the membership. Further, Brickman claimed that any move in a new direction could easily get lost or misconstrued in the welter of outlets available to publicize it. He added that in many NEA publications, particularly in its flagship *NEA Journal,* the tendency was toward a chattiness, folksiness, and storybook quality that was ill-suited to a real consideration of important issues.[70]

The problems that the NEA had in moving in any direction, particularly in a direction toward more active pursuit of teacher welfare, were illustrated, though unwittingly, in a state education association executive's article about relations between the national association and its constituent bodies. Lyndon U. Pratt clearly intended his article to be supportive of the NEA and its policies. However, he also identified the specific problems that plagued an organization as large and complex as the association. While the NEA had only one constitutional policy-making body, the Representative Assembly meeting formally at the annual convention, Pratt added that several commissions, committees, and departments also issued policy statements that could cloud or distort the official association policy thrust. In considering the NEA's relations with its state associations, Pratt discussed two problems. First, he claimed that at times the NEA had bypassed its state associations and dealt directly with the local associations, even to the point of providing specific field services that overlapped with the state association. While he did not state that this move was taken mainly in the field of teacher welfare, Pratt's statement of the second problem clearly implied that conclusion. He remarked that the classroom teacher movement that had blossomed within the NEA since 1940 had provided opportunities for what he considered unnecessary images of conflict and controversy to develop between teachers and administrators. This was especially the case, for Pratt, when the "presence of labor-affiliated teacher unions" intensified matters. In these cases, said the NEA state leader, the threat to the NEA's program of unity and cooperation between teachers and administrators was substantial. Thus, even this intended-to-be friendly account of the NEA and its activities exposed, though unintentionally, the cumbersome structure and the dual commitment to teachers and administrators that prevented the NEA from responding effectively to teachers and their concerns.[71]

NEA RESPONSE TO CRITICISM

The arguments that Myron Lieberman and other critics raised about the NEA proved prophetic of troubles that the association would encounter in the next fifteen years. Many teachers, especially men in the nation's large cities, were suffering the consequences of two decades of almost uninterrupted inflation, the shortage of colleagues needed to staff the classrooms crowded by the offspring of the baby boom of the post–World War II era, and the general lack of respect and responsibility that teachers experienced from their own administrative superiors as well as from the pubic at large.

The NEA hierarchy, however, at least as measured by the commitments of its highest appointed officer, was unphased by any of the criticism. In an article published in an issue of *School and Society* that contained some criticism of the association, NEA executive secretary William G. Carr weighed in with a ringing defense of its structure, programs, and policies. Though he mentioned no critics by name, he managed to respond to several of the points that many of them had made. In considering the issues of size and diversity, Carr turned what critics saw as weakness into strength. While size and diversity might have some problematic aspects, argued Carr, they were far outweighed by what the association's many members contributed to the organizational ethos. He linked the unity of the diverse elements in the NEA to the larger American polity's incorporation of diverse groups. The representation of many, sometimes conflicting, points of view in the various NEA bodies was, for Carr, a recognition of the democratic character of the organization, a proper symbol of strength, not weakness. The lack of a monolithic voice in the NEA was analogous to the educational situation in the country at large. While the nation had no formal educational policy, it had a national educational system that functioned through the actions of its constituent state and local bodies. The NEA's triple-tiered organization mirrored that of the nation's schools and shared, with those schools, in the production of national educational excellence.[72]

In discussing the association's positions on teacher welfare, Carr began by noting the distantly related matter of the many ways that the NEA sought to improve the educational service offered by teachers. Continuing to ignore the welfare issue he had raised, Carr next considered the crucial issue of relations between teachers and administrators. He defended the NEA's commitment to unity between the two groups, arguing that it prevented teacher myopia from becoming rampant. Teachers' views needed to be appropriately broadened by the variety of points of view and orientations they encountered elsewhere in the NEA, said the executive secretary. Moving beyond the issue of unity finally to a direct discussion of teacher welfare, he enumerated the various bodies, policies, and services in the NEA that were devoted to the protection of the teacher. On this point, he stressed the progress that had been made since the NEA reorganization of the post–World War I era. While there were many who might wish for the NEA to move further and faster in this area, the real acknowledgment of the strength of the NEA by national and state legislatures testified, for Carr, to the large measure of accomplishment that the association had achieved.[73]

While Carr's arguments were many and responded vigorously to the charges of the critics, they did not link the NEA convincingly to the issues that were then troubling many of the nation's school teachers. Similarly, his venture into the future of American education in an article published in the final 1957 issue of the *NEA Journal* was devoid of items of interest to the growing group of teacher activists. And even when he referred to NEA activities in the area of teacher welfare, as he did in a listing of association accomplishments in 1958, he did so using traditional categories that ignored the changing consciousness that was developing in many of the urban teacher groups throughout the nation.[74] The gap between the NEA's increasingly vocal minority of activist teacher members and Carr and other of the NEA's top leadership was illustrated in a survey in which delegates to the 1956 and 1957 Representative Assemblies were asked to state their priorities. Carr and the rest of the NEA staff were surprised to learn that the leading desire of the delegates was that the NEA pursue more vigorously the economic and social improvement of teachers.[75] Carr's inability or unwillingness to respond to this priority meant that the NEA was poorly positioned to deal with the wave of teacher militancy that was developing in the late 1950s and that would sweep the nation's schools in the next decade.

Another silence in Carr's stated and published commitments, a deafening silence, was his failure to comment or act in the area of race relations in education. While it is not absolutely certain that this silence reflected Carr's own personal beliefs, it did clearly mean that the association had failed to answer the challenge of the potent issue of school desegregation raised in the 1954 *Brown* decision. Separate consideration of the NEA's response to teacher militancy and its efforts to deal with the problems, within its own precincts as well as in the nation's schools, raised by the legal proscription of school segregation constitute the main focus of the next two chapters.

NOTES

[1]"We Want to Thank the NEA," *NEA Journal* 42 (March 1953): 164.

[2]Copies of all eight "Wage Stabilization Memos" are in the NEA Archives, box 762. Although the NEA argument was legally sound, it did not prevent school systems from rescinding salary increases or reducing them to comply with the "spirit" of the wage controls.

[3]For a summary of the NEA's international efforts, see Wesley, *NEA*, 357–62.

[4]Ruth Stout, "The 85th Congress: A Milestone in American Education," *NEA Journal* 47 (October 1958): 462–63. On the passage of the NDEA, as well as on the NEA opposition to the restricted spending it institutionalized, see Barbara Barksdale Clowse, *Brain Power for the Cold War: The* Sputnik *Crisis and National Defense Education Act of 1958* (Westport, CT: Greenwood Press, 1981): passim and 72–74.

[5]*NEA Research Bulletin* (April 1951) reported the results of the then latest biannual study. The results received further publicity in "Salaries *Lag* in City-School Systems," *NEA Journal* 40 (September 1951): 398–99.

[6]"The Effect of Class Size on Learning," *NEA Journal* 40 (March 1951): 215–16; "Class Size Is Out of Hand: We Must Help Bring to All the People the Realization That It Is Their Problem Too," ibid. 42 (December 1953): 555–56; "Teacher Load," ibid. 45 (February 1956): 96–97; "Class Size and Teacher Load: How Large Are Our Classes?" and "Teachers Speak," ibid. 46 (October 1957): 439.

[7]"A Minimum Scale of $3600 to $8200: What Does This Mean for Teachers?" *NEA Journal* 42 (December 1953): 569–70.

[8]"Professional Salaries for America's Teachers," *NEA NEWS* (March 26, 1954): NEA Archives, box 765.

[9]These and other "Special Memos" of the Research Division are all in the NEA Archives, box 762.

[10]"Quality-of-Service Recognition in Teachers' Salary Schedules" (July 1936), NEA Archives, box 762. Hazel Davis reported that much of her effort in the Research Division in the 1950s was devoted to the fight against merit pay: Hazel Davis interview (June 17, 1988), NEA Archives, box 3117.

[11]"The Financial Outlook for Public Education," *NEA Journal* 41 (September 1952): 363–64; "Equalization of Property Assessments," ibid. 47 (April 1958): 339; and "School Finance: A National Problem," ibid.: 340–41. John K. Norton, "Our Current Economy Can and Must Support Higher Salaries for Teachers," ibid. 46 (December 1957): 568–70.

[12]Each month from September 1955 to May 1956, the *NEA Journal* published a feature article on one of the topics.

[13]Joy Elmer Morgan, "The Second Half Million," *NEA Journal* 42 (September 1953): 329.

[14]"The Local and the CAP," *NEA Journal* 43 (November 1954): 516; and "Increased Dues for Increased Services," a three-part series advocating the dues increase in Ibid. 45 (November 1956): 484, 45 (December 1956): 571, and 46 (January 1957): 21. The membership decline after the dues increase is discussed in Ibid. 47 (February 1958): 78.

[15]"Legislative Spadework: A Job for Our Local Associations," *NEA Journal* 41 (January 1952): 44; "A Symposium: If I Were Planning a Local Meeting," ibid. 45 (March 1956): 172–73; "How We Got Our Salary Increases: A Symposium," ibid. 45 (September 1956): 371; and "Not Choked by Their Own Fewness: Our Local Associations," ibid. 42 (February 1953): 103–4.

[16]Samuel R. Rosen, " 'I Like Local Associations,' Says School Board Member," and Charles M. Rogers, " 'I Like Local Associations,' Says Superintendent," *NEA Journal* 41 (December 1952): 590, 591; "Symposium on Teachers Associations and Superintendents," ibid. 45 (December 1956): 589.

[17]"On the Question of Affiliating," *NEA Journal* 40 (October 1951): 481–82.

[18]"Scorecard for Our Local Associations," *NEA Journal* 40 (March 1951): 213; and "Size Up Your Local Association," ibid. 44 (April 1955): 238–39.

[19]"A Calendar for Local Associations," *NEA Journal* 41 (April 1952): 201; "Put New Life into Your Local by Using Group Technics Suggest Dorothy Stock and Helen K. Ryan," ibid. 44 (March 1955): 174–75; and "Local Association Handbooks," ibid. 45 (March 1956): 50.

[20]"Pedagog Pedro's Local Meeting," *NEA Journal* 46 (September 1957): 394; and Effie O. Stanfield, "Dues and Budgets," ibid. 47 (January 1958): 51.

[21]"A Quick Survey by the NEA Research Division: Major Activities of the State Education Associations, 1950–1951," *NEA Journal* 40 (January 1951): 53–55.

[22]"Teacher Welfare Activities of Our State Associations," *NEA Journal* 41 (October 1952): 422–23.

[23]May C. Smith, "A New Salary Schedule for New Jersey," *NEA Journal* 44 (February 1955): 94–95; "Professional Status Thru [*sic*] Unity: The Montana Association Stresses the 'U' in Unity and the 'US' in Status," ibid. 45 (February 1956): 99; Mary Josephine Wyles, "Teacher Welfare in New Mexico," ibid. 45 (February 1956): 102; George H. Deer, "The Louisiana Pattern for Broadening the Base of Educational Leadership," ibid. 45 (April 1956): 240; and James R. McDonough, "Hawaii's Teachers Win Political Freedom," ibid. 45 (November 1956): 507–8.

[24]NEA Research Division, *The Status of Field Work and Field Workers of State Education Associations* (Microfiche Document Catalog no. NEA 430, S53.1), NEA Archives, passim; quotation, 32.

[25]Ibid., 10, 12, and 18.

[26]NEA Research Division, "Staff Personnel Policies and Practices of State Education Associations," (n.d. [1956]), NEA Archives, box 518.

[27]Joy Elmer Morgan, "The Service of Willard E. Givens," *NEA Journal* 41 (May 1952): 267.

[28]Ibid.

[29]"In Appreciation of Outstanding Service," and "Willard E. Givens," *NEA Journal* 41 (May 1952): 268, 269–70.

[30]"William G. Carr," *NEA Journal* 41 (September 1952): 331.

[31]Carr, "NEA Staff Reorganization," *NEA Journal* (April 1955): 213, and "Did You Know [regional offices discussion]," ibid. 46 (October 1957): 468.

[32]"William G. Carr Discusses the Unique Character of NEA," *NEA Journal* 44 (December 1955): 575–76.

[33]Carr, "What Is a Member?" *NEA Journal* 45 (October 1956): 434, and "Teacher-Administrator Teamwork," ibid. 45 (November 1956): 506.

[34]Carr, "NEA Policies," *NEA Journal* 46 (September 1957): 386; my emphasis.

[35]Arthur F. Corey, "Professional Organizations and You," *NEA Journal* 46 (October 1957): 453.

[36]Bernard Baruch, "A Real Teacher: A Stirring Tribute to a Great Teacher by a Great Man," *NEA Journal* 39 (September 1950): 415.

[37]Eleanor Metheny, "I Like Teaching," *NEA Journal* 40 (December 1951): 612.

[38]Ibid. As will be shown shortly, the phenomenon of women teachers as earners of a second income in a family was on the rise in the 1950s.

[39]"Pedagogic Pulchritude," *NEA Journal* 40 (December 1951): 623.

[40]*NEA Journal* 40 (September 1951): 410–13.

[41]Kathryn E. Steinmetz, "Women in School Administration," *NEA Journal* 40 (October 1951): 488.

[42]Steinmetz, "Women Administrators in Higher Education," *NEA Journal* 41 (September 1952): 342.

[43]The accuracy of Steinmetz's data as well as her timidity can be ascertained by comparing her work with Blount, *Destined to Rule the Schools*. In her account

of the incidence of women in school administration throughout the twentieth century, Blount confirms Steinmetz's analysis but takes it substantially further along the road toward analyzing the problem.

[44]"Do We Need a New Curriculum for Women in Higher Education? Yes Says Louise Dudley, No Says Maribeth Cameron," *NEA Journal* 40 (October 1951): 452–53.

[45]"Meet the New Editor," *NEA Journal* 44 (April 1955): 193.

[46]Hazel Davis, "The American Public School Teacher at the Close of the NEA's First 100 Years," *NEA Journal* 46 (April 1957): 250–51.

[47]Isobel V. Brown, "The Trouble with Teachers," *NEA Journal* 47 (February 1958):107–8.

[48]William G. Carr, "Hilda Maehling Retires," *NEA Journal* 48 (December 1959): 501.

[49]"Supreme Court Decision on Desegregation," *NEA Journal* 43 (September 1954): 349.

[50]Ronald Gould, "The 'Closed Shop' and the Teacher," *Phi Delta Kappan* 33 (September 1951): 53, 64.

[51]"Should Teachers' Associations Have Compulsory Membership?—A Symposium," *Phi Delta Kappan* 33 (September 1951): 56–61.

[52]Ibid., 57–58. Since Phi Delta Kappa, the sponsor of the symposium and publisher of *Phi Delta Kappan,* was open only to men, it was not unexpected that the depiction of men's interests as in competition with those of women would come in a contribution to this publication rather than in a more general-interest educational forum.

[53]W. M. Schall, "In the Large City Local," *NEA Journal* 42 (January 1953): 48; and "The Second Half Million," ibid. 42 (September 1953): 329.

[54]"Big City Locals: A Tape Recording of a Discussion on Local Association Practices," *NEA Journal* 45 (October 1956): 433–34. The movie referred to in the text is *Cool Hand Luke.*

[55]Betty Stautzenberger, "We Are Proud of Our Building Representatives," *NEA Journal* 45 (May 1956): 314.

[56]"NEA in New York City," *NEA Journal* 47 (November 1958): 531.

[57]Wesley, *NEA.* Although the book was well documented and featured substantial use of primary sources as evidence for its conclusions, its uncritical boosterism of the association and its leaders was also clear. William Brickman identified this problem in "Toward an Evaluation of the Publications of the National Education Association," *Progressive Education* 34 (July 1957): 111–15.

[58]Myron Lieberman, *Education As a Profession* (Englewood Cliffs, NJ: Prentice Hall, 1956); Lieberman, "Teachers' Strikes: An Analysis of the Issues," *Harvard Educational Review* 46 (Winter 1956): 39–70; Lieberman, "Civil Rights and the N. E. A.," *School and Society* (May 11, 1957): 166–69; and Lieberman, "Introduction," *Progressive Education* 34 (July 1957): 97.

[59]Lieberman, "Teachers' Strikes," passim and especially 44–45, 49, and 65. In Chapter 3 I pointed to the NEA's unwillingness to publicize the Norwalk strike and the successful outcome achieved in Norwalk by the teachers' association.

[60]Lieberman, *Education As a Profession,* 335—quoting from NEA Executive Committee, "The Professional Way to Meet the Educational Crisis," *NEA Journal* 36 (February 1947): 47.

[61]Lieberman, *Education As a Profession,* 305–6.

[62]Ibid., 369–72. Lieberman made no mention of the difference between men and women teachers, a point that will be elaborated on in the next chapter.

[63]Lieberman, "Civil Rights and the N. E. A.," 166–69.

[64]Ibid., 168.

[65]George A. Male, "The NEA and the National Union of Teachers of England," *School and Society* (May 11, 1957): 163–66. Like Lieberman, Male was silent on the issue of gender differences in teaching and teacher organizations.

[66]Lieberman, "Introduction," 97.

[67]Lloyd P. Jorgensen, "The Social and Economic Orientation of the National Education Association," *Progressive Education* 34 (July 1957): 98–101.

[68]Maurice P. Hunt, "The NEA's Neglected Role of Critic," *Progressive Education* 34 (July 1957): 105–8.

[69]George A. Male, "The National Education Association and Teacher Welfare," *Progressive Education* 34 (July 1957): 108–11.

[70]Brickman, "Toward an Evaluation of the Publications of the National Education Association."

[71]Lyndon U. Pratt, "The Impact of the National Education Association on State Education Associations," *Progressive Education* 34 (July 1957): 116–18.

[72]William G. Carr, "The N. E. A.'s Service to American Education," *School and Society* (May 11, 1957): 160–61.

[73]Ibid., 163–66.

[74]Carr, "What's Past Is Prologue," *NEA Journal* 46 (December 1957): 604–5; and Carr, "So Far We Have Come During the First Year of the Expanded Program," ibid. 47 (September 1958): 428.

[75]On this survey and the Carr reaction, see Gabriel Steven Pellathy, "The National Education Association: A Political System in Change" (Ph.D. diss., New York University, 1971): 72.

CHAPTER 5

The Making of a Teachers' Union
The National Education Association, 1960–73

Between 1960 and 1973 the NEA remodeled itself, becoming an organization of teachers, first and foremost. It clearly moved away from its existence as a cooperative, nonconfrontational, professional association, a position that it had cultivated since its reorganization in 1917. The main tasks of this chapter are to chart the ascent to dominance of a militant, urban-oriented movement for teacher power within the NEA, to analyze this movement and identify its supporters and detractors among teachers and NEA officials, to show how the thirst for teacher power altered the relations among local, state, and national levels of organization within the association, and to show also how teacher power changed the operation of NEA headquarters and its staff.

In 1957 all but one member of the NEA cabinet, the high-level advisory and executive group established by Executive Secretary William Carr, were old enough to reach the mandatory retirement age of sixty-five within a decade; the exception would become sixty-five years old in thirteen years. Carr himself turned sixty-five in 1967. The pattern, then, was staff management of the association and its affairs by an aging group, almost all of whom were white males, often with minimal experience in the schools. This experience consisted quite often of a few years as a teacher and then some time as a school administrator, prior to a long tenure on the NEA staff.[1] Thus the NEA in the late 1950s, like many large organizations in the private sector, was clearly dominated by an appointed staff leadership that headed its organizational bureaucracy. Though the NEA had elected officers, a formal legislative body (the Representative Assembly), and an executive committee, the short terms of its elected officials and the cumbersome character of the relations between the Executive Committee and the Representative Assembly and the other decision-making segments of the organization—the board of directors and the board of trustees—combined to dilute the power of members and elected officers and to strengthen the power of the staff and its ability to frustrate change initiated or advocated by the membership. State education associations provided another effective brake on change. These NEA affiliates, even more than the national organization, were led by school administrators who agreed with NEA staff in their suspicions about teacher power. The two groups together managed to exercise an effective veto over NEA policies and actions they considered undesirable, especially the establishment of any independent teacher voice.

Empowered by their places at the top of the NEA hierarchy, William Carr and his lieutenants were in no hurry to respond to the desires or demands of classroom teachers or their local education associations. Events in the late 1950s and early 1960s, however, mandated a response. In the next section of this chapter, I describe the particulars of the more than decade-long unionization process that culminated in a new constitution for the NEA early in the 1970s. Then I look at the embrace of a new form of political action that accompanied the move to unionization and away from cooperative professionalism. Next come descriptions of the changes that unionization meant for relations between state and local affiliates of NEA and for the NEA staff. Finally, I consider the relationship between the militant unionization movement and the historic, though flawed, commitment of the NEA to women teachers.

TURMOIL IN THE NEA IN THE 1960s

If any single set of occurrences can be said to mark the beginning of the change toward militant unionism in the NEA, it was the series of teachers' strikes that took place in New York City, beginning in the late 1950s and continuing into the 1960s. While these strikes, like most strikes, originated in local conditions and were affected primarily by local circumstances and concerns, the failure of the NEA to respond effectively to those conditions and circumstances for its own national organizational advancement—and the contrasting success of the AFT in capitalizing on the New York situation to build itself—is the main circumstance that shaped the history of both organizations in the 1960s.

The New York teachers' strikes accompanied the organization of a powerful AFT local in that city, the United Federation of Teachers

(UFT). That body received recognition as the bargaining agent for the city's teachers through its victory in a strike-induced representation election, in which the UFT soundly defeated a competing NEA body. The UFT then negotiated a series of collective bargaining agreements that spoke directly to teachers' economic grievances as well as to their desire for recognition as legitimate actors in the city's educational affairs.[2]

The AFT victory in New York was repeated in many other big cities, meaning that the teachers' union was becoming a formidable rival to the NEA in terms of numbers of teacher members for the first time since the post–World War I era. Whereas in 1960 the AFT had 59,000 members and the NEA 714,000, by 1970 the union counted the allegiance of 205,000 teachers, an increase of close to fourfold, while the NEA's membership stood at 1.1 million.[3] The NEA total included school administrators, college professors, and assorted other nonteachers, while the AFT was strictly a teachers' organization. One of the main reasons for the union's defeat of the NEA in New York and other large cities was the weakness of the association's local affiliates compared with their AFT counterparts. It was not only in comparison with their competitors that the NEA locals were weak, however. Within the association itself, they paled in power and influence when compared with the more conservative, administrator-dominated state education associations, as well as with the NEA Board of Directors, which the state associations controlled through election of its members.

Representation elections and collective bargaining agreements in public school systems were local affairs. The AFT had traditionally relied on strong locals, particularly in contrast to its relatively weak state-level bodies. This practice, combined with the AFT's ties to the organized labor movement, which had substantial experience in conducting successful representation campaigns and negotiating collective bargaining agreements, helped the teachers' union to repeatedly defeat the association in the big cities. NEA reaction to these AFT victories was slow and clumsy; however, the association did eventually mount a campaign of its own among teachers at both the local and national levels.

The NEA action was hampered, however, by the lack of fit between the typical NEA local and the qualities that were needed in a big city fight with an AFT local in a collective bargaining representation election. The problems were clearly illustrated in a 1960 survey of local NEA affiliates, conducted by the association's Research Division and entitled "Local Associations—Organization, Practices, and Programs, 1958–59."[4]

The report, prepared by longtime Research Division staff member Hazel Davis and a research assistant, revealed much about the NEA's existing local affiliates, their relations with the developing militant teacher movement in the nation's large cities, and the views of Davis and others in the NEA hierarchy about the urban teacher movement. Fewer than 10 percent of the responses to the questionnaire on which the report was based came from city associations with more than one thousand members, a clear indication that the NEA's membership was concentrated in rural areas, small towns, and medium-sized cities, not in large urban centers where the militance was centered. Just as significant, the preponderance of the local associations that responded to the questionnaire were what Davis and the NEA called "all-inclusive" groups—that is, associations that enrolled administrators alongside teachers as members, as opposed to organizations comprising "classroom teachers" only. Further, the majority of members in the NEA local groups, wherever they were located, was made up of elementary teachers with a minority made up of high school teachers and, in all-inclusive organizations, school administrators. All of this indicated that the main affiliates of the NEA at the local level were substantially different in composition from the local teacher union groups that were either already affiliated with or soon to join the AFT. Union affiliation, not allegiance to the NEA, was the major characteristic of the local organizations that sparked the bargaining elections, conducted the strikes, and negotiated the contracts with school boards in the nation's largest cities in the 1960s and 1970s.[5]

The presence and role of paid staff was another characteristic discussed in the NEA report that differentiated association locals from the emerging union groups. Hazel Davis noted that less than 7 percent of the NEA locals employed paid staff and, of those that did so, most local employees were involved in clerical rather than leadership activities. In contrast, big city teachers' unions often featured full-time executive staff and full-time, paid organizers who conducted union membership campaigns and other activities. Of the few NEA locals that employed staff, by far the majority were the city organizations that were, or were soon to be, fighting the union in representation elections. In describing the activities of NEA locals, Davis noted that relatively few (about one-fourth) tried to represent teachers before superintendents and/or boards of education, the service that undergirded the very existence of a teachers' union local in this and subsequent periods. Another revealing statistic showed that more than 77 percent of the local associations responding to the survey reported conducting social functions as a major item of business. Interestingly, in spite of this relative lack of representational activity and the corresponding preponderance of social activity, the greatest single item of business mentioned by NEA locals was the pursuit of teacher welfare activities, with 72 percent reporting such efforts.[6] The effectiveness of those efforts, however, was not reported and must be doubted given the course of events in the 1960s.

Davis's conclusion from the above evidence was optimistic, but unfortunately, it proved unreliable as a guide for future activities: "Certainly the full picture of the strength, representative nature, organizational structure, and complexity, and wide scope of activities would indicate clearly the strong position held and meaningful role played in the professional lives of teachers by the local education associations."[7] In reality the NEA locals were poorly positioned in almost every respect when taking into account the collective bargaining and job action agenda that dominated the big city unions in the 1960s, garnered media attention, and jolted American politicians as well as the American populace for the next two decades. Davis's own approval of the NEA's approach and its results was reflective of the point of view that characterized almost the entire NEA central office staff. Needless to say, it was not surprising that the NEA was trounced a number of times in the representation elections that were fought for the organizational allegiance of city teachers in the early 1960s.

Within the NEA and its myriad subgroups, the thrust for change to combat the AFT came from teacher activists in cities like those that were directly experiencing the competition from the teachers' union. These activists began cooperating with one another in the late 1950s to pursue the interests of city teachers, an agenda that had been largely ignored by the staff and state association–dominated NEA. One revealing example that illustrated the militant activity, the state association's ineffectiveness, and the NEA's initial indifference to the urban militants occurred in 1958. In that year, the Las Vegas, Nevada, local affiliate of the NEA attempted to negotiate an agreement with its board of education. As part of this effort, the Las Vegas group attempted to divorce itself from what it considered a completely unresponsive Nevada Education Association and to disaffiliate from both the state association and the NEA. The NEA response, rather than to try and mediate or arbitrate the situation, was simply to disallow the actions taken by the Las Vegas association.[8]

Similarly, after the New York City teachers had chosen to have a formal representation election that was needed before any move to bargain collectively, but before the election was held, resulting in a resounding defeat for the NEA by the AFT, an article in the *NEA Journal* about the election was devoted largely to an indictment of the nefariousness of the union instead of making any positive statement about the association. This article focused on the recent "illegal" strike conducted by the union, charging that a vote for the union in the representation election was a vote for the strike and that a vote for the NEA was a vote "opposing strikes by teachers as unjustifiable repudiations of professional responsibility." The problem with this approach was that it ignored completely the reality that the strike had been successful in that it paved the way for the very representation election in which the NEA was then involved. Teachers, in New York City and in other large cities, were coming to the position that Myron Lieberman had posited a few years earlier: extraordinary measures such as strikes were sometimes necessary to secure legitimate objectives for teacher welfare, and an association that was flat-footed in its stand against recognizing this reality was unworthy of support.[9]

Other early attempts to get the NEA to respond to the urban teacher crisis were, at best, only partially successful. For example, in 1961 the Representative Assembly, reflecting the views of many of the women elementary teachers and school administrators who far outnumbered the urban activists in the NEA, voted against doubling the sum of money appropriated through the regular budget process for urban activities. One year later the Representative Assembly voted not to respond to objections from the Department of Classroom Teachers, a body within which the militants had made some inroads, to the lack of teacher representation on the NEA's Board of Directors. In both of these situations, the delegates preferred to go slowly rather than to respond to what seemed, to many of them, to be shrill demands for immediate action from a group of loud-mouthed urban teacher militants.[10]

These activists gradually infiltrated the elected offices of the NEA, however, working their way particularly into the ranks of the Executive Committee, a body elected by the Representative Assembly. The urban teachers also eventually succeeded in formally organizing their own subgroup within the NEA, the National Council of Urban Education Associations (NCUEA). It was this group that spearheaded the reconstruction of the NEA in the late 1960s and early 1970s.[11]

The overwhelming victory in 1962 of the New York AFT affiliate in the election of an organization to represent the city's teachers in negotiations with the school board provided a wake-up call that the NEA seemed ready to ignore. As James Carey, the president of the International Union of Electrical Workers told the NEA convention in 1962, "What happened in New York City, and you know it deep down in your hearts, is no accident or temporary phenomenon." He went on to criticize the NEA's antipathy to labor unions as a misguided ideology inappropriate for the conditions under which teachers found themselves working in the 1960s. Further, he lampooned the NEA's fear of "labor bosses" like himself and fear of the control by the "bosses" that labor organizing among the ranks of the nation's teachers would bring. He argued that his personal morality and the morality of his actions were in no way inferior to those of the leadership of the NEA.[12]

The NEA staff response to both its own NCUEA group of activists and the larger teacher union challenge was slow, halting, and ineffective. Executive Secretary William Carr initially followed the traditional strategy in urban locals that was geared to building the number of individual NEA members, not to increasing the strength of the services provided by the local affiliates. Further, Carr seemed personally uncomfortable with collective bargaining for teachers, the goal of most union locals and of many NEA urban locals. Under his leadership, the NEA developed a policy advocating "professional negotiations" as its own alternative to collective bargaining. Also, NEA policy featured "sanctions" applied against offending school districts—that is, provisions such as precluding members from accepting jobs in a sanctioned district, as its alternative to strikes. One high-ranking NEA staff member was assigned responsibility for these two sets of activities, and he devoted the majority of his time to their pursuit.[13]

The policies of "professional negotiations" and "sanctions" were developed as alternatives to union-oriented collective bargaining and strikes, alternatives that paid allegiance to the NEA's traditionally stated priority, or, perhaps more correctly stated, its ideology of building an educational "profession." This ideology rhetorically sought to tarnish AFT union activities as antiprofessional and to prevent teacher affiliation with the organized labor movement—the AFT and its parent organization, the American Federation of Labor–Congress of Industrial Organizations (AFL-CIO).

The fact that in practice—that is, in the settings where contracts were negotiated—the agreements reached by NEA locals differed hardly at all from AFT contracts belied the significance of the different terms the association leadership developed to distinguish its approach from that of the union. As the NEA finally reorganized itself in the early 1970s, it joined the Coalition of American Public Employees, a group that involved the NEA with the American Federation of State, County, and Municipal Employees (AFSCME) and other public employee unions but operated outside of the AFL-CIO. Thus, the NEA ultimately cooperated with other unions while staying outside of the official organized labor umbrella, thereby continuing to honor its ideological revulsion to trade unionism at the same time that it embraced the phenomenon.

The corresponding NEA movement away from sanctions and professional negotiations and in the direction of the countenance of work stoppages and the straightforward advocacy of collective bargaining took a number of years to accomplish. Much of that accomplishment required getting around or pushing through the opposition of William Carr, his supporters, and his immediate successor. Carr's backing was strongest in several of the state affiliates, particularly those in the South and in border areas of the nation.[14] He astutely used that support to combat the plans of the activist elements in the NEA. In fact, the history of the association throughout the 1960s and into the early 1970s can be read largely as a war between the pro- and antiunion elements within the group—or a conflict pitting the militant, largely urban, local leaders along with the national officers they were able to elect with increasing frequency in the 1960s against the more conservative state associations, the board of directors and the board of trustees, both of which were chosen by procedures that reflected extensive state association influence, and the appointed NEA staff.

The unionists managed to win a substantial victory at the expense of William Carr in the mid-1960s. In spite of his own misgivings, Carr was forced to acquiesce in the hiring of several labor organizers as part of the NEA staff. These organizers were recruited from other trade unions, and they brought trade union values and orientations with them to the NEA staff. They soon sparked the formation of the NEA Staff Organization (NEASO) and, in 1966, Carr was forced by action of the NEA Executive Committee and a vote of the Representative Assembly, both of which were bodies that were increasingly being influenced by the teacher militants, to recognize NEASO as the bargaining agent for employees of the NEA in Washington. Not only did the Representative Assembly rebuff Carr with its vote on this issue, but it refused even to allow him to comment from the floor on the situation.[15]

This vote was one significant step in the larger organizational struggle to limit the power of the executive secretary, a process that gathered momentum in the mid-1960s. In 1965, one year before the vote on recognizing the NEASO, delegates to the Representative Assembly passed a resolution recommending an increase in the number and proportion of teacher members on all NEA boards and committees. Three years later they made the recommendation into a requirement. In that same year, 1968, delegates to the Representative Assembly engaged in a serious discussion of the legitimacy of teacher strikes and passed a resolution on the "Withdrawal of Services" that for the first time sanctioned the use of the strike and put the association on record in opposition to legislation banning teacher strikes. This action occurred, at least in part, in reaction to a statewide strike that had taken place earlier in 1968 in Florida, led by the NEA's affiliate there, the Florida Education Association.[16]

The individuals and groups involved in the classroom teacher movement in the NEA were not confident about their prospects unless and until William Carr was replaced, however. This was not an easy task to accomplish. The Representative Assembly took a preliminary step down this road when it changed the body that approved the appointment of the executive secretary from the conservatively oriented board of trustees over which Carr had great influence to the more member-responsive Executive Committee.[17]

In the same year that this was accomplished, 1966, NEA President Richard Batchelder made a militant speech to the Representative Assembly putting conservative elements in the association—the staff leadership, school administrators, and the state association hierarchies, which were almost always dominated by administrators—on notice that the NEA was intent on becoming a true teachers' organization. In his own speech to the convention that year, William Carr struck a different note, cautioning teachers who were "withdrawing their services" not to engage in such an act precipitously. Carr maintained that teachers had not lost their ideals and stressed that they should keep their ethical commitments and obey the law—words that many of the militant teachers in his audience considered a tiresome repetition of outworn ideas.[18]

Within a year of this speech, William Carr resigned his position with the NEA. He had served beyond the normal retirement age; his contract had been renewed past the age of sixty-five by the board of directors even though he himself enforced the retirement age for his own staff.[19] Despite his ability to survive and to hold on to his office, he had reached the point where more often than not he was losing battles within the association to the organizational militants. The Executive Committee, responsive to the teacher activists, was now in control over the process for choosing the next executive secretary.

The person chosen to succeed Carr was Sam Lambert. In some ways Lambert resembled his predecessor. Lambert had been a mathematics teacher in West Virginia, worked for the state association there, and then took a position on the NEA staff in the Research Division. He quickly rose through the ranks in the Research Division to become director and, subsequently, an assistant executive secretary to Carr. He was much younger than his superior, however, and he was somewhat in touch with the teacher militants in the urban NEA locals. Shortly after his selection, Lambert met with the Executive Committee and agreed to a series of changes that made it clear that a new day was dawning for the NEA. The Executive Committee, elected by the members of the Representative Assembly, was now in control of its own agenda and unresponsive to a set of issues determined by the chief NEA staff officer. Also, the Executive Committee would meet more frequently and would exercise financial control over the association. The elected NEA president was to take more control over his or her own actions, rather than, as in the past, have them scheduled and overseen by the executive secretary. In addition to these changes, the Educational Policies Commission (EPC) was abolished. A body born of the depression era crisis in education and functioning to consider larger educational questions, the EPC was a symbol of the Carr era and its high-level, pie-in-the-sky priorities. Another factor no doubt related to the demise of the EPC was that one of its leading members had been an opponent of Lambert in the contest to succeed William Carr.[20]

In describing the organizational changes that had been instituted shortly after his accession to the top staff position in the NEA, Sam Lambert, speaking to the Representative Assembly in 1968, identified the major force behind them. "This reorganization, fellow teachers, recognizes one very important NEA fact of life: Most of our members are classroom teachers, and they should have a place at the top." He went on to indicate at least one concrete way of realizing that priority when he noted that the staff member responsible for the Department of Classroom Teachers was now to be promoted to the rank of an NEA cabinet officer. Lambert addressed that individual in front of the convention with the following words: "Welcome to the executive suite, fellow teacher."[21]

In his speech to the Representative Assembly after his selection, Lambert also indicated the substantial progress that had been made in accomplishing still another organizational change desired by the militants in the NEA, the unification of membership. Unification, the payment of dues to local, state, and national associations at one time, had been a stated priority of William Carr and his predecessors but primarily for the purpose of increasing the number of members at the national level. This large national membership could be used rhetorically to counter the AFT member increases that were obtained through organizing and negotiating collective bargaining agreements at the local level. Under Lambert, the thrust to unify was mandated for the first time and proceeded, under the mandate, at a much more rapid pace. It was part of a larger alteration of the NEA, undertaken in order to respond to the AFT.

Sam Lambert's accommodation to the program of the militant elements in the NEA proved to be short-lived, however. One reason for this was that he was not as strongly committed to militancy in practice as he was in his statements. Shortly after assuming leadership of the NEA, he was confronted with the statewide walkout of the Florida teachers. The Florida Education Association (FEA), acting in an unprecedented manner for an NEA state affiliate, followed the lead of its militant urban local associations in Miami, Tampa, Jacksonville, and elsewhere, and struck the entire state. Lambert did not advocate the actions that the FEA undertook enthusiastically, and his hesitancy to embrace the Florida teachers wholeheartedly can be contrasted with the position of one of his assistant executive secretaries, Cecil Hannan. Appointed to the NEA staff in an effort to be responsive to the NEA militants eager to see one of their own in the leadership ranks, Hannan came to NEA headquarters from a position on the staff of the association's militant affiliate in the state of Washington. He was much more in tune than Lambert with the teacher power movement that was animating teachers in Florida and throughout much of the rest of the NEA. Hannan, not Lambert, was the leading NEA official on the scene in Florida during the walkout.[22]

Like William Carr, Lambert reacted in a viscerally negative fashion to the AFT. In the late 1960s and early 1970s AFT leaders like David Selden and Albert Shanker undertook several attempts to discuss a merger between the union and the NEA. These attempts were initially successful at the local level in Los Angeles, California, and at the state level in the state of New York. Ultimately, however, Lambert's opposition to cooperation between the NEA and any group affiliated with the American labor movement, as represented by the AFL-CIO, carried the day in the NEA. Even some of the NEA's militant urban teachers, along with most of the rest of the members, balked at what they saw as being officially incorporated into the organized labor movement. Though his side eventually won the battle over AFL-CIO affiliation, Lambert lost the larger war for control of the NEA. He was deposed as executive secretary in 1972 at the same time that the NEA was revising its constitution and adopting a new form of organizational structure and leadership geared to responding effectively to a burgeoning teacher militancy.[23]

CONSTITUTIONAL REFORM AND ITS CONSEQUENCES

The adoption of a new constitution in 1973 was the culmination of numerous changes that had taken place within the association in the 1960s. The new constitution completed a process that began in 1964 when a study of the restructuring of the NEA was authorized. Initially, the executive secretary, then William Carr, had control over the process. He first placed responsibility for reorganization with a staff committee and then turned the matter over to a group of outside consultants. That consulting process resulted in a report that was rejected convincingly by the Representative Assembly because rank-and-file NEA members had not been involved in the deliberations. The Executive Committee then assumed responsibility for the constitutional change, taking it away from the executive secretary. The Executive Committee soon created the Committee on Planning and Organizational Development (CPOD) to move the matter forward. After two years of that group's activity, the militant teachers, in 1969, moved the issue to the floor of the Representative Assembly.[24]

The delegate who introduced the 1969 measure to establish a constitutional convention (Con-Con) to consider the issue of reorganizing the NEA provided a rationale for his initiative that connected the revision to the crises facing the nation's teachers and schools. He also raised the banner of teacher power as the vehicle to use to solve the crisis:

> Mr. President, today . . . when our very existence suffers widespread abuse, our performance is fragmented, thin, inadequate. The present, cumbersome machinery of old respected honor in an exhausted NEA cannot catch the pace, the velocity with which . . . school districts in America are wasting away, which is affecting 75 percent of America's students and 300,000 teachers.
>
> I believe there are teachers on this very floor, thousands across the nation, who have waited for two decades for a select, efficient, effective vehicle to help them negotiate the time to teach, the funds for teaching, the public understanding they need to teach. This is a first, a first and historic, stunning challenge for teachers to vote "aye" now for their commitment to strike an ongoing role in their responsibility for the education of all kids today. Teacher delegates shall in fact, not in speeches or beautiful program notes, be the determiners of their leadership in all education matters.[25]

The floor debate on the Con-Con proposal showed clearly that teacher activists were behind it and that opposition was concentrated among administrators and in the state associations, particularly the more conservative southern state groups. The opponents to the Con-Con argued effectively that its cost was unknown, and therefore, that approving it represented signing a kind of blank check to be cashed by the developers of the proposal. The vote on the issue in 1969 was a victory for the opposition. The matter was referred to the board of directors, a body still responsive to the state associations since its members were chosen through a state election process. The directors made a recommendation to the next Representative Assembly in 1970 that basically temporized on the issue of a Con-Con.[26]

At that same convention, however, the president of the NEA, George Fischer, made a militant speech endorsing a longer term for the president than the then current one year in office. This longer term would allow continuity in the top elected office of the NEA and enable the president to assume more significant duties, including some that had been the property of the executive secretary. This provision was subsequently approved a few years later as part of an eventually successful Con-Con initiative. Also in 1970 a candidate for the NEA Executive Committee from the militant NCUEA made the passage of the Con-Con part of his campaign platform. Despite this support, more lengthy debate occurred, and the resulting committee to plan the Con-Con was constituted to represent both the interests of activist teachers intent on change and those of the opponents of change.[27]

One year later, at the 1971 Representative Assembly, the struggle over the Con-Con continued, with teacher militants seeking to alter the direction of the temporizing trends of a year earlier and move toward the goal of making the NEA a representative organization of classroom teachers only. It would take one more year, however, for the teacher militants to achieve their objective. Finally, in 1972, a Con-Con proposal was passed that began the revision process and pursued it to a culmination that responded to the teachers who composed a majority of the delegates chosen to conduct the deliberations.[28]

Opposition to the Con-Con was energized at the 1972 Representative Assembly when Executive Secretary Lambert spoke against it in his annual address to the group. In his remarks Lambert regretted the 1968 Florida teacher walkout, charging that since the NEA had made a loan of $2 million to its Florida affiliate that had yet to be repaid, the national association was in serious financial trouble. Lambert linked the expensive militancy in Florida with the attempts at merger with the AFT, another initiative that he opposed passionately. He saw these unhappy events as directly related to the proposed constitutional revision, arguing that it would emasculate the state teacher organizations and lead the NEA down the road to teacher unionism. He stated his unalterable opposition to the entire process. A subsequent address to the delegates by the elected president of the NEA opposed Lambert on almost every particular. NEA convention delegates also heard a speech by Jerry Wurf, president of the AFSCME, a labor body that the NEA would shortly join in creating the Coalition of American Public Employees.[29]

The Con-Con was clearly the decisive formal step in the evolution of the NEA into a teachers' union. When the new constitution it produced was formally adopted in 1973, it prescribed a substantial reduction in the number of policy-making bodies in the NEA and an increase in presidential power at the expense of the power of the executive secretary. The president was elected to a two-year term, instead of the previous one year, and was to be the major spokesperson for the NEA. In the midst of the final battle over the passage of the Con-Con, Sam Lambert resigned as executive secretary of the association. His successors would never wield the power within the NEA that he and his predecessors had enjoyed. Teacher militancy had finally won the battle with the NEA staff bureaucracy and the state associations for control of the association.

THE NEA AND POLITICAL ACTION

The creation of a national Political Action Committee for the NEA and its teachers in 1972 was another significant outcome of the teacher militancy movement within the association in the 1960s. The movement that culminated in the creation of the Political Action Committee began in 1957 when the Representative Assembly passed a resolution on the "Teacher As a Citizen." The resolution sought to institutionalize the possibility that "every teacher may become an active participant in government and an active voter at the polls." On its face, the resolution seemed relatively noncontroversial, asking mainly that teachers behave in the same way that the most conscientious ordinary citizens acted. Its absence from the NEA agenda in prior years, however, indicated that the association was altering a situation in the past of a lack of official interest in political activism by its teacher members.[30]

The teacher-as-citizen resolution remained unchanged among the official NEA resolutions passed or reaffirmed for the next decade or so, as it took a back seat to the turmoil developing over collective bargaining, strikes, and other aspects of teacher militancy. In 1968, however, in the aftermath of the Florida teacher walkout and as a culmination of diverse attempts both nationally and locally to involve teachers more actively in politics, the NEA began development of a Teachers in Politics (TIP) program. This effort was accompanied by a flurry of related political activity, mainly weekend workshops on the political process, in forty-five states. As a culmination of these activities, a recommendation was presented to the NEA Board of Directors that a national political advocacy group be created.[31]

This action represented a substantially new direction for the NEA in at least two respects. Although the association and its affiliates had long practiced the art of political lobbying, that activity usually took the political composition of the legislative and executive political bodies as a given rather than as an arena for association influence. A political advocacy group meant more direct involvement in the entire political process, not just an attempt to pass or prevent legislation but also an effort to influence the election of those who made and executed the laws. Establishing a political advocacy body at the national level, in turn, threatened the state associations, especially those with a substantially more conservative political leaning than the NEA. The problem for the states was that militant teachers in their association might act in response to national directives or desires rather than conform to the often more cautious state association guidelines.

These and other fears were rampant among the board of directors, a large body whose members were chosen by the state associations. In 1969 the board of directors failed to approve a task force report recommending the creation of a national political action group. A minority on the board of directors, mainly those from the states where teacher activism was on the rise, spoke out against the majority's action. The minority directors also had support from the NEA president and a substantial number of delegates to the 1970 Representative Assembly. The president and minority directors offered a resolution that again came up before the full board of directors advocating creation of the national group. If the board refused to pass the resolution, it could and surely would be introduced at the Representative Assembly meeting by one of the minority directors acting, in conformity with NEA rules, as an individual. If the resolution were to be approved by the Representative Assembly, then the national political action body would be established. Evidently, the conservatives on the board of directors were convinced that if they voted no on the political action group, then the Representative Assembly would override their vote. Instead of this action, then, the board passed a compromise resolution continuing for another year the task force that had recommended creating the political advocacy group and mandating a pilot program of political action in one state during the year.[32]

Members of the board of directors and state association executives were not the only ones who feared a national political action movement in the NEA. A Washington staff member whose bailiwick was political action enumerated a number of other groups that were opposed to national political action: "traditional teachers, school administrators, school boards, state legislators, some office holders at every level, and provincial localities (primarily in the southern states)." All of these groups echoed the ideology behind the opposition to collective bargaining within the NEA and charged that, like collective bargaining, political activity was unprofessional and, therefore, inappropriate for teachers.[33] The same staff member quoted above, a relatively recent addition to the NEA's Washington office, identified the supporters of NEA political action as "militant teachers, public employee groups, liberal politicians, and labor unions."[34] The campaign for the national Political Action Committee within the NEA was clearly part of the same battle that was being waged within the association over teacher militancy, collective bargaining, and trade union tactics. Both of these disputes represented complementary aspects of the alteration of the association's leadership, ideology, and programs in this period. The NEA presidents in the early 1970s provided much of the leadership for the adoption of the national Political Action Committee. To achieve this result, they had to marshal the power of the large number of teachers who wanted to change things in the association and overcome the opposition of conservative elements in the state associations as well as in the national organization. Another aspect of the situation that made passage of the national political action body difficult was that in some of the more liberal state associations, existing political action committees feared competition for influence over their teachers from a national political action group that might have a different agenda.

Supporters of political advocacy at the national level sought to neutralize much of the state opposition by holding regional meetings on the topic of political action throughout the country. In tandem with these meetings, most of the NEA's elected officers, by now stalwarts in the campaign, proved able to maneuver the creation of the national political advocacy group through the cumbersome process of Representative Assembly approval in 1971 and 1972.[35]

Even as it was created, however, the National Education Association Political Action Committee (NEAPAC) was structured for restrained action, an indication that the victory was far from complete. Control over the NEAPAC and its activities was lodged in a group of individuals chosen through a process controlled by the state associations. State associations also put other obstacles in the road to the accomplishment of national political action. An important problem facing the NEAPAC was how to raise funds for its activities. The states sought to limit, if not to prevent, meaningful funding. By 1973, however, the financial backing for the NEAPAC was secured by the Representative Assembly, which approved a policy that authorized the solicitation of one dollar from every NEA member and also contained a provision that made sure that the states had to implement the policy.[36]

The early accomplishments of the NEAPAC were substantial. Created in June 1972, it quickly prepared for the fall congressional elections in that year. The committee decided not to endorse a presidential candidate in the 1972 election, even though NEA officers and activists clearly favored the Democratic candidate, George McGovern, over the incumbent president, Richard Nixon. The NEA leaders did not believe that McGovern could win the election and, thus, did not wish to risk alienating the winner with their endorsement of his opponent. In the congressional elections of 1972, however, the NEAPAC actively supported 184 candidates for office. Of the 165 NEA-endorsed candidates for the House of Representatives, 128 were elected; thirteen of the nineteen NEA-backed senatorial candidates were winners. In the 1972 election the NEAPAC spent a total of $30,000, and more than 25,000 NEA members worked actively in congressional campaigns. All this activity constituted a substantial positive outcome for the political action effort in its first year, and the NEA leadership made sure that all members were apprised of the outcome.[37]

The results of the 1974 congressional elections and of the 1976 congressional and presidential contests were even more impressive. In 1974 the NEA made more endorsements than it had in 1972 and was just as successful in picking winners as it had been the first time. In 1976 the NEA and its NEAPAC received substantial media attention for their support of the successful campaign of the Democratic presidential candidate, Jimmy Carter. The support was openly and appreciatively acknowledged by Carter and was a significant factor in the former Georgia governor's creation of a U.S. Department of Education in 1979, the fulfillment of an NEA objective that had been advocated continuously since 1917.[38]

Thus, the NEA's political action effort represented a change at the national level of organizational activity as significant as unionization was for many NEA locals. There was a negative impact, however, from both of these changes on many state associations and on many NEA staff members.

CHANGES IN THE RELATIONS OF LOCAL AND STATE ASSOCIATIONS

As discussed earlier in this chapter, the militant teacher movement in the NEA had originated in the local associations, particularly those in urban areas. The state associations, also as discussed earlier, were the sources for much of the opposition to the rising teacher power movement. This is not to say that all state associations sought to block change; those state associations with large numbers of activists among their members tended eventually to adopt the activist point of view, as illustrated by the actions of the Florida Education Association in its 1968 statewide strike. What must be understood, however, is that any organization at the state level had a different set of priorities and a different agenda than a local-level association. A state association was largely a lobbying entity that sought to influence state educational legislation and the administration by the executive branch of the results of that legislation. The state association had no role in local collective bargaining, except in trying to bring about state legislation that enabled the activity and in encouraging its improvement. The state associations were largely isolated from the collective bargaining process itself, which took place strictly between the local association and the local board of education.

Thus, in a very real sense, the changes described in this chapter represented a shift in power within the NEA from the state-level associations and down to the locals (as well as up to the national). The reality of this shift was illustrated in the course of the unification movement in this era. Unification, as already discussed, was a long-sought objective of the NEA. In this period its enforcement meant that individuals could no longer belong only to their state association without belonging to a local or to the NEA. Before this mandate, even delegates to the Representative Assembly did not have to be NEA members. Rather, the requirement for participation in the assembly was that delegates be members in good standing of the state association that elected them to represent the state at the national meeting. Unification, in the eyes of the militant reformers who saw the states as a major obstacle to change, cured this abuse.[39]

A structural alteration of staffing at the NEA headquarters also indicated that the local and national levels of the association were the places where the action would be taken in the 1970s. In 1970 the Representative Assembly engaged in a lengthy discussion of a proposed staffing program, the United Staff Service Program, known more popularly as the UniServ program. In describing UniServ, the NEA president noted that it was "a program of service to local teachers and their local associations— a program to serve teachers at the local level, where decisions vital to teachers are made." Help in several areas associated with the formal negotiations process was foremost among the needs of local associations. The areas of need ranged

> from the painstaking research that must precede successful performance at the negotiating table to the subtleties of behavior at the table to the public relations programs that must support the negotiating team. School boards and administrators increasingly use public moneys—the taxpayers' dollars—to hire professional negotiators to work against teachers. UniServ will place a trained and skilled negotiator on the other side of the table, facing down the board's hired gun and working with expertise for teachers.[40]

Negotiations, however, were not to be the only responsibility of a UniServ staff member. In addition, "UniServ representatives will be responsible for administering the whole range of policies and programs established by the local association." In terms of their employer, UniServ staff would be responsive to local, state, and national associations, but the NEA president made it clear that "the purpose of UniServ is to build strong local associations" and that "the typical representative will be accountable to the local association, not the state or national NEA."[41] This statement was a clear indication that, after 1970, the local association was truly a priority of the NEA.

The association also spoke with its purse regarding the UniServ program, providing that UniServ staff be paid in part by a grant from the national level. The state was not omitted entirely in the UniServ program, though its role was less important than that of either the local or the national. While UniServ staff were local employees, paid by the local with financial support from the NEA, "the state groups will have primary responsibility for the professional guidance, supervision, and evaluation of UniServ representatives," according to the NEA's president. Even in this area, however, the most important function, the training of staff, was performed by the national association, not the states: "the NEA will be concerned especially with the UniServ man's training."[42]

State association interests, including the official organization of state NEA affiliates (the National Council for State Education Associations) and the associations in southern and other states where collective bargaining was illegal and unlikely to become legal, balked at the UniServ plan. The state associations wanted any national funding apportioned not to the local associations but to the states on the basis of membership in the state associations. A graphic illustration of the opposition between the interests of state associations and those of urban activists in their locals came in the discussion of UniServ at the 1970 NEA convention. Delegates learned that although the Tennessee Education Association opposed the UniServ plan to fund locals, the Metropolitan Education Association (MEA), the local group in Tennessee's capital city of Nashville, dissented from the decision of the other Tennesseeans and supported the UniServ proposal. The MEA had already begun to employ its own staff to support Nashville's teachers, and UniServ promised national funds to aid in the effort.[43]

UniServ, then, institutionalized a direct and largely unmediated relationship between the NEA and its active local associations. These two levels of organization emerged strengthened as a result of all of the structural alterations of the NEA in the 1960s and early 1970s. The militant teachers who animated the activist locals were the major force behind the changes and the major beneficiaries of those efforts. Losers in influence during this era were the state associations and the appointed NEA staff members. School administrators had exercised influence both in the state associations and over the NEA staff. The administrators' own subunit of the NEA, the American Association of School Administrators (formerly the Department of Superintendence), reacted to the teacher militancy that was taking over the NEA by first weakening and then severing its ties with the parent association. Several other of the many NEA-affiliated departments also followed suit in the early 1970s.[44] With the passage of the Con-Con in 1972, there was no room left in the NEA for any subgroup that did not speak directly to the occupational interests of classroom teachers.

Like his predecessors, William Carr had developed and maintained close ties to the leading administrators in America's public school systems and had made the NEA a voice for the established educational leadership of the nation. Sam Lambert, though he courted the teacher militants for a brief time, did not loosen the ties with school administrators drastically. After Lambert, however, the NEA staff's role and orientation changed substantially. With the constitutional change of 1973, the staff, including the executive secretary, was made clearly subservient to the elected leadership. That leadership and its staff employees were there to serve teachers who were asserting their own occupational interests. These interests were often, though not always, opposed to the interests of school administrators.

The state associations, like the NEA prior to the Con-Con, were closely associated with the school administrators of their states. Teacher militancy, however, meant that the teachers were developing ways of representing their own interests in their states, rather than following the lead of their local administrators or those who staffed the various state departments of education. Still controlled by these two groups of administrators, the state associations often acted to block, delay, or dilute the various changes proposed by teacher militants for the NEA. By and large, however, their efforts were unsuccessful. The teacher-activist NEA, created in the 1960s and early 1970s, was much less responsive to the interests of the state associations than it had been at any time since its reorganization in 1917.

MILITANCY AND THE NEA STAFF

As the NEA remade itself organizationally in the 1960s and early 1970s, the Washington headquarters staff, including many of its most senior members with decades of experience, responded ambivalently, at best, to the situation. The response was often a cosmetic alteration of activities to appease advocates of change rather than a substantive attempt to deal with the situation. Of course the staff could do little that was not sanctioned by its leader, the executive secretary, who, as we have seen, was an obstacle for the organizational militants to overcome throughout the period. The actions of the executive secretary and the similar actions of the staff eventually left staff members in a position of poor relations with the teacher activists who were remaking the association. The course taken within the Research Division during these years serves as a case study of the forces and factors behind the staff lethargy that was characteristic of the operation of almost the entire NEA headquarters.

One of the oldest and most prestigious of the NEA's staff groups, the Research Division had enjoyed high status within the NEA central office since its inception in 1922. Part of that status was due to the quasi-academic work it undertook for the NEA, and another part was due to its close association with the Department of Superintendence in the 1920s, 1930s, and 1940s. Research Division staffers were treated with respect throughout the NEA headquarters, and directors of the Research Division were often on a fast track to the top spot in the NEA staff hierarchy. William Carr and Sam Lambert, the two executive secretaries of the NEA in the period from 1960 to 1973, had both risen to their leadership position from service as director of the Research Division. Carr's implacable opposition to the teacher militants and Lambert's initially conciliatory position and eventual conflict with them, characterized the range of reactions within the Research Division and much of the rest of the NEA staff in these years.

Sam Lambert became director of the Research Division in the late 1950s. Less than a year after taking this position, he undertook a redesign of the division's flagship publication, the *NEA Research Bulletin*. This was an unprecedented development, since the *Bulletin* had remained largely unchanged in format from the time of its initial publication in 1922. In the period since the first issue, five and later four issues of the publication appeared in each calendar year, with each issue devoted to an elaborate presentation of a single large-scale study, most often on topics such as salaries, retirement, or some other aspect of teacher welfare.

In 1958, however, Lambert changed the *Research Bulletin* dramatically. The foreword to the initial issue of that year was written by Lambert's predecessor, Frank Hubbard, who had assumed a position in Executive Secretary William Carr's cabinet. Hubbard described the rationale for the new format, which substituted several shorter articles often devoid of technical apparatus for the long articles replete with elaborate technical appendixes and tables that had been the pattern. Lambert believed that information needed to be provided much more rapidly in the middle of the twentieth century, in order to be of use to decision makers and teachers intent on improving their working conditions. If this approach meant the sacrifice of technical details in presentation, for Lambert it was a loss that was worth the cost. Providing simplified information to a more general audience, then, was the task of the new *Research Bulletin*.[45]

In his own account of his entire NEA career, Lambert stated that the change in the *Research Bulletin* was one of several ideas he had when he became director of the Research Division that sought to "jazz up" its products and thus to make its work available to a broader audience than had previously been the case. This, in turn, allowed the publication to serve as a recruitment vehicle for the NEA in its never-ending search for new members and their dues payments. Lambert had some experience in newspaper work, and it was this background that prompted him to attempt to popularize the work of the NEA Research Division.[46] It was also one visible way that the NEA could be seen as responding to challenges from the urban teacher militants to become more responsive to their concerns.

Changing the image of the *Research Bulletin,* however, was more a cosmetic than a substantive alteration. The longer, more technical studies of the Research Division that had occupied the pages of the *Bulletin* now appeared in a series of *Research Reports.* These documents were mirror images of the previous issues of the *Research Bulletin.* The *Reports* were substantial efforts devoted to topics familiar to longtime readers of the *Bulletin,* as typified in the first issue of the 1959 year entitled "Analysis of Salary Schedules, 1957–58."[47] Thus, Lambert's popularization of the work of the division was accomplished without sacrifice of the earlier focus on comprehensive studies.

Lambert also initiated a regular procedure of polling teachers on a variety of issues that resulted in a continuing database of teacher opinions that could be used by NEA for a variety of purposes. According to Lambert, staff could use the polls to check for the relationship between the policies and procedures adopted by the NEA Representative Assembly and the views of those policies by the larger teaching force. He added that, by and large, the Representative Assembly acted in conformity with the wishes of the membership, at least as they were measured by the opinion poll. He also noted that teachers in their political and occupational orientations were more conservative than might have been believed in the era of teacher militancy.[48] He did not discuss the relationship between this conservatism and the views of the NEA staff leadership, including himself and William Carr, or between it and the views of the militant teachers in the urban caucus of the NEA who were intent on remaking the organization.

The procedures undergirding the teacher opinion poll and the models for its development were described in a one-page article in the *NEA Journal.* Justified in the first place as an attempt to validate new sampling techniques, the teacher opinion poll was also important substantively "because teachers have valuable opinions on current educational issues and . . . it is possible to sample and report these opinions with speed and accuracy." The goal was to "provide the teaching profession with surveys similar to the well-known Gallup and Roper polls of public opinion."[49]

One of the important ways that these data were used was in the development of a long-standing column in the *NEA Journal* that simply printed the results of one or another part of a given poll. This feature ran in the *Journal* from the early 1960s through the 1970s. The teacher opinion poll was one of the few aspects of the Research Division's activities that survived the NEA staff shake-up of 1972–73, which followed almost immediately the passage of the teacher militants' constitutional alteration of the association. The longevity of the teacher poll indicated that teachers, and especially militant teachers, enjoyed seeing how they and their colleagues viewed issues such as teacher strikes that were then animating the occupation and were the subjects of numerous reports in the poll.[50]

Hazel Davis, a longtime Research Division staff member discussed in previous chapters, continued her service in the division during Lambert's years as director in the 1960s. In those years she enthusiastically pursued the same avenues of activity that she had traveled during her previous years in the division. She continued her studies of salaries, salary scales, and related areas of what she called teacher personnel issues. The one area in which she thought that she had accomplished something novel, the study of the status of school teachers, began in 1956 in an issue of the *Research Bulletin* published before Lambert changed its format.[51] This study built on Davis's earlier work on teachers' salaries and allied issues, adding to it consideration of other teacher characteristics to produce a broader profile of the occupation. The results, however, still emphasized the issues and the approach that Davis had long been pursuing, an emphasis that would fall out of favor in the eyes of the new urban militants. Davis's concern for topics such as comparing the salaries of married teachers and single teachers, or of women teachers and men teachers, was not a priority for those who sought to install a new order in the NEA.

In discussing her long tenure in the Research Division, Davis remarked that the division in the 1920s had not been set up to work with teachers in their classrooms. She characterized the work in the division as follows: "We were concerned with the status of the teaching profession." As examples of this concern, she cited work on the legal status of teachers, her own work on teachers' minimum salary laws, analyses of teachers' retirement provisions, and studies of social security. She saw the Research Division's main focus as being on economic issues and employment conditions, including tenure and rating scales.[52]

Tension or conflict between teachers and administrators had never been a matter of concern for Davis. Having never worked as a teacher, and having come to the NEA after a brief period as a secretary to the superintendent of schools in the District of Columbia, she saw little if any reason to expect conflict between these two groups. For her, information useful to teachers was useful to administrators as they fought for improvements in teachers' pay and working conditions. It never occurred to her to see teachers and administrators as even potential enemies. It did, however, occur to others, particularly to the urban teacher activists in the NEA in the 1960s.

The Research Division was not completely bereft of contacts with those who were intent on reshaping the NEA. Two of the subjects that had been and still were occupying some of the attention of the association's research staff were related to the slowly growing militancy. One was the already discussed effort to study and aid the locals of the NEA, beginning in the late 1930s and continuing in the next two decades; the other was the work with state associations, a few of which were responding to the advocates for change. These were two sectors of the NEA's sprawling organizational apparatus, along with the Representative Assembly, where the teacher militants were seeking to have a direct impact.

Hazel Davis continued to spearhead the Research Division's participation in the local association arena in the early 1960s, as she had done in the previous decades. Because of her expertise in studying local associations, Davis was one of the NEA staff members sent to New York City to work in the campaign against the AFT for the right to determine who would represent the city's teachers in negotiations with the school board. Davis's evaluation of the New York representation campaign and election, the event that constituted the NEA's most significant loss to the AFT in this period, was enlightening both for its analysis of the situation and for what it revealed about herself and other staff members called on to participate. She reported that the union resorted to misinformation on countless occasions and that her own efforts and those of other members of the NEA staff were too frequently concentrated on correcting that misinformation.[53] While Davis's charge was, no doubt, largely accurate, the decision by the NEA to concentrate on countering the union's claims with what the association judged to be the "facts" of the matter, one endorsed by Davis and her colleagues, both illustrated a historical commitment of the association to this principle and betrayed a stunning naïveté in organizational combat. Thus, the union was allowed to maintain the initiative in the situation and, thereby, to control the agenda of both groups. It should not have surprised anyone, then, that the NEA lost the New York City election and most other big city representation elections in the 1960s.

Davis and her colleagues acted professionally, perhaps morally, but also as political innocents. These actions stood in stark contrast to those of the AFT staff assigned to the New York representation election. In his memoir about his years in the AFT, David Selden, who eventually rose to the union's presidency, reports that his organization had a relationship with the custodian of the building in which the NEA maintained its headquarters during the period of the New York representation campaign and election. The reports to the union from its "mole" in the opposition camp, who daily read the copies of documents of the NEA staff left on desks or put into the trash, enabled the AFT to learn the details of association strategy and tactics as they evolved and to prepare specific responses to association actions almost instantaneously.[54]

Hazel Davis's experiences in New York were echoed in the participation of another Research Division staff member, Simeon Taylor, in the state of Florida during the 1968 teacher walkout there. Taylor was the member of the Research Division whose primary responsibility was to work with the state associations in developing their research efforts. He was sent to Florida as part of the NEA's contingent to aid the Florida Education Association as it conducted its statewide job action. Taylor's particular responsibility was to monitor the situation in two of Florida's sixty-eight county school systems where the boards of education were trying to prevent teachers who had walked out of their classrooms, and then returned, from being reemployed. In addition, he collected a variety of information on the efforts of Florida's business and governmental power structure to break the teacher walkout. Taylor documented numerous examples of people of inferior or no qualifications being hired to replace teachers who had left their classrooms and of businesses and businessmen intimidating teachers with threats of various kinds, including dismissal of their spouses employed in business, if they did not return to their classrooms.[55]

Taylor's reports and their accounts of the situation reveal at least two things. First, they show the genuine affinity he developed for the teachers who had walked out and then came face-to-face with the chilling result they faced as a consequence of this action. Second, his preparation of numerous reports and their formal acceptance and filing by the director of the Research Division testify to the tendency of staff to believe again in the "facts" as an ultimate arbiter in controversial situations. Until these reports were unearthed as part of the research effort for this study, however, they lay dormant and unexamined in the NEA archives, long after the fate of the Florida teachers had been decided, in many cases with the loss of their jobs. The reality was, and still is, that in teachers' organizational conflicts, either with other teacher groups or with boards of education, the game is such that the facts often take a back seat to strategy and tactics that can be used to manipulate a situation and leave the actual facts simply as one element in a much larger context.

As the urban militants moved into the NEA spotlight in the late 1960s, change was in the air at the Research Division, as it was in other divisions in the NEA headquarters and in the state associations. A letter from Sim Taylor to the Research Division staff in December 1971 discussed the new situation as it was unfolding. He noted that the meaning of the developments in the locals for the state and national research efforts was at least twofold. First, there was a need for much more coordination among all levels of the planning and conduct of research. For the Research Division, this meant clearing all questionnaires and other research materials with state research officers as soon as, if not before, they were sent to local associations. Also, similar designs and data collection procedures needed to be considered for research at all levels to help streamline the entire research effort. Second, and most important as a harbinger of the future for the Research Division, a needed outcome was thorough study and recommended procedures on "how research at the local, state, and national level can better meet the changing needs of the unified teaching profession."[56]

In her one year as director of the Research Division, 1966, Hazel Davis undertook a step that constituted a substantial attempt to respond to the urban militant teachers. She hired Donald Walker, who had a background in labor relations in the trucking industry, to work for the NEA. Walker's initial title was research assistant, a designation that did not differentiate his work in any way from that of others in the Research Division, most of whom possessed a doctoral degree, which he lacked. Soon, however, Walker was given a responsibility that was unprecedented in the history of the Research Division. In April 1967 Davis's successor as director of the Research Division announced a new divisional publication, the *Negotiations Research Digest*. This publication was the responsibility of a new unit in the Research Division, the Negotiations Research Unit, which was to be directed on a full-time basis by Donald Walker.[57]

In a circular describing the new unit, its responsibilities were enumerated as the storing, analyzing, and reporting of material relative to professional negotiations over the conditions of teachers. The output of the unit appeared in the Research Division's existing series of *Research Reports,* as well as in the new monthly publication, the *Negotiations Research Digest.* The purpose of this publication was to "provide maximum utility and reference" to "leaders of the teaching profession, to school officials, and to interested laymen."[58] Thus, the Research Division attempted to respond to the new circumstances of militant teachers with a new product devoted to a new topic but using a tried-and-true NEA approach: a publication for a wide-ranging readership that would provide the "facts" relevant to the situation.

The initial issue of the *Negotiations Research Digest,* dated April 1967, reported that the first major study by the new unit had begun in December 1966. It was "a comprehensive national survey of staff–school board negotiation in public education" based on a questionnaire mailed to superintendents in more than seven thousand school systems that enrolled one thousand or more pupils. In addition to the questionnaire results, the survey requested copies of the agreements negotiated with employee groups in the school systems. These agreements were collected and coded "for speedy search and summary by the Research Division's electronic computer." The unit's efforts were characterized as being geared to "reporting objectively and comprehensively all significant data, trends, and developments concerning professional negotiation, collective bargaining, and similar types of group action procedures relating to members of the teaching profession." The *Digest* was divided into sections reporting respectively on the description and analysis of agreements, judicial decisions and opinions relative to the agreements, the text of the agreements themselves, and special items.[59]

The development of the new unit and the new publication constituted a relatively successful effort by the Research Division to react to the challenge presented by the priorities of the NEA's militant teachers. The *Digest* was one of the few Research Division publications to survive intact after the NEA changed its internal governance and structure through the new constitution of 1973. This survival was a concrete sign that the *Digest* and the Negotiations Research Unit were indeed responsive to the new wave.[60] Yet the new unit also betrayed the limits of the traditional approach of the NEA and its Research Division in at least two ways. First, the *Digest* continued the long-running tendency of the Research Division to see publication as a form of, if not a substitute for, action. Second, the NEA continued to rely on superintendents as the conduit for information it needed on agreements, a reliance that betrayed the association's continuing dependence on school administrators, even as it moved to enhance its efforts to serve teachers who were becoming the formal adversaries of superintendents in the negotiations process.

The NEA's resorting to a publication in the effort to gain support from teachers in a war with another occupational organization seems naive, at least when viewed retrospectively. NEA leaders like Sam Lambert loved to point out that one of the major groups of subscribers to their own negotiations research service were AFT locals, which paid fifteen dollars for their subscription and thereby benefited considerably from the efforts of the NEA Research Division. The irony of the situation went unnoticed, however. The NEA leadership did not grasp the point that open subscription, the traditional device of the Research Division and the NEA, might be a liability in an occupational war in that the opposition was provided the same information as NEA affiliates who were competing with the opposition.

In a very real sense, nothing in the history of the Research Division or in the career of Sam Lambert had prepared either the agency or the individual for the kind of struggle that would consume the NEA for the next several years. The publication of the *Negotiations Research Digest* as well as the organizational changes devised by Sam Lambert were certainly sincere efforts in keeping with the tradition of the Research Division to meet the challenge of a new situation. Both Lambert and the division undertook these efforts without fully understanding the process and the priorities to which they were addressed, however.

The process and priorities underlay the concern that teacher activists in the association had with a number of specific aspects of educational research and the work of the NEA Research Division. In spite of this concern, the NCUEA, the body within the NEA in which teacher militancy was incubated, was relatively silent on the topic of the services of the Research Division. The NCUEA's focus was on obtaining adequate field services from the association to prepare for and to conduct local representation elections and negotiations with school boards. This focus entailed working to hire new staff in the field services area rather than criticizing the work of another division in the NEA's headquarters operation.

A few individuals did, however, discuss the Research Division's efforts in ways that revealed teacher suspicions of that enterprise. In 1971, for example, a query was made from the floor of the NEA Representative

Assembly about the studies of the Research Division, particularly those being made in conjunction with state and local associations. The delegate who spoke raised two specific questions: "Is this a new study or the same studies that have been made over the past years?" and "Is there any accountability of the Research Division by the other units requesting the information?" The director of the Research Division responded that "the research studies with the states and locals provide for some new studies as well as continuing studies" and that "there is accountability by the units requesting services."[61] What bothered the questioner and many others in the NEA was their perception that the Research Division did the same things over and over again without really trying to tailor the work to the needs of the group that requested it. The director's rather formulaic answer did little to mollify those who were concerned.

The Executive Committee of the NEA, the governance group that was most influenced by the urban militants, had raised similar issues regarding the work of the Research Division earlier in 1971. The committee asked Executive Secretary Lambert "to prepare a plan for conducting outside surveys on the use of Research Division publications by affiliates and individual members."[62] Although the decision was reached eventually not to go outside for the information, the consideration of such a move spoke loudly to a cloud that was developing in the minds of many NEA activists over the Research Division and its work. The specific concern was that the Research Division's traditional ways of doing business were too dependent on school administrators, too responsive to their agenda, and inattentive to the demands and desires of teachers. The NEA was choosing sides in the battle between teachers and administrators that was being waged in American school districts, and the Research Division was perceived as being on the wrong side of the battle lines.

In March 1972 a series of meetings took place between the Research Division and the Urban Executive Directors' Association (UEDA), a group of paid staff leaders from the increasingly militant urban education associations. From those meetings, a list of suggestions emerged, stated in the form of a series of requests. Among the several items raised by the UEDA, the following were significant in terms of the issue of divisional responsiveness to teachers: "Could they (the UEDA) receive more data concerning strikes?" "Could the Research Division staff be reoriented toward a teacher advocate role and limit distribution [of its materials] to associations—only?" And finally, "Could the Division restrict distribution and use of information regarding negotiation?"[63]

Here was a clear indication of the direction in which the Research Division had to move in the next several years in order to survive in the new NEA. It dispensed largely with its own publications program and remade itself into a service agency for local and state associations. Specific harbingers of these changes also occurred in 1972. The *Research Bulletin,* the flagship serial of the Research Division, which had been published continuously since 1922, expired with the May 1972 issue. One year later the *Research Reports* series also ceased publication. The year 1972, then, marked the end of an era for the Research Division, just as it did for the other operational divisions in the NEA headquarters. The association was fast becoming a teachers' union, indistinguishable in many ways from the AFT. The main difference in the two groups was now narrowed to the issue of the AFT's affiliation with the organized labor federation, the AFL-CIO. The NEA was an independent labor union, one not affiliated with the labor movement but one that resembled other labor unions in many particulars. Yet the NEA also still contained members and affiliates in states, mainly in the South and the West, that had no collective bargaining laws and, realistically, lacked the prospect of passage of such laws. Despite this fact, the NEA as a whole was becoming an organization committed to servicing local affiliates that bargained collectively as their major activity and expected assistance in this endeavor.

GENDER, MILITANCY, AND THE NEA

Why did it take the NEA more than a decade to remodel itself? One answer to this question, discussed in the preceding sections, was the conservative influence of the NEA staff and the administrator-dominated state education associations, particularly those in the South and elsewhere, that did not embrace the new gospel of collective bargaining. Another part of the explanation for the long period of reconstruction, however, deserves extended discussion and analysis; that is the role of gender in the phenomenon of teacher militancy.

There is little doubt that the teacher activism that developed in the early 1960s was largely a phenomenon that originated in the ranks of male high school teachers. In his analysis of the New York situation during the 1950s and 1960s, sociologist Stephen Cole highlighted the grievances that high school males in the city schools harbored after the imposition of equality in income and status between them and women elementary teachers achieved in the 1950s with the single salary scale.

According to Cole, in many respects the strikes and union affiliation of the city's teachers were the actions of men in the high schools and junior high schools who were responding to what they perceived as their own immiseration. The teachers' union appealed directly to high school males when it advocated restoring a salary increment for advanced degrees. The benefits of such a policy would go largely to the high school men who possessed those degrees in much larger proportions than any other group of teachers and not to the elementary women who were least likely to hold advanced degrees.[64] In contrast, the NEA's close identification over a three-decade-long time span with the single salary scale surely did not help in its campaign to keep the high school men out of the AFT in the nation's largest city.

The male-oriented quality of union support and militancy was present in other places besides New York City. In most settings, union membership was strongly related to the level at which a teacher taught—that is, high school teachers constituted the bulk of early union activists. In turn, this aspect of the situation meant that unionism was related to maleness and to devotion to the cause of material betterment. All three of these variables were sufficiently closely related to one another that they were difficult to separate, either in theory or in practice. Several investigations into union affiliation and teachers' willingness to strike also correlated those qualities with gender, with teaching in high schools, and with concern over salary increases.[65] It is not that all men were militant and that no women were militant; rather it is that militancy, defined as a willingness to join a teachers' union and to engage in a teachers' strike, both in support of one's economic improvement, was significantly overrepresented among high school males and underrepresented among elementary school females.

Another study of teachers, this time in the state of Oregon, looked closely into the patterns of identification between men and women teachers and their NEA-affiliated teachers' associations. Males were more likely to distrust their teachers' association while females were, conversely, more trusting of theirs. Economics was not the only factor behind these preferences, however. The dominance of school administrators, both on the job and in the teachers' association, was perceived differently by men and women. These differences in perception pointed to larger concerns in the occupational consciousness of both groups of teachers. Men teachers, who often aspired to administrative status, were prone to see administrators, whom they considered both potential and actual rivals, as a direct threat to their own occupational independence. Women, in contrast, did not see administrators as threatening occupationally and, thus, found little that was problematic in administrators' exercising leadership in the teachers' association. This difference held in both large cities, where the administrators were less likely to dominate an association, and in small towns, where indeed administrators dominated the teacher groups. The actual circumstances of whether administrators dominated the associations were less important than the differing perceptions of men and women about the situation.[66]

The difference in views over the issue of unionization between men and women who were active in the teachers' associations was another topic explored in the Oregon study. Only 3 percent of women activists in the teachers' associations favored unionization, while 33 percent of the men who were active in the associations did so. This was a remarkably large disparity that was likely representative of the perceptions of nonactivist men and women teachers about their lives and work that had a direct impact on their occupational consciousness.[67]

The situation in NEA affiliates in Oregon was similar to that in its local associations in much of the rest of the country. While the NEA's own study of its locals in 1960 did not address the gender of members in the affiliates or their attitude toward unionization, it did identify the preponderance of elementary teachers in its affiliates. This surely signified that women were the majority of NEA members. Further, given the Oregon study, it is likely that the men and women in most affiliates viewed quite differently the dimensions and the consequences of the challenge presented to the NEA from militant unions in large cities.

The NEA leadership had courted women teachers successfully for several decades and, in those decades, as well as in the 1960s, it had subtly appealed to women members as a brake against the mounting challenge of unionism. Since the NEA had revamped itself in the post–World War I years, it had relied on the women teacher members to form a bulwark against the tide of unionism. NEA's support of the single salary, beginning in the 1920s and lasting through its widespread implementation by the 1950s, its cultivation of a cooperative image and amicable relations between teachers and administrators in the schools and within the association, its pursuit of salary increases and other occupational improvement through the use of nonconfrontational "professional" methods, and its identification with small towns and state associations all inspired images of propriety and comity. These orientations clashed with urban-based appeals to militancy and unionism that were all geared to appeal to the interests and beliefs of men teachers.[68]

Analysts of the entire process of change in the NEA in this period are clear in their identification of gender, as represented by the increasing influence of male NEA members in the militant movement, as an important causal factor in explaining the organization's development.[69] The NEA leadership knew that what was happening in the association was significantly related to gender differences in the organization's members and in their activities. In 1962, for example, the NEA Research Division undertook a study of "Angry Young Men in Teaching," the results of which were summarized in a February 1963 article in the *NEA Journal*. A decade later, the Research Division prepared a survey of NEA members and leaders for the Con-Con committee that was planning the organizational reform that responded to the urban militancy in the association. In this survey the affinity of men teachers and high school teachers for an NEA merged with the AFT was noted, as well as the opposition of women teachers and elementary teachers to such an arrangement.[70]

The issue of gender seldom surfaced openly in the NEA in the 1960s, however. Within NEA publications, there was a diminution of the attention given to women and women's roles, in teaching and in the larger society, and the discussions of women that were undertaken were unrelated to their role and future in teaching. The most notable article on women's issues in the NEA's magazine occurred early in the decade, in April 1960. It was a discussion by six experts, three men and three women, of a recent foundation report on women's education. The discussants all advocated more and better education to combat the phenomenon of women ending, interrupting, or delaying their education in order to marry and have children. In several places the contributors endorsed an enlarged role for women as both wives-mothers and as workers. The only attempt to relate the discussion to teaching was in the last few paragraphs, where the decline in the number of women engaged in educational administration was discussed, though somewhat gingerly. The article was geared much more to the interests of a general audience of educated women readers than it was to women teachers interested in coming to terms with a potentially wrenching change in their own occupation.[71]

Near the end of the 1960s gender emerged as a rhetorical weapon in the campaign to remake the association. In 1969 George Fischer, the president of the association, a male, advocated the massive organizational alteration of the NEA that bore fruit four years later, as the way to meet the demands of militant teachers. In his speech he remarked that the teachers of the NEA were "no longer" interested in serving as the "kept women" of the communities in which they worked. He went on to advocate a change in the long-standing (since 1915) NEA custom of alternating a man and a woman in the position of association president: "The time has come for us to stop playing the game of boy-girl, boy-girl presidents." While the policy he advocated was avowedly nonsexist—choosing the best individual for the job, regardless of gender, and allowing that person to serve longer than one year—his language portrayed a symbolic, long-standing commitment of the association to gender equity in choosing its highest officer as a frivolous "game," rather than as a stand for an important principle.[72]

Thus, a subtle but real gender conflict was one of the aspects of the NEA's embrace of teacher militancy in the 1960s. Implicit in the change of the association from one dominated by state associations and oriented toward small towns to one that looked to big city militants for leadership and direction was a denigration of the orientations and preferences of many of its women teacher members. In contrast to this decrease in the NEA's attention to and recognition of women teachers, the association as it was unionizing in the 1960s and early 1970s began to pay substantial attention to its black teachers.

NOTES

[1]Wesley, *NEA,* 379–80.

[2]On New York and the UFT, see Stephen Cole, *The Unionization of Teachers* (New York: Praeger, 1969); Philip Taft, *United They Teach: The Story of the United Federation of Teachers* (Los Angeles: Nash Publishing, 1974); and David Selden, *The Teacher Rebellion* (Washington, DC: Howard University Press, 1984).

[3]Murphy, *Blackboard Unions,* 277.

[4]"Local Associations—Organization, Practices, and Programs, 1958–59," Microfiche Document no. 430, S60.1, C1, NEA Archives.

[5]For a description and analysis of these groups, see Ronald G. Corwin, *Militant Professionalism: A Study of Organizational Conflict in High Schools* (New York: Appleton-Century-Crafts, 1970).

[6]"Local Associations."

[7]Ibid., 27.

[8]*NEA Proceedings* 97 (1959): 252.

[9]*NEA Journal* 50 (October 1961): 64; and Lieberman, "Teachers' Strikes: An Analysis of the Issues," *Harvard Educational Review* 46 (Winter 1956): 39–70.

[10]*NEA Proceedings* 99 (1961): 156–60, 222–27; and ibid. 100 (1962): 200–21.

[11]Robert W. Bogen, "Organizational Change: Emergence of the Urban Movement in the National Education Association" (Ed.D. diss., George Peabody College for Teachers, 1970). Bogen was a staff officer of the Nashville local of the NEA in the 1960s, and his dissertation functions often as a primary account of the activities of the urban caucus in the association.

[12]*NEA Proceedings* 100 (1962): 51–52.

[13]T. M. Stinnett, Jack H. Kleinman, and Martha L. Ware, eds., *Professional Negotiations in Public Education* (New York: Macmillan, 1968). Stinnett was the NEA assistant executive secretary who was assigned the responsibility for professional negotiation activities. His coedited book, along with another he wrote, *Turmoil in Teaching* (New York: Macmillan, 1968), provides comprehensive summaries of the NEA's position on professional negotiations.

[14]For example, in 1968–69, more than 40 percent of the NEA's membership came from eleven southern and four border states. These members were able to cooperate with like-minded conservatives from the Midwest and West to fight the movements for change at NEA conventions. *Handbook of the National Education Association* (Washington, DC: The Association, 1968–69): 396.

[15]*NEA Proceedings* 104 (1966): 217; also see Bogen, "Urban Movement," 234–35.

[16]*NEA Proceedings* 103 (1965): 180, 417; and ibid. 106 (1968): 529, 526–27. On the Florida strike, see Wayne J. Urban, "Power and Ideology in a Teacher Walkout: Florida, 1968," *Journal of Collective Negotiations in the Public Sector* 3 (Spring 1974): 133–46.

[17]*NEA Proceedings* 104 (1966): 476.

[18]Ibid.: 7–27.

[19]Gabriel Steven Pellathy, "The National Education Association: A Political System in Change" (Ph.D. diss., New York University, 1971): 223–24.

[20]*NEA Proceedings* 106 (1968): 342–46; and Pellathy, "A Political System in Change," 237–38.

[21]*NEA Proceedings* 106 (1968): 18.

[22]Urban, "Power and Ideology in a Teacher Walkout."

[23]On merger, see Selden, *The Teacher Rebellion,* 175–224, and Marshall O. Donley, *Power to the Teacher* (Bloomington: Indiana University Press, 1975): 141–73.

[24]*NEA Proceedings* 102 (1964): 219; ibid. 103 (1965): 305–6; and ibid. 105 (1967): 299–302. For a quick history of the organizational reform, see the remarks by Florida teacher activist Pat Tornillo in *NEA Proceedings* 107 (1969): 105.

[25]*NEA Proceedings* 107 (1969): 100.

[26]Ibid.: 162–73.

[27]Ibid. 108 (1970): 7–17, 47–48, 107–24, 133–64.

²⁸Ibid. 109 (1971): 99–104, 152–53, 419–25, 433–49; and ibid. 110 (1972): 106–11, 138–62, 212–15, 229–331, 396–97, and 673–76.

²⁹Ibid. 110 (1972): 14–23, 7–13, 75–77.

³⁰Ibid. 95 (1957): 192.

³¹*NEA Reporter* 7 (October 25, 1968). This publication was developed as a supplement to the *NEA Journal* in the early 1960s. It was shorter, more headline and publicity oriented, and a major vehicle through which the NEA tried to become more popular with teacher readers, particularly militant teachers. Constance Trishler Shott, "The Origin and Development of the National Education Association Political Action Committee, 1969–1976" (Ed.D. diss., Indiana University, 1976), 3.

³²*NEA Proceedings* 108 (1970): 352–55, 373. President George Fischer, in his remarks to the Representative Assembly, contended that the board's action had been taken to prevent the approval of the political action body outright. For Fischer's remarks and their significance, see Shott, "Political Action Committee," 52.

³³Shott, "Political Action Committee," 55.

³⁴Ibid.

³⁵*NEA Proceedings* 109 (1971): 308–10, 384; and ibid. 110 (1972): 277–80.

³⁶Shott, "Political Action Committee," 60.

³⁷"Accomplishments in the 1972 Elections," *Today's Education* 62 (January 1973): 46. The renaming and revamping of the NEA's magazine in this period was part of another attempt to reach more teachers with a simplified, effective message of militancy. See also "Get Ready for a Lot More POW in Teacher Power," *American School Board Journal* 161 (October 1974): 32.

³⁸Shott, "Political Action Committee," 78–84; and David Stephens, "President Carter, the Congress, and NEA: Creating the Department of Education," *Political Science Quarterly* 98 (Winter 1983–84): 641–43.

³⁹*NEA Proceedings* 104 (1966): 217–21.

⁴⁰Ibid. 108 (1970): 214.

⁴¹Ibid.

⁴²Ibid. The implicit gender bias in the use of the term *man* at the NEA convention will be discussed in the final section of this chapter.

⁴³Ibid., 216–17.

⁴⁴Pellathy, "A Political System in Change," 149–64.

⁴⁵Frank W. Hubbard, "The Need for Inquiry," *Research Bulletin* 36 (February 1958): 3–4.

⁴⁶Sam Lambert interview (February 20, 1987), typescript, NEA Archives, box 3117. Unless otherwise mentioned, all citations for Lambert are to this interview.

⁴⁷Copies of this and other issues of the *Research Reports* are in boxes 764 and 765 of the NEA Archives.

⁴⁸Lambert interview (February 20, 1987).

[49]Glen Robinson and Chester H. McCall, Jr., "What Do Teachers Think?" *NEA Journal* 49 (April 1960): 31. Robinson at that time was assistant director of the Research Division. Later he became director when Sam Lambert was promoted to the position of executive secretary of NEA.

[50]For one example, see "Teacher Opinion Poll: Should Teachers Strike?" *NEA Journal* 57 (September 1968): 85–86. This particular report was longer than the usual half page or less given to results of teacher opinion polls in the *Journal.*

[51]"The Status of the American Public School Teacher," *Research Bulletin* 34 (February 1956). The theme of this publication was followed a few years later in "The American Public School Teacher, 1960–61," a *Research Monograph 1963-M2,* which was coauthored by Hazel Davis and another Research Division staff member. This publication is Microfiche Document no. 430 S63, c 1, NEA Archives.

[52]Hazel Davis interview (June 17, 1988), NEA Archives, box 3117.

[53]Ibid.

[54]Selden, *Teacher Rebellion,* 56–58.

[55]Sim Taylor to Glen Robinson (February 21, 1968), NEA Archives, box 1201. This box is full of various incident reports filed by Taylor about conditions in Florida during and immediately after the walkout.

[56]Sim Taylor to Professional Staff (December 6, 1971); and Taylor to Research Division Staff (January 26, 1972), both in NEA Archives, box 713. The quotation is from the second memo.

[57]"To Selected Leaders in Education" (April 1967), NEA Archives, box 797.

[58]"Negotiations Research Unit Established" (n.d. [April 1967]), NEA Archives, box 797.

[59]*Negotiations Research Digest,* no. 1 (April 1967): A-1, A-2.

[60]In fact, the *Digest* would continue publication through 1976. A complete run of its issues can be found in the NEA Archives, boxes 797 and 798.

[61]*NEA Proceedings* 109 (1971): 496.

[62]Ibid., 617.

[63]"Memorandum," Sim Taylor to Research Division Staff (April 18, 1972), NEA Archives, box 713.

[64]Cole, *The Unionization of Teachers,* 31–40, 54–63.

[65]Ronald G. Corwin, *Education in Crisis: A Sociological Analysis of Schools and Universities in Transition* (New York: John Wiley, 1974): 235. Also see William T. Lowe, "Who Joins Which Teacher Groups?" *Teachers College Record* (April 1965): 614–19.

[66]Harmon Zeigler, *The Political Life of American Teachers* (Englewood Cliffs, NJ: Prentice-Hall, 1967), 55–91.

[67]Ibid., 90.

[68]Ibid., notes the effectiveness of NEA antiunionism in Oregon.

[69]Pellathy, "A Political System in Change," 27.

[70]Sam Lambert, "Angry Young Men in Teaching," *NEA Journal* 52 (February 1963): 17–20; and "Survey of NEA Members and Leaders: Future Association Development," prepared by the NEA Research Division for Committee on Planning and Organizational Development (February 1972), NEA Archives, box 1465.

[71]"Education and the Role of Women: A Symposium," *NEA Journal* 49 (December 1960): 48–53.

[72]*NEA Proceedings* 107 (1969): 14, 15.

CHAPTER 6

Desegregating the National Education Association, 1954–78

In addition to the turmoil that characterized the NEA's dispute over unionism in the 1960s, there were other matters of conflict that occupied the association during that decade. The rise of a student movement on college and university campuses and the connection between this movement and the opposition to the Vietnam War resulted in a controversy that sometimes reached below the college and universities and down into the nation's K–12 schools. The NEA's conventions reflected this turmoil at times—for example, on several occasions when they considered motions against the war in Vietnam. Added controversy accompanied a motion to give power within the organization to the increasingly visible student movement then developing in the nation's schools and in the NEA, in imitation of the student movement on the nation's college and university campuses.[1] These activities provided one direct and visible link between the rising teacher militancy in the NEA and the political activism that was at large, particularly among various minority groups, in the nation during the 1960s.

The NEA's position on another set of controversial issues, that associated with the race question within the association and also in American society, was at best indirectly linked to the rise of teacher militancy within the association during the 1960s. While teacher militants often took a positive stance on matters of racial equity for black teachers in the NEA, the militants acted in a way that indicated that they saw little direct connection between their fight and that of minority teachers. However, the affinity between teacher militancy inside and outside of the NEA and its psychic and symbolic forerunner, the civil rights movement of the

nation's black minority, was well understood by the urban teacher militants. When black Americans, the most visible oppressed minority in the
nation, moved to redress their grievances through legal actions and then
through direct actions such as sit-ins and political demonstrations, the effect on other oppressed groups, including other ethnic minorities and
even public school teachers, was dramatic.

In public schooling itself, race relations became an overtly controversial issue with the declaration of the *Brown v. Board of Education*
decision by the United States Supreme Court in May 1954, a clear
statement that the days of segregation in public education were num-
bered. The NEA's organizational rival, the AFT, seized the initiative on
the issue of race in 1955 by mandating that all of its locals be desegregated in conformity with *Brown.* This action on desegregation reflected
the AFT's historic liberalism on the issue of race, particularly when compared with the NEA, as well as the more pragmatic reality that the teachers' union had hardly any southern affiliates. The few southern AFT
affiliates were forced from the union in 1956 when they chose not to
comply with the racial desegregation mandate passed by the national organization.[2]

The NEA was far larger than the AFT and far more diverse geo-
graphically. The association contained a substantial number of racially
segregated southern state and local affiliates, and these groups contained
relatively large numbers of members. This fact meant that the NEA had
significantly more to lose from pursuing a desegregationist stance than
did the teachers' union in terms of member allegiance in the South as
well as in other conservative state and local settings where the Supreme
Court's action was not universally admired. Also, the NEA lacked the
AFT's history of relative enlightenment on racial issues. For all of these
reasons, the association temporized on the issue of race after *Brown,* as it
had done on black-white relations through most of the century.

Segregated black teachers' associations existed in all the southern
states and in some border states at the time of *Brown.* Many of these
black associations were represented in the NEA, thereby creating a situation where the association had "dual" affiliates in several states. Southern
politicians stated their intention to close the public schools in response to
any desegregation initiative that came because of *Brown,* a threat that
teachers and their associations in the South had to take seriously. The
political climate created by this "massive resistance" movement threatened any state or local teachers' association in the South that expressed
interest in desegregating the schools, or its own membership, with legal

sanctions as well as, possibly, a violent physical reaction from many southern white citizens emboldened by the actions of their region's political leadership.[3] Thus, the NEA's caution in moving on the racial front at the national level after *Brown* was, in a real sense, a pragmatic response to social reality within the association, especially within its southern affiliates.

But there was more than pragmatism behind the NEA's actions on the race issue. In 1926 the association had entered into a relationship with the American Teachers Association (ATA), the national organization of black teachers, through the establishment of a Joint Committee on Problems in Negro Education and Life. This group's initial efforts were devoted to seeking the same accreditation for black high schools in the South that was available to white high schools. While this objective perpetuated the principle of separate but equal racial provisions enunciated in the 1896 *Plessy v. Ferguson* decision (and subsequently overturned in *Brown*), it was a goal earnestly desired by black teachers and the southern black citizens who sought school improvement within the existing segregated racial arrangements. Partial accomplishment of this accreditation objective, and satisfaction on the part of both the NEA and the ATA with that achievement, led to permanent status for the joint committee of the two organizations within a year of its founding.[4]

Participation in the joint committee constituted practically the entirety of NEA efforts to establish relations with black teachers and their associations until the 1960s. As noted in earlier chapters, the NEA was conspicuously lacking in enthusiasm for the cause of salary equity and other improvements in the conditions of black teachers and their students in the 1930s and 1940s, particularly when compared with its relative enthusiasm for the cause of women teachers. For example, in the years after the 1920s, when the association began to gather salary data on the nation's teachers, it chose not to publish the salary information it had relating to black teachers, while it repeatedly publicized the salaries paid to white teachers and almost as frequently suggested that women teachers suffered from severe salary inequities. Thus, the diffidence in the NEA's reaction to the *Brown* decision continued a long history of neglect of the nation's African American teachers, even though the NEA had the data to make their case for salary equity.[5]

The action of the 1954 NEA Representative Assembly in reaction to the *Brown* decision, which had been announced a little more than a month before the convention, was, in obvious deference to its southern affiliates, simply to resolve that the matter of desegregation was a national problem. Amendments to this resolution were proposed in most of the rest of the 1950s, seeking to put the association in one way or another on record as in favor of the desegregation of public schools mandated by the Supreme Court. These amendments were all unsuccessful, though the sentiment of acting favorably toward recognizing desegregation seemed to increase somewhat as the decade wore on. Generally, pro-desegregation sentiments were expressed by northern and western delegates to the NEA convention while southerners defended the status quo by pointing out that those in favor of a pro-desegregation policy were not the ones who would have to live with the consequences of that preference. As the NEA entered the 1960s, however, it had to contend with an increasingly powerful movement spearheaded by those committed to change of its long-established policy of what might be described as less-than-benign neglect in the racial arena.[6] It would take this movement more than a decade to transform the NEA from an institution that opposed the trend toward racial justice to one that stood in the forefront of the thrust for racial equity. By the end of the 1960s, the NEA had enacted relatively radical resolutions on proportional representation relating to the conduct of its own business that guaranteed the rights of black minority teachers, and it had endorsed increasingly controversial school desegregation measures such as mandatory busing plans. Also by this time the association was well on the way toward completion of the process of desegregating its segregated state affiliates.

DESEGREGATION OF THE NEA: BEGINNINGS

The year 1960 marked the beginning of a process of desegregating the NEA and its affiliates that would take almost two decades to implement completely. The initial change seemed hardly significant; there was only a minor alteration in the wording of the NEA's resolution on desegregation in 1960. More significant, however, the forces seeking a substantial alteration were about to become more powerful. A coalition began to develop between the black teachers in the association, the northern and western liberals who had been outspoken on the issue of desegregation, and some of the urban militants who were soon to remake the association into a powerful teachers' union.

Much of the opposition to becoming more forceful in opposing segregation came from delegates from the white southern state education associations. Their argument was basically that they could not themselves proceed faster than their communities were proceeding in the matter of desegregation. The consequence they feared was that an angry white South, fired by the doctrine of massive resistance, would move to close the public schools rather than desegregate them.

At the 1960 convention a white Louisiana delegate, who was also a member of the NEA Board of Directors and its Executive Committee, expressed southern sentiments at some length. He spoke against strengthening the desegregation resolution beyond the 1954 statement that the issue was a problem. He argued that differences on the issue were not mainly sectional, or even over matters of principle; rather, they were "differences in opportunity to experience at firsthand those overwhelming problems that our [southern] professional leaders must face in their daily work." He added that, in the South, where the problems were most acute, they were "not likely to be solved by passing resolutions at a national convention, or by emotional debate." He pointed out that the existing resolution on the topic, basically unmodified since 1954, had been "generally accepted" in southern communities. Additional specifications in the resolution, he believed, were likely to be counterproductive, hardening the climate of "resistance" and making "constructive educational goals more difficult to achieve." He concluded that the "real issue involved here today, then, is whether the action taken by the Delegate Assembly may help or hinder professional leadership in those communities in their one bitter task—to keep the public schools open and operating."[7] While this Louisianan certainly pointed to a real problem for the southern state and local associations, his devotion to the status quo and unwillingness to consider any additions or alterations to the NEA's position hardly seemed the kind of position that would influence others to favorably consider his reservations about changing the policy.

But there was more to the NEA's hesitancy on the issue of desegregation than recalcitrant southerners. The executive secretary of the association, William Carr, was quite sympathetic to the views of the white southerners. Though by no means an overt racist, Carr was the type of person who was unlikely to move to the front on a public policy issue where he and his organization might be seen as controversial and, thereby, be threatened with a loss of influence or membership. Carr was particularly anxious not to offend state education officials from the South and the members of his white southern affiliates. Thus, he could be counted on to try and block any attempt, from within or without the NEA, to move the organization to a position on the racial issue that was in any way in advance of the practical situations that his southern state and local affiliates were then confronting.

Carr's tendency to temporize rather than to act was illustrated in several of his speeches in the 1960s, until his eventual retirement from the position of executive secretary shortly after the middle of the decade. For example, in 1960, when a delegate to the Representative Assembly asked what the NEA had done in response to the closing of the public schools in Prince Edward County, Virginia, an action taken solely to avoid desegregation, Carr responded: "The staff has received no request from an affiliated organization, either in the State of Virginia or in the county, for action, and has taken no action." The questioner replied that it seemed odd that the NEA had recently embarked on an expensive, two-year study of "the needs of the space age" without an official request from any affiliate to do so and had done nothing about the situation in Virginia because it had not received such a request. Carr made no response, indicating that he had none to make. He used the press of continuing the convention's business as an excuse not to respond.[8]

In his final speech to the NEA convention in 1967, as that group contemplated action to force desegregation on southern state affiliates, Carr responded with a declaration in favor of continuing to go slowly on the issue: "The association is today able to exert . . . influence on a nationwide basis only because in the past it has moved with restraint and patience." Confronting his critics directly, Carr added: "Some, perhaps many, have felt that Association policy in civil rights should be more radical and rapid. In my view, however, the achievement of the widest possible consensus has been, and is, the price of continued effectiveness."[9] Thus, in his final years at the helm of the NEA, as in his earlier career, Carr was a brake on the movement to do something about putting the NEA on record in favor of the meaningful desegregation of the nation's schools.

In spite of Carr's reluctance, the movement for change toward active pursuit of desegregation gathered momentum as the 1960s wore on. The first real break in the dike of resistance came in 1961. In that year a lengthy resolution on "desegregation in the public schools" was drafted after consultation with both the black and white affiliate associations in the southern states. The resolution expressed "deep concern" for the problems in the schools in the aftermath of the Supreme Court's *Brown* decision and added a statement of principles and one of actions to the statement of concern. After voting down an amendment that directed the NEA staff to act positively on desegregation, another motion from the floor to amend the resolution was proposed, adding to it the following sentence: "The National Education Association pledges continued support of the United States Supreme Court decision on public school de-segregation." Passage of this amendment and the resolution to which it was attached finally put the NEA on record as favoring school desegre-gation, seven years after the highest court in the nation had ruled on the matter.[10]

In the following year, 1962, the resolution was again approved by the Representative Assembly, this time supplemented by an amendment commending communities "which have made progress toward" desegre-gation in their schools. This amended resolution passed with substan-tially less discussion than had accompanied the resolution in the previous year—a sign, perhaps, that the association was moving toward a real consensus, at least in determining its official statement on the topic.[11]

In 1963 the previous year's resolution was again presented to the NEA Representative Assembly, this time accompanied by an endorse-ment from the joint NEA-ATA Committee that it be passed. With pas-sage of the resolution for a third consecutive year, it would become part of the permanent platform of the NEA and would no longer have to be voted on. Before approval in this year, however, a delegate from the black teachers' association in Texas proposed an amendment calling for: "Extension of the principle of desegregation as it applies to the profes-sional membership in organizations affiliated with the NEA."[12] The passage of this amendment paved the way for the most significant activ-ity that the NEA would engage in regarding the race issue for the rest of the decade and most of the next decade: the desegregation of its own affiliates.

In 1964 the NEA president informed the Representative Assembly that substantial action had been taken in response to the previous year's mandate to desegregate the association's dual affiliates. By the middle of 1964, the number of states having racially segregated affiliates had di-minished from eighteen at the time of the *Brown* decision a decade ear-lier to eleven. The association's highest elected officer also announced that the NEA and its affiliates had contributed more than $75,000 "to the Prince Edward [County, Virginia] Free School Association," a group that had set up a private school for black children in the county that had closed its public schools rather than desegregate them.[13]

In considering the resolution on desegregation at the 1964 conven-tion, the NEA Representative Assembly approved an amendment that mandated the merger of segregated affiliates. It called for "all affiliated associations . . . to take immediate steps to remove all restrictive mem-bership requirements dealing with race," to "develop plans to effect the compete integration of all local and state affiliates whose memberships are now limited to specifically designated racial . . . groups," and to set a deadline of "July 1, 1966," by which time the Executive Committee of the association was to deal with any failure to implement the mandated plans.[14]

This action by the 1964 NEA convention occurred almost immediately after the U.S. Congress, spurred by President Lyndon B. Johnson, passed a landmark Civil Rights Act. The two events combined to add momentum to the movement to desegregate the remaining dual NEA affiliates as well as to facilitate further desegregation of the association itself.

DESEGREGATION AT THE NATIONAL LEVEL

Technically, one could not say that the NEA was a segregated organization. It had substantial numbers of black members and black delegates to its conventions, most of whom came from the southern states. It also had, however, an independent association of black teachers functioning in a parallel relationship with itself. And it had dual affiliates in several southern and border states—that is, separate black and white state (and some local) education associations. A merger between the two national associations, the NEA and the ATA, constituted a significant step toward the desegregation of the remaining dual state and local affiliates. In 1963 the Representative Assembly had urged the Joint NEA-ATA Committee to consider the issue of merger between the two associations.[15] The 1964 convention action turned the consideration into a mandate.

It took two full years after the mandate was passed for the national merger to be accomplished, however. Most of the reasons for the delay were related to the concerns of the ATA that it simply not be absorbed into the NEA and thereby disappear without a trace. One issue of special concern for the black teachers was the ATA's long-standing support of the National Association for the Advancement of Colored People (NAACP) and its Legal Defense Fund (LDF). The fund had been the prime mover in waging most of the salary equity suits on behalf of black teachers in the 1940s, had also sparked the initiatives that resulted in the *Brown* decision, and had taken the lead in pursuing school desegregation suits in school districts throughout the nation in the 1960s and 1970s, efforts to gain compliance with *Brown*. After long negotiations the NEA responded to this issue by agreeing to accept responsibility for cases "involving the defense of teacher rights." What this stipulation meant in practice was that henceforth the NEA was to take responsibility for defending black teachers who were often confronted with the loss of their jobs as desegregation was implemented in ways that catered to white parents' fears of blacks teaching white students. A similar but substantially less controversial accord was reached by which the NEA would take over support for the Association for the Study of Negro (later Afro-American) Life and History.[16]

Behind these and other ATA concerns was the frustration that many black teachers felt over the decade-long record of noncompliance or minimal compliance with the *Brown* mandate. They feared that, given their relatively small numbers, black teachers would have little influence in the merged NEA. To respond to this concern, the NEA Executive Committee provided for "periodic evaluations" of the national merger as well as of the mergers of state affiliates that were to follow, evaluations that could be used to respond to continuing and new black grievances. In spite of this action, black teachers still felt ill at ease with their prospects in a merged national teacher association. Yet, putting aside their fears and responding to a larger issue of principle, the members of the ATA approved the merger with the NEA at their last national convention in June 1966. Less than one month later, the NEA approved the merger at its Representative Assembly meeting.[17]

Significant conditions were attached to the merger agreement. One, and perhaps the most obvious, provided that all ATA members in good standing become members of the NEA. A second and less obvious but perhaps equally significant provision was that the staff members of the ATA be employed in the southeastern regional office of the NEA in Atlanta, Georgia.[18] As will be illustrated shortly, the employment of black staff and officers was also a significant issue in the mergers of state affiliates that followed the national merger. And, as already suggested, this issue spoke indirectly but importantly to the concern for the employment prospects of black teachers in school desegregation plans.

The NEA's southeastern regional office had been established as the sixth regional office of the association in 1965, in response to the urging of the Joint NEA-ATA Committee. Its task was to facilitate the delivery of services from the national office to state and local affiliates in the region that it served. Shortly after its establishment, a biracial advisory board for the office was formed to make sure that "no racial incident would mar the spirit of harmony" that the NEA was seeking to encourage in the Southeast.[19]

In that same year Irvamae Applegate was elected to the NEA vice presidency and thus was in line to take over the NEA presidency. Applegate would vigorously push the mergers in the state association arena.

During her presidential year, 1966, she announced the formation of a Compliance Committee to monitor and supervise the merger plans of the remaining dual state affiliates. When her successor then appointed Applegate to that Compliance Committee, she became intimately associated with the merger negotiations in the states that followed upon the national merger and was a force for continuation and intensification of the merger momentum.[20]

EARLY STATE MERGERS

As the movement for a merger between the NEA and the ATA gathered momentum in 1964, seven of the eighteen dual associations that had existed at the time of the *Brown* decision had already merged. These seven included the associations in six border states—Missouri, Maryland, West Virginia, Kentucky, Oklahoma, and Delaware—and in the District of Columbia. These early mergers were usually accomplished simply by the white association removing racial restrictions from its constitution and/or bylaws and inviting members of the black association to join. Generally speaking, these mergers were relatively easily accomplished, with the smaller group of black teachers simply being absorbed into the white association.[21] This situation reflected the relatively low proportion of minority citizens in the border states and, also, the relatively successful experience they had in desegregating their schools.

The remaining eleven states with dual affiliates, however, the eleven states of the old Confederacy, had substantially different sets of circumstances that caused their black teachers to voice concerns very much like those expressed by the members of the ATA before its merger with the NEA. These eleven states had significant black populations and large numbers of black students enrolled in segregated schools. Their black teachers' associations represented a considerable number of black teachers who were teaching in the segregated schools. The black teachers' associations also had substantial assets, extensive programs for their members, and commitments that they wished to protect in any merger with their respective white association. Merger took place relatively rapidly in four of these eleven states: Florida and Texas completed merger agreements before the end of 1966, and Virginia and Tennessee brought the process to closure in 1967.

In these states there were some tough negotiations between the dual associations before the completion of the merger agreements. In Florida the black association had a strong financial and emotional commitment to its headquarters building that it wanted, somehow, to be honored before the merger. Similarly, in Texas, the substantial financial assets of the black association, rather than simply be turned over to the merged association with a white majority and thereby lost in the larger budget, were given over to a Commission on Democracy and Human Rights. This group had been created in response to an initiative from the black association to continue the fight to protect the rights of black teachers in the state.[22]

In three of these four states—Florida, Virginia, and Tennessee—the employment of the paid staff members and some high-ranking elected officers of the black teachers' association was an issue. This was resolved differently in each situation. In Florida the chief executive of the black association obtained a position as an assistant superintendent in Dade County, the largest school system in the state. Another leader from the black Florida teachers' association was employed as a member of the field staff of the merged state association. In Virginia two leaders from the black association were employed by the merged association and the NEA, respectively. The new black employee of the merged Virginia association became its director of special services. In Tennessee the merger contained a stipulation that the new association have an integrated and racially balanced staff. The head of the black association took a position with the Tennessee State Department of Education, while another staff member was employed as a field staff representative of the merged association.[23] These appointments, especially those in local and state administrative positions, reflected the NEA's continuing relationship with school administrators, a relationship that would end in the early 1970s. The administrative appointments also may have reflected the reality that the states themselves were moving positively toward desegregation in response to the mandate of *Brown* and the force of the civil rights movement.

There was some negative feeling in the ranks of black educators that accompanied the mergers in these four states, however. It generally arose out of concern that the immanence of merger had weakened the black association and forced it to accept an agreement that reflected more a situation of absorption than a marriage of equal partners. In Texas, for example, announcement of merger talks in 1963 led to a substantial drop in membership in the black association from more than ten thousand shortly after the announcement to seven thousand at the time of the actual merger. This drop hampered the black association's ability to provide for its members during the period before merger and weakened its ability to bargain with the white group over merger terms.[24]

Similar weaknesses characterized the situations for the black associations in all four of these states and were reflected in the black leaders moving to positions of lesser prominence in the staff of the merged association than they had enjoyed in their own group. Each successive merger that occurred without a black executive in the top leadership position of the new group increased the concerns of the black officers, staff, and members in the remaining black associations. In response, they attempted, in a variety of ways, to reach agreements that were stronger in their recognition of the assets, talents, and reputations of black associations and leaders than had been the case in the four early merger states.

These sentiments were crystallized at the national level in a working paper on the topic of state mergers prepared by Samuel Ethridge, the highest ranking black staff member in the NEA headquarters. This paper suggested that more careful attention was necessary in relation to several specific issues in planning and implementing the merger process. First, Ethridge noted that the actual name given to the process was important; a term like *unification* carried far fewer negative connotations than did *dissolution, absorption,* or even *merger.* Also, he argued that an explicit rationale for the process was helpful in each case, a rationale that went beyond the existence of NEA mandates and emphasized the things to be gained by both groups in the process of merger. Additionally, Ethridge highlighted the importance to the new association of its role as developer of policies relating to teacher welfare in desegregated school systems, a role that needed to be stressed in order to win the positive allegiance of black teachers. The new association, Ethridge believed, needed to recognize that it was indeed a new body and not something created by a minor alteration in the existing policies and procedures of either the black or white association. Finally, Ethridge suggested that sensitivity was necessary to the negative connotations of seemingly universal phrases like *All are welcome* to black teachers who had experienced the euphemistic character of such language since the adoption of the separate but equal principle in the 1890s and its application in the field of education. Several specific suggested outcomes followed from Ethridge's stated concerns. They included constitutional provisions proscribing racial restrictions, the dissolution of both existing groups in favor of a genuinely new organization, a new name that reflected the new association and not either of its predecessors, the pooling of the assets of the two organizations, a joint committee to conduct the affairs in the interim before the final agreement, and agreements on the representation of both groups on committees in the new organization and the rotation of key officers by race for a period of years during which "race will not be an issue in election to office."[25]

Both the length of the list of concerns outlined in this document and the specificity of solutions it advocated indicated that further mergers would be more difficult to achieve than those that had previously taken place. The first example of a more equitable merger, from the point of view of the black association, came in the state of South Carolina.

Accomplished in 1968, the South Carolina merger responded to several of Ethridge's concerns. It was developed by a committee comprising six members from each existing association. The committee provided for a one-year period in which the constitution of the new association was to be developed. The eventual agreement also provided some protection for the leadership of the black association in attaining both the highest elected office of the new group and its chief staff position. The president-elect of the white association became the first president of the merged group, while the president of the black association became the vice president, and presumptively, president-elect of the new association. Similarly, the executive secretary of the white association became the new executive secretary, while the chief staff officer of the black association became associate executive secretary of the merged group, with responsibility for special services. The merger agreement also provided for proportional representation from each association on the committees of the merged group, as well as equal (and thus more than proportional) representation from each association on the important (especially to the black association) Defense Committee of the new association. Another provision specified that the first chair of the Defense Committee be black.[26]

Not all whites in South Carolina were comfortable with these guarantees, and there was considerable dispute over how long they were to last. Initially, the guarantees were to end with the implementation of the agreement. Eventually, a variety of adjustments to maintain a visible black presence in the highest circles of the merged association was made, adjustments that were to be in force for a nine-year period following merger.[27]

Blacks also had concerns about the South Carolina merger. They included the disposition of the black association's legal defense fund, the name of the new association (blacks desired a new name rather than keep the name of the white group), and assurance about the automatic ascension of the president of the black association to the presidency of the merged association after the term of the white association's president as head of the new organization expired. Disposition of these issues reflected a compromise that had some bitter aspects for blacks. A positive outcome was that the defense fund was designated to remain for its specific purpose by a majority vote of the merger committee. The other two proposals were not positively resolved from the black point of view, however. The president of the black association believed that she had a tacit agreement with whites to succeed to the presidency, but the white members of the merger committee disputed that belief. This dispute, along with misunderstanding regarding the duties that the black association's staff leader had as associate executive secretary of the merged association, led to some substantial bad feelings about merger on the part of black educators.[28]

Two things became clear from the South Carolina agreement. First, extended negotiations between more equal partners had yielded a stronger agreement on behalf of the black partner in the merger. Second, the development of clear, specific provisions in the merger plans became an obvious priority for all interested parties. Both of these points became significant in the process that yielded agreements in the remaining states. These agreements all took place under intensified pressure from the national level to accomplish merger. This pressure took the form of mandated completion dates and sanctions against groups that did not merge.

NEA CRITERIA FOR MERGERS

Continuing concern on the part of black teachers and their associations about the terms of recently enacted mergers, along with concern expressed on the floor of the 1968 NEA convention about the slow pace of negotiations in the remaining six unmerged states, combined to intensify the movement for mergers in these states. Earlier in the year the Executive Committee and the NEA president, perturbed at the slow pace of the negotiations in the yet-to-be merged states and the reluctance of NEA staff to facilitate the mergers, had created a Compliance Committee and appointed Irvamae Applegate as its chair.

In her report on the committee's activities to the 1968 national convention, Applegate stressed several points. First, she noted that the Compliance Committee had responsibility for evaluating those merger agreements that were being implemented. She added that this evaluation process had revealed that there were some problems left unresolved by the mergers, but that they were not insurmountable nor were they drastically different from the problems evident in associations that had not experienced the merger process. In the interest of eliminating these problems in the mergers still to be enacted, however, she announced that the Compliance Committee had "retained, or made the decision to use, the American Arbitration Association to bring about further progress." She added that the group had also decided to establish definite guidelines for the remaining mergers by October 1968.[29]

What Applegate referred to as guidelines were modeled on some "Criteria for Evaluating Merger Agreements" that had been developed initially in 1965. At the NEA Executive Committee meeting in October 1968, these criteria became the official standards to be used to evaluate the fairness of the remaining mergers. The official name of the standards as adopted was "Criteria for Evaluating Merger Plans and Compliance with Resolution 12 [the resolution on merger]." These criteria specified that the remaining merger plans adhere to nine conditions. The first was that the merged association needed to represent the formal dissolution of both previous associations and "the creation of a completely new one." The second criterion provided for a grievance procedure to be available for those who objected that a merger did not comply with the NEA resolution on the topic. Third, the rights of minority group members in policy making, participation in activities, and office holding were to be protected. The next stipulation was that mergers at the local level were to take place within one year of a state association merger. Another provision followed calling for the representation of "black and white personnel" on all levels of staffing in the new association.[30]

Another criterion for evaluating a merger plan covered the increasingly sensitive issue of the selection of the chief staff officer of the new association. It specified that the existing chief executive officers of the two associations being merged were to be the candidates for the new position. Additionally, it mandated that the one officer not chosen for the new position was to be provided an appropriate position, "reporting to the Executive Secretary, with a salary which is at least equal to the person who is second in command." The NEA was working hard here to protect the staff leader of the black association from demotion and the humiliation that resulted from not being chosen for the top position in the merged association and instead being "kicked downstairs" to a position of slight responsibility and small remuneration.[31]

The remaining criteria spoke to what would happen if a merger were not completed by the mandated date. One called for third-party assistance if the merger was still uncompleted on December 1, 1968, and specified that if the two associations in a state could not agree on a third party, then the NEA would choose the individual or agency. Further, if the issues were not resolved by December 15, 1968, the recommendation was that the NEA would "require that the remaining issues be submitted to binding arbitrations under the rules and procedures of the Center for Dispute Settlement of the American Arbitration Association." The final two specific criteria pertained to the final approval process of merger agreements. One required that any agreement be approved by the NEA Executive Committee before its final approval by the legislative bodies of the to-be-merged associations. The second specified that the merger plan needed to be in the hands of the Compliance Committee by January 1, 1969, and to be approved by the to-be-merged associations by the end of the 1968–69 school year.[32] While the language of the criteria was quite specific, the adoption of the criteria as "guidelines" indicated that there would be room for negotiation on every matter included within them. Clearly, then, the national body was encouraging and, to some extent, threatening the states where merger had not yet taken place to implement the process expeditiously.

The NEA Representative Assembly gave further indication of its endorsement of the NEA's pressure on unmerged affiliates to merge when, in 1967, it elected Elizabeth Duncan Koontz, a black educator from North Carolina as vice president and, thus, president-elect of the association. The symbolic importance of this choice was understood by all participants in NEA affairs and particularly by those in the still unmerged state associations. Yet, in spite of this affirmation of progress in black-white relations in the NEA, the complete desegregation of all dual affiliates was not achieved for several more years. That outcome was to involve extensive, detailed, and sometimes acrimonious negotiations between the remaining unmerged state associations.[33]

Desegregation Efforts under the Criteria for Merger

The criteria for merger adopted by the NEA in 1968 affected the situation in six states where merger had not yet taken place: Alabama, Arkansas, Georgia, Louisiana, Mississippi, and North Carolina. The national mandated deadline for merger in these states was for the process to be completed by the time of the July 1969 NEA national meeting. The provision for outside mediators or fact finders to be used to assist the merger negotiations was employed in all of these states except Arkansas, where it did not seem necessary.[34] This was one indication that there was substantial difficulty that attended the process of reaching an agreement in these states. By the end of 1969, however, merger agreements had been negotiated and approved in three of the six states—Alabama, Arkansas, and Georgia.

The merger agreement in Arkansas was formally approved by the black and white associations on March 1, 1969, with the provision that it take effect officially on July 1 of that year. The Arkansas merger proceeded relatively amicably, in contrast with the situation in the other two states. The final agreement, contrary to the criteria specified by the NEA, kept the name of the white association, the Arkansas Education Association, for the merged group. It called for membership on all committees of the merged association in proportion to its racial composition. Additional black members were also approved on the new association's Commission on Professional Rights and Responsibilities, as had been the case in other states. The joint merger committee that had hammered out the agreement was to continue its existence over a five-year period, in order to help resolve any differences in interpretation of the agreement that might arise. The executive secretary of the white association became the chief executive officer of the new group, while the executive secretary of the black association was appointed to the position of assistant executive secretary for human relations. While the white headquarters building was the designated location for the merged group, the agreement provided that the black association's headquarters building not be disposed of without an approval process that recognized the special interests of the former members of the black association.[35]

Delegates to the 1969 NEA meeting were informed of the successful Arkansas merger, which officially came into existence during the convention. In reporting about the merger, the leader of the newly merged Arkansas association remarked that the "members of our association are dedicated to the quest for equality in educational opportunity for the youth of our state," thereby linking the desegregation of the teachers' associations to the larger task of the equitable desegregation of his state's schools. He concluded his remarks by celebrating his state's accomplishment in the racial arena and, in a nod to traditional NEA professionalism, by noting the link between teachers and student welfare: "Arkansas has made tremendous progress over the years. We have a long way to go but we will make it by the dedication of the teachers of Arkansas for the improvement of the educational opportunities of our students."[36]

Alabama's merger agreement was also approved prior to the 1969 NEA convention, on May 16, with the effective date to be in August of that year. A major stumbling block to merger in Alabama had been the desire of the black association that its role as a plaintiff in several

Alabama school desegregation suits be assumed by the merged organization. This was an especially difficult situation, since litigation over desegregation might well involve the merged body representing black and white teachers who were competing for the same jobs. After considerable negotiations, the matter was finally resolved shortly after the 1969 NEA convention. The settlement provided that the NEA agree to take over the status of plaintiff from the black association.[37]

The Georgia negotiations yielded the most comprehensive and controversial agreement of any of the state mergers up to that point. It followed a long, intense, and often acrimonious period of meetings between representatives of the black and white affiliates in the Empire State of the South, aided at strategic moments by outside mediators from the NEA. Unprecedented in the other mergers, but following the NEA merger guidelines, the agreement in Georgia gave the merged association a new name, the Georgia Association of Educators (GAE). Additionally, the merger provided a series of nine-year guarantees on the issues of alternating the presidency by race, the racial composition of the board of directors and the Executive Committee of the GAE, and the composition of other committees and commissions of the new group. Generally, black representation was guaranteed at levels beyond those that were "proportional" to the number of blacks in the new organization.[38]

On the matter of the location of the GAE headquarters, the agreement stipulated that a new location be found and that the facilities of each separate group be protected from sale for a five-year period before their final transfer to the merged association. Given that the location of the new headquarters building had yet to be chosen, the agreement specified that the top two officers of the GAE, one white and one black, were to have their offices in the same place. The choice of the top executive officer for the GAE was a major problem in the negotiations, especially after the chief executive officer of the white Georgia Education Association, an individual quite close to retirement age, announced his resignation before merger and was replaced by a considerably younger man. The black chief executive officer, Horace Tate, was an experienced leader and a tough negotiator who feared that this change in leadership in the white association was engineered to keep him (Tate) out of the highest GAE office for many more years. The final choice of the GAE executive secretary came after a long period of difficult negotiations, culminating in the appointment of a three-person selection committee composed of one member chosen by each association and a third member chosen by the first two. When that committee chose the new white leader as the GAE's executive secretary, difficult negotiations over Tate's position, duties, and remuneration followed.[39]

When agreement on Tate's status was reached, final approval by the boards of directors of the black and the white association was the next step. The white association quickly gave its approval, but the black group, the Georgia Teachers and Education Association, balked. Blacks objected to the lack of regular grievance provisions in the agreement as well as to the absence of any provision for grievances in the years after the nine-year implementation period had elapsed. Further negotiations resulted in creation of the Grievance Committee, which had an annual meeting as well as a concession to black members to protect their rights after the nine-year implementation period expired. Given these changes, the merger was quickly approved by both boards of directors and then by the members of both associations.[40]

Negotiators in the state of North Carolina had also reached a merger agreement before the 1969 NEA convention, which was quickly ratified by the white association but turned down by the black group. A black North Carolina delegate to the NEA convention indicated a major concern of black teachers in his state and elsewhere when he proposed an amendment to the NEA continuing resolution on fair employment practices. The amendment stated: "The Association further deplores the discriminatory practice of eliminating Negro educators [in desegregation settlements] by not hiring them or by hiring limited numbers of black educators. The Association recommends that the minimum hiring of black educators be in proportion to the composition of the black-white ratio of the pupil population." The amendment added that "Until such time as the ratio of black and white educators reaches the ratio proportions of the student racial populations, steps should be taken to employ black educators to correct the existing inequities." In discussing his proposal, the North Carolinian pointed out that black teachers had lost nearly half of their teaching positions because of desegregation in one North Carolina city. He also noted that in that city, and in another of the state's largest school districts, far fewer than 10 percent of the new teachers hired were black. Subsequent discussion revealed that North Carolina was not the only state where black teachers had lost jobs because of desegregation and further, that black administrators also often found themselves unemployed after implementation of a desegregation mandate.[41]

The amendment was discussed during the late stages of the convention, and its failure to pass may have been as much due to a time squeeze as to any other factor. Still, at least one white delegate to the convention voiced an objection to the amendment on the grounds that it substituted one form of employment discrimination for another.[42] Thus, two decades before the controversy over affirmative action reached full flower nationally, the NEA was encountering the "reverse discrimination" argument that was to carry the day in the conservatively dominated federal courts of the 1990s. The NEA, however, was not dominated by conservatives, at least not at its national conventions. Final approval of the North Carolina merger by the black association also indicated that at least some protection had been provided for black teachers in that state as part of the merger agreement.

Two other actions at the 1969 NEA convention are worthy of mention here. The first was the Representative Assembly's repudiation of the actions of the Richard Nixon administration that had delayed the specific deadline of September 1, 1969, that had been set by the Department of Health, Education, and Welfare (HEW) for compliance by school districts with HEW desegregation guidelines. An amendment added to the NEA's desegregation resolution stated: "The National Education Association insists that there be no deviation by the federal government from the established timetable for desegregation established by the HEW guidelines." A second sentence in the amendment specified that "The Association directs its officers and staff to exert every effort to reestablish the September 1969 deadline for full compliance." The day after the passage of this resolution, the NEA president read to the delegates a stinging telegram that he had sent to the Nixon administration as a follow-up to the amended resolution on desegregation.[43]

In another discussion late in the 1969 convention, the NEA Representative Assembly considered a motion to specify that mergers in the states that had yet to approve agreements mandate a new name for the merged association as well as a fifty-fifty membership of blacks and whites on all boards, committees, and commissions, and binding arbitration of any impasses. In discussion of this amendment, prominent NEA leaders who had served as fact finders and mediators in several merger negotiations spoke against it, arguing that the good-faith efforts of both black and white negotiators were negated by such mandates. Others also pointed out that the amendment narrowed considerably the role of the NEA Executive Committee in carrying out its assigned oversight of the remaining mergers. Whether these specific arguments proved decisive, the Representative Assembly rejected the amendment.[44] The rejection, however, did not indicate any lessening of the fervor for mandated mergers on the part of the Representative Assembly. Rather, it indicated that the delegates had some sensitivity for the variations in situations in states, variations that were ignored by such blanket mandates.

By the end of 1969, the NEA had successfully sponsored agreements in all but three of its segregated state affiliates—Louisiana, Mississippi, and North Carolina. In North Carolina the merger was concluded satisfactorily in 1970. In Louisiana and Mississippi, however, merger was far from completion at the end of the 1960s. In conformity with the guidelines for merger adopted by the Representative Assembly, the white associations in Mississippi and Louisiana were expelled from the NEA in 1970 because of their failure to approve a merger agreement. The black associations in those two states, which had approved a merger proposal, were not expelled. Since merger was not achieved, they were charged to continue reporting to the national association on events in their states relating to merger until negotiations reached a successful culmination.[45]

Three other matters discussed at the 1970 NEA convention pointed to present and future difficulties that were encountered as the association and its affiliates wrestled with the issue of school desegregation. One was a proposal that "The National Education Association believes that educators must have a voice in any decision-making process that involves transfers of educators to achieve racial balance," proffered by a delegate from Georgia and seconded vigorously by a delegate from New York state. While subsequent discussion revealed that the matter was addressed in another part of the NEA's complicated roster of resolutions, the offering of such a proposal showed that the issues raised in settling school desegregation suits affected the job security of both black and white educators. So, the relatively straightforward and consistently principled approval of school desegregation by the NEA was now confounded by the issue of problematic transfers of both black and white teachers because of desegregation mandates and other employment provisions that affected the opportunities, security, and future of both black and white teachers. While in particular situations the negative impact might be on only one of the two groups, the general prospect of desegregation potentially threatened each group's employment prospects.[46]

Another discussion at the 1970 convention related to the school desegregation resolution considered for adoption. In an obvious move to strengthen the resolution, explicit acknowledgment was made of the *Holmes v. Alexander* (1969) Supreme Court decision calling for immediate school desegregation and promulgated because of official reluctance in most school districts to implement the process in any expeditious fashion.

Additionally, the convention delegates also approved a proposal that the association endorse the availability of mandatory busing as a means of achieving school desegregation. Thus, the NEA was moving increasingly forcefully to endorse the more controversial desegregation efforts by the federal courts.[47]

Still another matter considered at the 1970 convention related to the implementation of desegregation. The Representative Assembly approved a new business item relating to the "Misuse of the National Teachers Examination [NTE]." Discussion of this item revealed that the NTE was being used in several southern school districts to discriminate against black teachers in initial employment, continuation of employment, and promotion decisions. It called on the NEA to notify the Educational Testing Service (ETS), which had taken over development of the NTE, of the action taken at the convention. Further, it asked that the ETS take steps to stop the racially discriminatory use of its instrument in several southern states. Discussion of this item was brief before its passage, an indication probably that widespread knowledge of the discriminatory uses of the NTE existed or that the entire matter was so obscure that delegates did not see fit to consider its many ramifications extensively.[48]

The result of all of these actions was that by 1970 the NEA, in direct contrast to the situation that it had found itself in ten years earlier, and for several decades before 1960, was firmly aligned with desegregation and other particulars of the movement to achieve racial equity in education. The problems encountered in achieving both racial equity and desegregation, though by no means uncomplicated, were relatively mild in 1970, particularly when viewed from the perspective of subsequent decades when the actual mixed results of the implementation of desegregation mandates and the increasingly novel measures invented to avoid their reach became known widely enough to muddy the waters surrounding this policy issue.[49]

THE NEA AND DESEGREGATION IN THE 1970s

Merger of the final two dual-affiliate states, Mississippi and Louisiana, did not take place until well into the second half of the 1970s. Mississippi finally achieved its merger in 1976, and Louisiana completed the process one year later.

Progress in Mississippi proved extremely slow when the merger issue became confounded with a court mandate to desegregate the schools throughout the state. White reaction to the mandate fueled antimerger elements in the Mississippi Education Association (MEA), the white group that was expelled from the NEA when it failed to approve a merger agreement at the end of the 1960s.

The black and white Mississippi education associations had carried on serious negotiations with each other over merger terms in the late 1960s, with help from NEA mediators. As the mid-1969 deadline for merger (or expulsion) approached, the two groups appeared on the verge of an agreement, the particulars of which had emerged from a process that involved the latest effort of an NEA mediator. The proposed agreement called for a three-phase merger process. Initially, a joint council of the two associations would embark on a one-year development of a final plan, to include several particulars specified by the mediator. Among these provisions were several that related to the second phase of the plan, encompassing a six-year period. In this phase, a board of directors, a representative assembly, and an executive leadership were all to be fully provided for, with guarantees of equality for blacks in some of the bodies and proportionality in others. In the third phase, which was to culminate before the end of the six-year period, a revised constitution was to be presented to the renamed group, the Mississippi Association of Educators, in which the percentage guarantees for black representation of the earlier phases could be reconsidered.[50]

Although this plan seemed to bypass several difficult issues and left much to be decided in the future, prospects for its approval looked good when the two presidents and the two executive secretaries of the separate associations announced their endorsement. At subsequent meetings of the two groups' legislative bodies, the black association approved the agreement overwhelmingly, while the white association rejected it by a more than eight-to-one (468 to 60) margin. According to a knowledgeable NEA official's account of events in Mississippi, the reason for the action by the whites was the failure of their leadership to "openly advocate or urge support for the plan," in spite of their endorsement. After some dawdling within the NEA over expulsion of the white affiliate—caused by the hope that a resolution still might be attained—and following another negative white vote on a modified merger plan, the NEA Executive Committee voted on April 12, 1970, to expel the MEA.[51]

In early 1969, some months before the NEA's mid-year deadline for merger or expulsion, the white and black associations in the state of Louisiana were substantially further from resolution than they appeared to be in Mississippi. The NEA responded to this situation by appointing a fact finder in an effort to jump-start the stalled negotiations. A major obstacle to settlement was the position of the two associations on black representation in the merged group. The white association insisted on representation achieved through the usual election procedures, thereby seeming to assure a limited black presence in the new leadership. The black association demanded equal representation on the board of directors of the merged association and concessions in the direction of more than proportional representation on some of its other committees. Given this dispute, the fact finder devised a plan that tried to split the difference between the two groups. While the NEA Executive Committee approved the fact finder's plan, neither of the two Louisiana associations consented. As a result, before the July 1969 NEA convention, both groups were suspended from the national association, though not yet expelled. In subsequent meetings to again consider the fact finder's plan, held late in 1969, the black association approved the recommendations while the white association again rejected them. In response to these actions, the NEA Executive Committee expelled the white Louisiana Teachers Association shortly after it had expelled the white Mississippi association.[52]

The response of the white Louisianans, following up on a threat they had made earlier, was to sue the NEA on the grounds that expulsion was an illegal action. This effectively ended the merger negotiations in Louisiana and put the dispute into the courts, as a matter between the national group and its white Louisiana affiliate. It took several years to get the issue out of the courts and back into an arena where the two Louisiana associations could again begin to deal with each other.[53]

Thus, at the beginning of the 1970s, for somewhat different reasons, the NEA was stymied in completing its drive to desegregate all of its southern affiliates by its failures in Mississippi and Louisiana. This, however, did not prevent the national body from moving ahead in its efforts to support school desegregation wherever and whenever it could and to provide for a strong African American and other minority presence in its own leadership and policy bodies.

One example of this thrust was provided at the 1971 convention when the Representative Assembly considered the following provision, proposed by a delegate from Michigan:

> That the NEA actively recruit and provide on-the-job training or a defined intern program specifically designed to expedite the hiring process of minority group persons—ethnic minorities (Afro Americans, Spanish speaking Americans, native Americans, and . . . Asian Americans) and women for UniServ staff positions. And that the Asso-

ciation strongly urge coordinating councils to post and/or list a nondiscriminatory clause when requesting applicants to interview for staff positions.

Discussion of this proposal revealed that few minorities had filled any of the many positions opened by the recent development of the UniServ program, which provided national funding for staff for local associations. One opponent of the proposal charged that naming specific ethnic groups to be favored countenanced the very discrimination that the proposal claimed to be redressing. This argument became a bulwark of the opposition in later years to affirmative action on behalf of minorities in employment and admission to educational institutions. Another opponent of the proposal chided the Michigan association, from whence it had come, for lacking a substantial minority presence in its own delegation. In direct response, and turning the criticism in a direction in which it had not been intended, a Michigan delegate acknowledged his own group's poor record in minority hiring but also argued that this was a reason for support of the proposal. After another statement of support for the proposal, this time from a Nebraska delegate who pointed out that it was also supported by the National Council of Urban Education Associations (NCUEA), the group that was leading the movement to remake the NEA into a militant teachers' union, the proposal was adopted.[54]

Later on in the 1971 convention, a move to recognize the claims of Mexican Americans to special consideration in attaining NEA staff positions was also approved. The NEA president-elect stated his own support for the principle involved and spoke for the Executive Committee of the association: "I personally, and I think every member of the Executive Committee, would welcome being armed with a mandate to make the staff a little browner, a little redder, and with better-looking eyes." Additionally, in response to this statement and to the minority hiring proposal for the UniServ program, the NEA executive secretary provided delegates to the convention with the actual numbers of various minority groups on the NEA staff. The numbers, in every case, were remarkably small, at least when considered from the perspective of those who sought a meaningful minority presence on the NEA staff.[55]

At the same convention, in direct response to the issue of the mergers of dual affiliates that had taken place in all states but Louisiana and Mississippi, the NEA Executive Committee approved a proposal that histories be written of the black associations covering the period before merger. This action was undertaken so that the particulars of the rich experience of the black associations not be lost. Noting that these histories would parallel in significance, as well as supplement, the history of the ATA that was prescribed in the NEA-ATA merger agreement, the measure was approved without any dissent.[56]

The next year, 1972, saw further progress in achieving a significant minority presence within the NEA. For example, at one of the meetings of the NEA Board of Directors, the large and relatively conservative policy-making group chosen through elections in the various state associations, the group heard a report on the NEA's plan to intervene as a friend of the court in the Richmond, Virginia, school desegregation suit. At that point, the issue under consideration in the Richmond case was whether to consolidate the majority black Richmond school district with two large majority white suburban districts for school attendance purposes, thereby facilitating substantial desegregation. The NEA intended to stand in support in federal court of the cross-district desegregation effort, a policy that was quite controversial at the time and remained so in the late twentieth century. After considerable discussion, including a stated objection to the NEA participation from one of the state of Virginia's members on the board of directors, the board defeated a motion sponsored by the Virginian to oppose the NEA's participation in the case. Thus, even in this heretofore conservative body, support for action in the desegregation arena was increasing.[57]

Additionally, at its 1972 annual convention, the NEA Representative Assembly approved strong resolutions on school desegregation, on civil rights, and on proportional representation for minorities in "every phase of governance" of the association and its affiliates. Still other resolutions provided for the evaluation of merger agreements to ensure that "the unique contributions, history, and flavor of each former organization be retained and be visible in the new merged association" and that all affiliates in states that had not undergone merger provide and implement "at least proportionate minority participation in every phase of governance." Other resolutions in that year endorsed the racial balancing of school staffs to help achieve desegregation, Chicano self-determination in education, and the noncooperation of NEA and its affiliates with any organizations that discriminate in membership "on the basis of race, creed, sex, or ethnic background."[58]

Thus, the NEA was moving to a consistent position of approval of desegregation and affirmative action on behalf of racial minorities at the same time that those policies were quite controversial, and would become increasingly controversial, in the nation's school districts and in other arenas of American life. The one remaining major item on the NEA's internal agenda in minority relations that was still unresolved was the successful completion of mergers in Mississippi and Louisiana.

Merger in Mississippi and Louisiana

The stymied merger of the dual associations in these two states at the turn of the 1970s left the NEA in an awkward position in both of them. While the majority of teachers in each state was white, the official NEA affiliate in each state was the previously segregated black association, which in neither case had more than a few white members. The NEA faced a situation of severely diminished influence in educational affairs in each state, given that its affiliate contained mainly minority group members. The national group worked assiduously to remedy the situation. This effort finally bore fruit in the second half of the 1970s.

The Mississippi merger was finally achieved in 1976. It was the result primarily of the black and white associations, in spite of their impasse, continuing to talk with each other, aided by the offices of the NEA. Eventually, this communication dispelled the ignorance and accompanying negative attitudes of the two sets of teachers toward each other. The terms of the final Mississippi merger provided for a new name for the new group, the Mississippi Association of Educators (MAE), following the Georgia precedent and conforming to the earlier Mississippi merger agreement that had been turned down by the white association. Additionally, it had a complicated set of provisions to ensure more than proportional black representation on the MAE Board of Directors. At the end of five years, black representation on the board, at the least, would have to remain proportional to the black membership in the MAE.[59]

Also, according to the merger agreement, the Executive Committee of the MAE was to reflect the more than proportional racial composition of the board of directors. The delegates to the Representative Assembly of the new organization were to be chosen to reflect the racial balance in the merged group. MAE committees were all to have at least 40 percent minority membership, except for the Merger Review and Teacher Rights Committees, both of which were to have equal representation of blacks and whites.[60]

The approval of the Mississippi merger in 1976 was a welcome occurrence for all those interested in public education in the state, since the public schools of the Magnolia State were facing substantial enrollment losses of white students to private, church-related "segregation" academies that sprang up in response to court-ordered desegregation plans. Although the relations between black and white teachers that had been strained by court-ordered desegregation were still not completely amicable, the leaders of the new MAE reported substantial progress in this regard. They were optimistic about the future both of the schools in their state and of the MAE.[61]

Louisiana proved a more difficult problem for the NEA to solve. The legal suit filed by the white association against the NEA's intervention in Louisiana was eventually settled through an agreement reached between the two parties "out of court" in 1973. This paved the way for subsequent NEA-sponsored intervention in the merger negotiations by an arbitrator appointed by the American Arbitration Association. The arbitration continued over a five-year period and eventually led to the final settlement of the merger issue in 1977. As in Mississippi, the main difficulty was less over specific provisions of an agreement than it was one that was caused by attitudes of suspicion and distrust on the part of black and white teachers that reflected the long years of separation between the two groups.[62]

The final settlement in Louisiana was patterned on that achieved in Mississippi. It contained a name change for the new association as well as guarantees for black representation in all of the new group's major executive and policy-making bodies. The eventual favorable outcome in Louisiana required substantial cooperation on the part of the executives of the black and white associations, as well as skillful involvement on the part of the NEA staff: the NEA attorney, the southeastern regional director, and the recently appointed new national executive director. Still, the final merger agreement was marred by a legal objection filed by the long-time executive secretary of the black association. Although this legal initiative failed, it reflected the fact that many black teachers in Louisiana, as well as many whites, felt betrayed by the merger plan.[63] Given the heatedness of the issues, the long period of wrangling, and the wounds suffered by many on both sides, it is difficult to imagine a settlement that could have been achieved without some damage occurring.

ORGANIZATIONAL CONSEQUENCES OF MERGERS

Thus, by the end of the 1970s, the NEA had competed the desegregation of its racially segregated affiliates. At the same time, the association was publicly on record in strong support of school desegregation and a wide variety of related measures supporting minority rights inside and outside of the schools and the association. The alteration in the association's position since 1960 in the entire area of civil and minority rights was remarkable. The NEA went from a stance of noninvolvement in school desegregation in deference to its white segregated state affiliates in the South to one of active intervention on the side of African Americans and other minority groups in its own affairs, in school desegregation, and in other areas unrelated to education.

This change was accompanied by the successful merger of all of the NEA's segregated affiliates and provisions, with some resistance to those mergers being accomplished through the simple absorption of minorities into the larger associations that diluted their voice. Various plans to protect and enhance minorities within the merged associations, as well as in other NEA affiliates, were approved enthusiastically.

The alteration that the NEA experienced on issues related to race and education in the period from 1960 to 1980 was as remarkable as the transformation of the NEA from a hesitant professional association to an activist trade union that took place almost simultaneously. While the two movements proceeded on parallel paths, they were not movements that coincided with each other completely.

In fact, after the NEA became a teachers' union in the early 1970s, it was mainly in its southern affiliates, especially in those that had merged and thereby ended the divisiveness of racial separation, that the unionization movement foundered. Except for Florida, all of the southern states refused to pass legislation enabling the collective bargaining of their teachers. Many NEA members in these states, black and white, approved the action of their legislatures. In spite of this phenomenon, it seems fair to conclude that the desegregation of the NEA could not have occurred without the agitation in the association for an activist, militant brand of teacher unionism. As the thrust for change embodied in the unionization movement was fueled by the civil rights movement and the *Brown* decision, it in turn helped to alter the climate within the NEA toward the acceptance of desegregation.

While there was a significant shift in race relations and racial attitudes in the NEA between 1960 and the 1970s, there was an equally significant and ironic change in the way that race was used in the NEA-AFT fight for the allegiance of teachers in this period. Recall that the AFT straightforwardly advocated swift compliance with *Brown* almost immediately after the decision was announced in 1954. In 1961, in the battle with the NEA for the allegiance of the teachers in New York City, the AFT pointed to its own support of desegregation and to the NEA's hesitancy on the issue to win the allegiance for the union of the city's black

teachers. The AFT also used this issue to woo black teachers, mostly successfully, in other major cities during the rest of the 1960s.[64]

The ironic twist in the situation occurred in 1968 in New York City.
Here the New York AFT local, the United Federation of Teachers (UFT),
found itself pitted against a vocal segment of the city's black community
in the dispute over community control in the predominantly black Ocean
Hill Brownsville attendance district, chosen as a pilot for the city's innovations in decentralization and community control. Charges of racism
were leveled at the teachers' union for its refusal to grant the community
school board in Ocean Hill Brownsville the right to transfer from its
schools white teachers it considered racist. These charges and the rancor
that accompanied the union's strikes over the issue of community control
severely tarnished the union's record of enlightenment on civil rights and
other racial issues. This chain of events, combined with the successful
mergers of the segregated NEA affiliates and other steps taken by the
NEA in the late 1960s and 1970s in the interest of desegregation and the
occupational concerns of black teachers and the larger black community,
left the association in a more advantageous position with minority teachers in its continuing battle for their allegiance with the AFT. Like the
AFT in the 1960s, the NEA used its advocacy and its successes in minority relations in the 1970s and subsequent decades to depict itself positively in contrast with the union in the battle for the allegiance of black
teachers and in the larger public relations war that the two groups waged
frequently, if not constantly.[65]

Within the NEA in the 1960s and 1970s, advocates of democratiza-
tion, in addition to pointing out the increase for teacher power achieved
by the movement to remake the association into a union to compete with
the AFT, also pointed to the increased power and influence exercised by
minority groups that had been energized by the merger movement. There
were a few other more tangible outcomes of the merger movement, however, especially in the states where they took place, that also deserve
mention here.

Most significant, an eventual increase in membership was achieved
in most, if not all, of the merged states. While opponents of merger, or
those who wished to stop or slow the process, could and did point to
membership loss as a major negative consequence, in the long run this
proved not to be the case. By 1979 membership in all of the merged
states had increased well beyond the level that had existed before merger.
The lowest percentage increase in the merged states was achieved in the
state of Florida, where a wrenching statewide teacher walkout and its

aftermath combined to estrange teachers from one another. A subsequent battle for a statewide collective bargaining statute and, after its achievement, bitter and often unsuccessful fights with the AFT over who would represent teachers in collective bargaining, cost the Florida Education Association a substantial loss of members to the union. In spite of these impediments, the merged Florida affiliate's 1979 membership total of approximately thirty thousand was nearly four thousand more than the total membership of the racially separate affiliates before the merger. At the other end of the spectrum, the merged North Carolina affiliate in 1979 had more than twice as many members as the separate affiliates had enrolled prior to merger. The increase in membership in all affiliates after merger compared with membership in the separate affiliates before the process was 87 percent.[66]

Just as important, the quality and quantity of the interactions between the races in the merged associations reflected a substantial, positive change. Individuals learned to deal with one another in ways that they had never before experienced. The progress in race relations within the merged NEA affiliates echoed progress in numerous southern school districts where desegregation occurred successfully. While the region's large cities remained troublingly segregated for the most part, as did most of the large cities in the rest of the nation, progress in some southern cities such as Charlotte, North Carolina, and in many small southern towns and rural school districts was substantial. This is not to say that the South's schools were completely or even largely desegregated in the 1970s, but rather that far more progress along the road to racial equity in education was achieved in the region than in any other area of the nation. Further, the progress toward desegregation that was achieved in the South confounded the pundits and analysts who predicted that desegregation would fail completely. Similarly, in the southern affiliates of the NEA, racial progress was accomplished through the merger of segregated affiliates, an outcome that many, if not most, observers thought beyond the reach of the teachers.[67]

By the late 1970s, then, the NEA had completely accomplished the merger of its segregated affiliates and significantly altered its reputation as an organization indifferent to racial justice. Also by that time, the association had accumulated almost five years of experience in its new, more unionlike organizational structure and stance.

Ironically, however, the NEA's earlier commitment to women teachers had apparently receded in significance, a development that accompanied the moves to unionization and to desegregation. It seemed almost as if recognition of the less powerful elements of the teaching force were a zero-sum game. As blacks and other ethnic minorities were given more recognition within the NEA, the attention to women teachers tended to fade from the association spotlight.

These shifts provide the backdrop for a look at the NEA in the years since merger and unionization, as well as a final evaluation of the association as an actor in the twentieth-century world.

NOTES

[1]In most of the conventions of the 1960s, the NEA's discussions about students concentrated on the issues of the composition and program of its affiliate student organization, the Student National Education Association (SNEA). In the late 1960s, however, the student antiwar movement and other aspects of student activism provoked spirited debate on the convention floor. A task force was assigned to report on ways that the NEA could respond to student activism; see *NEA Proceedings* 108 (1970): 211–12, and ibid. 109 (1971): 131–36. On the Vietnam War debate, see ibid. 109 (1971): 282–86.

[2]Murphy, *Blackboard Unions,* 196–99.

[3]On the phenomenon of massive resistance, see Numan Bartley, *The Rise of Massive Resistance: Race and Politics in the South During the 1950s* (Baton Rouge: Louisiana State University Press, 1969). For a full treatment of the NEA's response to desegregation, see Michael John Schultz, *The National Education Association and the Black Teacher: The Integration of a Professional Association* (Coral Gables, FL: University of Miami Press, 1970).

[4]Allan M. West, *The National Education Association: The Power Base for Education* (New York: Free Press, 1980), 117–18. This volume, written by an associate executive secretary of the NEA shortly after the change of the association toward teacher unionism and reflecting the perspective of one actively involved in that change, is particularly informative on the racial desegregation of the association in the 1960s and 1970s. It functions as a quasi primary source on the subject, as well as a secondary account of the association's history.

[5]The failure to publish data relevant to black teachers' salary inequities was reported by longtime NEA Research Division staff member Hazel Davis in her oral history interview that is preserved in the NEA Archives (Hazel Davis interview [June 17, 1988], box 3117). Davis noted that in the early 1940s Thurgood Marshall, legal counsel for the NAACP (National Association for the Advancement of Colored People) Legal Defense Fund, visited the Research Division to review the unpublished information it had relating to the salaries of black teachers in relation to those of whites. This was vital information to Marshall as he prepared and pursued various salary equity initiatives through the courts in this period.

[6]West, *The National Education Association,* 93–99.

[7]*NEA Proceedings* 98 (1960): 169.

[8]Ibid.: 148.

[9]Ibid. 105 (1967): 19.

[10]Ibid. 99 (1961): 193–211; quotation, 210.

[11]Ibid. 100 (1962): 171.

[12]Ibid. 101 (1963): 232–36; quotation, 233.

[13]Ibid. 102 (1964): 19–21.

[14]Ibid.: 179.

[15]Ibid. 101 (1963): 166.

[16]West, *The National Education Association,* 121. On the NAACP, see Mark Tushnet, *The NAACP's Campaign Against Segregated Education, 1925–1950* (Chapel Hill: University of North Carolina Press, 1987).

[17]West, *The National Education Association,* 121–22.

[18]*NEA Proceedings* 104 (1966): 15.

[19]West, *The National Education Association,* 123.

[20]Ibid., 123–24.

[21]Ibid., 122.

[22]Ibid., 126–27.

[23]Ibid., 126–29.

[24]Ibid., 128.

[25]Samuel B. Ethridge, "Working Paper on Ending Dual Associations" (June 8, 1966), NEA Archives, box 1012.

[26]West, *The National Education Association,* 129–30.

[27]Ibid., 130.

[28]Ibid., 130–31.

[29]*NEA Proceedings* 106 (1968): 133.

[30]West, *The National Education Association,* 265–67.

[31]Ibid., 267.

[32]Ibid., 267–68.

[33]Schultz, *The NEA and the Black Teacher,* 187–89; *NEA Proceedings* 106 (1969): 268–70; and ibid. 107 (1970): 346–48, 613–14, 632.

[34]West, *The National Education Association,* 132–44.

[35]Ibid., 141–42.

[36]*NEA Proceedings* 107 (1969): 55–56.

[37]Ibid., and West, *The National Education Association,* 144–46.

[38]West, *The National Education Association,* 136.

[39]Ibid., 137–38.

[40]Ibid., 138–39.

[41]*NEA Proceedings* 107 (1969): 252–53. For subsequent scholarly confirmation of the grievance of the black North Carolina teacher, see David Cecelski, *Along Freedom's Road: The Hyde County School Boycott* (Chapel Hill: University of North Carolina Press, 1994).

[42]*NEA Proceedings* 107 (1969): 253.

[43]Ibid.: 143, 215.

⁴⁴Ibid.: 268–70.

⁴⁵Ibid. 108 (1970): 613–14, 632.

⁴⁶Ibid.: 170.

⁴⁷Ibid.: 173–74.

⁴⁸Ibid.: 300. Subsequent scholarship has shown that the NTE indeed was put to racially discriminatory uses throughout the South, especially in the state of South Carolina; see Scott Baker, "An American Dilemma: Teacher Testing and School Desegregation in the South," in Wayne J. Urban, ed., *Essays in Twentieth-Century Southern Education: Exceptionalism and Its Limits* (New York: Garland, 1999): 163–98.

⁴⁹For contemporary scholarly accounts that examine basically the same phenomena and reach diametrically opposing conclusions about school desegregation, see David Armor, *Forced Justice: School Desegregation and the Law* (New York: Oxford University Press, 1994); and Gary Orfield, Susan E. Eaton, and the Harvard Project on School Desegregation, *Dismantling Desegregation: The Quiet Reversal of* Brown v. Board of Education (New York: New Press, 1996).

⁵⁰West, *The National Education Association,* 147–48.

⁵¹Ibid., 148; and *NEA Proceedings* 108 (1970): 613–14.

⁵²West, *The National Education Association,* 153–54; and *NEA Proceedings* 108 (1970): 632.

⁵³West, *The National Education Association,* 154–55.

⁵⁴*NEA Proceedings* 109 (1971): 295 (quotation), 297–98.

⁵⁵Ibid.: 317–318 (quotation, 318), 320.

⁵⁶Ibid.: 528. Histories were prepared for every state except Georgia and are available at the NEA Archives.

⁵⁷*NEA Proceedings* 110 (1972): 408–9.

⁵⁸Ibid.: 692 (quotation), 699, and 702 (quotation). Despite the wording, it seems fair to conclude, as I do at the end of this chapter, that the NEA diminished its attention to women teachers and their work lives as it increased its sensitivity to black teachers and other ethnic minorities.

⁵⁹West, *The National Education Association,* 151.

⁶⁰Ibid., 151–52.

⁶¹Ibid.

⁶²Ibid., 155–56.

⁶³Ibid., 157.

⁶⁴Michael John Schultz, author of *The NEA and the Black Teacher,* discussed this development in "After All," *Today's Education: NEA Journal* 60 (November 1971): 80.

⁶⁵For an insightful account of the change in the two groups on civil rights and in other areas, see Maurice Berube, *Teacher Politics: The Influence of Unions* (New York: Greenwood Press, 1988), 106–11.

⁶⁶West, *The National Education Association,* 159.

⁶⁷Ibid., 160–61.

CHAPTER 7

Back to Professionalism
The National Education Association
in the Past Twenty-five Years

This chapter differs substantially from the previous chapters in the content it covers, the material it uses for documentation, and the approach it takes in analyzing that material. The first two matters of difference mentioned, the content of the chapter and its documentation, are the result of a change in the sources available for analysis.

The documentary record for the period since the early 1970s that is available to students of the NEA is markedly inferior, in both quantity and quality, to what is available for the earlier years. One need only look at the volumes of the *NEA Proceedings* for the years up to 1972 and compare them with those since that year to understand this point. The volumes for the earlier years are larger, filled with verbatim discussions of the Representative Assembly, and replete with speeches from elected officers, reports from high-level appointed NEA staff, committee and commission reports, and remarks from distinguished visitors. The volumes starting with 1973 are substantially smaller, devoid of extensive firsthand discussions and debates, and contain far fewer reports and speeches. These latter volumes seem "sanitized" in relation to their predecessors, revealing little about any controversies and making it appear as if there were but one point of view present in the NEA.

In a very real sense, this change in the *Proceedings* is a reflection of the successful remaking of the association into a teachers' union in the 1970s. Unlike in the previous years, particularly the immediately preceding decade of the 1960s, the NEA after 1972 chose not to hang its dirty linen to dry in its written records, not to publicize its divisions over issues and its vigorous internal arguments about how it should conduct itself. The reason for the change is that such records, if available, might be used by NEA opponents in various educational arenas—school administrators whom its negotiators faced directly in formal adversarial proceedings in local school districts, conservative politicians convinced that teacher unionism was a dangerous development, or the AFT, its rival for the allegiance of teachers. The particulars of unionization that explain this shift in approach will be explored more fully in the discussion of collective bargaining in this chapter and in other sections. It is sufficient to say here that the NEA's somewhat paternalistic confidence in its version of educational professionalism that animated the association from 1917 until 1960 and that confidently allowed it to make its *Proceedings* a recorded forum for a wide variety of discussions and debates was replaced by a single-minded devotion to educational unionism in the years after 1972 that made it equally determined to keep those discussions and debates "in house" and not available for general public consumption.

Similar to the change in the *Proceedings,* the *NEA Journal,* in addition to changing its name to *Today's Education* shortly before the change to unionism in the early 1970s, also underwent a substantial alteration in its content and approach. Moving to a more popularly accessible format through an increased emphasis on graphics as well as a shortening of article length and a preference for immediate impact as opposed to complexity and nuance, the new magazine was designed to appeal directly, rather than reflectively, to teachers and to serve their occupational interests first and foremost. This change has made it a less valuable source for scholars to use in analyzing the NEA than was its predecessor publication. Finally, the alteration of the Research Division from the position of a bounteous provider of published information about American education into a body that provided much less published material and much more direct service to other elements of the NEA deserves mention. For the published material of the Research Division also revealed much about the NEA and its organizational agenda and priorities that was not made available after its change in orientation under the unionist leaders and its cessation of much of that publication. Fortunately for the student of the NEA's most recent history, some primary source material relevant to the operation of the Research Division in these years does exist in the NEA Archives. It provides most of the primary source material that is used for the documentation of the discussion of the Research Division, and other discussions, in this chapter.

The difference in the content of this chapter and that of the others in this volume deserves a separate discussion. The already mentioned dearth of primary source documentation outside of the material relevant to the NEA Research Division makes impossible a detailed chronology and analysis of the association in these years, like that undertaken for the previous periods. Instead, this chapter will settle for a more impression-istic picture painted in broad strokes that seeks to suggest the larger meaning of events rather than to describe them in detail or to argue con-vincingly for a single interpretation. Because of the shortage of available primary source documentation for this more recent era in the associa-tion's history, the commentary in the later sections of this chapter will rely to a greater extent on a few extant secondary discussions of the NEA and its organizational rival, the AFT, than on primary sources. One virtue of using other secondary sources is that my own interpretation of the NEA and its evolution can be compared with that of other scholars, hopefully leaving the reader with a richer understanding of the issues under discussion.

The issue of the hesitancy of many historians to comment on the contemporary meanings or current applications of their work must be discussed briefly here, especially in relation to the analysis in this chap-ter. For these reluctant scholars, events that are contemporary or are barely one or two decades old are just not history in the same sense that events of more distant times are. Historians of this point of view find it difficult to develop the same sense of "perspective" on more recent events that they can reach in dealing with more distant happenings. The distance they can maintain from past events gives them some confidence in the soundness of the evaluations they offer about the past that they do not have in commenting on more recent happenings. They worry that their analysis of more recent events is driven directly by their own ideo-logical perspectives and is less likely to take into account material that does not fit that perspective than analysis of more distant events. Part of being distant from an event is allowing its consideration to be subject to a passage of time that permits consideration of more than one perspective. I myself confess to considerable affinity for this point of view, and read-ers of earlier chapters of this volume may well have detected its presence in many of those chapters.[1]

There is a disingenuous aspect in this reluctance to deal with the contemporary or the very recent past, as well as in the hesitancy to con-front the present meaning of one's historical research, however. As many have pointed out, it is often, almost always, a concern with current issues or problems that drives any good historical work. If this is the case, then not to study the recent past and not to make an explicit commentary on the present ramifications of one's historical work is to walk away from that work without exploring perhaps its most interesting and important aspect. Persuaded by this argument, I will consider the recent history of the NEA in this last chapter and, especially in the final sections, offer some commentary on what it means, from my perspective, for the association's present and future prospects.

THE 1970s AND THE 1980s: AN OVERVIEW

As already indicated, the major change in the NEA in this period was its transformation into a full-fledged teachers' union that competed vigorously and effectively with the AFT for the formal allegiance of American teachers. This change had profound implications for the NEA's central office staff and will be discussed in the next section of the chapter.

Given this transformation into a trade union, the most important change in the NEA's organizational structure was not in its organization or staffing arrangements but in its leadership. The move toward elected presidential leadership and away from control of the association by the executive secretary was a significant alteration; however, it was also one that took place gradually over a number of years. The 1972 constitutional convention, as described in the previous chapter, increased the term of the president from one to two years and allowed the president to succeed himself or herself for one term. The presidents who first came into office under these changes, however, functioned more like their predecessors as honorific symbols than like the strong leaders that the architects of the change envisioned. Thus, the first executive secretary to serve under the new constitution, Terry Herndon, continued the tradition of strong staff leadership of the NEA through the 1970s, though he took the association clearly along the path to the teacher unionism that had been feared and loathed by his predecessors.

Subsequent constitutional change in the 1980s paved the way for the era of strong presidential leadership desired by the reformers of 1972. The latter changes, to a three-year presidential term and including the possibility of two terms, allowed a president the possibility of up to a six-year tenure in office in which to make a mark as the leader of the association and to influence the larger world of American education. The first individual to use this longer term to increase her visibility and her stature both in the association and in the larger educational world was an African American woman, Mary Hatwood Futtrell. She gave the NEA an extended period of strong presidential leadership, which increased her visibility to the point that she was as identifiable as a leader to the educational community and to the larger American public as was the AFT's longtime president, Albert Shanker. Further, her visibility as a female and an African American reinforced the image of the NEA, established through its substantial desegregation of its segregated affiliates, as a leader in the movement for equity in American education and American society.

Futtrell's successor, Keith Geiger, served his full two terms, remaining in office until 1996. His service in the interest of an even stronger teachers' union, added to that of Futtrell, gave the NEA well over a decade of strong presidential leadership. Geiger's successor, Robert Chase, has continued that tradition of strong presidential leadership through the end of the 1990s and, with the death of Albert Shanker shortly after Chase's own accession to the NEA presidency, made the contemporary NEA leader into an even more formidable national educational spokesperson. The final sections of this chapter will discuss two of Chase's most important initiatives and their present and prospective impact on teachers and the schools.

With the ascent of three strong leaders to the presidency, each serving a lengthy period in office, the position of executive secretary of the NEA clearly diminished in terms of its leadership responsibilities, especially in relation to external affairs. The top-ranking staff member of the NEA is now just that, the appointed NEA official who is responsible for ensuring that the rest of the NEA staff is mobilized to follow the policies mandated by the Representative Assembly and instituted under the guidance of the elected leadership, particularly the president.

After considering the impact of this new leadership and other structural changes on the activities and orientations of the Research Division, as an example of what happened throughout the NEA's central office staff in response to unionization,[2] this chapter then looks thematically at three other aspects of NEA affairs since the advent of unionization. The topics of collective bargaining, political action, and educational reform will each be considered in some detail for what they show about the nature of the NEA as a union. Finally, the program of current NEA president Robert Chase will be analyzed, especially his advocacy of a "new unionism" for the NEA and his pursuit of a merger with the AFT. The prospects for success, or lack of success, in each of these ventures reveal much about the contemporary NEA as both a teachers' union and as an association of educational professionals not unlike that begun by J. W. Crabtree in 1917 and continued by his successors until 1972. In a way, then, the current NEA is a successor to both of its predecessors, or, at the least, Robert Chase would like it to be.

One final point must be made here. It relates to the political climate in which the NEA has functioned in the past quarter century. The high tide of the period for the NEA was in the middle and late 1970s, when the association became a union and earned substantial political influence as it supported Jimmy Carter's successful presidential campaign in 1976. Four years later, however, the political climate changed in an entirely different direction with the election of Ronald Reagan to the nation's highest office. The two Reagan administrations, and that of George Bush, covering the period from 1980 to 1992, were a bleak time for the NEA. The occupants of the nation's highest executive office were often openly disdainful of the unionized NEA and saw it as one of the leading causes of a deterioration of quality in the nation's schools. The particulars of their view and the NEA's at best partial success in rebutting it will be discussed later in the chapter.

What remains for this initial discussion is to consider what the Clinton presidency, begun in 1992 and continued in the election of 1996, meant for the NEA. On the surface, it was a substantial victory for the association, which backed a winner in the presidency for the first time in more than a decade. Turning that victory into tangible rewards for the nation's teachers proved a more difficult proposition, however. The Republican ascendancy to the position of majority party in the two houses of Congress in 1994 also hampered the NEA severely. Clinton's need to reach some accommodation with the Republicans, along with his ability to promise much and to deliver much less, meant a struggle for his and for the NEA's educational priorities. Thus, although the association was no longer under the gun of presidential disapproval, it has continued to struggle to find its role in the new political alignment. The contours of that struggle are described in the latter sections of this chapter.

Before considering them, however, a look at the early years of this period, the time of the unionization of the association, and how it changed the NEA's central office, is in order. The nature of this change is revealed fully through a close look at one division of that central office, the Research Division, in the 1970s and 1980s.

UNIONIZATION AND THE NEA RESEARCH DIVISION

In the aftermath of the constitutional alteration of 1972 and the subsequent reordering of NEA priorities to conform to the new constitution, the NEA Research Division underwent a substantial change in its role and activities. Before the change, and since the Research Division's inception in 1922, it served mainly as a publishing arm of the association. Its published products were available to all educators, to the public at large, and, just as important, to the scholarly community interested in both the association and in larger American educational issues. The output of the Research Division in these years represented a substantial scholarly accomplishment, as well as an organizational one. Understanding and acknowledgment of the Research Division's significance and achievement on the part of the rest of the NEA staff made it the most prestigious component of the NEA headquarters operation, a sort of first among equals within the NEA central office.[3]

When the NEA began to turn itself, in the early 1970s, into a full-fledged trade union committed to collective bargaining for its local affiliates and to overt political action for itself and its state affiliates, both the emphasis in the activities of the Research Division and its primacy of place in the NEA staff pecking order changed drastically. Whereas formerly the Research Division published its information so that all who were interested could have access to it, in the era of unionism and collective bargaining, information became a resource the scarcity of which was a virtue. Information became a weapon to be used in waging a variety of occupational wars on behalf of NEA members.

In the 1960s early criticism of the public information focus of the NEA Research Division had come, though hesitantly, from the ranks of the teacher activists who were intent on remaking the association into a teachers' union. In the latter part of the decade, within the NEA staff, this criticism of the division came from the organizers who were being hired in the increasingly powerful Field Services Division. Their job was to conduct the representation election battles with the AFT for the right to bargain on behalf of school teachers in school districts. They went to local communities to organize teachers, to negotiate contracts, and to provide contract administration and other services in the interest of building strong local teachers' associations affiliated with the NEA.

In the pre-union era, from 1922 to 1972, the NEA through its Research Division had provided information to both teachers' associations and to school administrators in conformity with the association's larger commitment to unity in outlook between these two sets of actors. This commitment had provoked few complaints and provided few negative consequences. In the collective bargaining era of institutionalized adversarial relations, however, NEA organizers and local association leaders were more and more frequently taken aback at finding, in the midst of a political battle or a hard-hitting round of negotiations with a superintendent or a board of education, that the administration was using figures provided by the NEA Research Division to counter an argument the teacher representatives were making about salaries, benefits, or some other aspect of the negotiation.

This point was eloquently made by the director of NEA Field Services in a 1974 conference on the role of research in the new NEA. In discussing the need for confidentiality in the information provided to NEA affiliates, the top association organizer and negotiator[4] negatively described the old system in which the Research Division had provided information to administrators as well as to teacher representatives. He complained that this situation often caused the NEA field staff no end of embarrassment and frustration:

> But why give them, the opposition, the use of our own information, that prevents them from working. The old salary book is a good example which we used to face at the bargaining table. Now the NEA did all the work and they [the opposition] utilized that information, and it seems to me that they ought to be utilizing their own research facilities and their own staffs and their own efforts to gather that information rather than sitting down at the bargaining table and having the *NEA Research Bulletins* come across the table as evidence in their favor to support an argument or in a fact-finding hearing.[5]

Opponents of the NEA Research Division used this complaint as an argument around which to anchor a rebuilding of the division into an entity whose primary allegiance was to NEA local and state affiliates. This in turn meant that, given its rebuilt structure and focus, most of the division's publications were intended for and restricted to an internal NEA audience.

The move toward more privacy in the conduct of NEA research and the dissemination of its results was clearly reinforced in a memo circulated in May 1974 that discussed the design and implementation of research in the association. The memo assigned coordinating responsibilities to the Research Division but added that the actual research activities were to be undertaken only in response to specific requests from other areas and agencies of the NEA. Discussions about publication or other use of research results were no longer to be made by the Research Division: "Publication or the release of findings will be solely the responsibility of the initiating . . . area unless it desires to involve NEA Research in this aspect of research utilization."[6]

As this change of orientation in the Research Division and in the rest of the NEA staff apparatus unfolded, Terry Herndon, the director of the Field Services Division who had complained about opponents' access to NEA research materials, was chosen as the new executive secretary of the association. Before becoming director of NEA's Field Services staff, Herndon had served as executive director of the Michigan Education Association, one of the most advanced of the NEA's state affiliates in the collective bargaining arena and one from which much of the impetus to unionization and much of the criticism of the old NEA had originated.

Herndon's accession to the top position in the NEA headquarters meant that the Field Services staff's antagonism toward the NEA Research Division's approach to information gathering and publicity was now dominant in the highest circle of the association. What the field staff representatives meant when they discussed responsiveness was substantially different from what NEA's Research Division had been providing for seventy years: copious amounts of statistical data with a minimum of interpretation—all of which was available to anyone who requested it. Organizers needed data with interpretation that showed how it was immediately useful in an organizing campaign or a representation election. If this meant that the data needed to be reconfigured, at the least, or perhaps to be reconceived so that they meant something other than what they appeared to mean, then so be it.

The repudiation of the old style of widespread dissemination of information was clearly typified in the wording of a phrase appended to the bottom of the title page of the Research Division's June 1974 "Summary of Teacher Opinion Poll and NEA Membership Survey" document. The same phrase would be found on the title page of many NEA research documents in the next two decades. It read as follows: "Confidential and not for publication or dissemination without permission of the Director of NEA Research."[7] Needless to say, the NEA research director, now chosen by and responsible to Terry Herndon, was increasingly careful that valuable information be kept in-house and not be made available widely, as it had in the past.

In 1977 Herndon communicated with the entire NEA staff about some important new procedures relating to surveys and polls that were to be conducted by the NEA. He remarked that various units of the central office staff had too often moved independently to conduct their own surveys of affiliates and their members. This practice had resulted in increased expenses and a poorer return rate in the conduct of NEA surveys. In the future he directed that surveys were to be submitted to the NEA Research Division for review and approval, and results were to be obtained through the NEA Research Division unless problems of scheduling necessitated use of an outside contractor. This change in policy, which might on its face seem like support for the Research Division from the NEA's chief executive officer, represented instead a continuation of the restriction of the research group. Herndon indicated this when he added that he would be responsible for adjudicating any conflicts that developed over the policy: "If the program area is dissatisfied with the service of the Research area, then the matter should be referred to me for resolution."[8]

Thus in the late 1970s and early 1980s during Herndon's tenure as leader of the operation of the NEA's headquarters, the Research Division's function was altered drastically from that of a quasi-scholarly enterprise dedicated to the provision of information for a wide audience to one of a service unit for field staff in organizing and in other NEA units. In fact, two of the directors of the Research Division in the 1980s came not from a background in research but rather from other sectors of the association, one from the Field Services unit that had long been critical of NEA Research. Their main qualification for the directorship was their commitment to changing the Research Division. Distinct public service–oriented activities within the Research Division, such as those provided by the archives and the library, were either abolished or severely curtailed and moved out of the research unit. This trend continued after Herndon left the NEA in the mid-1980s. It lasted at least until the end of that decade and continues, with some modifications, to the present.[9] The result for the NEA Research Division, as for most of the rest of the NEA staff, was a turning inward in attention and a move away from traditional public service as a major aspect of operations.

COLLECTIVE BARGAINING

As shown earlier in this volume, the NEA had to overcome many internal obstacles in order to embrace the process of collective bargaining. The major difficulty for opponents of collective bargaining was that it embodied a trade union approach of adversarialism that deviated strongly from the cooperation between teachers and school administrators that had underlain the NEA's commitment to professionalism since the 1920s. Yet embedded within that professionalism was a notion of consultation of teachers by administrators and school board members that was not abandoned but was often institutionalized in the formal negotiations conducted and agreements reached under collective bargaining. Thus, advocates of collective bargaining within the NEA could and did argue that adoption of collective bargaining was not a repudiation of professionalism but rather the road to its meaningful accomplishment. This argument was never effectively answered by NEA opponents of collective bargaining, and that failure had much to do with the association's eventual embrace of collective bargaining as a desirable way to achieve occupational goals, including the achievement of genuinely professional relations with administrators and lay boards.

Well before the constitutional change of 1972, the NEA had been forced to plunge into the arena of collective bargaining competition with the AFT with the passage of public employee representation and negotiation statutes in many states and the resulting needs of many local associations to respond to them. Hiring organizers with backgrounds in collective bargaining in many different trade unions and little or no background in education meant the triumph of the needs of the adversarial process over the ideology of cooperative professionalism in the association. When those organizers were not out in the field in school districts but were spending time in the Washington offices of the NEA, their interactions with longtime NEA staff members imbued with the traditional ideology of professionalism were not uniformly amicable. Yet, the dominance of organizing and collective bargaining as priorities of the NEA was clear, as illustrated in the immediately preceding discussion of changes in the Research Division.

The increasing presence of organizers in the NEA was directly related to a developing militancy in the NEA's own staff organization (NEASO).[10] This organization waged a strike against the NEA management in 1971 over pay and benefits that was a wrenching experience for many longtime NEA staff members. The settlement of the strike did not signal a return to good relations between NEA staff and NEA management, as evidenced by a subsequent Reduction in Force (RIF) of staff by management. In 1973, in response to the RIF and shortly after the NEA constitutional revision, the NEASO affiliated with the Communications Workers of America. Thus, in its own relations with its staff, the NEA was becoming an employer and was being drawn into the hard-boiled labor relations activities that it had opposed as inappropriate for teachers for several decades.

While commitment to collective bargaining clearly was increasing as a priority of the NEA in the 1960s and 1970s, there were several factors that still made it more of a problem for the association than it was for the AFT. One major factor was the masculine ideology implicit and occasionally explicit in the essentials of the collective bargaining process. The very notion of institutionalized adversarial relations, two sides negotiating with each other in "smoke-filled rooms," along with the threat of a strike that was present in the background or the foreground of the negotiations, represented an approach to work relations that made many women teachers uncomfortable. In Newark, New Jersey, for example, the Newark Teachers' Union, according to a recent oral history of its activities, spoke "the hard boiled language of masculine independence." In marked contrast to the Newark unionists were the "straight-laced Wasps," including the women members of the Newark Teachers Association, to whom the "concept of a union was based on the fact that a member of the union was a laborer, a workingman—not a professional, not a college graduate."[11] The affinity of junior high school male teachers and high school males for the AFT and its pursuit of collective bargaining in New York City is another example of the gendered aspect of unionization and collective bargaining. There is no reason to believe that the Newark and New York gendered divisions among teachers over the issues raised by unionization were not present in many other settings where the NEA battled with the AFT over the right to represent teachers.

A second difficulty that had to be overcome before the NEA could completely embrace collective bargaining was the relationship between the national organization and its numerous affiliates. While the NEA remade its national organization and its central office thoroughly in ways that facilitated collective bargaining, it was not as successful in remaking all of its state affiliates into effective advocates and supporters of the process. From the beginning of its first reorganization in 1917, the NEA had been an organization that depended primarily on its state affiliates. When the association moved to strengthen its local associations in the 1940s and again in the 1960s, it did so in top-down ways such as the UniServ program, which provided staff from the national to assist locals, with the entire process brokered through state associations. The complexity and clumsiness of the triple-tiered arrangement hindered the effective pursuit of collective bargaining, just as it had hampered the effective pursuit of many other association programs.

In contrast to the NEA's three-level (national, state, and local) organizational arrangement, collective bargaining is a process that is conducted almost completely on the local level. In collective bargaining states, once an enabling law is passed by the state legislature, the state-level organization is all but superfluous. While it can and does function as a source of advice and support for local collective bargaining activities, the state-level organization is structurally unrelated to the process. State associations in strong collective bargaining states have circumvented this difficulty by working in the legislature for improvements in the collective bargaining laws and, like associations in non–collective bargaining states, for benefits unrelated to collective bargaining such as tenure and retirement laws.

In non–collective bargaining states, however, the state education association has a special and more functional role to play in teacher advocacy. These states, most in the Southeast but also some in the West, are in conservative areas where teachers' unions and collective bargaining are unpopular. Associations in these states often wield substantial power as a lobby in the state legislature. When performing their role as a lobby, these associations push for a wide variety of state laws to win salary gains, improvements in working conditions, grievance provisions, and retirement benefits for teachers. Yet the absence of collective bargaining in these states means that the NEA, which is the strongest teacher organization in most if not all of them, contains different if not competing organizational agendas within two groups of its state affiliates. The states that have collective bargaining must have state associations with distinctly different agendas and priorities from those that do not have collective bargaining. Thus, NEA's commitment to collective bargaining can never be as total as the AFT's, as long as it has a substantial number of affiliates that cannot legally engage in the process.

The one creative response that the NEA, given its powerful lobbying status at the national level, might have made to collective bargaining was passage of an enabling statute at the federal level that superseded state prohibitions of the process. Unfortunately for this objective, the political tide after the NEA achieved its major victory in the federal arena, creation of the U.S. Department of Education in 1979, moved in an opposing direction. The Department of Education that Jimmy Carter and Congress created was a far cry from the powerful entity that the NEA desired. Many federal educational programs remained outside of the new department, and it did not receive either the funding or the prominent leadership that the NEA sought for it. Nevertheless, it represented a "foot in the door," an agency that could have been given more power by subsequent administrations and congresses. Alas, for the NEA, the future of the Department of Education was dimmer rather than brighter. The association spent much of the 1980s fighting the effort of the two Reagan administrations to abolish the Department of Education. Although this fight was successful, the ascendancy of political conservatism represented by the election of Ronald Reagan meant that the prospects of a federal collective bargaining statute became increasingly remote.[12]

Thus the NEA, even as it embraced collective bargaining in the 1960s and 1970s, never embraced it as fully, as wholeheartedly, as singlemindedly as did the AFT. This lack of a complete embrace of collective bargaining, as we will see later, had some positive ramifications, as well as the negative result of hamstringing the NEA in its drive to become the leading advocate for all of America's teachers.

POLITICAL ACTION AND THE AFT

Despite its inability to obtain a federal collective bargaining statute, the NEA has proved a formidable political actor at the national level as well as in many states. When the NEA moved its headquarters to Washington, D.C., in 1917, it set a goal for itself of national political influence. It is mildly ironic that the particular achievement that signified the ultimate fulfillment of this goal, the creation of the Department of Education in 1979, was achieved by the unionized NEA that repudiated, at least in part, the rest of the professional agenda of its predecessor organization. The ascent of the NEA Political Action Committee in the early 1970s came with unionization, but it was not a necessary accompaniment to the rise of collective bargaining. In a sense, it represented a combination of the NEA's preunion and union agendas.

The AFT's opposition to the U.S. Department of Education was a policy that echoed its suspicion of Jimmy Carter, whom it had held at arm's length during his campaign of 1976 and his term in office. In 1980 the AFT supported Carter's most formidable opponent in the Democratic primaries, Edward M. Kennedy of Massachusetts. Carter's victory over Kennedy in the nominating process, again with substantial NEA support, continued the association's string of victories over the AFT in national politics. Those victories were substantially short-circuited, however, by Carter's close-to-landslide loss of the presidency to Ronald Reagan in the 1980 general election.

Events since that election have dimmed the NEA's luster as a national political force. The AFT, in contrast, proved much more able than the association to sustain itself publicly as an agency that spoke for American teachers in the era of conservative educational policies and priorities of Ronald Reagan and his Republican successor, George Bush. Perhaps this success was due, in some part, to the fact that the AFT spoke publicly with one strong voice, that of its able and articulate president,

Albert Shanker. Shanker's views on education, politics, and any other topic he chose to consider were published in a weekly column in the Sunday edition of the *New York Times*. Though this "column" was actually an advertisement paid for by the teachers' union, it quickly became much more than a paid ad, because the AFT chief executive weighed in with measured assessments on a variety of educational issues.

The NEA, in contrast, never could gain the attention at the national level that one consistent voice, speaking on a regular basis in a prestigious national outlet, gained for its rival organization. As already mentioned, the personal dominance of Shanker as spokesman for American teachers was mitigated somewhat by the long tenure of Mary Futtrell and of Keith Geiger; however, even these substantial personal rivals could not find the outlet that allowed them the regularity of attention and the prestige in the educational community that Shanker garnered from his column.

To return to a consideration of national politics, it seems fair to conclude that the NEA, in the period of Republican ascendancy, maintained its edge over the AFT in Democratic Party politics. The result, however, was that the association became almost completely identified with the Democrats, while the teachers' union was viewed less skeptically by Republicans and others committed to an educational agenda that was not that of the Democrats. The Clinton administrations of the 1990s have paid proper homage to the NEA's political clout by verbally acknowledging the association and its priorities.[13] Clinton's relative lack of educational initiatives as president, other than protection of existing programs against congressional Republicans intent on aborting or diminishing their funding and impact substantially, has meant, however, that in a very real sense the political configuration of educational priorities inherited from his Republican predecessors has held relatively constant.

Like the NEA, the AFT is oriented primarily to the commitments of the Democratic Party but with some substantial differences in its relation to the other political party. The AFT did not simply oppose the Republican educational initiatives of the 1980s but tried to work with some Republicans in their mutual interests. Perhaps some of the explanation for the AFT's willingness to work with, or at least not simply to oppose, Republicans comes from its large presence in New York State, where Republicans are more moderate and less influenced by the ideological conservatism of the Christian right that affects, if not dominates, Republicanism in the South and the West. The AFT has often supported Republicans in New York City and politicians in New York State who have agreed with the union on parts of its agenda and conducted their campaigns for office as individuals who represent something more than reflexive opponents of public employee unionism.

Before discussing further NEA-AFT differences in the period of Republican ascendancy in the 1980s and early 1990s, the point must be made that the two groups are in substantial agreement on most of their political priorities. Equity in school finance—increased funding for poorer school districts to bring them close to parity with wealthier districts—is a cause that both groups support wholeheartedly. Similarly, they agree in their opposition to the three core planks of the Republican educational platform of the 1980s and 1990s: tuition tax credits for private school parents, prayer in the public schools, and any version of a voucher or choice plan that provides public money for private schools.

One area of difference in the commitments of the organizations that has spilled over into the political arena was discussed in the previous chapter: their responsiveness to racial and ethnic minority concerns and to gender concerns. Since the 1968 dispute in New York City over community control and the right of the minority-dominated board of education in the experimental district of Ocean Hill Brownsville in Brooklyn to transfer from the district white teachers it considered racist, the AFT has taken a more conservative line in regard to minority claims for equity. When affirmative action on behalf of minorities in the area of admission to professional schools was contested before the Supreme Court in the *Bakke* case of the 1970s, the AFT supported the white plaintiff who claimed that he was being discriminated against by the University of California medical school, which preferred, he contended, less qualified minority applicants for admission. The NEA, in contrast, reflecting the change it underwent as it merged its segregated affiliates, vigorously supported affirmative action in this and other cases.

Another difference between the two groups was evident in their consistent advocacy of rather different curricular orientations. The AFT has strongly voiced allegiance to a single curriculum that emphasized the basic subjects in elementary education and the more academically oriented studies in the traditional subjects of mathematics, the sciences, and the humanities in high schools and colleges. In contrast, the NEA has vigorously supported multicultural curricular emphases and has sometimes challenged the idea of an essential core of knowledge, particularly Eurocentric cultural knowledge, for all students.

The clash of the two organizations in relation to minority claims for equity was also sharpened in the debate over the policy of bilingual education. Generally, the AFT opposed bilingual programs for both political and educational reasons. The federation's educational argument was that bilingual education was a policy not supported by research findings and one that distracted attention from the essential educational task of gaining competence in the English language. Politically, the AFT argument was that bilingualism was really a movement to establish language minorities as culturally separate groups that pursued their own interests in ways that alienated them from the larger American culture. In contrast, the NEA took the position that bilingualism was an educationally appropriate way for non-English speakers to learn both their own language and the English language. Politically, the NEA saw bilingualism as a device that language minorities could use to defend themselves against prejudicial attitudes on the part of so-called mainstream Americans and against policies that catered to those prejudices.

The NEA has also been a consistent supporter of policies directed to protecting and enhancing the rights of women in educational institutions and in the larger society, while the AFT has been more selective in its advocacy of women's issues. And in the same vein, the NEA has consistently supported special education initiatives to "mainstream" handicapped and other special students into regular classes, while the AFT has worried more about the negative effect of these policies on the academic progress of regular, as opposed to special, students. All of these orientations, when combined with the visibility of NEA president Mary Futtrell, an African American woman, propelled the association to a position of leadership in the minority rights movement in the 1980s. Under her white male successors in the 1990s, the orientation toward minority rights did not diminish. Affirmative action personnel commitments in the NEA's own national office have also resulted in a staff that has a large and visible minority contingent, including some minority members in leadership positions.

The NEA, then, has emerged in the late twentieth century as a consistent supporter of the campaigns of African Americans, of other ethnic minority groups, and of women as they all sought to preserve or expand on gains won in the 1960s and 1970s. The AFT, in contrast, has been much more open to the counterclaims of white males who charge that, as a rule, policies that seek to protect or advance minority or women's interests represent "reverse discrimination."[14] The AFT's position, which might be compared with that of many of the "Reagan Democrats" who defected to the Republican candidates in the elections of the 1980s and early 1990s, is a traditional trade unionist defense of principles such as seniority rights in employment relations that prominority policies often seek to abrogate. The most publicized arena for these clashes has been in the public employment and advancement of policemen and firemen, occupations where minorities have become present to any substantial degree only in the fairly recent past. The NEA, reflecting the longtime presence and influence of women in its affairs, as well as its own commitments to minority teachers in the desegregation of its affiliates, has been more willing to consider alternatives to seniority that seek to balance the claims of minority workers less likely to have attained the amount of seniority that yields effective job security.

The two organizations have also clashed over political issues seemingly unrelated to education. On foreign policy the AFT took a relatively consistent anticommunist stand in the 1970s and 1980s, while the NEA was more suspicious of anticommunism as a reflexive response and more willing to entertain foreign policy alternatives. The NEA, or at least those visible in its leadership positions, vigorously embraced the peace movement and offshoots such as the nuclear freeze movement in the 1970s and 1980s. The 1981 NEA convention saw the members endorse this leaning on the part of their leaders when delegates approved a resolution opposed to nuclear war.[15]

Two years later the positions of the two groups on foreign policy had educational ramifications in their battle with each other for members and primacy of place. In 1983, when the NEA published a teachers' manual on nuclear war that clearly opposed the use of atomic weapons, the AFT charged that the pamphlet represented one-sided "propaganda" rather than a legitimate approach to the teaching of controversial material.[16] Again, the AFT's position represented the relatively conservative but long-standing position on foreign policy followed by the AFL-CIO hierarchy under its venerable leader, George Meany. Many think that Albert Shanker's frequently talked about accession to a role in the highest circles of the AFL-CIO might have been a factor in the AFT's conservative foreign policy views. Yet, they also may have truly reflected Shanker's own orientation. The NEA, in contrast, was much more venturesome in entertaining more liberal alternatives in the foreign policy arena.

THE NEA, THE AFT, AND EDUCATIONAL REFORM

One outcome of the years of Republican dominance of the presidency, 1980–92, was a change of the agenda in the national discussion of education, particularly in the debates on educational reform. While educational equity and equality dominated the reform agenda in the 1960s and the 1970s, the Reagan administration was able to make "excellence" the prime focus of educational reform discussions in the 1980s and early 1990s. The excellence movement received a large boost in 1983, when a Reagan administration commission published the pamphlet, *A Nation at Risk*.[17] The reactions to the pamphlet on the part of the NEA and the AFT are instructive in illustrating further the differences between the two groups in the 1980s and early 1990s.

In one sense, *A Nation at Risk* represented the attempt of Reagan's first secretary of education, Terrel Bell, to move the Republican educational agenda away from a reflexive negativism represented most graphically in its desire to abolish the recently established Department of Education.[18] The other Reagan educational policies—tuition tax credits, prayer in the public schools, and vouchers or other choice plans by which public funds could be used to send children to private schools—also appeared to offer precious little to those interested in the educational reform priorities of the 1960s and 1970s. The most vocal and articulate advocates of Reagan's educational agenda included advocates of private school interests and neoconservative intellectuals disenchanted, mainly on cultural and/or intellectual grounds, with public education.

A Nation at Risk managed to raise the issue of educational excellence in broad enough terms that it appealed, at least in part, to many reformers concerned with improving American education. The pamphlet argued that as a nation the United States had slipped badly in the educational realm. Using international measures of subject matter achievement, it claimed that the United States was lagging behind its economic competitors, particularly many of the European nations and, most important, Japan. Skillfully using the language of international economic warfare, the pamphlet dramatically intensified points that had been made earlier in several articles and books praising the educational system of Japan. Given the status of the Japanese as the most visible and most successful competitor of the United States in the emerging global economic order, the pamphlet aroused substantial concern over American education.

The response of the NEA and the AFT to the excellence movement that was given dramatic impetus by *A Nation at Risk* was quite disparate. Generally, the NEA reacted negatively, seeing educational excellence as a continuation and intensification of the Republican attacks on public schools and school teachers. While on the whole the association may have been correct in this assessment, its shrill opposition to the pamphlet and the excellence movement tarnished its public image, making it seem an impediment to sensible discussion of the issues raised. The AFT, in contrast, was much more measured in its discussion of educational excellence, thereby allowing development of its public image as a group willing to examine criticism judiciously and to respond to it in a statesmanlike way.

The difference is easily illustrated further through a discussion of the attention paid in *A Nation at Risk* to the issue of higher standards for students and teachers. The pamphlet called for the strengthening of the academic curriculum in the schools and, in turn, for a renewed emphasis on examinations and standardized tests to measure the results. Both of these emphases had some attraction for Albert Shanker and the AFT. Shanker, and the scholars in the educational and academic community who had his ear, had been concerned for some time about the educational flabbiness of American schools and colleges. Particularly, they worried about the educational institutions' unwillingness to counter the diluting of the curriculum that was occurring because of vocationalism and, even more important, because of multiculturalism.[19]

Shanker also astutely linked the standards movement that was approved in *A Nation at Risk* to the fears of many teachers for their mental and physical welfare in classrooms that were increasingly populated by minority students and others seemingly unmotivated by traditional academic commitments. In many of his columns in the *New York Times,* Shanker emphasized school discipline in addition to academic standards. His willingness to entertain the possibility that the schools were indeed failing intellectually contrasted sharply with the NEA's ringing defense of public education. While the association's commitment to the public schools was laudable, its seeming willingness to ignore the problem of grievous and what many thought obvious academic deficiencies tarnished it as an organization unwilling to look at real problems and uninterested in trying to solve them.

The contrast between the NEA and the AFT was just as sharply, though more subtly, illustrated in their reactions to the call in *A Nation at Risk* for raising the standards of preparation for school teachers. Again, the NEA appeared simply defensive in the face of plausible, if not demonstrable, criticism. Shanker, in contrast, used the pamphlet's drive for higher teacher standards to pursue an idea for teacher reform with which he had recently become enamored. The AFT participated enthusiastically in discussing and planning the National Board for Professional Teaching Standards (NBPTS), a body that was in the process of developing a national certification instrument for teachers. While the NBPTS's activities were certainly in line with the NEA's long-standing desires for occupational improvement and for a more powerful national role in educational affairs, the failure of the national board to go on record against the principle of merit pay, a concept long opposed by both the NEA and the AFT, caused the association to react skeptically to the initial national certification efforts. The AFT, in contrast, pragmatically ignored the issue of merit pay and concentrated on the ways that national certification could increase the professional standards and standing of the teaching occupation. The NEA eventually adopted the position of conditional support for the NBPTS and for national teacher certification but with reservations that related to some internal dissent in the association on the issue. The entire episode furthered the association's image as a reflexive naysayer to educational reform efforts and the AFT's image as a more judicious organization that seriously looked at proposals for reform and backed those with which it agreed.[20]

Thus, on the educational reforms promulgated by advocates of educational excellence, as on the race issue, the NEA and the AFT can be seen to have reversed their long-held positions. Albert Shanker skillfully guided the federation to the support of stronger classroom discipline, stronger academic standards, and more rigorous certification for teachers, along with other attempts to improve teaching, all as part of the necessary advocacy of teacher professionalism that seemed appropriate given the political climate and the occupational conditions teachers faced in the 1980s. The AFT's commitment to professionalism in teaching was enhanced by some of the bargaining agreements reached by its locals. Some of these agreements implemented career-ladder plans by which senior teachers mentored, served as consultants to, and in some cases evaluated their junior colleagues. The NEA, in contrast, hewed closer to a trade union line—one that advocated more traditional protectiveness of teachers against threats to their jobs from outsiders such as reformers for excellence.

The above analysis, in drawing the contrast between the two groups, is overgeneralized in several ways. For example, it ignores successful cooperation between NEA state affiliates and educational reform governors in states such as South Carolina and Tennessee. These states, with NEA approval, instituted a more rigorously academic curriculum, an intensified commitment to standardized testing, and a variety of plans for teacher improvement including career ladders that in a sense institutionalized a merit pay principle.

Also, this analysis of different responses to educational issues allows Albert Shanker to speak for all the members of the AFT and the leaders of the NEA to speak for all of its members, which ignores the diversity of opinion on educational excellence and educational reform present among the teachers who compose the NEA and the AFT memberships.[21] And finally, this analysis lets stand oversimplifications of complex issues on the part of both organizations that represented positions often taken more with the objective of countering the views and positions of the other organization or of garnering positive public attention, in preference to taking a judicious stand on an educational matter.

In spite of these complexities in the position of both organizations, it is also the case that Albert Shanker effectively advocated educational reform and teacher professionalism that gave him, and to a somewhat lesser extent, his organization, an image of wise statesmanship that in an earlier era was the self-proclaimed property of the NEA. Raising the standards for new recruits to the teaching occupation, a policy that Shanker repeatedly endorsed, also enhanced the AFT's image while in no sense repudiating traditional trade union priorities. Increasing standards for new recruits helps protect the existing practitioners of the occupation by making entry more difficult. Higher standards for entry was a long-sought goal of most of the craft unions that helped to found and to develop the American Federation of Labor as an organization that protected the rights and sought the economic benefit of skilled workers. What Shanker managed to do was to market his clearly conservative, craft-oriented views on a variety of issues, packaging most of them as a professional approach to educational reform and downplaying their more socially regressive aspects. A clear example of that social regression is that raising standards for new teachers presents a further obstacle for minority members who want to become teachers.

In contrast to Shanker and the AFT, the NEA was still hamstrung by its size, the diffusiveness of its leadership, and the variety of opinions on the part of the many national and state leaders who could be considered spokespersons for the association. Because of these conditions, the NEA failed to publicize effectively the "professionalism" that was implicit, at least, in its own cornerstone approach to educational reform of advocating teacher participation in decision making in schools and school systems. It was not clear that the NEA would prove capable of establishing a position of judicious critic of some reform measures, enthusiastic advocate of others, and careful evaluator of all proposals for change, given its record on reform issues in the 1980s.

The ascendancy to the presidency of Robert Chase in 1996, a candidate who called for the association to take more leadership in educational reform and for an era of "new unionism" in which the NEA would attend to teachers' professional needs as well as to their salaries and benefits, indicates at the least that there is an awareness of this problem in the association's highest circles. Two of Chase's priorities, merger with the AFT and the "new unionism," are the subject of the next two sections of this chapter.

MERGER WITH THE AFT

The possibility of a merger between the two national teachers' unions has been a part of the American educational scene for the past quarter century, since the NEA remade itself into a union in the early 1970s. And even more than a decade before that change, in the 1950s Myron Lieberman was discussing the pros and cons of a possible merger that neither organization appeared ready to consider.[22] Lieberman's insight at that time, namely that competition between the two organizations for the allegiance of the nation's teachers was as much of a drain on the resources of each body as it was a set of circumstances that provided them with the possibility of invigorated activity, has proved generally correct. Further, the negative aspects of organizational competition have increasingly been noticed in the highest inner circles of both the NEA and the AFT and have sparked a series of attempts at merger over the years.

Shortly after the NEA's change to union status in the early 1970s, there was a merger of the New York affiliates of both the association and the federation at the state level. The enormous difference in power between the two groups, with the AFT being far more visible and active in the merger, resulted in the eventual takeover of the NEA affiliate by the federation rather than a genuine merger of equals. What were considered machinations at the NEA convention by the New York affiliate, at least in the eyes of NEA leaders, along with suspicions of the agenda of Albert Shanker, still the most powerful and visible teacher unionist in New York State, caused the NEA to create a new affiliate in New York to compete with the merged organization. A similar set of events occurred in Florida a few years later—merger of the two affiliates at the state level, dominance by the AFT side, and the subsequent creation of a new NEA state affiliate. This time, however, the result was as much the outcome of bad blood created by the statewide teacher walkout as it was of any actions or policies of the merged group.

After these two aborted state mergers, though discussion of the issue of merger remained alive within the NEA, any actual initiatives toward implementing the discussion were unsuccessful. The financial cost to each organization of competing with the other, and the nonfinancial consequences of not competing, continued to burden both groups, however. In the late 1980s, affiliates of the organizations began to take matters into their own hands at the local level, where the costs and other debilities of frequent competition in representation elections were felt most acutely. In the two most prominent cities in California, San Francisco and Los Angeles, NEA and AFT affiliates merged at the local level. Although these mergers were largely successful, they presented some difficulties for the local groups in apportioning which national organization would get what part of dues money in a dual affiliation as well as who would be delegates to which convention.

The success of the local mergers, as well as a realization of the complications that they created for the national groups and the continued costs of not being merged, caused NEA president Keith Geiger to rekindle merger negotiations with the AFT in the early 1990s.[23] Geiger's initiative met with a positive response from the AFT, and the two groups engaged in substantial preliminary talks that culminated in a set of formal negotiations over merger that began in 1993. These negotiations lasted for more than a year, but ultimately the two sides failed to reach an agreement. Much of the responsibility for that failure came from the NEA side of the negotiating table. The NEA negotiators were confined by a set of preconditions that had been placed on their work by the 1993 NEA convention, which formally authorized their participation in the talks. These preconditions were based on issues of substantial importance to the NEA, its leaders and its members, as well as on some longstanding fears of the association. Among these were concerns based on the New York and Florida mergers that the NEA not be taken over by the AFT, a devotion to the longtime tradition in the NEA that voting at the convention by secret ballot be maintained in the new organization, and a firm conviction that Albert Shanker not be the president of the new organization.

After the 1994 failure of the merger talks, the 1995 NEA convention opted to reconsider their preconditions of two years earlier and gave their negotiators more flexibility if a new set of negotiations were to occur. Those negotiations eventually did begin, and before they ended, the death of Albert Shanker in 1996, though it cast a pall over the union and robbed American educational discourse of a powerful voice, increased the chances of a positive outcome. At about the same time, Keith Geiger retired as NEA president and was succeeded by his vice president,

Robert Chase of Massachusetts. Chase quickly gained enormous visibility for his effort to infuse a "new unionism" into the NEA, which will be discussed in the final section of this chapter. Another part of Chase's commitment to change within the NEA was to intensify the pursuit of merger, which was in the midst of being negotiated.

Some political and economic factors underlying the merger negotiations of the 1990s deserve at least brief mention here. Both the NEA and the AFT have spent the past two decades under the political gun, so to speak, as the Republicans first dominated the White House for a twelve-year period and, two years after losing the presidential election of 1992, won both houses of Congress for the first time in several decades. These election victories reflected, if they did not create, a general public mood of antiunionism. This antiunionism and conservative political climate fueled a substantial reduction in the percentage of private sector workers in trade unions and a distinctly intensified negative public image for public employee unions. The Republican ascendancy also abetted a trend in educational finance that was already in place before 1980—the increase in the state-level portion of funds for public education and the corresponding decrease in both the federal and local financial effort. All of these factors, added to the realization of the economic costs of continued organizational competition, were on the minds of association and federation leaders, members, and negotiators.

Antiunionism, however, at least in the form of opposition to participation in the AFL-CIO, was still a distinct part of the worldview of substantial segments of the NEA in the 1990s. The southern and western affiliates led the way in this regard, but even members from some of the more labor-oriented states were not immune to fear of the dominance of "blue collar" orientations, values, and status in a merged organization. When the NEA allied itself in the 1970s in a Coalition of American Public Employees with the American Federation of State, County, and Municipal Employees and other public employee unions, antiunionism as a hallowed NEA principle was dealt a substantial blow. Subsequent state-level agreements between NEA affiliates and various unions, some affiliated with the AFL-CIO and some independent, also eroded the principle of antiunionism. Still another factor mitigating antiunion ideology in the NEA was the successful move within the association to organize educational support personnel, undertaken to compete with the AFT for the allegiance of school bus drivers, cafeteria workers, teachers aides, and clerical staff. And finally, antiunionism took an important symbolic blow when the NEA was itself declared a union that came under the terms of the federal labor law, the Landrum Griffin Act, in terms of its tax status and political activities. While all of these developments softened antiunionism in the NEA, they did not destroy the phenomenon completely, as we will see shortly.

Given all of these changes, it was not surprising when the latest round of negotiations between the NEA and the AFT yielded an agreement early in 1998 that promised to merge the two organizations by creating a genuinely new teachers' union. All that stood between the agreement and its implementation was approval by the NEA and the AFT at their summer conventions. The AFT convention, as expected, approved merger overwhelmingly a few weeks after the NEA meeting. In the case of that NEA convention, however, the merger was rejected by a substantial margin. The convention, which was required to approve the merger by a two-thirds vote in order for it to be implemented, instead turned it down by a margin of 58 to 42 percent. This overwhelmingly negative vote was a surprise, at least when considered against the backdrop of public optimism on the part of President Chase and other NEA supporters of merger regarding the chances for its approval.

Given the secret ballot as the way of conducting NEA business, the identity of those who voted against the merger, as well as the reasons for their vote, are not likely ever to be known completely. In fact, AFT analysts of the situation charged that the lack of accountability between representatives and the constituencies that elected them was precisely what allowed delegates to the NEA convention to use the secret ballot to vote down the merger, which was desired by the membership.[24] This argument is countered by NEA members who claim that the public vote of the AFT at its conventions allows the leadership of the union to maintain a stifling control over its delegates who, if they vote against the wishes of the leadership, do so in a public forum where they can be identified and marked for reprisal.

One analysis of the NEA vote, by a longtime NEA staff member with a background and commitment to the labor movement, revealed several points that should not surprise the readers of this volume. That analyst identified fear of blue collar trade unionism, particularly in the Southeast, as a substantial part of the reason for opposition to merger. Other factors that motivated NEA delegates to oppose merger, according to this analysis, included objection to the lack of term limits for the presidency, allegiance to the secret ballot, and insufficient commitment to minority teachers in the merger.[25] The lack of provision for term limits alarmed the NEA leaders, who did not want presidential domination of their organization like that which they saw as characteristic of the AFT in the Shanker years. Any teachers' organization, they believe, must be more than the property of one person. The allegiance to the secret ballot is also, as just discussed, a priority of those who object to one-person rule. The minority representation concern is one that the NEA of the past twenty years has honored more substantially than the AFT has, as pointed out in the previous chapter and earlier in this one. The fear here is that a merged organization that does not provide solid guarantees of minority representation might well follow the AFT path of diffident response and diminished commitment to that concern.

Whatever the configuration of motives that supported the vote against merger, it meant a substantial rejection of the proposal by the NEA convention. And yet, certain other aspects of the situation complicate this relatively simple conclusion. Particularly important is the commitment that was reiterated by the same NEA convention that rejected merger: to continue to act cooperatively with the AFT. Also important is the NEA delegates' concern for preservation of the organization that they know and to which they are committed, as opposed to one that, if merger had been approved, would have been substantially different though not necessarily more like the AFT. And finally, the statement of one NEA delegate that he was opposed to affiliation primarily because it fueled those opponents of teacher unionism who would argue that affiliation was merely a power grab and not a commitment to educational improvement, echoed the stated commitments and a substantial part of the real agenda of the preunion NEA.[26]

The current state of this historic commitment to the professional goals of educational reform and educational improvement bears discussion as the final part of this analysis of the NEA in the 1990s. To discuss the NEA's commitment to reform in this decade, however, requires consideration of the "new unionism" argued for so eloquently and enthusiastically by NEA president Robert Chase since his election in 1996.

THE NEW UNIONISM AND THE OLD

The new unionism that has been coined as a term in the statements of Robert Chase since his ascendancy to the presidency of the NEA in 1996, has roots in association activities earlier in the 1990s as well as in earlier decades of the twentieth century. Before discussing those particulars, the contours of the concept of new unionism must be outlined. Briefly, the new unionism is that set of orientations, goals, and commitments that seeks to add something significant to the pursuit of teacher benefits through the collective bargaining that has characterized the NEA since the 1970s. What the new unionism adds is variable, depending on the circumstances that teachers and schools face in any particular setting, but the variety can be summarized under the labels of "educational reform" and "quality education."

One of the aspects of the development of a more diverse agenda for the association in the early 1990s was the contextualizing of the traditional union objective of economic improvement in ways that looked at its larger impact. Implicit, if not explicit, in this effort was an attempt to show how teacher and school improvement can serve democratic objectives as well as teacher needs. For example, beginning in the late 1980s and continuing into the 1990s, the NEA's Research Division began a series of publications called *Eye on the Economy,* which sought to encourage the NEA and its affiliates to link its traditional pursuits to consideration of the larger economic picture within which they were taking place. Other examples of this phenomenon of seeing the NEA and its economic activities in a larger context included publications that explored the link between education and economic development and that looked critically from an equity perspective at various types of taxation policies in relation to support of public schools. The similarity of this activity to that which had been undertaken in the NEA in the 1930s in reaction to the depression was either unknown, or known and not remarked on, in NEA circles.[27]

The search for new directions also invaded the most traditional union activity in which the NEA engaged, collective bargaining. Here the association looked for broader categories in which to analyze and to characterize its activities, categories that spoke at least potentially to non–collective bargaining as well as to collective bargaining states. The effort was to conceptualize and extend services to all of its affiliates. Particularly important in this light was the consideration of nonadversarial approaches such as interest-based bargaining or "collaborative bargaining," the topic of an NEA publication in 1991.[28] Both these activities and the attempt just discussed to consider the wider economic context in which affiliates existed were undertaken at least in part because of the largely negative political climate in which the association functioned in the 1980s. Yet these relatively creative responses to that adversity showed that the NEA was capable of thinking about itself and its affiliates in new ways that might allow adversity to be the spark for innovations that promised productive outcomes.

The heart of the new unionism, however, is more than a broader contextualization of traditional unionism. It is a commitment to educational reform. And this aspect of the movement also preceded President Chase's rise to the top of the NEA hierarchy in 1996. In the 1995–96 report on the *Status of the American Public School Teacher,* a report of results of a survey of teachers that the NEA has conducted at regular intervals since 1956, substantial attention was paid for the first time to issues of the quality and the improvement in quality of education. For example, the survey contained items relating to the availability of such instructional resources as computers, videocassette recorders, instructional software, and other teaching aids. Also included in the survey items were such topics as shared authority between teachers and administrators for decisions about pedagogy, variety in teaching methods, flexibility in scheduling classes and classroom activities, and assessment of instruction.[29]

Since 1996 Robert Chase has made the commitment to educational reform a cornerstone of his presidency of the NEA, and he has publicized that commitment indefatigably in association activities and in larger forums. Coining the term *new unionism* as the watchword of his commitment to a changed NEA, Chase has outlined his ideas for that change at great length.

First, for Chase the new unionism means a reconfiguration of the adversarial relations that have been institutionalized in the collective bargaining process. What Chase seeks are partnerships between teachers and administrators—cooperative relationships that allow them to act together for their mutual benefit and, most important, for the benefit of the schoolchildren who are their charges. Included in this commitment to changed relations between teachers and administrators is a commitment to restructuring in school organization that empowers all actors to participate creatively and productively in the educational process. The affinity between Chase's desires and the teacher participation movement of the preunion NEA bears mention. Chase's new relationships resemble, in part, structural change proposals—such as site-based management, which seeks to empower teachers to conduct education in those institutions productively—that have been voiced for at least the past decade and that have received support from the NEA. Chase, however, has made it clear that he is willing to entertain proposals far beyond teacher participation or site-based management, proposals that might reconstruct the very concepts of schooling and teaching in ways not yet tried in any setting.[30]

For Chase and his new unionism, the goal of restructuring, or of any other educational reform, is increased educational opportunity and increased educational achievement for students in public schools. This commitment has caused the NEA to embrace the reform proposal for "charter schools" in many states, including my own state of Georgia. Charter schools are creatures of the legislatures or other regulatory bodies that charter them, usually freeing them from many if not most of the state regulations as well as the local district rules that traditionally regulate public education. While many see the charter school movement as another attempt by the political right to disestablish the public school system in states, Chase and his reform-minded NEA colleagues embrace it for its potential to improve public education. The intent of association members applying for charters is stated as a desire to conduct truly innovative public schools that will serve as models for the betterment of the entire enterprise.

There is little doubt that Robert Chase seems fully committed as an individual to the cause of school reform and that this commitment from the highest elected position in the NEA may well mean a new day for the association. What Chase also understands but does not emphasize in his presentations is that the new unionism he advocates is in many ways a return to the NEA as it existed before the 1970s. Cooperative relationships between teachers and administrators and an allegiance to educational improvement were two of the fundamental commitments by which the NEA defined itself for more than four decades in opposition to the AFT. And if the analysis in these pages is in any way faithful to the forces it has tried to describe and evaluate, then those commitments were important to a number of teachers, particularly to many women teachers, throughout much of the twentieth century. The economic and social upheavals of the 1960s, however, exposed much that was faulty in the NEA's commitments, including those to cooperation and to school improvement. Too often, those commitments masked a situation of gross inequality in school relations, a dominance over teachers by administrators. They also hid a worsening economic situation for teachers, largely because the school districts were uninterested in contending with or unable to keep up with the negative impact on teachers of inflation in the larger economy.

The challenge for Robert Chase and his new unionism is to try and blend creatively the two aspects of the new and old unionism, commitment to educational improvement for students and to economic improvement for teachers. It is at least mildly ironic that in the NEA, the new unionism represents to a significant extent the values espoused by the old NEA, the professional association of the preunion era. As described in these pages, that old NEA had mixed results in achieving its objectives. It was more successful for years at keeping the AFT at bay and at assuaging, if not answering, the status and equity concerns of women teachers than it was at genuinely accomplishing substantial improvement in either teachers' conditions or educational achievement. In a very real sense, then, Chase poses a challenge for which the precedents are close to useless. An NEA that is able to serve teachers economically and professionally—through material and educational improvement—has never existed. What did exist before the union era was an NEA that talked persuasively about education and about professionalism without attending successfully to the concerns of either of these priorities.

If the NEA at the turn of the twenty-first century is successful in accomplishing the objectives outlined by its new president, then it will truly occupy the position of a genuinely "new union." President Chase's advocacy of merger with the AFT might have been undertaken in an effort to eliminate the obstacle that occupational rivalry poses to the prospects of a genuinely reformed teacher organization. His members, however, evidently responded to concerns that were based on traditional NEA fears of a self-interested trade unionism that does not allow, in their minds, substantial consideration of reform. At least on this issue of merger, Chase's lack of success does not bode well for his other efforts at leadership.

Still, his new designs for the NEA are interesting, promising, and at the same time, filled with the same signs of wishful thinking that surround almost all attempts at reform of the public schools at the end of the 1990s. The contours of school success are well illustrated in many segments of American educational enterprises—private schools and suburban public schools continue to do a relatively good job of preparing students for university study and success in later life. The places where these objectives are not so readily accomplished—the public schools of our nation's larger cities and older suburbs, where the members of the two teachers' organizations are concentrated—are the places where Chase's hopes and plans will be tested. One can only hope that he and the NEA will be successful.

NOTES

[1]"Presentism" has been a contested issue in the historiography of American education at least since the charge of distortion of the past in the interest of the present was leveled at Ellwood Cubberley by Bernard Bailyn and Lawrence Cremin in the 1960s. For a provocative account of this dispute, one that is more balanced and less critical of Cubberley than were Cremin and Bailyn, see Sol Cohen, "The History of the History of American Education: The Uses of the Past," in Cohen, *Challenging Orthodoxies: Toward a New Cultural History of Education* (New York: Peter Lang, 1999): 3–29. For the fears of an Australian educational historian who wrote about nineteenth-century women that she could not do historical justice to women teachers in the twentieth century, see Marjorie Theobald, "Writing Landscapes for a Good Teacher," *History of Education Review* 27 (1998): 29–36.

[2]My own experience as historian of the NEA Research Division has allowed me to conduct comprehensive interviews with many of its present and former staff members, the results of which inform many of the judgments reached in this chapter, and to consult the division's own formidable records of both its past and present accomplishments. Also see Urban, *More Than the Facts.*

[3]Ibid.

[4]This individual, Terry Herndon, would shortly become the executive director of the NEA and thus the individual in charge of the fate of the Research Division.

[5]Terry Herndon to Participants in the Research Role Conference (October 21–22, 1974), NEA Archives, box 713.

[6]Guidelines for Coordination of Research Studies (May 28, 1974), NEA Archives, box 174.

[7]NEA Archives, box 786.

[8]Terry Herndon to Executive Staff (September 7, 1977) NEA Archives, box 174.

[9]Urban, *More Than the Facts,* ch. 6.

[10]The development of the NEASO, from its beginnings as a largely social organization to an independent union to a union affiliated with an international labor organization, can be followed through its newsletter, *Staff Line.* A complete file of the newsletter is in the NEA Archives, box 404.

[11]Stephen Golen, "Race, Class and Classroom: The Newark Teachers and Their Union, 1937–1969." Paper delivered to the Organization of American Historians, Chicago, Illinois, 1995, p. 2.

[12]On the NEA's failure to enact a collective bargaining statute, see West, *The National Education Association,* 246–47.

[13]Keith Geiger's acceptance of a position in the Clinton administration after his NEA presidential term ended indicated that Clinton acknowledged NEA influence in more tangible ways also.

[14]In this discussion as well as in much of the other discussion in this chapter, I borrow from Berube, *Teacher Politics,* especially 106–16.

[15]Ibid., 119–21.

[16]Ibid.

[17]National Commission on Excellence in Education, *A Nation at Risk: The Imperative of Educational Reform* (Washington, DC: Government Printing Office, 1983).

[18]Terrel Bell, *The Thirteenth Man* (New York: Basic Books, 1988), is a fascinating memoir of Bell's attempts to save the department and public education from the attacks of the more ideologically conservative members of the Reagan administration who could abide no public enterprise other than defense.

[19]Diane Ravitch, an educational historian who became the director of research in the Office of Educational Research and Improvement of the Department of Education in the Reagan administration, was closely aligned with Shanker. While on the faculty at Teachers College, Ravitch, along with Chester Finn of Vanderbilt University, had established an Educational Excellence Network of scholars and educators that preceded *A Nation at Risk* by several years.

[20]Berube, *Teacher Politics,* 101–2.

[21]The NEA Research Division continued to conduct studies of teachers and their opinions, though without making them as widely available to the public, in the 1980s and 1990s. For example, see the *1987 Survey of NEA K–12 Members,* the *Status of the American Public School Teacher, 1990–1991,* and the *Status of the American Public School Teacher, 1995–96,* all published by the Research Division. Surveys like these, on occasion, revealed differences in opinion between a majority of NEA members and the official position of the organization.

[22]Lieberman, *Education As a Profession.*

[23]This discussion relies on Sam Pizzigati, "The Merger Fails—What Next for Education Unions?" *Working USA* (November–December 1998): 11–22. Also, in working for the NEA Research Division, I have on several occasions discussed merger with NEA staff members.

[24]Pizzigati, "The Merger Fails," 20.

[25]Ibid., 17–18.

[26]Ibid., 17.

[27]For example, see *Eye on the Economy* (May 1995). For this activity in the 1930s, see Chapter 2 of this volume.

[28]Urban, *More Than the Facts,* 133–34, 143 n. 14.

[29]Ibid., 132.

[30]Chase has expounded on the new unionism in speeches in many forums, including the National Press Club. He has also published his views in a wide variety of forums. For example, see Mardell Raney, "Technos Interview: Bob Chase," *Technos: Quarterly for Education and Technology* 7 (Spring 1998): 4–10.

Epilogue

I begin this concluding discussion by recapitulating the major argument in the book and then restating how the argument accounts for the ebbing and flowing of three major thematic elements—professionalism, race, and gender. The main argument in this account has been threefold, dealing with the distant past, the recent past, and the present moment in the twentieth-century history of the NEA. My claim is that the NEA initially remade itself into a professional association in the post–World War I era and maintained this position, largely through successfully courting women teachers to be members, until the 1960s. In that decade, under the leadership of militant men who came from junior high and secondary schools, the NEA turned itself into a militant trade union, though one not affiliated formally with the labor movement. In the 1990s, under its current president, the NEA seeks once again to remake itself, using the term *new unionism* to describe what it seeks to be—an organization responsive to claims for school improvement and quality education, just as it is responsive to the occupational needs of its members.

Professionalism was the consciously stated priority of the NEA from the time of its remodeling in 1917 until the 1960s. In that latter decade, the process of unionization began and was eventually completed with the constitutional change in 1972. An outcome of that process was a perhaps unconscious but no less real movement to hold the professional agenda of the NEA in abeyance and to embrace militant unionism and collective bargaining as the goals of the newly unionized association. In the 1990s, after two decades of this tough-minded unionism, the NEA's president is attempting to establish a "new unionism" agenda that seems

to resemble in many of its particulars the preunion professional orientation that animated the association for four or five decades before unionization.

Race has been a difficult factor to account for in the twentieth-
century history of the NEA. Just about a decade after the end of World
War I, in 1928, the largely white professional association began a long-
term but timid relationship with the black American Teachers' Association. For the next three decades, the two associations cooperated in rather
innocuous attempts at racial amelioration, but the NEA made sure that
the interaction was never controversial. Though it was aware of salary inequities experienced by black teachers, the NEA seldom publicized these
inequities, thereby refraining from embracing the agenda for racial improvement advocated by the black teachers' association that threatened
some segregated white NEA affiliates. Given this situation, one should
not be surprised that the NEA temporized in response to perhaps the
major educational policy event of the twentieth century, the 1954 *Brown
v. Board of Education* Supreme Court decision, which signaled the death
knell for state-supported racial segregation in public schools.

After several years of hesitancy and an increase in pressure from the
ranks of black and some white teachers, the NEA began in the 1960s a
process of desegregation of itself and its segregated southern affiliates
that by the 1970s had achieved remarkable results. This process had no
logical or coherent relationship with the unionization of the association
that took place at roughly the same time, but it did benefit from the climate of change that unionists forged in the NEA. Furthermore, occasional cooperation between the desegregationists and the unionists
hastened the desegregation effort. In the aftermath of unionization and of
its own desegregation, the NEA became a leader in the push for the
meaningful desegregation of the nation's schools. It also stood strongly
for other equity-oriented policies such as affirmative action on behalf of
blacks, other minorities, and women in admission to educational institutions and in employment, promotion, and job retention.

The gender issue developed in almost a reverse pattern compared
with what happened to the NEA in the racial arena. From the time of its
remodeling in 1917, the professional NEA went out of its way to court
women teachers. Although this attempt was not the result of social or political enlightenment nor of an affinity for the social or political equity
causes of activist women, the NEA pursued women earnestly as the
group most needed to build the membership in the association that would
make it the leading institutional voice of the nation's educators. NEA

support for a single salary scale, its attention to the plight of married women teachers in the 1930s and 1940s, and its recognition of the accomplishments of several of its women staff members in these decades all testify to the importance of women for the association and its recognition of that importance. Although this activity never reached the stage of encouraging conflict between the predominantly female teaching force and the predominantly male ranks of school administrators who firmly controlled both the nation's schools and the NEA, the association did as much as it could for women without disturbing the patriarchal nature of educational power relations.

The unionization of the NEA in the 1960s and 1970s, as described in Chapters 5 and 6, was a distinctly masculine phenomenon. Thus, it should not be surprising that in the immediate aftermath of that unionization, the NEA's preunion commitment to women was de-emphasized. It is not that the association completely ignored women teachers but rather that it promoted their interests and spoke to them as teachers—and paid less attention to them as women teachers. Women's rights and women's concerns were supported but usually as a part of the NEA's larger commitment to equity for racial and ethnic minority groups.

Women, of course, are not a minority group, though they share with ethnic and racial minorities a stigmatization and the experience of discrimination in the workplace and elsewhere. Yet, if the depiction of women teachers in the earlier chapters of this book, and in the work of other authorities such as Kate Rousmaniere[1] is accurate, then they are substantially a middle-class population that cannot necessarily be expected to support wholeheartedly an association that portrays itself as a militant cadre of activists or one that takes a high-profile role as a zealous advocate of socially and occupationally disadvantaged minority groups. Nor can white women be expected necessarily to react enthusiastically on behalf of increasingly controversial policies such as affirmative action for minorities.

Of course, most of the evidence to support the characterization of women teachers as middle class is relatively old, dating to the early and middle parts of the twentieth century. The most recent profile of teachers by the NEA, however, provides more up-to-date descriptions of teachers and of women teachers, that lead to the conclusion that the historic characterization of women teachers as middle class is still relevant.

First, the makeup of the teaching force reported recently by the NEA reinforces the significance of gender for the groups like the NEA that seek to represent teachers. In 1995–96, the latest year for which data have been reported, the teaching force was 74.4 percent female and 25.6 male. This is the largest percentage of women in the teaching force since the NEA began compiling this sort of data on teachers in the 1950s. Further, the increase in the percentage of women is most significant in the most recent decade, the period from 1986 to 1996, going from 68.8 in the former year to 74.4 in the latter.[2]

Interestingly, the percentage of men in teaching in the 1961–96 period peaked in 1971 at 34.3, then fluctuated for the next decade before declining steadily from 33.1 percent in 1981 to 31.2 percent in 1986, to 27.9 percent in 1991 and, finally, to 25.6 percent in 1996.[3] An important parallel development is the decline in men in secondary teaching from a majority of 56.8 percent in 1961 to a smaller majority of 50.4 percent in 1986 and then, dramatically, to a minority of 43.8 percent in 1991 and of 41.1 percent in 1996.[4] These numbers lend strength, I believe, to my description of the militancy of the 1960s and 1970s as a male phenomenon. They also indicate that the increasing recent feminization of the teaching force is a factor worthy of consideration on the part of leaders of teachers' associations, such as Robert Chase, as they form their policies for the next century.

In terms of the class makeup of teachers, the evidence is less dramatic but still suggestive. From 1966 to 1991, the latter year being the last year for which father's occupation was recorded in the NEA survey of teachers, the most dramatic decrease was in the percentage of farmer fathers, declining from 26.5 percent in 1961 to 10.8 percent in 1991. The most dramatic increase in the category of father's occupation was in the portion coming from professional or semiprofessional work, which increased from 14.5 percent in 1961 to 25.6 percent in 1991.[5] In 1991 more than 75 percent of teachers came from families where the father was either a skilled or semiskilled worker, a professional or semiprofessional worker, or a managerial worker or self-employed. Forty-seven percent of teachers came from the latter two categories, which, I would argue, can be described as white collar, middle class. Those two white-collar categories are also even more characteristic of women teachers than of men teachers: 49 percent of women teachers in 1991 had fathers whose occupations can be classified as white collar, middle class, while 42 percent of the fathers of men teachers had that occupational background. In contrast, the more blue-collar but perhaps still middle-class category of skilled or semiskilled worker described the fathers of 30 percent of men teachers and 25 percent of women teachers. More significant, the category of unskilled worker accounted for the fathers of 12 percent of men teachers and 8 percent of women teachers.[6] While these differences in background are not overwhelming, their significance is increased when one remembers that women teachers now outnumber men by a three to one ratio. With this in mind, I read the figures to show that teachers of the late twentieth century continue their historic tendency to come from families with middle-class status and that contemporary women teachers are even more representative of this tendency than men.

Another variable related to teachers' class or status is the level of education attained by their parents. This variable is included in both the 1991 and 1996 NEA teacher status reports, as well as in earlier ones. Measures are given of both father's and mother's educational attainment. In the former category, the percentage of fathers of women teachers in the three categories of highest educational attainment—those possessing at least some college education, a college degree, or some graduate work—exceeded the percentage of fathers of men teachers in both years, 41 percent to 35 percent in 1991 and 42 percent to 38 percent in 1996.[7]

In terms of the educational attainment of the mothers of teachers, the years 1991 and 1996 reveal that in both years 35 percent of the mothers of teachers were in the same top three categories. This was in rather strong contrast to the percentage of mothers in those three categories in 1971—27 percent—the first year in which this information was recorded.[8] Also in 1996, the percentage of mothers of women teachers in the top three categories of educational attainment exceeded that of men teachers by 38 to 29.[9]

I offer these figures first to suggest that there is substantial evidence to conclude that, if anything, teachers are becoming increasingly middle class and that women teachers are more middle class than men teachers. More important, this evidence more than suggests that the historic depiction of teachers as predominantly female and oriented to middle-class notions of culture and propriety is as apt a characterization of late-twentieth-century teachers as it is of their predecessors.

But what can these statistics mean for the contemporary programs of teachers' associations and unions? Here again, I can only be suggestive. It seems appropriate to me, however, to suggest that the demographic trend in the teaching profession, one that certainly points in the direction of an increasingly female occupation and almost as certainly in the direction of a stable, if not increasingly, middle-class occupation, can provide fertile soil for the implementation of a more "professional" agenda such as that proffered by NEA president Robert Chase in the late 1990s. While contemporary concerns about equity might preclude Chase from speaking specifically to women teachers, rather than to teachers in general, and while the immediate past of the NEA might also lead him to prefer the term *new unionism* to the term *professionalism,* there is some reason to believe that there may well be a fit between Chase's new ideology and his membership. Both the content of Chase's message and the composition of the teaching force resemble to a substantial extent the circumstances in the preunion era of the NEA, when it proclaimed professionalism as its operative ideology and when that professionalism appeared to be embraced enthusiastically by a predominantly female teaching force. Thus, Robert Chase's calls for educational reform as well as material occupational improvement may well be received favorably by his own membership and by other teachers. The articulateness of his ideas, of course, as well as the choice of forums in which they are delivered, will have much to say about their reception or lack of reception.

Returning to the topic of race, and considering its possible interaction with the new unionism agenda of the NEA, the evidence from the teachers' survey tells a somewhat different story. Demographically, the teaching force in the past thirty years has become slightly whiter, increasing from 88.3 percent in 1971 to 90.7 percent in 1996. Correspondingly, the black percentage of teachers has decreased from 8.1 percent in 1971 to 7.3 percent in 1996.[10] These changes are small in terms of the numbers involved, but when compared with the demographics of the public school population, they loom larger in significance. The percentage of black and other nonwhite minority students in our public schools is growing rapidly, to the extent that many are predicting a nonwhite student majority in the schools by the middle of the twenty-first century. Although I would not want to claim that white teachers cannot teach black or other minority students, I do believe it is important that minority students see enough minority faces in the teaching ranks to believe that there are teachers who understand from experience and background what minority students are facing in school and who can demonstrate that academic achievement is an attainable goal for minority populations.

In terms of the productive interaction of Robert Chase and the NEA's new unionism with racial and ethnic minority populations, I would make two proposals. First, I would suggest that the association's commitment to affirmative action, even in a period where it is becoming an increasingly controversial and questioned policy, be reinforced. Even though affirmative action is not an integral part of any new or professional unionism, it is critical to the success of that or any other enterprise that seeks to improve public education in the twenty-first century. The reason I say this is that support of affirmative action is one way, no doubt an imperfect way, to show the association's commitment to minority students and to facilitate an increase in the percentage of minority teachers. Second, I would suggest that in addition to concentrating on educational reform and educational quality as appropriate goals to be pursued under a "new unionism," the NEA might increase its steps to bring the crisis in educational quality of our inner-city schools, where the poor and underachieving minority populations are concentrated, to a place of greater prominence in its reform effort. I understand that the association has not ignored this aspect of the situation, but I would think that an even greater stress on quality education in poor communities, as an integral part of the larger campaign for educational improvement, would provide both enhanced chances for a better education for the students who need it most and a socioeducational agenda, aiding poor children, that would be supported enthusiastically by teachers.

Although these suggestions are less than earth shattering, I think that they forge a productive link between the history of the NEA as described in these pages and the present and future challenges that face the group. While others may draw other connections between past and present from my work and that of other historians, these are the ones that strike me as especially warranted given the educational challenges of the turn-of-the-century era in which I, the NEA leaders and staff, and public school teachers work. I think that a "new teacher unionism," or, in other terms, an increasingly professional teacher unionism, is desirable. I hope that it is attainable. I know that without it we are likely not to achieve the educational accomplishment that most, if not all of us know is necessary for our national welfare.

NOTES

[1]Rousmaniere, *City Teachers.*

[2]*Status of the American Public School Teacher, 1995–96* (n.p.: National Education Association, 1997), 16.

[3]Ibid.

[4]Ibid., 77.

[5]*Status of the American Public School Teacher, 1990–1991* (n.p.: National Education Association, 1992), 79. Whether because of concerns about gender equity that might be characterized by opponents as "political correctness" or because of an understanding that fathers' occupation was less cogent as a status variable, the NEA stopped including it in its surveys of teachers in 1991. The 1995–96 survey contains no such category.

[6]*Status of the American Public School Teacher, 1990–1991*, 79 and 179.

[7]Ibid., 181; and *Status of the American Public School Teacher, 1995–1996,* 235.

[8]*Status of the American Public School Teacher, 1995–1996,* 76. Mothers' educational attainment in the three highest categories—that is, some college education, a college degree, or some graduate work—increased substantially in 1986 from its 1981 level of 27 percent to 31 percent.

[9]*Status of the American Public School Teacher, 1995–1996,* 233.

[10]Ibid., 75.

Bibliography

PRIMARY SOURCES

There are three major sets of primary sources for this volume. I will say a bit about each of them and their utility for studying the NEA.

The *Journal of the Addresses and Proceedings of the National Education Association,* cited in this volume as *NEA Proceedings,* is a verbatim record of all the actions undertaken at the annual convention of the NEA until 1973. It contains the speeches, the committee and commission reports, and the record of the business conducted at the NEA meetings, including debates on the floor of the convention. It also includes the minutes of the NEA's Board of Directors, Board of Trustees, and Executive Committee for the years in which these bodies held meetings and conducted business. Additionally, the *Proceedings* contains the record of the meetings of the Department of Superintendence, when they were held separately from the NEA meeting. After 1973 the *Proceedings* are less comprehensive, a truncated record that I refer to as sanitized. Although this seems a harsh judgment, the point is that the *Proceedings* until 1973 are a valuable source for historians, and after that year, are much less valuable. The *Proceedings* have been published and distributed widely to libraries, so they are easier to obtain than most collections of primary sources.

The *Journal of the National Education Association,* cited in the text as the *NEA Journal,* is another extremely valuable source for studying the history of the NEA. Revamped shortly after the association remodeled itself in 1917, and again near the time when the association became

a union and the *Journal* was retitled *Today's Education,* this periodical
provides a copious record of what the association leadership thought
worthy of communication to its members over the years. Although its
journalistic character makes it less of a comprehensive source than the
Proceedings, its monthly publication makes it a more frequent and diverse record of the NEA than the other publication. Like the *Proceedings,* the *Journal* is widely available in libraries. Like the *Journal,* the
NEA Research Bulletin and other publications of the NEA Research Division were distributed widely when published and can be found in many
libraries.

Finally, the enormous variety and complexity of the materials contained in the NEA Archives mark this collection as enormously important for both the NEA and its many departments for most of the twentieth
century. The significance of this collection cannot be overestimated, and
the student of the NEA, of one or more of its departments, or of numerous other aspects of the American educational enterprise in the twentieth
century, can find much material of benefit in this collection. It is difficult
to access, however, now that the archives are no longer within the NEA
Research Division. The various boxes in the collection are stored in a
warehouse away from the NEA headquarters in Washington, D.C., and
researchers must request boxes to be transported from the warehouse to
headquarters, where they can be perused. These difficulties are more
than compensated for, however, by the value of the materials contained
in the various NEA collections.

References in the notes of this book to various items in these three
sources are not listed in the enumeration of sources that follows.

OTHER SOURCES

Almack, John C., and William G. Carr. "The Principle of the Nomograph in Edu-
cation." *Journal of Educational Research* 12 (December 1926): 340–55.
Armor, David. *Forced Justice: School Desegregation and the Law.* New York:
Oxford University Press, 1994.
Baker, Scott. "An American Dilemma: Teacher Testing and School Desegrega-
tion in the South." In Wayne J. Urban, ed., *Essays in Twentieth-Century
Southern Education: Exceptionalism and Its Limits,* 163–98. New York:
Garland, 1999.
Bartley, Numan. *The Rise of Massive Resistance: Race and Politics in the South
During the 1950s.* Baton Rouge: Louisiana State University Press, 1969.
Bell, Terrel. *The Thirteenth Man.* New York: Basic Books, 1988.
Berube, Maurice. *Teacher Politics: The Influence of Unions.* New York: Green-
wood Press, 1988.

Blount, Jackie M. *Destined to Rule the Schools: Women and the Superintendency.* Albany: State University of New York Press, 1998.

Bogen, Robert W. "Organizational Change: Emergence of the Urban Movement
in the National Education Association." Ed.D. diss., George Peabody College for Teachers, 1970.

Brickman, William. "Toward an Evaluation of the Publications of the National
Education Association." *Progressive Education* 34 (July 1957): 111–15.

Buchanan, Frederick S. "Unpacking of the N. E. A.: The Role of Utah's Teachers
at the 1920 Convention." *Utah Historical Quarterly* 41 (1973): 150–61.

Callahan, Raymond E. *Education and the Cult of Efficiency.* Chicago: University
of Chicago Press, 1962.

Carr, William G. *Education for World Citizenship.* Palo Alto, CA: Stanford University Press, 1928.

———. *John Swett: An Educational Pioneer.* Santa Ana, CA: Fine Arts Press,
1933.

———. *The Continuing Education of William Carr: An Autobiography.* Washington, DC: National Education Association, 1978.

———. "The N. E. A.'s Service to American Education." *School and Society*
(May 11, 1957): 160–66.

Cecelski, David. *Along Freedom's Road: The Hyde County School Boycott.*
Chapel Hill: University of North Carolina Press, 1994.

Clifford, Geraldine Joncich. "Home and School in Nineteenth Century America:
Some Personal History Reports from the United States." *History of Education Quarterly* 18 (Spring 1978): 3–34.

———. "Man, Woman, Teacher: Gender, Family, and Career in American Educational History." In Donald R. Warren, ed., *American Teachers: Histories
of a Profession at Work,* 293–343. New York: Macmillan, 1989.

Clowse, Barbara Barksdale. *Brain Power for the Cold War: The* Sputnik *Crisis
and the National Defense Education Act of 1958.* Westport, CT: Greenwood
Press, 1981.

Cohen, Sol. *Challenging Orthodoxies: Toward a New Cultural History of Education.* New York: Peter Lang, 1999.

Cole, Stephen. *The Unionization of Teachers.* New York: Praeger, 1969.

Corwin, Ronald G. *Education in Crisis: A Sociological Analysis of Schools and
Universities in Transition.* New York: John Wiley, 1974.

———. *Militant Professionalism: A Study of Organizational Conflict in High
Schools.* New York: Appleton-Century-Crafts, 1970.

Counts, George S. *Dare the School Build a New Social Order?* New York: John
Day, 1932.

Crabtree, J. W. "The School Board Journal and the N.E.A." *American School
Board Journal* 82 (March 1931): 61.

———. *What Counted Most.* Lincoln, NB: University, 1935.

Donley, Marshall O. *Power to the Teacher.* Bloomington: Indiana University
Press, 1975.

Dumeil, Lynn. "'The Insatiable Maw of Bureaucracy': Antistatism and Education Reform in the 1920s." *Journal of American History* 77 (September 1990): 499–524.

Eaton, William Edward. *The American Federation of Teachers, 1916–1961: A History of the Movement.* Carbondale: Southern Illinois University Press, 1975.

Fenner, Mildred Sandison. *NEA History: The National Education Association: Its Development and Program.* Washington, DC: National Education Association, 1945.

"Get Ready for a Lot More POW in Teacher Power." *American School Board Journal* 161 (October 1974): 32.

Golen, Stephen. "Race, Class and Classroom: The Newark Teachers and Their Union, 1937–1969." Paper delivered to the Organization of American Historians, Chicago, March 1995.

Gould, Ronald. "The 'Closed Shop' and the Teacher." *Phi Delta Kappan* 33 (September 1951): 53, 64.

Herbst, Juergen. *And Sadly Teach: Teacher Education and Professionalization in American Culture.* Madison: University of Wisconsin Press, 1989.

Hoffman, Nancy, ed. *Women's True Profession.* Old Westbury, NY: Feminist Press, 1981.

Hofstadter, Richard. *The Age of Reform: From Bryan to FDR.* New York: Knopf, 1955.

Hunt, Maurice P. "The NEA's Neglected Role of Critic." *Progressive Education* 34 (July 1957): 105–8.

Jorgensen, Lloyd P. "The Social and Economic Orientation of the National Education Association." *Progressive Education* 34 (July 1957): 98–101.

Kaufman, Polly Welts. *Women Teachers on the Frontier.* Hartford, CT: Yale University Press, 1974.

Krug, Edward A. *The Shaping of the American High School, 1921–1940.* Madison: University of Wisconsin Press, 1972.

Lawn, Martin, ed. *The Politics of Teacher Unionism: International Perspectives.* Dover, NH: Croom Helm, 1985.

Lieberman, Myron. "Civil Rights and the N. E. A." *School and Society* (May 11, 1957): 166–69.

———. *Education As a Profession.* Englewood Cliffs, NJ: Prentice Hall, 1956.

———. "Introduction." *Progressive Education* 34 (July 1957): 97.

———. "Teachers' Strikes: An Analysis of the Issues." *Harvard Educational Review* 46 (Winter 1956): 39–70.

Lowe, William T. "Who Joins Which Teacher Groups." *Teachers College Record* (April 1965): 614–19.

Male, George A. "The National Education Association and Teacher Welfare." *Progressive Education* 34 (July 1957): 108–11.

———. "The NEA and the National Union of Teachers of England." *School and Society* (May 11, 1957): 163–66.

Mattingly, Paul. *The Classless Profession: American Schoolmen of the Nine-teenth Century.* New York: New York University Press, 1975.

Murphy, Marjorie. *Blackboard Unions: The AFT and the NEA, 1900–1980.* Ithaca, NY: Cornell University Press, 1990.

National Commission on Excellence in Education. *A Nation at Risk: The Imperative of Educational Reform.* Washington, DC: Government Printing Office, 1983.

Norton, John K. "A Survey of the National Education Association." *School and Society* 36 (July 16, 1932): 74–75.

———. "The Ability and the Effort of the States to Support Education." *Journal of Educational Research* 16 (September 1927): 88–97.

Ogren, Christine. "Where Coeds Were Coeducated: Normal Schools in Wisconsin, 1870–1920." *History of Education Quarterly* 35 (Spring 1995): 1–26.

Orfield, Gary, Susan E. Eaton, and the Harvard Project on School Desegregation. *Dismantling Desegregation: The Quiet Reversal of* Brown v. Board of Education. New York: New Press, 1996.

Ozga, J. T., and M. A. Lawn. *Teachers, Professionalism and Class.* London: Falmer Press, 1981.

Pellathy, Gabriel Steven. "The National Education Association: A Political System in Change." Ph.D. diss., New York University, 1957.

Pizzigati, Sam. "The Merger Fails—What Next for Education Unions?" *Working USA* (November–December 1998): 11–22.

Pratt, Lyndon U. "The Impact of the National Education Association on State Education Associations." *Progressive Education* 34 (July 1957): 116–18.

Quantz, Richard A. "The Complex Vision of Female Teachers and the Failure of Unionization in the 1930s." *History of Education Quarterly* 25 (Winter 1985): 439–58.

Raney, Mardell. "Technos Interview with Bob Chase." *Technos: Quarterly for Education and Technology* 7 (Spring 1998): 4–10.

Rousmaniere, Kate. *City Teachers: Teaching and School Reform in Historical Perspective.* New York: Teachers College Press, 1996.

Russell, Francis. *A City in Terror: The Boston Police Strike.* New York: Viking Press, 1975.

Scharf, Lois. *To Work and To Wed: Female Employment, Feminism, and the Great Depression.* Westport, CT: Greenwood Press, 1980.

Schultz, Michael John. *The NEA and the Black Teacher.* Coral Gables, FL: University of Miami Press, 1970.

Selden, David. *The Teacher Rebellion.* Washington, DC: Howard University Press, 1984.

Shankland, Sherwood D. "The Department of Superintendence—1891–1931." *American School Board Journal* 82 (March 1931): 61, 120–21.

Shott, Constance Trishler. "The Origin and Development of the National Education Association Political Action Committee, 1969–1976." Ed.D. diss., Indiana University, 1976.

"Should Teachers' Associations Have Compulsory Membership?—A Symposium." *Phi Delta Kappan* 33 (September 1951): 56–61.

Sizer, Theodore. *Horace's Compromise: The Dilemma of the American High School.* Boston: Houghton Mifflin, 1984.

Smaller, Harry. "Teachers' Protective Associations, Professionalization and the 'State' in Nineteenth Century Ontario." Ph.D. diss., University of Toronto, 1988.

Spaull, Andrew, ed. *Australian Teachers: From Colonial Schoolmasters to Militant Professionals.* Melbourne: AE Press, 1986.

———. *Teacher Unionism in the 1980s: Four Perspectives.* Hawthorn, Victoria: Australian Council for Educational Research, 1986.

Stephens, David. "President Carter, the Congress, and NEA: Creating the Department of Education." *Political Science Quarterly* 98 (Winter 1983–84): 641–43.

Stinnett, T. M. *Turmoil in Teaching.* New York: Macmillan, 1968.

Stinnett, T. M., Jack H. Kleinman, and Martha L. Ware, eds. *Professional Negotiations in Public Education.* New York: Macmillan, 1966.

Taft, Philip. *United They Teach: The Story of the United Federation of Teachers.* Los Angeles: Nash Publishing, 1974.

Theobald, Marjorie. "Writing Landscapes for a Good Teacher." *History of Education Review* 27 (1998): 29–36.

Tushnet, Mark. *The NAACP's Campaign Against Segregated Education, 1925–1950.* Chapel Hill: University of North Carolina Press, 1987.

Tyack, David. *The One Best System.* Cambridge, MA: Harvard University Press, 1974.

Tyack, David, and Elisabeth Hansot. *Managers of Virtue: Public School Leadership in America: 1820–1980* New York: Basic Books, 1982.

Tyack, David, Robert Lowe, and Elisabeth Hansot. *Public Schools in Hard Times.* Cambridge, MA: Harvard University Press, 1984.

Urban, Wayne J. *Black Scholar: Horace Mann Bond, 1904–1972.* Athens: University of Georgia Press, 1992.

———. "History of Education: A Southern Exposure." *History of Education Quarterly* 21 (Summer 1981): 131–45.

———. *More Than the Facts: The Research Division of the National Education Association, 1922–1997.* Lanham, MD: University Press of America, 1998.

———. "New Directions in the Historical Study of Teacher Unions." *Historical Studies in Education* 2 (Spring 1990): 1–15.

———. "Organized Teachers and Educational Reform in the Progressive Era, 1890–1920." *History of Education Quarterly* 16 (Spring 1976): 35–52.

———. "Power and Ideology in a Teacher Walkout: Florida, 1968." *Journal of Collective Negotiations in the Public Sector* 3 (Spring 1974): 133–46.

———. "Teacher Activism." In Donald Warren, ed., *American Teachers: Histories of a Profession at Work,* 190–209. New York: Macmillan, 1989.

———. "Wayne's World: Growing Up in Cleveland, Ohio, 1942–1963." *Educational Studies* 26 (Winter 1995): 301–20.

———. *Why Teachers Organized.* Detroit, MI: Wayne State University Press, 1982.

Urban, Wayne J., and Joseph W. Newman. "Communists in the American Federation of Teachers: A Too Often Told Story." *History of Education Review* 14 (1985): 15–24.

Urban, Wayne J., and Jennings L. Wagoner, Jr. *American Education: A History.* New York: McGraw-Hill, 1996.

Wesley, Edgar. *NEA: The First Hundred Years.* New York: Harper, 1957.

West, Allan M. *The National Education Association: The Power Base for Education.* New York: Free Press, 1980.

Whitehead, Kay. "The Women's Teachers' Guild, 1937–1942." In Adrian Vickery, *In the Interests of Education: A History of Education Unionism in South Australia,* ch. 4. St. Leonard's, New South Wales: Allen & Unwin, 1997.

Williams, Charl O. "A Message for American Education Week." *Independent Woman* 17 (November 1934): 338.

———. "A Wise Economy in Education." *Child Welfare* (May 1932): 531–32.

———. "Are You Posted on Committees? Department of Education." *Child Welfare* (October 1932): 88–89.

———. "How Professional Are Teachers?" *Peabody Journal of Education* 16 (September 1938): 118.

———. "Teacher Ethics and Professionalization." *Illinois Education* (March 1942): 198–99.

———. "The Challenge." *Child Welfare* (July–August 1931): 662–63.

———. "The Legend of Miss Bonny." *The National Elementary Principal* 23 (June 1944): 41–42.

Zeigler, Harmon. *The Political Life of American Teachers.* Englewood Cliffs, NJ: Prentice-Hall, 1967.

Name Index

Almack, John C., 48
Anthony, Susan B., 108, 149
Applegate, Irvamae, 219, 224

Bagley, William C., 46
Barton, Clara, 108
Baruch, Bernard, 147–148
Batchelder, Richard, 179
Beauchamp, Edward, xx
Beecher, Catherine, 109
Bell, Terrel, 263
Blake, Katherine Deveraux, 147–148
Blount, Jackie, xvi, 167–168n
Bond, Horace Mann, xiv
Brickman, William, 162
Brown, Isobel, 152
Burr, Samuel, 54
Bush, George, 250, 258
Burstyn, Joan, xvii

Carey, James, 176
Carr, William G., 44, 129, 144–147, 171, 180, 190, 192
  answers critics of NEA, 163–166
  attitude of, toward women teachers, 153

background and education of, 47–48
early work of in Research Division, 49
establishes NEA cabinet, 149
as Executive Director of Educational Policies Commission, 153
international interests of, 48
opposes desegregation, 215–216
retirement of, 179
Carter, Jimmy, 187, 250, 257, 258
Carver, George Washington, 112
Chase, Robert, 249, 250, 266–267, 269, 270, 271–275, 282–284
Clifford, Geraldine, xiii, xx
Cohen, Sol, xv
Cole, Stephen, 201
Counts, George S., 54
Crabtree, James W., 10–20, 28, 34, 36, 44, 91, 143, 249
Crissman, George R., 4
Cubberley, Ellwood P., 28, 48

Davis, Hazel, 70–73, 118–119, 171–175, 194–196
Dewey, John, 109
Dix, Dorothea, 108
DuShane, Donald, 84–87, 91

295

Subject Index